UNCROWNED QUEEN

UNCROWNED
QUEEN

The Life of
MARGARET BEAUFORT,
Mother of the Tudors

NICOLA TALLIS

BASIC BOOKS
New York

Basic Books
Hachette Book Group
1290 Avenue of the Americas, New York, NY 10104
www.basicbooks.com

Printed in the United States of America

First Edition: June 2020

Published by Basic Books, an imprint of Perseus Books, LLC, a subsidiary of Hachette Book Group, Inc. The Basic Books name and logo is a trademark of the Hachette Book Group.

The Hachette Speakers Bureau provides a wide range of authors for speaking events. To find out more, go to www.hachettespeakersbureau.com or call (866) 376-6591.

The publisher is not responsible for websites (or their content) that are not owned by the publisher.

Print book interior design by Trish Wilkinson

Library of Congress Cataloging-in-Publication Data
Names: Tallis, Nicola, author.
Title: Uncrowned queen : the life of Margaret Beaufort, mother of the Tudors / Nicola Tallis.
Other titles: Life of Margaret Beaufort, mother of the Tudors
Description: First edition. | New York : Basic Books, 2020. | Includes bibliographical references and index.
Identifiers: LCCN 2019054272 | ISBN 9781541617872 (hardcover) | ISBN 9781541617889 (ebook)
Subjects: LCSH: Beaufort, Margaret, Countess of Richmond and Derby, 1443–1509. | Great Britain—History—Wars of the Roses, 1455–1485—Biography. | Mothers of kings and rulers—England—Biography. | Great Britain—History—Lancaster and York, 1399–1485. | Great Britain—History—Henry VII, 1485–1509. | Tudor, House of. | Nobility—Great Britain—Biography.
Classification: LCC DA330.8.R5 T35 2020 | DDC 942.04092 [B]—dc23
LC record available at https://lccn.loc.gov/2019054272

ISBNs: 978-1-5416-1787-2 (hardcover), 978-1-5416-1788-9 (ebook)

LSC-C

10 9 8 7 6 5 4 3 2 1

*In the hope that they would be proud, this book is dedicated
to the memory of my dearly loved grandparents,
to whom—like Margaret—family meant everything.
Richard and Sylvia Howard
Brinley and Joyce Tallis*

CONTENTS

Contents

DRAMATIS PERSONAE

UNCROWNED QUEEN FEATURES A GREAT number of personalities, all of whom had varying impacts on Margaret Beaufort's life. To help familiarize the reader, I include below a brief biographical sketch of some of the main characters in Margaret's story.

Beauchamp, Margaret, Duchess of Somerset (c. 1420–1482)

Margaret's mother was the daughter of Sir John Beauchamp and Edith Stourton. She was married first to Sir Oliver St John, by whom she had seven children. Following her brief marriage to John Beaufort, which produced a single daughter, Margaret, she remarried in 1447. Her third husband was Lionel, or Leo, Lord Welles, by whom she had a son. Margaret Beauchamp died prior to 3 June 1482.

Beaufort, Edmund, Second Duke of Somerset (c. 1406/7–1455)

The younger brother of Margaret's father, Edmund was granted the dukedom of Somerset in 1448. A favourite of both Henry VI and his queen, Edmund was unpopular with many of his fellow nobles—most significantly the Duke of York, who tried to have him imprisoned on several occasions. Edmund participated in the first battle of the Wars of the Roses at St Albans in 1455, where he was killed.

Beaufort, John, First Duke of Somerset (1404–1444)

Margaret's father was the grandson of John of Gaunt and Katherine Swynford. Somerset spent much of his youth imprisoned in France as a result of his capture at the Battle of Baugé. He was ransomed in 1438, and in 1442 he married Margaret Beauchamp. In July 1443 he led a military campaign to France, but it ended in disaster. He returned six months later, in January 1444, and was met with disgrace. In May—just days before his infant daughter's first birthday—Somerset died, possibly by his own hand.

Bray, Sir Reginald (c. 1440–1503)

Margaret met the man who would become one of her most trusted servants and lifelong friends following her marriage to Henry Stafford. Bray acted as receiver general to the couple and managed Margaret's estates for around two decades. He served Margaret loyally and conspired on her son's behalf in the Buckingham Rebellion of 1483. Following Henry VII's accession in 1485, Bray was handsomely rewarded and became one of the king's most influential advisors. He died childless on 5 August 1503.

Cecily of York (1469–1507)

Margaret was extremely fond of the third of Edward IV's daughters, who she is likely to have come to know well during her time at the court of the Yorkist king. It was probably under Margaret's auspices that Cecily was married to John Welles, Margaret's half-brother, in 1487. Following Welles's death, Cecily wed Thomas Kyme without seeking Henry VII's consent. The king was outraged, but Margaret did her best to protect the former Yorkist princess, interceding on her behalf. Cecily lived out the remainder of her days quietly.

Edward IV (1442–1483)

The son and heir of Richard, Duke of York, following a victory at the Battle of Mortimer's Cross in February 1461, in March Edward declared himself king. His victory was consolidated after the bloody Battle of Towton on 29 March. Edward secretly married Elizabeth Wydeville in 1464, and together the couple would produce ten children—eight of whom survived infancy. In 1470 Edward was briefly deposed and fled abroad, but he returned the following year to fight for his throne. After two successful victories at Barnet and Tewkesbury, he regained his crown. Edward died unexpectedly in 1483, the results of which led Margaret Beaufort to spy an opportunity for her son.

Elizabeth of York (1466–1503)

The eldest daughter of Edward IV and Elizabeth Wydeville, Elizabeth was betrothed to the French dauphin in 1475 as part of her father's peace negotiations. The betrothal was broken off in 1482, and the following year Margaret plotted to marry Elizabeth to her son, Henry. Their marriage finally took place in January 1486, and in September Elizabeth gave birth to the first Tudor heir, Arthur. Together she and Henry sired seven children, four of whom survived infancy. Elizabeth died nine days after the birth of her final child, Katherine.

Fisher, John, Bishop of Rochester (c. 1469–1535)

The son of a Yorkshire merchant, Fisher first met Margaret in 1494 when he was senior proctor at Cambridge. The two struck up an immediate friendship, and before long Fisher had assumed the role of Margaret's chaplain and confessor. In 1504 Fisher was created Bishop of Rochester and remained a close friend of Margaret's for the rest of her life. So much so that he was one of the executors of her will, and it is from him that much of the information about her life stems—largely related by Margaret herself.

George, Duke of Clarence (1449–1478)

A younger brother of Edward IV, it was to Clarence that Henry Tudor's title of Richmond was given in 1462. Clarence was treacherous and rebelled with the Earl of Warwick against his brother in 1469. He was later reconciled with Edward IV and became a recipient of the king's favour. He was married to Isabel Neville, and the couple had two surviving children: Margaret, later married to Sir Richard Pole, and Edward, Earl of Warwick, executed in 1499. Following the death of his wife in 1476—probably as a result of childbirth—Clarence's behaviour became increasingly erratic. He was arrested and tried on charges of treason, of which he was found guilty. He was executed on 18 February 1478, reportedly by being drowned in a butt of Malmsey wine.

Henry VI (1421–1471)

Margaret's kinsman was the only child of Henry V and Katherine of Valois. Gentle and pious by nature, Henry was completely unsuited to the task of ruling a country. Under his rule, the Wars of the Roses broke out in 1455. Henry was deposed in 1461 and spent the next nine years either in hiding or imprisoned. Though he was briefly reinstated in 1470, the following year he was deposed once more and murdered in the Tower of London on 21 May 1471.

Henry VII (1457–1509)

Margaret's only son was born at Pembroke Castle two months after the death of her husband, Edmund Tudor. His birth was traumatic, but in spite of this Henry grew to be a healthy boy. Much of his early life was spent under the protection of his uncle, Jasper Tudor, but in 1462 Henry became the ward of William Herbert. He was treated kindly, and kept in contact with his mother, though he seems to have seen her but rarely. In 1471, at Margaret's urging, Henry fled abroad with Jasper Tudor, spending fourteen years in exile in Brittany and France. He returned at the head of an army in August 1485 and successfully defeated Richard III at the Battle of Bosworth. In January 1486, Henry married Elizabeth of York, thereby uniting the Houses of Lancaster and York. The couple had four children who survived infancy, chiefly his successor, Henry VIII. Henry died at Richmond Palace on 21 April 1509.

Henry VIII (1491–1547)

Henry was the second of Margaret's grandsons and was raised with his sisters, primarily at Eltham Palace. As with all of her grandchildren, Margaret was fond of Henry, and her accounts show that she sometimes bought gifts for him. Following the death of his elder brother Arthur in 1502, Henry became Henry VII's sole surviving male heir. He succeeded his father as Henry VIII in April 1509 and married Katherine of Aragon soon after. At the time of his death in 1547, he had married six times and produced three legitimate children.

Herbert, William, Earl of Pembroke (c. 1423–1469)

In 1462 William Herbert, a loyal supporter of Edward IV, became the guardian of Margaret's son, Henry Tudor. The boy was brought to live with Herbert and his family at Raglan Castle and was treated kindly by his guardian and his wife, Anne Devereux. Herbert eventually hoped to arrange for Henry's marriage to his daughter, Maud. In July 1469, Herbert partook in the Battle of Edgecote, taking young Henry with him. He was captured and executed the day after the battle.

Katherine of Aragon (1485–1536)

The Spanish bride of Margaret's eldest grandson, Arthur, arrived in England in October 1501. The following month, Katherine and Arthur were married in a lavish ceremony in St Paul's Cathedral, but the marriage was cut short when Arthur died in April 1502. Katherine was then betrothed to Margaret's younger grandson, Henry, but he repudiated this in 1505. She nevertheless remained in England, despite being poorly treated by Henry VII and forced to endure a great deal of financial hardship. Shortly after his father's death, Henry VIII resolved to marry Katherine, and the couple were quietly married on 11 June 1509. In spite of numerous pregnancies, Katherine produced just one surviving child, a daughter named Mary. By 1526 her marriage to Henry had begun to fall apart, and she was later forced to endure a very public and painful separation from him.

In 1533 Katherine and Henry's marriage was declared invalid, and three years later she died a lonely death at Kimbolton Castle.

Margaret of Anjou (1430–1482)

Henry VI's French-born queen was the daughter of René of Anjou and Isabella, Duchess of Lorraine. Married to Henry VI in 1445, she rather than her husband came to be a dominant force in the Wars of the Roses. Following the Lancastrian defeat at Tewkesbury in 1471 that saw the death of Margaret's only child, Prince Edward, Margaret became Edward IV's prisoner. In 1475 she returned to France, having been ransomed to Louis XI, and died there in poverty on 25 August 1482.

Morton, John (c. 1420–1500)

Hailing from Dorset, Morton rose steadily to prominence under Henry VI and was appointed chancellor to his heir, Prince Edward, on 26 September 1456. Following the Lancastrian defeat at Towton, Morton was captured while attempting to flee to Scotland and was imprisoned in the Tower of London. Incredibly, he managed to escape and hurried to join Margaret of Anjou in France. He remained there until Henry VI's readeption, but after his master's murder he reconciled with Edward IV and was pardoned in July 1471. He became one of Edward's most trusted advisors but was later imprisoned by Richard III. Morton supported Henry Tudor's claim and was a key conspirator in the Buckingham Rebellion. Following Henry VII's accession, Morton was appointed Archbishop of Canterbury in 1486 and Lord Chancellor the following year.

Neville, Richard, Earl of Warwick (1428–1471)

The man who became known as the Kingmaker supported Edward IV during the first years of his reign. He became the most powerful noble in the realm but was incensed when he discovered that Edward had married Elizabeth Wydeville in 1464. Five years later, he rebelled against Edward and succeeded in capturing him, but an attempt to rule in Edward's name failed. Though he and Edward were reconciled, it was short-lived, and in 1470 Warwick supported the readeption of Henry VI. When Edward IV returned to claim his throne the following year, his army met with that of Warwick at Barnet on 14 April. During the course of the battle, Warwick was killed.

Richard III (1452–1485)

The younger brother of Edward IV, Richard—following the king's unexpected death in April 1483—moved quickly to take control of his nephew, Edward V, and eventually, the realm. He was proclaimed King of England on 26 June and crowned alongside his wife, Anne Neville, on 6 July, with Margaret in attendance. Three months later, Richard was forced to deal with the Buckingham Rebellion, of which Margaret was one of the leading conspirators. The rebellion was a failure, and Richard confiscated all of Margaret's goods. The remainder of his reign was plagued by unrest, and in the summer of 1485 Richard prepared to face Henry Tudor on the battlefield. He was killed in the battle, and his naked body slung over the back of a horse—several humiliation wounds were inflicted after his death. Richard's remains were discovered in 2012 and identified the following year. He was interred in Leicester Cathedral in 2015.

Stafford, Henry (c. 1425–1471)

Margaret's third husband was the second son of Humphrey Stafford, Duke of Buckingham. He and Margaret were married in January 1458, and they seem to have enjoyed a genuinely happy marriage. The couple spent a great deal of time together, but after thirteen years of marriage Stafford died in October 1471 as a result of injuries inflicted at the Battle of Barnet.

Stafford, Henry, Second Duke of Buckingham (1455–1483)

As the grandson of Humphrey Stafford, Duke of Buckingham, Henry was Margaret's nephew by marriage and also her cousin through his mother.

Following the death of Edward IV in 1483, Buckingham became the chief ally of Richard, Duke of Gloucester, and fully supported his usurpation of the throne in June. Before long, though, Buckingham began plotting with Margaret for Richard's overthrow, and he planned a rebellion. When this failed, Buckingham was captured and executed on Richard III's orders on 2 November 1483.

Stanley, Thomas, Earl of Derby (c. 1433–1504)

Margaret married her fourth husband in June 1472, a match made—as with her other marriages—for political advantage rather than personal preference. Stanley was a man of dubious political allegiance, but following Henry VII's accession he was richly rewarded as the king's stepfather. Though Margaret was declared *femme sole* (a sole person) in 1485 and later took a vow of chastity, she and Stanley remained on good terms and continued to work together. Following his death on 29 July 1504, Stanley was laid to rest in Burscough Priory, Lancashire.

Stanley, William (c. 1435–1495)

The younger brother of Margaret's husband Thomas Stanley, William was instrumental in Henry Tudor's success at the Battle of Bosworth. He was rewarded for his good service, being appointed Chamberlain of the king's household and becoming immensely wealthy. At the beginning of 1495, however, Stanley was arrested on suspicion of supporting Perkin Warbeck. He was executed on 16 February.

Tudor, Arthur (1486–1502)

Margaret and her family had high hopes for the firstborn child and heir of Henry VII and Elizabeth of York—Margaret's grandson. In 1493 Arthur was sent to Ludlow Castle to continue his education and prepare for the task of kingship that awaited him. He rarely came to court, and thus Margaret saw little of her eldest grandson. On 14 November 1501, Arthur married the Spanish princess Katherine of Aragon, and soon afterwards the newlyweds returned to Ludlow. Tragically, before long Arthur fell ill and died on 2 April 1502.

Tudor, Edmund, Earl of Richmond (1428/30–1456)

Through his mother, Katherine of Valois, Edmund was the half-brother of Henry VI. It was thanks to the king that Edmund was granted the earldom of Richmond, and it was under his auspices that Edmund's marriage to Margaret Beaufort was arranged in 1455. The newlyweds moved to Wales, but their marriage was short-lived; on 1 November 1456 Edmund died of plague at Carmarthen Castle, leaving Margaret pregnant at the age of thirteen.

Tudor, Jasper, Earl of Pembroke and Duke of Bedford (c. 1431–1495)

The younger brother of Edmund Tudor, Margaret's brother-in-law was a devoted and trusted figure in her life. Not only did he support Margaret throughout the trying days that followed Edmund's death in 1456—including offering her shelter at Pembroke Castle, where she gave birth to her son—he also guarded Henry Tudor and stayed by his side following their foreign exile in 1471. Jasper remained loyal to Henry following his accession to the throne in 1485 and was greatly loved by both his nephew and Margaret. He died childless in December 1495.

Tudor, Margaret (1489–1541)

Margaret always held an especial fondness for her eldest granddaughter and namesake, and showed great concern for her welfare. In 1503 Margaret left England and travelled to Scotland to marry James IV. Her husband was killed at the Battle of Flodden in 1513, leaving Margaret a pregnant widow with a small son—James V. She endured a turbulent marital history, marrying twice more—as a result of her marriage to Archibald Douglas, she had a daughter, also named Margaret. She died at Methven Castle, Perthshire, on 18 October 1541.

Tudor, Mary (1496–1533)

The youngest surviving daughter of Henry VII and Elizabeth of York joined Margaret to entertain Philip of Castile at Croydon in 1506. The following year she was betrothed to his son, Charles, but the negotiations never came to fruition. Instead, in October 1514 Mary married Louis XII of France, but he died after just three months of marriage. Shortly after—probably in February 1515—Mary clandestinely married Charles Brandon, Duke of Suffolk. Their union produced two surviving daughters, Frances and Eleanor. Frances was the mother of Lady Jane Grey and her two sisters.

Welles, Lionel or Leo (c. 1406–1461)

Margaret's stepfather married her mother in 1447, having been previously married to Joan Waterton. He was a strong supporter of the House of Lancaster and served as Joint Deputy of Calais in the 1450s. Welles was created a Knight of the Garter in 1457 and fought for Henry VI at the Battle of Towton in 1461. It was there that he was killed, and later that year he was attainted by Parliament. Welles was buried alongside his first wife in St Oswald's Church, Methley.

Wydeville, Elizabeth (c. 1437–1492)

The first commoner to become Queen of England was married secretly to Edward IV in 1464. Though her union with Edward was successful, Elizabeth and her family managed to alienate many of her husband's nobles. The result was that, following Edward's death, the Wydeville family had little support in their attempts to secure power in the name of Elizabeth's son, Edward V. Elizabeth and her remaining children fled to sanctuary, where she plotted with Margaret to overthrow Richard III. Following Henry VII's accession and the marriage of her daughter, Elizabeth of York, to the king, Elizabeth reappeared at court. However, in 1487 she removed to Bermondsey Abbey, and it was there that she died in 1492.

TIMELINE

31 August 1422	Accession of Henry VI
31 May 1443	Margaret Beaufort is born at Bletsoe Castle
27 May 1444	John Beaufort, Duke of Somerset, dies in Dorset
23 April 1445	Henry VI marries Margaret of Anjou
22 May 1455	First Battle of St Albans
June–August 1455?	Margaret marries Edmund Tudor
1 November 1456	Edmund Tudor dies at Carmarthen Castle
28 January 1457	Henry Tudor is born at Pembroke Castle
3 January 1458	Margaret marries Henry Stafford
10 July 1460	Battle of Northampton
2 February 1461	Battle of Mortimer's Cross
3 February 1461	Execution of Owen Tudor at Hereford
4 March 1461	Accession of Edward IV
29 March 1461	Battle of Towton
12 February 1462	Henry Tudor's wardship granted to William Herbert
11 February 1466	Birth of Elizabeth of York
26 July 1469	Battle of Edgecote
3 October 1470	Readeption of Henry VI
11 April 1471	Second reign of Edward IV begins
14 April 1471	Battle of Barnet
4 May 1471	Battle of Tewkesbury

21 May 1471	Henry VI is murdered at the Tower of London
2 June 1471	Henry Tudor flees abroad
4 October 1471	Henry Stafford dies at Woking
June 1472	Margaret marries Sir Thomas Stanley
9 April 1483	Edward IV dies at the Palace of Westminster
26 June 1483	Accession of Richard III
6 July 1483	Coronation of Richard III
2 November 1483	Execution of the Duke of Buckingham
7 December 1484	Henry Tudor denounced as a rebel
22 August 1485	Henry Tudor defeats Richard III at the Battle of Bosworth
30 October 1485	Coronation of Henry VII
18 January 1486	Henry VII marries Elizabeth of York
20 September 1486	Prince Arthur born at Winchester
16 June 1487	Battle of Stoke
25 November 1487	Coronation of Elizabeth of York
28 November 1489	Princess Margaret born at the Palace of Westminster
28 June 1491	Prince Henry born at Greenwich Palace
2 July 1492	Princess Elizabeth born at Sheen Palace
16 February 1495	Execution of Sir William Stanley
18 March 1496	Princess Mary born at Sheen Palace
21 February 1499	Prince Edmund born at Greenwich Palace
23 November 1499	Execution of Perkin Warbeck
28 November 1499	Execution of the Earl of Warwick
14 November 1501	Prince Arthur marries Katherine of Aragon
January 1502?	Margaret travels to Calais
2 April 1502	Prince Arthur dies at Ludlow
2 February 1503	Princess Katherine born at the Tower of London
11 February 1503	Elizabeth of York dies at the Tower of London
29 July 1504	Thomas Stanley dies
1505	Margaret founds Christ's College, Cambridge

21 April 1509	Henry VII dies at Richmond Palace
11 June 1509	Henry VIII marries Katherine of Aragon at Greenwich Palace
24 June 1509	Coronation of Henry VIII and Katherine of Aragon
29 June 1509	Margaret Beaufort dies at Westminster Abbey

INTRODUCTION

Amid the modern-day bustle of Central London, the Palace of Westminster—the seat of government for centuries—dominates the scenery. Adjacent to the palace stands the imposing Westminster Abbey, the magnificent setting for the coronation of English monarchs since William of Normandy conquered England in 1066. Fifteen monarchs lie buried inside its ancient stone walls, alongside consorts, royal children, and others who have played pivotal roles in shaping England's history.

Prominent both within and without the abbey is the spectacular Lady Chapel, whose fan-vaulted ceiling and stained-glass windows provide a splendid example of late medieval architecture. Begun by Henry VII in 1503 as a permanent and tangible memorial to the Tudor dynasty, the chapel was described by the awestruck Tudor traveller John Leland as 'the wonder of the world'. It is also the final resting place of some of history's most illustrious figures, several of whom were a part of the famous Tudor family: Edward VI, Mary I, Elizabeth I and the chapel's founder, Henry VII, who lies entombed with his wife, Elizabeth of York.

In the south aisle of the chapel, set apart from the grand, tourist-crowded monuments, stands a black marble tomb-chest. Atop the chest lies a skilfully crafted bronze effigy of a woman: she is dressed simply in a widow's wimple with a long mantle, her head resting on two intricately designed pillows that show a portcullis and a Tudor rose. A coronet—long since lost—once lay above her head in an indication of her noble status.

Lines and wrinkles that hint at years of stress and anxiety are etched on to her face—probably moulded on a death mask—serving as a permanent and tangible reminder of the extraordinary and perilous events that shaped her life. Her small, delicately crafted hands, showing signs of age and the arthritis that plagued her towards the end of her life, are raised in prayer, and a mythical yale (a creature with the head of a goat with swivelling horns, body of an antelope, and tail of an elephant) that once boasted horns sits at her feet. The black marble tomb-chest contains sculpted bronze shields with arms that proudly proclaim the woman's heritage. Most prominent among them are the Royal Arms. Adorning the tomb is a Latin inscription composed by the celebrated Dutch humanist scholar Desiderius Erasmus, which begins with a proclamation of the woman's defining legacy: 'Margaret of Richmond, mother of Henry VII, grandmother of Henry VIII'.

The regal Margaret of Richmond—better known as Margaret Beaufort—lies resplendent, her tomb embellished with symbols that emphasise the identity that she created. Few of the abbey's visitors recognise that the tomb of this small, simply garbed lady is that of the mother of Henry VII and grandmother of Henry VIII—the notorious Tudor king. In contrast to the awe-inspiring double tomb of her son and daughter-in-law that dominates the Lady Chapel, Margaret Beaufort's memorial attracts little interest.

Yet, following her son's accession to the throne until her death, Margaret's birthday was proudly celebrated in the abbey each year, in fitting recognition of a woman who was instrumental in founding England's most famous dynasty. Descended from a line of English kings, and the great-granddaughter of a royal duke, Margaret—against quite incredible odds—raised herself to become the mother of a king. Her life reads like an episode of a modern-day soap opera. War was a common theme. Born into the midst of the Hundred Years' War that raged between England and France, Margaret soon saw bloodshed spread to English soil. Political tension spilled over into civil war, destroying families and tearing apart the country and those who sought to rule it.

Margaret would not have recognised the terms 'the Cousins' Wars' or 'the Wars of the Roses' by which the conflict became known, for these are the products of a later age, but the bloody twists and turns of the struggle between her own house—that of Lancaster—and her enemy's—York—dominated and shaped much of her life. It was a war in which most of the noble families of England would become hopelessly embroiled. In 1976, J. R. Lander suggested that by 1461 at least forty-nine out of sixty peerage families were involved in the wars—Margaret's most of all.[1]

From the outset, her life was overset with obstacles, all of which she was forced to negotiate. A marital pawn since the earliest days of her childhood, she was just thirteen when she was widowed and gave birth to her only child. These circumstances forced Margaret to take an active role in seeking a protector both for herself and for her son, while ingratiating herself with kings from a rival house in order to safeguard her son's and her own future. It was finally a scheme Margaret initiated that began to settle the conflict and brought the son of a Welshman born with no expectations of kingship to the throne of England, ushering in—at least in part—an era of peace.

'Henry VII's devout and rather awesome mother' is the description the historian Neville Williams offers of Margaret Beaufort in his 1973 biography of the king.[2] Both adjectives in this statement are true, but neither does full justice to the woman who forms the subject of this book. Williams's assessment does, however, accurately summarize the way in which Margaret has often been portrayed: a religious fanatic who was obsessively ambitious on her son's behalf and who dominated his court, an image compounded by the effigy upon her tomb as well as the surviving portraits, which show her wearing widow's weeds and a barbed wimple, on her knees in prayer. This is the image often conjured up when the name Margaret Beaufort is mentioned. Yet it is as two-dimensional as the paintings themselves, frequently used as a convenient shorthand when relating the tales of the period. Margaret's own story and her true character as a living, breathing woman are a far cry from such flat representations.

My first proper introduction to Margaret Beaufort came when I was researching the jewel collections of the queens of England in the period 1445 to 1548. Throughout my exploration, I was struck by how different the Margaret who was emerging from the pages of archival material was to the traditional figure. Her image has been through some revisions over the years since her death, but the popular one has rarely been accurate. Furthermore, in spite of the impact Margaret made on English history, she has often been little more than a footnote, overlooked and ignored. In recent years this has begun to change, and she is now starting to feature more prominently in the narratives that she helped to shape.

In the years following Margaret's death, though she was remembered and her memory revered by those whose lives she touched, she failed to attract the attention of poets, playwrights and artists. Given the impact she made on her son and his court, it is somewhat surprising that her story did not inspire William Shakespeare enough to consider her inclusion in any of his plays. She was referenced on brief occasions in *Richard III*, in which her husband Thomas Stanley was afforded a role. Considering the part that Margaret played in the events of Richard's reign, her exclusion as a character in her own right is curious. It can perhaps only be explained as a desire of the playwright not to offend Margaret's great-granddaughter, Elizabeth I, by highlighting the disgrace of her ancestress following Richard's discovery of her treasonous activities—chiefly, her plotting to overthrow the Plantagenet king and replace him with her own son, for which Richard placed her under house arrest.

It was not until the twentieth century that Margaret would re-emerge from the shadows into which she had been cast following her death. Since that time, she seems to have finally caught the attention of an array of novelists, writers and others. She has appeared regularly in popular culture, and today interest in Margaret persists. Curiously, she has been remembered in two very contrasting ways: sympathetically, as a pious and cultured lady who ought to be celebrated for her achievements and as the mother of the Tudor dynasty, and in an altogether more sinister light, as the woman who may have been responsible for the disappearance of the Princes in the Tower—a theory that we shall put to bed once and for all in the pages of this book.

There have been other layers of obfuscation as well, as novels have toyed with the idea of Margaret as a romantic heroine, deeply in love with her second husband, Edmund (Margaret's experience of love was never so conventional), whereas TV series have predominantly chosen to focus on her ruthless ambition.[3] More recently, there has been a wave of enthusiasm and interest in Margaret's story, sparked by Philippa Gregory's series of novels in which she features heavily. Indeed, *The Red Queen* is told from Margaret's point of view. Her portrayal in the accompanying 2013 drama series *The White Queen* is as a fanatic, obsessed with the idea that God intended her son to rule and working tirelessly to ensure that he fulfils his destiny. The series also wove a love story and affair into her relationship with her brother-in-law, Jasper Tudor. By contrast, the 2017 adaptation of Gregory's *The White Princess* saw Margaret smother Jasper to death upon his discovery of her involvement in the murder of the Princes in the Tower, as well as being publicly humiliated by her son. The trend of casting Margaret in a variety of guises depending on the dramatic leanings of the author/producer seems set to continue.

But her true story is far richer than any of these fictions. My impressions while interrogating Margaret's jewel collection only grew as I broadened my investigation. Indeed, the privilege of writing Margaret's story—and it has absolutely been a privilege—has been enhanced by the opportunity to delve into the wealth of source material that is extant. It has been both extremely challenging and exceptionally rewarding. The overwhelming sensation of experiencing history as it happened envelops the reader handling this treasure trove of Margaret's papers, and it becomes easy to immerse oneself fully in the fifteenth and early sixteenth centuries. A similar feeling occurs when studying the handful of Margaret's letters that survive, written in varying contexts to a number of recipients. These allow us to view different aspects of her character, for through these we can see how she conducted her business affairs, viewed her family and demonstrated her intense affection for her son.

I am not the first scholar drawn to Margaret, and neither will I be the last. The rich abundance of surviving primary source material, details of which can be found in Notes on Sources, has ensured that she has long attracted the fascination of biographers, and her prominent role in television series, such as those mentioned above, lends her considerable appeal among a wider audience. I must, however, take time to highlight the exceptional work of Michael Jones and Malcolm Underwood, whose 1992 joint study is considered—more than justifiably—to be the definitive work on Margaret's life. Following in their footsteps has not been easy. Other scholars have sought to highlight her educational and religious patronage, which, although covered in this book, are not the main focus. Instead, my aim is to dispel the many myths surrounding Margaret's life, and in their place offer a rounder, richer picture.

I have discovered a woman who started life playing by the rules: a marital pawn, defined by her wealth and bloodline. But, early on, the dangerous events that unfolded around her unleashed a new side of Margaret—one that sought a voice and independence. The fifteenth century was an extraordinary time for women and gave them hitherto unprecedented opportunities to make their voices heard, as Sarah Gristwood remarks in her exceptional work on the women of the Wars of the Roses: 'The second half of the fifteenth century is alive with female energy', and Margaret was one of its most potent forces.[4] Over time, Margaret pressed against the constraints imposed by her sex and society, slowly demanding more and more control over her life, until the crown on her son's head allowed her to make the unprecedented move for almost total independence: financially, physically and sexually. This is a woman who learned pragmatism very early on, who knew when to lay aside ego and finer loyalties for the sake of the long game—unlike so many of her male contemporaries. No doubt, the turning point was the birth of her son. His rights and very survival gave Margaret extraordinary energy and zeal, even when her own life was at stake.

Margaret's story is one of tragic lows and exceptional highs: it is a tale of war and peace told through the eyes of an extraordinary woman who played a leading role and became one of the most influential personalities of the late fifteenth century. Though in material terms she was privileged and never went without, emotionally she suffered heartache and loss, endured struggles and faced perils. Yet she survived; in time she thrived. In so doing she helped to lay the foundations for England's most famous dynasty. More importantly, though, she created a lasting legacy as an individual who ought to be remembered in her own right, thereby achieving more than she could ever have anticipated. Margaret's is, therefore, a life to be celebrated: it is the life of a woman who became a queen in all but name.

Nicola Tallis, Westminster Abbey

PROLOGUE

28 January 1457

As the bitter weather swirled, inside the strong stone walls of Pembroke Castle a thirteen-year-old girl was undergoing the worst ordeal of her life. The war that would tear apart the country had not long begun, but here, in the mighty Norman stronghold, situated in the midst of southwest Wales, close to the river estuary that opens into the Celtic Sea, two lives hung in the balance.

Lady Margaret Beaufort—a wealthy heiress with royal connections to the House of Lancaster—was just twelve years old when she married Edmund Tudor, half-brother to the Lancastrian King Henry VI, but her painfully tender age did not prevent the eager bridegroom from consummating the match, and Margaret quickly conceived. Her condition was soon fraught with danger and uncertainty when her husband died of plague on 1 November 1456, leaving his young wife alone and terrified of contracting the same disease.

The heavily pregnant teenager was far from her family and forced to seek aid from her brother-in-law, Jasper Tudor. She fled to his fortress at Pembroke. It was there that the young Margaret faced a terrible labour. Her underdeveloped body struggled to endure the strain of childbirth, and it was thought that neither mother nor child would survive. Her confessor, Bishop John Fisher, would later declare: 'It seemed a miracle that of so little a personage anyone should have been born at all'.

Yet after many traumatic hours, Margaret gave birth to a son. She named him Henry in honour of his Lancastrian forebears. This was the moment when everything changed for Margaret—and ultimately for England. The healthy baby she brought into the world must have seemed a true miracle, and as she cared for him over the following days and weeks, a love grew in her like none she had felt before. That love would once again bring Margaret close to death before culminating in a dramatic twist at Bosworth in 1485. For in her arms she held the future King of England, a man who would seek to end the bloodshed and unite the rival Houses of Lancaster and York.

But as Margaret recovered, sheltered for the moment inside the thick walls of Pembroke Castle, she faced many more trials to overcome before she—and her son—would truly be safe.

PART ONE

CHAPTER I

NOBLE BLOOD

I n the heart of the Bedfordshire village of Bletsoe, amid fragrant gardens, stood a castle surrounded by a moat. A comfortable three-story house with crenellations that were added in the fourteenth century, Bletsoe Castle was more of a fortified manor than a defensive structure. The castle had come into the hands of the Beauchamp family in 1359, and it was there that Margaret Beauchamp, Duchess of Somerset, spent much of her childhood.[1] With its warm family associations, it is little wonder that the duchess chose Bletsoe as the setting for the birth of her child in the spring of 1443. When her daughter arrived on 31 May, she chose to name her Margaret, perhaps after herself and in honour of the infant's paternal grandmother, Margaret Holland. The duchess carefully noted the arrival of baby Margaret—her only child by John Beaufort, Duke of Somerset— in her beautifully decorated Book of Hours, originally commissioned by her father-in-law. In time, her daughter, Lady Margaret Beaufort, would inherit and treasure this book, treating it as a family heirloom and using it to record the momentous events in her own family.[2]

'She came of noble blood lineally descending of King Edward III'.[3] This summary by John Fisher, Bishop of Rochester, of the prestigious origins of the baby born at Bletsoe, to whom he became a close friend in later life, perhaps pinpoints the most significant detail of Margaret's beginnings. Indeed, to understand Margaret fully and, in particular, how her sense of identity matured and made its mark, it is vital to trace her ancestry back to Edward III—a lineage that is more colourful than Bishop Fisher made out. Edward, who had become king at the age of fourteen, after his father, Edward II, was deposed, ruled England from 1327 until his death in 1377. The fifteenth century would be defined by a bloody conflict between his descendants, who came to form two rival houses stemming from two of Edward's sons: John of Gaunt, founder of the House of Lancaster, and Edmund of Langley, Duke of York, fourth son of Edward III and founder of the House of York.

Margaret, who was one of the most enduring victors of the conflict, belonged to the House of Lancaster. Her royal blood came courtesy of her father, who was the grandson of John of Gaunt (the name being an English take on Ghent, the place of his birth in 1340), himself the third of five surviving sons born to Edward III and Philippa of Hainault.[4] Despite being a younger son, Gaunt had once been the most ambitious and powerful nobleman in the realm, renowned for his courage and widely admired for his military prowess. Gaunt made three marriages during his life. The first, a love match to Blanche of Lancaster through which John became the Duke of Lancaster, produced two surviving daughters and a son—a son who would later turn the face of the English monarchy upside down by usurping the throne as Henry IV.[5] The second, after Blanche died in 1368, to Constance, the daughter of the murdered Pedro I 'the Cruel', King of Castile, was motivated by Gaunt's ambitious pursuit of Castile's throne.[6] The marriage of Gaunt and Constance was unhappy, which perhaps explains why, around 1372, he began a passionate affair with Lady Katherine Swynford.[7] The daughter of a knight from Hainault, Katherine had once served in the Duchess Blanche's household and was now governess to Blanche and Gaunt's two daughters, Philippa and Elizabeth.[8]

Like Gaunt, Katherine Swynford had been married before and widowed.[9] Gaunt and Katherine's widely known affair resulted in the births of four children: John, Henry, Joan and Thomas.[10] Because the nature of their parents' relationship rendered these children illegitimate, they were given the surname Beaufort after the lordship and castle that Gaunt had once owned in Anjou.[11] Unsurprisingly, her husband's infidelity caused Gaunt's wife Constance great distress. Matters came to a head in 1381, and Gaunt agreed to end his relationship with Katherine in order to further his claim to the Castilian throne. Their children, however, rendered him unable to sever all ties with her, and he continued to support them.

On 24 March 1394, Constance died.[12] Her death presented an opportunity for Gaunt to resume his relationship with Katherine Swynford, and it was not long before he did so. This time there was no reason why it should not be an honourable coupling, and in January 1396 Gaunt and Katherine were married at Lincoln Cathedral. The marriage received the blessing of Gaunt's royal nephew, Richard II, who had succeeded his grandfather Edward III in 1377, and who was fond of Katherine and her children. Just months after their wedding, the pope declared the couple's marriage valid and pronounced all their children—and any future children—legitimate. Then, in the Parliament of February 1397, Richard II 'legitimized my lord John Beaufort, his brothers, and his sister'.[13]

In one stroke, Margaret's ancestors were transformed from bastard stock to legitimate descendants of the great King Edward III. Still, in the years to come, the Beaufort siblings and their descendants were to discover that the stigma of illegitimacy persisted.[14] Indeed, during the reign of Richard III, when the king was eager to discredit Margaret's son, he took care to emphasise that 'his mother [Margaret] was daughter unto John Duke of Somerset', whose father had, he claimed, been conceived 'in double adultery'. Therefore, 'no title can or may be in him'.[15]

ON 3 FEBRUARY 1399, JOHN of Gaunt died at Leicester Castle at the age of fifty-eight.[16] His son by Blanche, Henry, Earl of Derby, was in exile in Paris following a quarrel with Thomas Mowbray, Duke of Norfolk. In recent years, the reign of Richard II had twisted into tyranny, and the king now refused to allow Henry to inherit the lands that should rightfully have passed to him at his father's death. It was this that prompted Henry to return to England at the head of a military campaign. In early

July, he landed at Ravenspur on the coast of Yorkshire. Richard II was on campaign in Ireland with most of his loyal lords, and before long Henry had gathered enough support not only to assert his rights as Duke of Lancaster but also to make a bid for the English throne. Support for Richard crumbled in the face of Henry's army, and having chased him to Conwy Castle in North Wales, Henry captured his royal cousin. Richard was imprisoned in the Tower of London, and on 13 October, Henry had himself crowned Henry IV. Before long, the dethroned Richard was sent north to Pontefract Castle, where, three months later, in January 1400, he died: many believed that he starved to death, either by choice or by design.[17]

John, the eldest of the Beaufort sons—Margaret Beaufort's grandfather—born somewhere around 1372 or 1373, had been well favoured by Richard II. In 1397, he was created Earl of Somerset, and later that year, he was named Marquess of Somerset, Marquess of Dorset, and Lieutenant of Aquitaine. Further good news was to come when, on 27 September— two days before his elevation to the rank of marquess—he married the king's niece and wealthy heiress Margaret Holland.[18] The marriage would in time enhance Margaret Beaufort's power, for she came to inherit many of her grandmother's manors.

Throughout the tumult of 1399, John Beaufort remained loyal to Richard II. Though he was later reconciled to his half-brother, Henry IV, his position nevertheless reverted from Marquess to Earl of Somerset. In other ways, however, he was well rewarded by the new regime, first becoming Chamberlain of England in 1399 and then Constable of England in 1404. Three years later, the king finally clarified his status and that of his siblings. On 10 February 1407, Henry IV reaffirmed the legitimacy of the Beauforts. This time, however, the words *excepta dignitate regali*— 'excepting the royal authority'—were added to the Letters Patent, thereby dictating that the Beauforts' legitimacy did not entitle them to stake a claim to the throne.[19] Given the manner in which Henry had acquired his crown, his measures are unsurprising. Crucially, however, his additions were never passed through Parliament and thus would emerge as a matter of contention in later years when the legitimacy of the Beauforts became of paramount importance to Margaret and her son—in his first Parliament of 1485, Henry VII took care to reaffirm Richard II's statute but unsurprisingly made no mention of Henry IV's added clause. The reinstatement of the Beaufort family's title had no impact on John Beaufort, for his exhaustive efforts in the king's service eventually undermined his health. He died on 16 March 1410 at the hospital of St Katharine by the Tower in London and was buried in Canterbury Cathedral.[20]

Margaret Holland remarried, this time to Thomas, Duke of Clarence, second son of Henry IV, but she had no more children, meaning that her wealth remained reserved for John Beaufort's children. Together, they had produced six children: four sons and two daughters.[21] Following the death of her eldest son, Henry IV's godson and namesake, Henry, in 1418, John—Margaret Beaufort's father—inherited the earldom of Somerset.[22] His tragic tale was to have far-reaching consequences in Margaret's early life.

John, Earl of Somerset, was born in 1404, and much of his life would be dictated by politics and war. In 1337 England became embroiled in the Hundred Years' War against its long-time enemy, France. Begun during the reign of Edward III, who believed that through his mother, Isabella of France, it was his right to be King of France, the war continued to rage even after the spectacular victory of Henry IV's son and successor, Henry V, at Agincourt in 1415.[23] At the 'tender age' of fifteen, the young Earl of Somerset travelled to France to engage in military service with his stepfather, Thomas, Duke of Clarence, and his younger brothers Thomas and Edmund.[24] Matters started well for young Somerset when Henry V—the second Lancastrian king and Henry IV's heir—knighted him at Rouen. However, disaster engulfed the family on 22 March 1421, when Somerset's stepfather Clarence was killed at the Battle of Baugé and Somerset and his younger brother Thomas were captured. As the highest-ranking prisoner,

Somerset was particularly valuable to the French, and numerous attempts to secure his release came to nothing. This was just the beginning of a series of disasters that were set to hover over his career; he would spend over seventeen years in French captivity. His brother Thomas was set at liberty in 1430 but tragically died the following year in battle at Louvier.[25]

When Somerset had been imprisoned for almost eighteen months after Baugé, news arrived that would change the whole course of the war. On 31 August 1422, Henry V died unexpectedly of dysentery at the Château de Vincennes, to the east of Paris.[26] Henry was just shy of his thirty-sixth birthday, and his death was met with 'great heaviness of all his people'.[27] Not only was the kingdom entrenched in a war with France, but Henry's heir was 'an infant still in his cradle'.[28]

The nine-month-old baby who succeeded his father as King of England was Henry V's only child by the French princess, Katherine of Valois. Henry VI had been born on 6 December 1421 at Windsor Castle, around eighteen months after his parents' marriage. He had never been afforded the opportunity to meet his father, who had been campaigning in France at the time of his birth. Just two months after the death of Henry's father, the French king Charles VI—Henry VI's maternal grandfather— also died, leaving the infant Henry the ruler of both England and France. Though the French would go on to crown their own choice—Henry's uncle Charles VII—in England, there was much deliberation over a successor to the crown. A child of this age was clearly incapable of ruling. Henry's mother, Queen Katherine, was twenty years old—old enough to rule—but her husband's subjects regarded her with suspicion because of her sex and foreign roots, rendering her an unsuitable candidate for a regent.

Instead, the next fifteen years were dominated by power plays of the young king's three uncles—John, Duke of Bedford; Humphrey, Duke of Gloucester; and Henry Beaufort, Bishop of Winchester—as well as by the shifting fortunes of the war in France. It was not until 12 November 1439 that the king, just shy of his sixteenth birthday, declared himself to have come of age.

AT THE TIME OF INFANT Henry VI's accession, Margaret Beaufort's father, Somerset, was still in the early days of his years-long captivity. Despite desperate pleas to the king's council begging for action to secure his release, it was not until 1438 that, after a series of complicated and drawn-out negotiations, he 'was ransomed for an immense sum of money', £24,000 (£15 million).[29] Unsurprisingly, he claimed that his ransom left him 'impoverished', but it was not only money that he had lost.[30] After seventeen years of imprisonment—the longest period of captivity endured by any English aristocrat during the Hundred Years' War—his youth had been irretrievably taken from him, and his health seems to have been undermined by the experience.[31]

Somerset's captivity and engagement in military action ensured there was no time for domesticity, although he had managed to sire a bastard daughter, Tacyn.[32] In 1442 his thoughts at last turned to marriage. His choice of bride was Margaret Beauchamp, who, according to Bishop Fisher, was 'right noble as well in manners as in blood'.[33] Though it was by no means the sort of prestigious match expected of someone so closely connected to the Crown, it was at least a respectable choice. Margaret Beauchamp, born around 1420, was the daughter of Sir John Beauchamp and his second wife, Edith Stourton, who resided at Bletsoe Castle in Bedfordshire.[34] Though Margaret Beauchamp's origins were hardly as illustrious as her husband's, she was rendered all the more attractive by the fact that in 1421 she had become the heiress of her only brother, John Beauchamp, who had died unmarried and childless. Margaret Beauchamp had inherited all of his lands, including Bletsoe, Lydiard Tregoze in Wiltshire, and manors in the Dorset and Bedfordshire regions. Though she was a few years Somerset's junior, she was already a widow; her marriage to Sir Oliver St John had produced six children: two sons and four daughters.[35] Sir Oliver had died in France in 1438—the same year as Somerset's release—leaving his wife with a large brood of young children to support. The need for a male protector was almost certainly the driving force behind Margaret Beauchamp's decision to remarry, although it is unclear how the match with Somerset came about.

The precise date of Somerset and Margaret Beauchamp's wedding is unknown, but it had taken place by July 1442.[36] The couple can hardly have known each other, yet in no time at all Margaret became pregnant. Though he was doubtless pleased with the speed at which his new wife conceived, Somerset's mind was very much occupied with other matters, chiefly paying off his crippling ransom. In an effort to raise funds, he had resorted to pledging some of his jewels: his wife would later try to recover a piece that had been sold to a London tailor.[37]

Another opportunity to bring in funds came about when Somerset was appointed to command the English force in a new campaign in France following Charles VII's invasion of Gascony in 1443.[38] Despite his limited military experience, Somerset negotiated hard to reach a suitable agreement. By the early months of 1443, he was busy making preparations to leave England once more. In April the king appointed him captain general of Aquitaine and Normandy, and there was a further honour to come. By act of Parliament, on St George's Day, 'from an earl he was created a duke, and God so ordaining it, was sent upon an expedition in the parts beyond sea'.[39] The new Duke of Somerset was nevertheless conscious that his wife would soon give birth to his first legitimate child, and his forthcoming absence prompted him to make provisions for his unborn heir if 'anything come to my said Lord of Somerset in the said voyage but good'.[40] At Somerset's instigation, the king agreed that Somerset's wife would be entrusted with the care of their child as opposed to a guardian, because 'she should by nature have it in more tenderness than any other creature'.[41] Matters having been settled to the best extent possible, Somerset continued with his preparations.

There were high hopes for the French campaign led by the newly created Duke of Somerset, but in a sign of what was to come, it started badly. Having finally joined his troops after a series of delays—perhaps partially accounted for by the birth of his daughter—Somerset left England in July. On 12 August, he reached Cherbourg with a force of approximately seven to ten thousand men (reports differ on the exact number) and he immediately began marching towards Brittany.[42] The campaign, however, brought nothing but disappointment. Though Somerset succeeded in taking some minor towns, he came nowhere near achieving the success that had been anticipated, never once engaging with the French army. To make matters worse, he allowed his men to pillage and plunder French towns and villages and squandered and misused Crown funds in an attempt to replenish his own coffers. His mission had never been easy, but the campaign was a dismal failure.

In January 1444, eight months after the birth of his daughter, Somerset returned home. In London, his reception was cold. The usually mild-mannered king was outraged. According to a contemporary chronicler, Somerset 'being accused of treason there, was forbidden to appear in the king's presence'.[43] His career seemingly in tatters, Somerset had no choice but to withdraw in shame, and he retired to one of his Dorset estates.[44] It is unclear whether Somerset's wife and infant daughter joined him in Dorset, but given what may have transpired, it seems improbable. It is related by a chronicler that Somerset, in a state of desperation and despair,

> the noble heart of a man of such high rank upon hearing this most unhappy news, was moved to extreme indignation; and being unable to bear the stain of so great a disgrace, he accelerated his death by putting an end to his existence, it is generally said; preferring thus to cut short his sorrow, rather than pass a life of misery, labouring under so disgraceful a charge.[45]

Margaret was just a few days shy of her first birthday when her father died on 27 May 1444, a tragedy that her mother would record in her Book of Hours. Given that suicide was considered a mortal sin, it is surprising that the Croyland chronicler—whose author was well placed to know the truth of the matter—reported the manner in which the disgraced man had met his death. Other contemporary sources ignore the matter entirely, simply stating that Somerset died, without making further comment.[46] This strongly suggests that he did indeed commit suicide, and if this was the case, then given contemporary attitudes, it says much about his tormented state of mind.

Somerset's death was not spoken of openly—another indication of the uncomfortable circumstances. As Margaret grew, she would have become aware of the rumours, although she never addressed them, in public at least. Throughout her life, Margaret's deceased father evidently held some place in her heart, for she would later order prayers to be said for his soul at Cambridge. Whatever the true circumstances, the loss of Somerset at such an early point changed the course of his infant daughter's life considerably. It left Margaret both vulnerable and in a dubious position, for though she was proud of her family, she was also forced to deal with the fact that she was descended from a family whose legitimacy would be continuously questioned.

It was in the Saxon minster at Wimborne, burial place of the Saxon king Ethelred and a royal peculiar (a church that falls under the direct jurisdiction of the Crown) since 1318, that Somerset was laid to rest.[47] At his daughter's cost and instruction, a magnificent tomb of Purbeck marble and Dorset limestone was later erected to his memory and that of his widow, still to be seen in the minster today.[48] Interestingly, the effigies of Margaret's parents show them clasping hands, clearly indicative of how Margaret herself chose to view her parents' marriage, in spite of its short duration. It may also be a significant attempt to emphasise her own legitimacy, for she—unlike some of her ancestors—had unquestionably been born within wedlock, and her parents' marriage, though short, was honourable. A memorial window depicting the couple and their daughter could once also be seen in the East Window but was moved to All Saints' Church, Landbeach, in the eighteenth century. There, the beautiful jumbled glass features the only known likeness of Margaret in her youth.[49] Margaret later founded a chantry within Wimborne Minster, and of the many she endowed, this was the most personal, giving some indication as to the sorrow she felt for the loss of a father she had never known.[50]

At the time of Somerset's death, the duchess was once again pregnant, proving that the couple were reunited at some point following Somerset's return from France.[51] Possibly the shock of her husband's death caused her to miscarry, or else the child was stillborn or died young, for nothing further is heard of this pregnancy.

As Somerset's only legitimate child, Margaret, though just an infant, became a wealthy heiress. Somerset may have struggled to recover from his imprisonment financially, but in landed terms his estates were vast, in large part inherited from his mother, Margaret Holland. Among others, he owned lands in the counties of Kent, Worcestershire, Lincolnshire, Norfolk, Somerset, Essex, and Sussex. However, his death left Margaret and her mother without a male protector in the vicious, backbiting world of fifteenth-century politics. The young heiress's inheritance made her a precious—and therefore vulnerable—commodity.

Moreover, though the legitimacy of the Beauforts in later years was questioned, Margaret's royal blood, which could be traced back to Edward III, made her even more appealing. In 1444, though, she was still a little girl, less than a year old. A little girl who had no voice and no say in her own future: a pawn in a much bigger game whose fate—at this time, at least—seemed set to be decided by others. Within no time at all it became clear that the decisions made in Margaret's girlhood would affect the course of the rest of her life.

CHAPTER 2

OF SINGULAR WISDOM

The day of 31 May 1444 marked Margaret's first birthday. Her father had been dead for only four days, yet in that time the king, residing at the royal castle of Berkhamsted in Hertfordshire, had already made a momentous decision about the infant's future.

> And forasmuch as our cousin the Duke of Somerset is now late passed to God's mercy, the which hath a daughter and heir to succeed him, of full tender age called Margaret. We considering the notable services that our cousin the earl of Suffolk hath done unto us, and tendering him therefore the more specially as reason will, have of our grace and especial proper motion and mere deliberation granted unto him to have the ward and marriage of the said Margaret, without anything.[1]

Prior to Margaret's birth, the king had agreed to grant the Duchess of Somerset control of Margaret's caretaking, but since then the duke had fallen into disgrace. Henry VI felt no compunction to uphold the agreement, and Somerset's death was recast as an opportunity. As a direct descendant of John of Gaunt, the child was, after all, a member of the royal family. Though her male Beaufort relatives were regarded as superior in rank by right of their sex, Margaret was now the most senior member of the Beaufort family in the female line. Furthermore, her blood connection to the king—her father's second cousin—and her lack of a male guardian had not gone unnoticed. Many were eager to obtain her valuable wardship in order to secure an interest in her lands. Bishop Fisher later confirmed that as a result of the 'likelihood of inheritance many sued to have had her to marriage'.[2]

The man upon whom Henry VI chose to settle his cousin's wardship, William de la Pole, Earl of Suffolk, was one of his great favourites. Described by Fisher as 'a man of great experience', Suffolk had been born in 1396 to Michael de la Pole, second Earl of Suffolk, and Katherine Stafford.[3] Like Margaret's father, Suffolk had been a soldier and had loyally served Henry V throughout the French campaign.[4] Suffolk's position was bolstered by his marriage in 1430 to the formidable Alice Chaucer, dowager Countess of Salisbury and granddaughter of the famous poet, Geoffrey.[5] Like that of Margaret's parents, their marriage produced just one child, a son, born in 1442. With a lone precious heir, it was only natural that Suffolk considered his son's marital prospects to be of the greatest importance. Fisher claimed that it was with this in mind that his thoughts turned to Margaret, and he 'most diligently procured to have had her for his son and heir'.[6]

This may have been Suffolk's initial motivation, and it did indeed eventually come to pass, but at one time his plans for his son's future lay elsewhere. In 1446 he had obtained the wardship of Anne Beauchamp, the sole heir of Henry Beauchamp, Duke of Warwick.[7] Sadly, the young girl died in 1449, bringing all hopes of a future matrimonial alliance to an abrupt end. These earlier plans would later gain grave significance for Suffolk, but this was all still to come. In the meantime, in 1449, Suffolk's attentions fell upon Margaret, though there is no evidence that he ever met her or that she left her mother's care.[8] He was aware, nonetheless, that she was a wealthy young heiress with prestigious connections and lands because he had been granted the keeping of her lands upon Somerset's death.[9] On Margaret's side, Suffolk's standing with the king made an alliance with the de la Pole family honourable. Still the advantage was mostly Suffolk's. Unlike Margaret, his family had no royal blood, being descended from wool merchants.[10]

AT THE TIME OF MARGARET Beaufort's birth, her kinsman and king, Henry VI, was twenty-one. To the disappointment of his subjects, he displayed none of the attributes of his warrior father, and it had long been clear that, by the standards of the time, he was of weak character. He displayed no leadership qualities and had no desire for military glory. Henry was learned, and education was one of his greatest passions—something he and Margaret had in common. Neither was this the only interest they shared, for, like Margaret, the king was exceptionally pious. His chaplain, John Blacman, later recalled that Henry was 'more given to God and to devout prayer than to handling worldly and temporal things, or practising vain sports and pursuits'.[11] Henry was also a kind man, a quality that Margaret cannot have failed to recognise—and undoubtedly appreciated—when she met him for the first time during her girlhood.

In 1441 Henry's thoughts turned to marriage, and he received portraits of several potential brides. In Henry's mind, the ideal candidate would bring an opportunity for peace with France, and in the autumn of 1443 his uncle Henry Beaufort—by now a cardinal who enjoyed significant influence with the young king—seemed to have found the perfect choice. His suggestion was Margaret of Anjou, the niece of Charles VII and daughter of René of Anjou, the titular king of Naples, Sicily, and Jerusalem (titular because, although he adopted these titles, they meant nothing and he ruled none of these kingdoms).[12] In May 1444 Suffolk agreed the Treaty of Tours, whereby Margaret of Anjou would be married to Henry VI and the English would return Maine and Anjou to the French. This was hugely unpopular in England, and matters were made worse by René's poverty, which rendered him unable to provide a dowry for his daughter. Regardless, the deal had been done.

Margaret Beaufort was just shy of her second birthday when, on 9 April 1445, the *Cock John*—part of an entourage consisting of fifty-six ships—docked on the south coast of England. On board was precious cargo—the king's bride-to-be, Margaret of Anjou, who had been escorted by Margaret Beaufort's guardian, Suffolk, and his wife Alice.[13] Her arrival signified a policy of peace between England and France, but it was not destined to last. It had not been an easy crossing for the fifteen-year-old French princess, who was feeling so unwell upon landing that Suffolk had to carry her ashore. When she recovered from the treacherous journey, the princess made her way to thirteenth-century Titchfield Abbey in Hampshire.[14] It was there that, on 23 April, Bishop William Ayscough solemnized her marriage to Henry VI: England had a new queen.

The Milanese ambassador later told his mistress that an Englishman had described the new queen as being 'a most handsome woman, though somewhat dark'.[15] In truth there are few clues as to Margaret of Anjou's appearance, but all surviving images of her portray her with blonde hair: whatever the truth, the king was certainly pleased with his new bride.[16] An exorbitant sum that included the commissioning of new jewels was laid out in preparation for the queen's coronation, which took place at Westminster Abbey on 30 May.

The new queen would come to know well—and favour—members of Margaret Beaufort's family, for they had always been close to the king. Indeed, members of the Beaufort family were by the young king's side from the moment of his accession. Margaret's great-uncle, Cardinal Beaufort, played an especially prominent role in the affairs of the realm until his death in 1447 and was a leading member of the king's council.[17] Following Cardinal Beaufort's death, Margaret's uncle, Edmund Beaufort—the youngest and only surviving of Somerset's brothers—assumed the role of head of the family. Edmund was around three years younger than Margaret's father and during Somerset's French imprisonment had distinguished himself so well in military affairs that he had been made first Earl and then Marquess of Dorset. He was steadfastly loyal to Henry VI and, unlike his elder brother, ingratiated himself with the king. Henry relied heavily on him, particularly in matters concerning relations between England and France. On 31 March 1448, when Margaret was four years old, her uncle Edmund was rewarded for his loyalty and created Duke of Somerset, the title once held by her father. It was an honour for which he would pay a high price.

THE PRIMARY SETTING FOR MARGARET'S childhood was Blet-
soe, the Bedfordshire place of her birth, where, as Margaret's nineteenth-
century biographer Caroline Halsted tells us, Margaret's mother lived in
'great pomp'.[18] Despite the tragic circumstances in which her father had
died, Margaret seems to have enjoyed a happy childhood. The family network was always strong and remained so until the end of her life. Raised
by her mother alongside her half-siblings, the St Johns, and her father's
bastard daughter Tacyn, Margaret was always close to her half-brothers
and -sisters.[19] Their appearances in her accounts bear witness to the bond
they shared—the names of John, Oliver, Edith, Mary, Margaret and Elizabeth St John all appear at various points. While at Bletsoe, Margaret,
worked on an embroidery that depicted the lineage of the St John family;
she would later present this to her half-brother John St John on the occasion of his marriage in 1498.[20] Given her many siblings, Margaret would
never have lacked for company during her childhood. Unlike them, however, Margaret alone could boast of her royal lineage and connections: it
was her career that had the most potential.

As a small child, Margaret could never have comprehended her own significance. Neither, in her early days, would this have been of great import
to her as she applied herself to her lessons. Not all girls were given an education; that Margaret was shows that her mother recognised how important it would be to her daughter's future. Practical skills, such as managing
lands and estates—in which Margaret later took such an interest—were
a crucial part of a noblewoman's life and would have been expected when
Margaret assumed the role of a wife. Her family were also great music
lovers, and Margaret would have become accustomed to the entertainers
who graced her mother's household from a young age. Indeed, in later life,
regular payments for minstrels appear in her accounts—they were not always her own; those of the king, queen, her granddaughter Princess Mary,
and the abbot of St Albans are mentioned, among others. Singers from the
king's chapel as well her own chapel at Collyweston also performed for her
entertainment and were referenced in her accounts.

Not all of Margaret's lessons were concerned with the practical, however. Her friend and admirer Bishop Fisher would later recollect that 'she was of singular wisdom' and that 'right studious she was in books which she had in great number both in English and in French'.[21] This was not mere flattery, for Margaret owned books in both languages and later commissioned them, too. Fluency in French was considered both desirable and necessary for men and women—particularly those with a future career at court—but Margaret, not content with French alone, was keen to learn another language. According to Fisher, 'Full often she complained that in her youth she had not given her to ye understanding of Latin wherein she had a little.'[22] Margaret's thirst for knowledge was impressive; perhaps she inherited some of the fervour of her paternal grandmother, Margaret Holland, who herself had been a great literary patron. Further evidence of Margaret's intellectual pursuits is given by her later inclusion in the will of her mother-in-law, the Duchess of Buckingham, from whom she had borrowed books on occasion.[23] The duchess was clearly aware of Margaret's enthusiasm and bequeathed her several items: 'To her daughter Richmond a book of English, being a legend of Saints; a book of French, called Lucun; another book of French, of the Epistles and Gospels; and a devotional book with clasps of silver gilt, covered with purple velvet.'[24] Margaret treasured her books, and she would later amass an impressive library consisting of all manner of subjects—primarily religious, but also romance and satire.

From an early age, religion played an integral role in Margaret's life, offering her both comfort and reassurance. Margaret's mother was herself a pious woman and may have instilled the importance of religion in her daughter. Margaret may also have been influenced by her half-sister Margaret St John, who became a nun and later Abbess of Shaftesbury.[25] While at Bletsoe Castle, Margaret would have become familiar with the nearby medieval church of St Mary the Virgin, which boasted a splendid fifteenth-century wall painting of Saint George and the Dragon.

Later in Margaret's life, she tried to make religion as accessible as possible and found that translating works from French to English provided her with an outlet to do so. Her choice to translate both *The Mirror of Gold for the Sinful Soul*, a religious work that had originally been translated from Latin into French, and Thomas à Kempis's *Imitation of Christ*, a devotional book composed just a few decades before Margaret's birth, may have reflected her piety and religious interests.[26] More than this, though, Margaret's translations were an attempt to make these religious texts accessible to a wider audience, something that she was later able to do as a result of her exalted wealth and position. In her mind, she was giving others the opportunity to educate themselves by the reading of such texts, thereby improving their own minds. It was thus part of a much broader scheme in which Margaret was able to use her influence for the bettering of the lives of others. Much later, Margaret's great-granddaughter Elizabeth I would skilfully emulate such projects. Margaret's mother, the Duchess of Somerset, to whom 'she was a very daughter in all noble manners', supervised all of Margaret's lessons and must have been delighted at the attentiveness her daughter showed in her education.[27]

When not at Bletsoe, Margaret and her mother's household would often reside at Maxey Castle. Located in the village of Maxey in rural Northamptonshire, the castle was another residence that formed a part of the duchess's inheritance.[28] Today, all that survives is the partial remains of the double moat that once surrounded it. It was in these residences that the duchess felt most at home and chose to raise her growing family.

Though she had lost her husband, Margaret's mother, the Duchess of Somerset, did not give up on matrimony: just under two years after the death of Margaret's father, the duchess fell in love. The object of her affection was Sir John Neville, and the relationship was serious. So much so that the couple decided to wed.[29] Because they were related in the second degree of affinity, they applied for a dispensation from the pope, claiming that they were motivated by 'the ardour of a singular affection'.[30] In addition to her feelings, the duchess, being a widow, evidently felt vulnerable, because the dispensation stated that the couple were prompted by 'the conserving of the divers domains which the said Margaret holds by right of dower in several dioceses, and for several other reasonable causes'.[31] The dispensation was duly granted on 5 April 1446, but for some unknown reason the marriage never took place. It is possible that Sir John Neville died, for there is no further mention of him in contemporary sources and nothing in regard to the Duchess of Somerset. The personal reasons for which the duchess chose to marry were ones that her daughter would never consider, for Margaret seems never to have fallen in love. Her marriages, instead, were all made with practicality in mind.

Whatever the circumstances surrounding the Duchess of Somerset's failure to marry Neville, by the following year she had moved on. On 14 April 1447, when Margaret was nearly four years old, her mother was once again granted a licence to remarry, taking as her third husband Lionel, or Leo, Lord Welles.[32] Margaret grew to be fond of the son—her half-brother John—that her mother's third marriage produced, but nothing is known of her relationship with her stepfather. Lord Welles was a loyal supporter of Margaret's paternal uncle, Edmund Beaufort, so it must have been a choice of which Edmund approved and perhaps even had some hand in arranging. Welles had been one of the king's privy councillors and had risen steadily in the king's favour. Like many of his contemporaries, he had served in military campaigns before joining the king's household, and in 1438 he took up the post of Lord Lieutenant of Ireland. Like Margaret's mother, Welles had been married before, to Joan Waterton, the daughter of a trusted retainer of John of Gaunt by whom he had one son and four daughters.[33] At a stroke, therefore, Margaret could add five step-siblings to her growing family, and there is evidence that she retained relationships with some of them in later life. Around 1450, when Margaret was seven years old, she was joined in the nursery by her half-brother, John. He was the last child that the Duchess of Somerset would bear, and it seems probable that he was named in honour of John of Gaunt in a proud declaration of the family's connections.

It is unclear how great a role Margaret's new stepfather took in her upbringing, but as he had his own burgeoning career to occupy his time, it is unlikely that it was particularly profound. Decisions concerning Margaret's future had been settled upon Suffolk, so there was no reason for Lord Welles to be involved in her rearing.

The complexities of her situation and the importance of her alliance with the heir of her guardian, William de la Pole, Earl of Suffolk, would have dawned on young Margaret—not yet six years old—when, early in 1450, sometime between 28 January and 7 February, she underwent a form of marriage ceremony with John de la Pole. Given the tender years of the bride and groom, who was just a year older than Margaret, the ceremony was never consummated and was instead *per verba legitime de presenti*—what would today be termed a common-law marriage. This was as far as the relationship would go, and in spite of the words that had passed between them, Margaret never considered John de la Pole her husband; contemporaries instead commonly referred to Edmund Tudor as 'her first husband'.[34] Likewise, John de la Pole, who lived until 1492 and whose descendants became dangerously entangled with Margaret's own, never claimed the contrary to be true. From what would soon transpire, however, it is evident that others were of a different mind.

IN THE YEAR OF MARGARET'S wedding ceremony, matters in England took a dangerous turn. Henry VI's ineptitude in governing his kingdom was plain for all to see; easily influenced and manipulated by those around him, including Somerset and Suffolk, Henry had allowed corruption and greed to fester within the court. Moreover, he had shown no interest in the military affairs of England, lacking both the understanding and the experience to command his army in France. As a result, in October 1449 Rouen fell to the French army. Then, in July Somerset surrendered Caen. By the end of August 1450, there were just two remaining English possessions in France: Calais and Aquitaine.

Margaret's guardian Suffolk—now a duke—had long been unpopular in England, having been apportioned much of the blame for England's wars with France by reason of his policy of peace and promoting Henry VI's marriage with a dowerless princess. Although Suffolk retained the king and queen's favour, Henry was under great pressure from the duke's enemies, as well as the common people, to punish him. Suffolk desperately protested his loyalty, citing that both his father and his brothers had died in royal service, while he himself had 'borne arms for 34 winters in the time of the king your father and your own time'.[35] He steadfastly declared, 'I may die protesting that I have always been true to you, sovereign lord, and to your land, and to your prosperity and welfare'.[36]

At the beginning of 1450, matters came to a head, and in spite of his protestations of innocence, on 28 January Suffolk was impeached by Parliament. The uncertainty of his fate no doubt hastened his need to ensure the security of his heir and thus prompted the marriage of his son to Margaret. Outraged that he had not been punished further, the commons demanded his arrest, leaving the king with little choice but to have his favourite placed in the Tower. On 13 March, accused of having 'falsely and traitorously plotted, contrived, proposed, envisaged, performed and committed various high, great, heinous and horrible treasons', Suffolk appealed to Henry. His accusers claimed that the duke, having procured Margaret's wardship, was

> proposing to marry her to his said son, claiming and pretending her to be the next to inherit the crown of this your realm, for want of an heir from you, sovereign lord, in order to accomplish his said traitorous purpose and intention; whereupon the same duke of Suffolk, since the time of his arrest, has caused the said Margaret to be married to his said son.[37]

On his knees before the king, Suffolk vehemently denied the accusations made against him:

> As for the second part of the first article, it is contrary to law and reason to consider the said Margaret so close to the crown; and for his acquittal, he had told to a large number of the lords that if the duke of Warwick's

daughter had lived he had intended to marry his son to her and not to the said Margaret.[38]

He was desperate to show that he had never intended to manipulate Margaret's royal blood to his advantage. Indeed, Margaret's lands, through which he could secure a handsome inheritance for his son, were of greater value to him than her bloodline.

As neither the king nor his nobles had any desire to drag the matter out publicly by putting Suffolk on trial, they instead banished him from England and France. Across the realm news of his exemption from capital punishment spread, inflaming public anger. On 30 April—just a month before Margaret's seventh birthday—Suffolk set sail for Flanders, but he did not make it far. Before long, a vessel, the *Nicholas of the Tower*, intercepted his ship. The unfortunate duke was taken on board, where he was immediately bade 'Welcome Traitor'.[39] He was then forced to undergo the humiliating spectacle of a mock trial whose outcome was a foregone conclusion. A correspondent of the Pastons—a Norfolk gentry family through whose copious surviving letters we owe a wealth of information about the tumultuous events of the fifteenth century—reported that Suffolk was 'drawn out of the great ship into the boat, and there was an axe and a stock; and one of the lewdest of the ship bade him lay down his head'.[40] Then, with a rusty sword, the executioner 'smote off his head within half a dozen strokes' before stealing his fine clothes.[41] His mutilated body was thrown overboard and washed up on the shores of Dover on 2 May. The disgraced duke's remains were laid to rest in the Church of St Andrew at Wingfield, Suffolk, where his father was also buried.[42] Though Suffolk's brutal murder shocked many, few of his contemporaries save for the king and the distraught queen—to whom Suffolk had been somewhat of a father figure—mourned his passing.

Margaret was probably too young to remember much about the fate of her guardian; it is possible that she had never met him. However, in the immediate aftermath of Suffolk's disgrace and murder, she remained married—in name—to his son. On 18 August, three months after the horrendous events that transpired on board the *Nicholas of the Tower*, Pope Nicholas V issued a dispensation to Margaret and her husband. This was in response to their petition—which likely stemmed from their concerned mothers—that 'they formerly contracted marriage *per verba legitime de presenti* in ignorance that they were related in the fourth and fourth degrees of kindred'.[43] Evidently, both parties were eager for the youngsters to remain married, for the petition had claimed that if the young couple were to divorce, 'grave dissensions and scandals would probably be stirred up between their parents and friends'.[44] Perhaps there had been concern as to the impact Suffolk's death would have on the marriage of these two young people, and as such it was feared that it would be annulled—which was clearly not the hoped-for outcome. As a result of the petition, the pope decreed that the youngsters were to 'remain in the said marriage, notwithstanding the said impediment' and that their offspring would be legitimate.[45] For the time being, however, the marriage was to remain as it had been made: *per verba legitime de presenti*—a marriage of words rather than deed.

SUFFOLK'S MURDER PROVED TO BE the first in a series of events starting in 1450 that turned the country upside down. Though the unpopular duke was now gone, the Crown was still bankrupt, resulting in harsh taxation, and corruption remained rife within the court. Henry VI's inability to solve these problems only made matters worse. By May, the commoners had had enough, and a rebellion broke out in Kent. The rebels began to march on London, demanding that the king dismiss his corrupt advisors.[46] It is highly improbable that Margaret, almost seven years old, would have been in the capital at this time, but she may nevertheless have been aware of the tension spreading across the country. Though the rebellion was crushed and order restored, tensions continued to run high.

The death of Margaret's father-in-law, Suffolk, left the way clear for her uncle Somerset to assume a more powerful role in government. His influence and favour with the king and queen continued to grow, but in spite of this, Somerset had a rival who was intensely jealous of the high regard in which the duke was held by the royal couple: Richard, Duke of York. York's father, Richard, Earl of Cambridge, was the son of Edward III's fourth son, Edmund of Langley, while his mother, Anne Mortimer, was the great-granddaughter of the king's second son, Lionel, Duke of Clarence. Such prestigious ancestry gave York a claim to the throne—and a strong one at that. In appearance York was short and unremarkable, but he was intelligent and well respected, if not amiable. His marriage to Cecily Neville, the mother of Margaret's great-aunt Joan Beaufort, with whom he would sire thirteen children, had bolstered his power and ambition. Having been appointed Lieutenant General of France on 2 July 1440, York had in recent years spent much of his time in France, gaining valuable military experience.

Queen Margaret greatly disliked and feared York on account of his open opposition to some of the king's policies and favourites. In 1447 he had therefore been created Lieutenant of Ireland—a post that had once been occupied by Margaret's stepfather, Lord Welles—in order to limit his involvement in parliamentary decisions. York sailed for Ireland in the summer of 1449, but having spent a fortune of his own money during his years in military service—for which he had never been recompensed—he was becoming increasingly alienated from the king's regime. To make matters worse, the queen's preference for Somerset was clear for all to see, as were her attempts to diminish York's role within the government. By the autumn of 1450, like many of the king's subjects, York had had enough. In September he returned from Ireland and demanded that the king's traitorous advisors, chief among them Somerset, be removed. York had gained the support of the commoners by promising to restore order to the realm. But the queen and Somerset suspected that York's motives were more ominous—after all, he had a good claim to the throne, and the queen had yet to bear her husband an heir.

York was not alone in his concerns about the government. Many believed that the king had lost any vestige of control. On 1 December, with

York's influence, Somerset was impeached by Parliament and sent to the Tower. But his imprisonment was short-lived, for the king and queen soon ordered that he be set free. In January 1451 Parliament demanded his removal, but still the king refused to renounce his favourite. Throughout the turmoil, Margaret's family remained unquestionably loyal to Henry VI. By now her stepfather Lord Welles was mostly absent, having been appointed Joint Deputy of Calais in 1451, alongside Richard Wydeville, Earl Rivers. There he would remain until 1455.

As tensions continued to grow, York was in a state of desperation and was anxious for the king to take action. With this in mind, he prepared for armed resistance. Despite the queen's and Somerset's warnings, Henry VI could not be convinced that York was intent upon taking his throne until the duke began marching with a force towards London in February 1452. It was an unpopular move amongst the people, and though Henry, keen to promote peace, pardoned York for taking up arms, the duke then found himself excluded from politics and humiliated. But that was not an end to his disgruntlement, and matters would soon become far worse.

It was against this backdrop of foreign war and political tension in a country that was swiftly being torn apart by inner strife, bankruptcy, and corruption that Margaret Beaufort was raised. Far away from the unrest, secluded in her mother's homes, Margaret would before long join her kinsmen and become fully immersed in the intrigues of the court, and with it the problems that were to envelop the country and her family—it was a destiny from which there was no escape.

CHAPTER 3

A MARVELLOUS THING

In February 1453, when Margaret was just a few months shy of her tenth birthday, the king commanded her mother to attend the court in London and to bring her daughter with her. This is likely the first occasion on which Margaret visited court, and possibly also London. If so, its bustling, overcrowded streets would have been a stark contrast to the quiet and peaceful English countryside to which she had grown accustomed. Dominating the skyline with one of the tallest spires in Europe was the cathedral of Old St Paul's, where her ancestor John of Gaunt lay entombed. Elsewhere, the banks of the Thames were lined with the resplendent houses of the nobility, with sprawling gardens that stretched down to the river. The rest of the city was a maze of twisting streets bursting with houses and shops where Londoners peddled their wares. The Palace of Westminster was the king's primary residence, located next to the magnificent abbey where England's monarchs were traditionally anointed. It is likely there that Margaret met her royal kinsman for the first time.

As Margaret was brought into the king's presence, she was confronted with a kindly thirty-one-year-old man who did not conform to the stereotype of a king. A sixteenth-century portrait of Henry that appeared in Henry VIII's inventory (perhaps based on a lost original) shows a richly dressed man with a thin face and dark hair.[1] Though the allures of fine clothes and costly jewels had once appealed to him, it was well known, as Blacman tells us, that from the king's youth 'he always wore round-toed

39

shoes and boots like a farmer's'.[2] These were coupled with 'a long gown with a rolled hood like a townsman, and a full coat reaching below his knees'. Henry rejected all of the fashionable and costly garments that were available to the highest ranks of society.[3] Even on the feast days, when custom dictated he should don his crown, Henry was known to wear a hair shirt 'that by its roughness his body might be restrained from excess'.[4]

The king's reason for summoning his young cousin to court was simple: though Margaret had been married to the heir of the Duke of Suffolk, it had been a marriage of words only—easily dissolvable. The king had decided—almost certainly at his own instigation—that the young couple would divorce and Margaret would marry his half-brother Edmund Tudor. The marriage would be advantageous for all parties. As a reward for his loyalty to the king, Edmund would accumulate all of the lands that Margaret had inherited upon the death of her father, and Margaret would benefit from the increased stature that accompanied proximity to the Crown.

According to a story later relayed by Bishop Fisher, who learned of it from Margaret herself, she may have had some choice in the matter. Being 'not fully nine years old', as Fisher remembered, Margaret was still a child.[5] He related that another candidate for her hand had been presented, for Henry VI 'did make means for Edmund his brother, then the Earl of Richmond'.[6] Margaret, however, being 'doubtful in her mind what she were best to do', had 'asked counsel of an old gentlewoman whom she much loved and trusted'.[7] If this story is true, then she was clearly torn between John de la Pole and the other candidate. Accordingly, the unnamed gentlewoman advised her to 'commend herself to Saint Nicholas ye patron and helper of all true maidens, and to beseech him to put in her mind what she were best to do'.[8] This was, so Fisher said, advice that the young and pious Margaret took to heart, and so 'she followed and made her prayer so full often, but specially at night when she should ye morrow after make answer of her mind determinedly'.[9]

Fisher continued: 'A marvellous thing that same night as I have heard her tell many a time, as she lay in prayer calling upon Saint Nicholas, whether sleeping or waking she could not assure, but about 4 of ye clock in the morning one appeared unto her arrayed like a bishop, and naming unto her Edmund had take him unto her husband'.[10] Margaret's reason for appealing to Saint Nicholas could be explained by the fact that he was believed to be the patron saint of children and was thought to perform miracles. Whatever the rationale, it is unsurprising, in light of later events, that she would tell such a tale, in so doing constructing a narrative around this time in her life whereby her fate was led by both God and destiny. It was a story that would later be recounted by other chroniclers and so was evidently well known. Though the narrative was clearly of use in supporting Margaret's ambitions, her own piety lends strong credence to her genuinely believing she had indeed had a vision. Even at this point in her life, she was deeply committed to her religion. And it pointed her firmly in one direction. For it was 'by this means she did incline her mind unto Edmund ye King's brother and Earl of Richmond'.[11] In truth, whatever spin Margaret later added, it is improbable that the king would have allowed her to make any other choice.

Edmund and his brother Jasper Tudor were Henry VI's younger half-brothers; though they shared the same mother, Katherine of Valois, on their father's side, their blood was neither royal nor noble. Following the death of her husband Henry V in 1422, Katherine of Valois, a young widow, soon became a willing participant in a dalliance with a squire named Owen Tudor. There is no surviving evidence of a marriage between the couple, and in the Parliament of 1427 it was declared that 'no man of whatever estate or condition make contract of betrothal or matrimony to marry himself to the queen of England without the special licence and assent of the king'.[12] The consequences for those who disobeyed were dire: 'duly convicted', one would 'forfeit for his whole life all his lands and tenements'.[13] If Katherine married Owen Tudor or was considering marrying him, then there was good reason for them to keep the marriage quiet. Polydore Vergil would later claim that, following the death of Henry V, his widow 'being but young in years', fell for Owen, 'a gentleman of Wales, adorned with wonderful gifts of body and mind, who derived his pedigree from Cadwallader'.[14] In truth, Owen Tudor was a Welshman who could trace his lineage from the prominent Tudor family that resided in Penmynydd in Anglesey and that counted Gronw Fychan ap Tudur—once the lord steward of Llywelyn the Great—among his ancestors.[15]

Katherine and Owen's union had resulted in the births of several children. Henry VI greatly favoured his younger half-brothers, both of whom were described as being 'sincerely beloved' in the Parliament of 1453.[16] In the spring of 1453, they joined the queen on progress, and later that year they both received great rewards as a result of their 'nobility of birth and proximity in blood'.[17] On 23 November 1452, Edmund and Jasper Tudor were raised to the peerage. Edmund was created Earl of Richmond, and Jasper was made Earl of Pembroke. New lands were given to the brothers to support their heightened status, in Jasper's case centring in South Wales, where he would become immensely popular. The king may already at this time have had young Margaret Beaufort in mind as a bride for the elder of his half-brothers, for what better way to reward Edmund than with the hand of a wealthy heiress with drops of royal blood? It has been suggested that Henry VI, with no male heir of his own, was considering naming Edmund his heir. Though this is unlikely to have been the case—after all, the Duke of York had the strongest dynastic claim and Edmund's royal blood came solely from his French-born mother, who had no claim to the English throne—Margaret's blood, stemming from John of Gaunt, would undoubtedly have strengthened any claim of Edmund's. Regardless, it would not be long before such a measure proved to be unnecessary.

Having spent a merry Christmas at Greenwich, where the entertainments included an elaborate disguising (a masque, an entertainment in which the participants wore costumes and were disguised), on 5 January 1453 the king knighted both Edmund and Jasper in an extravagant ceremony at the Tower. This could have been in preparation for what lay ahead: just two months later and within weeks of Margaret's divorce from John de la Pole, on 24 March she became the ward of 'the king's uterine brothers'.[18] Her lands were immediately divided between the Tudor brothers, making them both wealthy men.

Following the summons of the Duchess of Somerset to London, her daughter Margaret received an introduction to court life. As an impressionable girl of nine years, she would have been awestruck by the queen, who was twenty-three and a powerful figure at court. Despite the dismal state of Crown finances, Queen Margaret was fond of finery and frequently appeared bedecked in the richest clothes and jewels, surrounded by her loyal damsels. Young Margaret Beaufort was certainly in attendance for the Garter celebrations at Windsor Castle on 23 April and would have been dazzled by the splendours of the court and the sumptuous red costume worn by the queen. Around this time, Margaret is also likely to have been afforded the opportunity to meet Edmund Tudor—her future husband—probably for the first time. In honour of the occasion, the king made his 'right dear and right well beloved cousin Margaret' a gift of 100 marks for clothes on 12 May, in order to make a splendid impression.[19] In later life Margaret was exceptionally fond of clothes and a keen follower of fashion, an interest that probably stemmed from her mother's love of finery and her time in the court.

Though she was not yet ten years old, for the second time in her life Margaret's marital prospects had been settled, but there were no immediate plans for her wedding. Given her young age, it had probably been agreed that she could remain with her mother until she was old enough to fully cohabit with Edmund and fulfil her duties in every sense. It was not long, though, before events once again took an unexpected turn.

Henry VI's ongoing troubles swiftly turned into a crisis as matters both in France and at home spiralled out of control. In the autumn of 1452, John Talbot, Earl of Shrewsbury, had retaken Bordeaux from the French, but it was clear they were not going to permanently renounce it. To consolidate his victory, Talbot needed money and supplies, but as a result of England's bankruptcy, neither was forthcoming. In July 1453, terrible news arrived: the English army had suffered a crushing defeat at Castillon in Gascony. Talbot had been killed, and worse still, Calais was now the only remaining English possession in France. The Hundred Years' War had finally come to an end. It was a humiliating defeat.

That August, devastated by the summer's events, the king travelled to his palace at Clarendon to the east of Salisbury.[20] Clarendon had been a popular residence among Henry's predecessors and was often used as a hunting lodge. It was there that the king, complaining of extreme fatigue on the evening of 15 August, collapsed into what *John Benet's Chronicle* described as 'a major illness'.[21] Henry seems to have fallen into a stupor from which he could not be roused, leaving him seemingly conscious but unable to communicate or walk. This left his attendants both horrified and perplexed. His illness has been the subject of debate among modern historians, with some believing he was suffering from a mental breakdown and others suggesting it was catatonic schizophrenia. To Henry's doctors there seemed to be just one explanation: insanity.

For Queen Margaret, the news of her husband's illness was particularly distressing: after eight years of marriage, in April she had been able to deliver him the happy news that she was pregnant with her first child, due in the autumn. Yet, it soon became clear there was to be no quick recovery for the king. The situation became desperate, and to conceal his condition from his subjects, Henry was sent to the relative seclusion of Windsor Castle. His absence left the pregnant Queen Margaret to face the challenges of governing the realm alone. England had already emerged from the Hundred Years' War in a state of humiliation, but with the king's illness, the country was descending into chaos.

Queen Margaret's primary objective was to ensure that the Duke of York learned nothing of the king's incapacity, for she was fearful he would once more attempt to seize the reins of government. But matters were soon beyond her control, for on the morning of 13 October, at the Palace of Westminster, she was finally 'delivered of a fair Prince, whose name was called Edward'.[22] On a dynastic level, the birth of Prince Edward immediately settled the question of the succession, for the king now had a legitimate male heir. But what should have been an occasion of great joy was marred by Henry VI's continuing state of unresponsiveness. Secluded at Windsor under the supervision of his doctors and servants, the king had no idea that he was now a father. Matters were not helped by the circulation of rumours that the prince was the result of his mother's affair with Margaret Beaufort's uncle, Somerset.[23] There was certainly no truth to the accusations of his involvement with Queen Margaret, which stemmed purely from the favour in which the queen and her husband held him. As the political crisis grew, so too did the long-standing divide in the political structure. Two rival factions had emerged: on one side, the court party, headed by Queen Margaret and Somerset; on the other, York and his two key allies, the Earls of Salisbury and Warwick. There was no question as to where the loyalties of Margaret Beaufort's family lay.

Early in the new year of 1454, Henry VI was presented with his baby son. It was crucial that he acknowledge the prince, for until he did so vicious rumours about the infant's paternity would continue to circulate. Yet the king showed no signs of recognising the child, let alone acknowledging him. With no improvement in Henry's health, action needed to be taken to safeguard the government of the realm. Despite York's growing popularity among the nobles, the queen believed that she alone was the obvious candidate to head a regency, and so she made a bid for power. However, her arrogance and her contemptuous demeanour, coupled with the repugnance with which many viewed the idea of female rule, lost her a great deal of valuable support. The queen's foreign origins also worked against her, and it was obvious that nobody would rest easy with her at the forefront of affairs. Other arrangements would have to be put into place, but the queen was adamant that York should play no part in them.

When Parliament opened at Westminster on 14 February, the atmosphere was tense. Then, much to Queen Margaret's horror, on 27 March the Parliament appointed York Lord Protector of the realm during the king's incapacity. This was disastrous for Margaret Beaufort's family, and her uncle Somerset was promptly sent to the Tower. This time, Queen

Margaret was utterly powerless to prevent it. Indeed, she was now sent to Windsor to join her husband: the stage of power seemingly belonged to York alone.

The removal of the head of the family must have caused Margaret's mother a great deal of alarm, and, at ten years old, Margaret may well have sensed her anxiety. Who knew what the future held for her family? The wheel of fortune had turned in York's favour, and he proved himself to be a strong leader. Widely admired by the commons for his strenuous efforts to restore good government, he worked to repair the bankruptcy of the Crown.

Though their loyalty remained wholeheartedly with Henry VI, both Edmund and Jasper Tudor offered York their support. Unlike many of Henry VI's nobles, who were primarily motivated by self-interest, the Tudors seem to have been driven by a commitment to the fair governance of their half-brother's realm as well as his well-being, willingly complying with York's attempts to reduce the size of the royal household in an effort to restore Crown finances. Throughout York's protectorate, though he co-operated with the duke, feasibly Jasper was mistrustful of him. This would explain why he appears to have been particularly mindful of the importance of maintaining a presence in London, attending both Parliament and meetings of the council.[24] His brother Edmund was often absent for reasons that are unclear—possibly he was suffering from poor health.

Just as good order was being restored, the unexpected occurred. On Christmas Day, to the elation of the queen and her supporters, Henry VI made a recovery. Prayers were immediately offered up in thanks, and the king—who had no memory of what had happened to him—dispatched his almoner to Canterbury to make an offering on his behalf.[25] Still, recovery was gradual, and the king continued to suffer from bouts of ill health for the rest of his life. The court party were ecstatic that their king had regained his wits—after he had spoken to some of his lords 'as well as ever he did', the men were so overwhelmed that 'they wept for joy'.[26] Henry was at last able to meet—and more importantly, acknowledge—his young son, Prince Edward, much to Queen Margaret's pleasure. To the relief of Margaret's family, Prince Edward's birth signified the continuation of the Lancastrian royal family, yet unbeknown to them, all hopes that the arrival of an heir would bring security for the future were sorely misplaced.

With the king's recovery it was clear that York's nine-month protectorate would soon come to an end. Accordingly, on 9 February 1455, much to Queen Margaret's delight, he was formally discharged. Five days before York's protectorate was dissolved, Margaret's uncle Somerset was released from his imprisonment in the Tower and quickly restored to his former place by the king and queen's side, as were his supporters.[27] York was furious and withdrew to his stronghold of Sandal Castle, near Wakefield.[28] Though his power had dissipated, the queen's hatred of him had not. Intent on destroying him, she and Somerset began plotting his demise.

Henry VI may have been on the road to recovery, but he continued to display a lack of interest in the affairs of his realm. He turned more than ever to religion, leaving Queen Margaret and Somerset to run the kingdom. Queen Margaret's position had been immeasurably strengthened by the birth of her son, giving her more reason than ever to safeguard the Crown. And so she turned her attention to rallying as much support as possible, as well as to convincing her husband that York was vying for the throne. York, meanwhile, aware that his enemies would soon make a move against him, was not about to wait for them to strike. Together with Warwick and Salisbury, he began raising an army. All three men owned extensive estates in the north, and together, they were a force to be reckoned with.

The king's council planned to hold a great meeting on 21 May at Leicester, but York and his allies were deliberately excluded. Instead, they were all summoned to present themselves before the council. York, however, was wary. Fearing the consequences of Somerset's release, and suspecting that charges would be brought against him and his supporters, he took matters into his own hands: he and his army marched south, intent on securing his restoration to power and destroying Somerset for good.

On 1 May, Jasper Tudor left London with the king on the first stage of their journey to Leicester. When word reached them that York and his supporters were travelling south with an army, Henry immediately raised a force to defend the monarchy, fully aware that he was York's real target. War seemed inevitable.

On 22 May, the political tension between the court party and the Duke of York and his supporters finally erupted into violence. Accompanied by Jasper Tudor, Somerset and 'many lords', Henry VI had reached St Albans, twenty-two miles north of London, when York intercepted them.[29] Though he had the larger force, neither he nor the royal party wanted to fight. Instead, York persuaded Henry to hear his complaints: he wanted Somerset stripped of his power and punished. But his efforts were in vain, for the king—however weak—was not prepared to be dictated to and steadfastly refused to hand Somerset over. His response was clear: if York wanted to settle the matter, he would not be able to do so peaceably.

Seeing no alternative, York made the drastic decision to attack. According to a Milanese envoy, informed by a messenger, when the king's party 'were outside the town they were immediately attacked by York's men'.[30] York was fully aware that many would believe he had committed treason. The king's forces, led by Humphrey, Duke of Buckingham—a man who would later be closely connected with Margaret Beaufort—were ill prepared and taken aback by the strength of York's forces. Despite being caught off guard, the royal party initially held their own—that is, until Warwick quietly led a force into the town. The attack was disastrous for the royal army, many of whom fled when they perceived the direction that the battle was taking.

Realizing that the battle was lost, Margaret's uncle Somerset attempted to take refuge at the Castle Inn in the town. It was not long, however, before York's men had surrounded it: for Somerset—so long protected by the king and queen—this time there would be no escape. It was not long before he was struck down. As *John Benet's Chronicle* reported, 'All of the

Duke of Somerset's party were killed, wounded or at the least despoiled'.[31] With his death, the battle ended. The head of Margaret's family was now dead, and Vergil later claimed that

> king Henry conceived great and incredible sorrow for the loss of the duke of Somerset, because he had reposed all his hope in him, and for that such a noble captain, who had fought valiantly so many years against the French men, should now finally be killed of his own countrymen.[32]

But for the king, who had stood watching the violence play out around him, there were to be more direct consequences. On Warwick's orders, Yorkist archers shot and captured him. According to the Milanese ambassador, 'the Duke of York went to kneel before the king and ask pardon for himself and his followers, as they had not done this in order to inflict any hurt upon his Majesty, but in order to have Somerset. Accordingly, the king pardoned them'.[33] York had successfully eliminated his enemy, and in so doing knew that he had taken a huge step in securing his return to power.

Margaret's uncle Somerset was laid to rest in the abbey at St Albans.[34] Later, Margaret not only made offerings to the abbey but also on one occasion even rewarded the minstrels of the abbot. Whether the links with her uncle gave her a sentimental tie to St. Albans is unclear, but she was certainly aware that he had lost his life in the king's service there. Somerset's death meant that the head of Margaret's household—and a potentially powerful protector for her—was gone. Thus far, Margaret's short life had been punctuated by the deaths of some of the leading male figures in her life: her father, Suffolk, and now her uncle. In their place, Somerset's eldest son—Margaret's cousin Henry, who had fought and been injured at St. Albans—was the new head of the family. Like his father, Henry harboured a bitter resentment against the Yorkist regime, exacerbated by Somerset's murder, and would continue his family's struggle to hold on to the crown.

As those involved digested the outcome of the battle the following morning, York and his supporters escorted the king back to London. A contemporary chronicle claimed that Henry returned to the capital 'as king and not as a prisoner', but in the eyes of many the reality seemed otherwise.[35] The conclusion of the Milanese ambassador that 'now peace reigns' could not have been further from the truth.[36]

CHAPTER 4

AT WAR TOGETHER IN WALES

While the swords clashed at St Albans, Margaret Beaufort had probably remained with her mother and siblings in the Bedfordshire and Northamptonshire countryside. On 31 May, nine days after the Battle of St Albans, she reached her twelfth birthday, and it was probably soon afterwards that her marriage to Edmund Tudor was celebrated—it had certainly taken place by September. Margaret was not even a teenager, yet her marriage made her Countess of Richmond. It was a title that she retained even after Edmund's death, and the result of the marriage would determine the entire course of the rest of her life.

No details of Edmund and Margaret's wedding are known, and it is unclear precisely where and when it took place—possibly at Maxey or Bletsoe, Margaret's childhood homes. Her mother was probably present, as were Owen and Jasper Tudor. The experience must have been all the more daunting for Margaret given that she had only met Edmund once or at the most a handful of times prior to the ceremony. By the same token, given the age difference—Edmund was more than ten years Margaret's senior—they are unlikely to have had much in common. This was not unusual by contemporary standards but does give some insight into how the twelve-year-old Margaret must have felt as she promised to love, honour, and obey a man whom she barely knew. The conclusion of her marriage brought Margaret one step closer to Henry VI, who was already her kinsman by blood. Now, Henry was also her brother-in-law. No longer could she live at home under her mother's protection, sheltered from the events unfolding. As the wife of the king's half-brother, she would become directly involved in and witness firsthand the political turmoil that lay in store.

In spite of her adolescence, there was no question of Margaret's second marriage following a similar course to her first. From the start, Edmund Tudor fully intended that his young wife should fulfil her marital duties without delay. Chief among them was the consummation of her marriage, which took place either immediately or soon after the couple's wedding. The church declared that twelve was the age at which a girl was permitted to have sexual relations with her husband and cohabit, while fourteen was prescribed for boys. Nevertheless, many of Margaret's contemporaries still considered this to be painfully young and often chose to wait a few years. Mary de Bohun, for example, had been a similar age when she was married to Henry, Earl of Derby (later Henry IV), but had not given birth to her first child until six years after her wedding, indicating a delay in consummation.[1] So eager, though, was Edmund to secure an interest in Margaret's inheritance through consummation and the production of an heir that this was not an option. Despite being in his mid-twenties and between thirteen and fifteen years older than his bride, he wasted no time in making Margaret his wife in the fullest sense of the word. To the modern eye, Edmund's determination appears both horrific and brutal: indeed, Jones and Underwood have described his actions as 'ruthless and inconsiderate'.[2] His reckless disregard for Margaret's physical underdevelopment would leave her with deep emotional—and possibly physical—scars.

In spite of what happened, it is possible that Margaret harboured fond feelings towards her second husband. She frequently recounted the tale of choosing his suit by means of divine guidance and went to great lengths to identify herself with him. In her first will dated 2 June 1472, she left instructions for Edmund's remains to be removed from their resting place in Carmarthen and moved to Bourne in Lincolnshire, where she intended to be laid to rest beside him.³ Later, she also gave orders that prayers were to be said for her husband's soul at her foundation of Christ's College, Cambridge. Margaret's stipulations for her own memorial later changed, and as such this never transpired. She did, however, request that Edmund's arms be incorporated on her tomb, where they remain to this day. We will never know how far her initial request was based on the desire to be associated with Edmund—a desire intensified by the fact that their union led to the foundation of the Tudor dynasty—and how far, if at all, on true warmth of feeling, given that their marriage lasted for less than eighteen months, not all of which was spent together. The truth is that we know frustratingly little of Margaret and Edmund's relationship and thus can never be sure.

Likewise, it is difficult to get a sense of Edmund's character or appearance because there are no surviving portraits of him. The brass that adorns his tomb provides the only clue as to what he looked like and shows a rather harsh-looking man with dark, shoulder-length hair fully bedecked in armour—thereby emphasising his military prowess—his hands raised in prayer. But this was created at a later date so cannot be taken as an accurate reflection.⁴

Margaret's husband had not participated in the fighting at St Albans, but in the aftermath of the battle he was keen to show his support for his half-brother the king. Four days after the battle and prior to Margaret's marriage, Parliament was summoned: convening in July, it opened 'with the lord king sitting on the royal throne in the Painted Chamber'.⁵ Edmund had returned to the capital to attend and was there on 9 July to witness York and his supporters renew their oath of allegiance to Henry VI. The purpose of the Parliament was to find a way in which the government could move forward inclusive of York. Immediately after St Albans, the Milanese ambassador was of the belief that York would 'take up the government again'. 'Some', he wrote, 'think that the affairs of that kingdom will now take a turn for the better'.⁶ The duke had already taken steps to ensure his return to power, building a strong network of support. He had also been appointed Constable of England. At the same time, his ally the Earl of Warwick had been created Captain of Calais, further strengthening the position of York's supporters. Queen Margaret, meanwhile, had been left devastated by the death of Somerset, which only served to deepen her hatred of York. Like him, she now attempted to rally support, and she could certainly be assured of the loyalty of Margaret—though still a child—and her husband.

By the autumn, Margaret had bidden farewell to her mother and travelled with her husband to Pembrokeshire in West Wales. In September the newlyweds took up residence at the luxurious Palace of Lamphey, a bishop's palace that had been largely constructed by Henry de Gower, Bishop of St David's, in the fourteenth century. Featuring two courtyards, it was a regal and spacious residence that boasted an impressive eighty-two-foot-long Great Hall that provided the perfect space for entertaining. There was also a chapel, of which Margaret would have made full use, as well as comfortable apartments. Coupled with its lavish interiors, Lamphey's copious grounds contained orchards, fragrant herb gardens, and fishponds. Set in the vast and beautiful Welsh countryside, Lamphey had always been intended as a rural retreat, and thus it provided an idyllic setting for a newly married couple to get to know each other. Edmund, however, had more than recreation on his mind.

On 12 November, Parliament met again, but this time neither Edmund—in Wales with Margaret—nor his brother Jasper were present.[7] The king was also absent 'for certain just and reasonable causes', and it is wholly possible that he was once again suffering from a mental breakdown.[8] Soon after it had been convened, Parliament once more appointed York Protector of England. Yet again he made a concerted effort to resolve some of the realm's problems, particularly the improvement of Crown finances. His hard work paid off in terms of winning public opinion, and the commons loved him for it. Yet the queen and her supporters remained suspicious as to his true motives and were convinced that he had set his sights on the throne. Whatever her feelings, for the moment Queen Margaret was powerless to oppose York's rule. The fate of Margaret Beaufort's house, therefore, appeared to rest in the hands of another—one who had great personal ambitions of his own; it would only be a matter of time before he chose to pursue them.

THE ARRIVAL OF THE EARL and Countess of Richmond in Wales had never been intended purely as an opportunity for leisure. Instead, Edmund had been tasked with overseeing the king's authority in the area, though he was also prepared to lend his support once more to York in London. He had not been in Wales for long when it became apparent that to some his presence was unwanted. The most powerful magnate in the region was Gruffudd ap Nicholas, and friction immediately arose between the two men, presumably as a result of Edmund's determination to assert his authority. Thus far, Nicholas had always been loyal to the House of Lancaster, but as a result of their defeat at the Battle of St Albans he seems to have lost some of his possessions. Edmund's presence in Wales deepened his resentment. So much so that by the late spring or early summer of 1456, the tension had erupted into violence: at the beginning of June a correspondent of the well-informed Paston family reported that the two men 'are at war together in Wales'.[9]

Margaret, living in unfamiliar territory with a husband she barely knew, must have found the conflict unnerving at the very least. Despite her luxurious surroundings, it would have been a far cry from the relative serenity to which she was accustomed. Her husband was not prepared to back down in his war with Nicholas, and before long his efforts reaped a satisfying reward. By the beginning of August, he had taken control of Carmarthen Castle from his rival—a mighty twelfth-century stronghold that was key to government in that part of Wales, and of which York was constable.[10] Little did he know that his actions were to have detrimental consequences.

That summer Margaret had just passed her thirteenth birthday, and while Edmund was busying himself with military matters, she learned that she was pregnant with her first child. Tradition has it that she conceived at Caldicot Castle in Monmouthshire, but there is little evidence to support this. Given that Caldicot was over a hundred miles from Lamphey, it seems unlikely that she would have travelled this far.[11] The news would have come as a source of joy to Edmund, whose determination to secure an heir had been the driving force behind the early consummation of their marriage, but Margaret's own response is less clear. Her lack of physical development and small build had not prevented her from conceiving, but there was a long way to go. Mother and infant mortality were high and took no account of rank. Though a woman might survive labour, she ran the risk of becoming afflicted with a postnatal infection for which there was no cure. Likewise, possibly more than 30 per cent of children died before the age of seven as a result of disease or malnourishment.

While Margaret was taking in the reality of her pregnancy in the heart of the Welsh countryside, she was far from the court in London and news took some days to travel. She may not, therefore, have been immediately aware of the state of the government. In February, Henry VI—seemingly recovered—had dissolved York's protectorate in Parliament. The duke nevertheless remained a member of the council, despite the protestations of his bitter enemy the queen. Queen Margaret had ample reason to be wary of York, for he had already demonstrated that he was prepared to resort to warfare to retain his grip on the reins of power. But of greater concern to her was the dynastic threat he posed. It was clear that given the opportunity, he would not hesitate to press his claim to the throne.

Margaret's cousin Henry Beaufort, who had succeeded his father to the dukedom of Somerset following Edmund's fall at St Albans, had now ingratiated himself in the queen's favour and was one of her key supporters. In the summer, the king and queen moved with the court to Coventry, accompanied by Margaret's brother-in-law Jasper. Throughout that spring and summer, Jasper had been in almost constant attendance on the king, who clearly enjoyed his company and knew that he could trust him implicitly. It is not inconceivable that Jasper was keeping his brother Edmund abreast of affairs at court; if this were the case, then Edmund would have known that, though there was an uneasy peace between the queen and York, tensions between them had by no means been quelled. York, however, was quietly waiting for Queen Margaret to make the next move.

WHEN WORD REACHED YORK THAT Edmund Tudor had captured Carmarthen, of which he was constable, he was alarmed. Edmund's unshakeable loyalty to Henry VI was well known, and York was not prepared to risk him becoming too powerful a force in Wales, where he himself commanded support. With this in mind, he immediately assembled a force to take back Carmarthen and reassert his authority. Two thousand men led by Sir William Herbert and Sir Walter Devereux marched to the Welsh town and made straight for the castle. Edmund's men were unable to withstand such an attack, and on 10 August the castle was seized. Edmund was captured and imprisoned.

Back at Lamphey, Margaret—married for only about a year, and in the early months of pregnancy—was suddenly overcome with fear for her husband's life, as well as her own safety and that of her unborn child. But her distress would be of short duration, for before long Edmund was released. However, he remained at Carmarthen and, as the autumn approached, showed no signs of returning home. It may be that he was simply eager to remain to ensure that the king's interests were upheld, or else he was showing signs of illness that rendered him unable to travel. Whatever the circumstances, at some point Edmund did become unwell. It was alarmingly clear that he had contracted the plague, which had been mercilessly ravaging Wales. It was a deadly disease that swiftly claimed the lives of its many victims, which explains why there was no time for Edmund to prepare a will. Tragically, he soon succumbed, dying on 1 November at Carmarthen Castle.

Edmund's death left his pregnant teenage wife alone and vulnerable. Her residency in Wales rendered her completely isolated from her family in England, with no one to turn to for support. The timing could hardly have been worse, and Margaret was once again consumed with fear. Not only had she lost her husband, but she was also about to embark on the most perilous experience of her life—with no guarantee of survival.

MY GOOD AND GRACIOUS PRINCE, KING AND ONLY-BELOVED SON

As the bitter winter winds swirled, Margaret was ensconced at Lamphey when word reached her of the death of her husband at Carmarthen Castle. There is no indication as to how or precisely when Margaret was told of Edmund's death, or of her reaction to the news. She was, though, compelled by a sense of urgency to ensure her well-being and that of her unborn child. Her second husband was laid to rest in the Grey Friars at Carmarthen, but, later, more than two decades after Margaret's own death, his remains would be moved to St David's Cathedral during the Dissolution of the Monasteries on the orders of his grandson, Henry VIII. The inscription on his tomb offers little insight into Edmund's life or character, instead highlighting simply that he was the 'father and brother to kings'.[1] Later, Edmund's son would order ceremonies annually at Westminster Abbey to commemorate his father, and money was sent each year to Carmarthen to pay for daily prayers to be said for his soul.

But in 1456, Edmund's death left Margaret a widow at the age of just thirteen, and alone at Lamphey in the midst of an unknown Welsh region ravaged by plague. Left to fend for herself at a time when she was already fraught with anxiety, she showed her true strength of character and would shortly prove that she was a survivor.

There was no time for Margaret to grieve for the husband she had barely known, for she was nearly seven months pregnant and fearful for the safety of her unborn child. She was terrified of the plague, and in later years Bishop Fisher would relate to her son that 'while your mother carried you in the womb you narrowly avoided the plague of which your illustrious father died, which could so easily have killed an unborn child'. Given the fate of her husband and the virulence with which the plague spread, Margaret's fears were both understandable and justified. It was against the backdrop of disease and political unrest that Margaret was forced to consider her future—and quickly. Not only did her youth and pregnancy make her vulnerable to the plague, but her sex and widowhood made her a potential target for power-hungry men: it was evident that she could not remain alone at Lamphey. But her advanced pregnancy and the bleak winter weather ensured that there was no question of her undertaking the gruelling journey to her mother's estates in England, and thus she was forced to turn elsewhere.

THOUGH AN UNEASY PEACE HAD ensued, the divide between the Lancastrian court party and the Yorkists still ran deep and showed no signs of healing. It was clear that there was no middle ground and that choices would have to be made. For Margaret's brother-in-law Jasper, the decision was simple: though he had done his best to work with York and understood that his actions were for the good of the country, he had never wavered in his loyalty to Henry VI. Familial ties won the day, and there was no question of Jasper abandoning his half-brother now. This was all the more important given that the death of Margaret's husband Edmund deprived the king not only of his half-brother but also of a loyal and valuable ally whose allegiance had been unshakeable. At some point in November, word reached Jasper of the death of his beloved brother, and the news doubtless came as a bitter blow. Many years later, in a touching sign of his devotion to his family, Jasper would leave instructions in his will for four priests to sing perpetually in Keynsham Abbey for 'the well of my soul' and that of his parents and brother.[2] But in the winter of 1456, he was at once made aware of the plight of his sister-in-law—alone in Wales, heavily pregnant and fearful of the plague. Laying aside his grief, Jasper wasted no time: it was he who came to the pregnant Margaret's aid.

Margaret's relationship with her brother-in-law had always been amicable, and at twenty-five years old, he was both strong and brave. He was not yet married, and thus had no family of his own with which to occupy his time. Jasper was therefore an ideal choice of protector for Margaret, and although she did not know him well, she knew that she could trust him with her safekeeping and that of her unborn child. It was a task that he in turn approached with the utmost seriousness. Probably it was during this time that a bond of trust was forged between them—one that would endure for the rest of their lives and be of the utmost consequence in the coming years.

In normal circumstances, Margaret's thoughts at this time would have been occupied with plans for her confinement—plans that she later helped to ensure were put into practice with meticulous detail for the births of her grandchildren—but there was no time for that now. Similarly, the idea of travelling in winter through an unfamiliar landscape would have been unthinkable for a woman so far advanced in pregnancy. But in the circumstances, it was essential that she do so. As Jasper's horse clattered into the courtyard at Lamphey—the date unknown, but probably sometime in mid-November—Margaret prepared to bid farewell to the comfortable home in which she had spent much of her brief marriage.

Jasper's main seat was the stronghold of Pembroke Castle, situated on the banks of the river estuary in the town of Pembroke: André described it as being near to 'the source of a violent stream'.[3] At a little over two miles from Lamphey, it was a short journey, though given her pregnancy, it would have been far from comfortable for Margaret. She nevertheless arrived at Pembroke safely.

Of Norman origin, the towering five-storey stone keep, built by the mighty William Marshal in 1204, dominated Pembroke.[4] The castle was surrounded by thirteenth-century stone walls, encasing an impressive Norman great hall and a whole host of other buildings, including a dungeon—a gruesome reminder of Pembroke's violent past.[5] Its position on a high rock made it more easily defendable against potential attackers, and, given the uncertainty of the times, it was a wise choice of location for Margaret to spend the remainder of her pregnancy. The castle had been granted to Jasper in 1452 as part of the earldom of Pembroke, although his frequent presence at court makes it unlikely that he had been afforded an opportunity to spend much time there. He had nevertheless spent a great sum of money in an attempt to maintain Pembroke's defences and to ensure that it was a congenial residence. There was a fine chapel, accommodation for Jasper and his household, and a solar (an upper chamber commonly found in medieval homes) into which he had inserted a splendid oriel window.[6] Although not as luxurious or as peaceful as Lamphey, Pembroke was a secure and comfortable alternative.

In spite of her well-furnished and secure surroundings, in both physical and emotional terms Margaret was largely isolated—she had no family or friends to turn to for comfort or support, only the brother-in-law she can barely have known. And because Jasper was unmarried, there is likely to have been a distinct lack of noble female company at Pembroke—Margaret's own servants and the female household staff would have been all there were—making the experience even more isolating for her.

As Christmas, New Year and the onset of 1457 were celebrated at Pembroke, Margaret's due date quickly approached.[7] It was to be one of the first Christmases Margaret ever spent away from her family. At least, under Jasper's protection, she could feel relatively safe within Pembroke's walls—André tells us the castle was 'heavily fortified'.[8] Given that childbirth was an exclusively female process, Margaret would have been attended by at least one midwife, but no other details of the preparations put in place are known. Some women relied on holy relics in order to help them through the ordeal of childbirth, while others employed special amulets to protect them. In later life Margaret is known to have owned jewels featuring the likenesses of saints thought to aid pregnant women. However, she may simply have relied on prayer: a prayer book she later commissioned for her fourth husband, Thomas Stanley, contains a number of prayers aimed at protecting the user from all manner of dangers, including childbirth.[9]

At the end of January, Margaret's labour pains began, and she was confronted with the agonizing reality of childbirth. Always a pious woman whose religious devotion shone through for the rest of her life, providing her with a great source of comfort, Margaret would need all of her faith to get through this most difficult time.

On 28 January, the exhausted Margaret at last gave birth to a son. A tower still called the Henry VII Tower has traditionally been cited as the place of birth of Margaret's child, but recent excavations at Pembroke have shown that he is more likely to have been born in a lavishly decorated building that once lay inside the castle's outer walls.[10]

Bishop Fisher recalled the outcome of Margaret's labour:

Like Moses, [Henry] was wonderfully born and brought into the world by the noble Princess his mother, who was very small of stature, as she was never a tall woman. It seemed a miracle that, at that age, and of so little a personage, anyone should have been born at all, let alone one so tall and of so fine a build as her son.

Henry's biographer Neville Williams rightly observed that Henry's 'arrival in the world was not heralded by national rejoicing', for he was born as nothing more than the son of a deceased nobleman.[11] Nevertheless, André later did his best to emphasise his master's parentage, describing it as 'most noble'.[12] He took particular care to highlight Edmund Tudor's connections, boldly, and falsely, stating that they stemmed all the way back to the Roman politician Brutus, one of the key conspirators in the murder of Julius Caesar. When it came to Margaret, whom André described as Henry's 'most illustrious royal mother', he was careful to stress that she was 'a very noble woman, endowed with uprightness and virtue from above'.[13]

Though she had done her duty and produced a living child, the experience had been so difficult that, to begin with, both Margaret's life and that of her infant were believed to be at risk. But it was not long before the danger passed. The day of the birth was one that Margaret celebrated for the rest of her life, and in later years she wrote to Henry on his birthday remembering that it was 'this day of St Agnes, that I did bring into this world my good and gracious prince, king and only-beloved son'.[14] Margaret had suffered great trauma, and she faced the reality that—although just embarking on her teenage years—she had a new and important role to play: that of a mother. Yet this did not faze her, for from the moment of Henry's birth an extraordinary bond was forged between mother and son, one that would endure for the rest of their lives, perhaps later heightened by the knowledge that Henry was to be Margaret's only child—whether through choice or circumstance.

Rather than naming her son after the father who had died before he was born, in a proud declaration of her own heritage and loyalty to the royal family into which he had been born, the baby was christened Henry in honour of Margaret's kinsman Henry VI—the child's uncle and probable godfather. In light of her own origins it is unsurprising that Margaret chose to ensure that her son was closely associated with the king by bearing his name; moreover, many of Henry VI's predecessors with whom he shared his name had been strong leaders, and thus the name was a solid choice. Henry was a legitimate king, unlike Edmund Tudor who may have been born out of wedlock. The only association with baby Henry's father and the Tudor family was the title Earl of Richmond with which from the moment of his birth Henry was styled in right of Edmund Tudor. In the sixteenth century, however, the Welshman Elis Gruffydd, who hailed from Flintshire, recorded in his chronicle that the infant had first been christened Owen—probably at the request of his uncle Jasper as a compliment to his own father—but that during the course of the ceremony Margaret had insisted that the bishop should alter this to Henry. No other source makes any reference to this incident, so it is impossible to corroborate, but knowing Margaret's character, her insistent independence and fierce familial loyalty, there is certainly more than a hint of truth to it.

There is the possibility that the physical and psychological trauma of her son's birth caused Margaret permanent damage. It has often been said that the harm inflicted as a result of childbirth rendered her physically incapable of bearing another child. It is true that despite two further marriages, she is not known to have experienced any further pregnancies and certainly produced no more children. More than five hundred years later, it is impossible to know what the true long-term physical consequences of Henry's birth were, if indeed there were any. It is possible that Margaret had scar tissue or a damaged uterus that prevented her from carrying another child, but consideration must also be given to the psychological effects of giving birth at such a young age.[15] In years to come she would urge her son not to allow her granddaughter and namesake to be sent to Scotland for her marriage to James IV too early, in case in his haste to consummate their union he might 'injure her, and endanger her health'. Margaret was speaking from experience. With this in mind, it is hardly difficult to imagine that Margaret made a conscious decision not to become pregnant again. Such a prospect can only ever be speculative, but there is evidence in her later life, particularly with regard to her choice of a third husband, to support such a possibility. That Margaret chose not to have another child has never been mooted, but given what we know of her character, her circumstances and her later behaviour, it ought not to be ruled out. Unsurprisingly, there is also evidence that her experience of sex at such an early age made the thought of it completely abhorrent. A religious book that she later bequeathed to Christ's College, Cambridge, contained a section on frigidity. This was annotated, possibly in Margaret's own hand, with a poignant question: Was it a sin to loathe sex?[16]

In spite of the physical and psychological impact of Henry's birth—whether temporary or permanent in either sense—from the start Margaret adored him. She 'wisely attended to the care of her son', nursing Henry devotedly in his early days.[17] Nevertheless, in the same manner as all noble children, her baby would have been entrusted to the care of nurses—presumably including a wet nurse to suckle him—who were responsible for his everyday care. Margaret knew all too well, though, that these precious days at Pembroke were not destined to last for long.

Shortly after Henry's birth, thoughts turned to Margaret's future. Though she was now a mother and fell under the protection of her brother-in-law, her age and position as a widow made her vulnerable. This was only exacerbated by the growing tension within the realm in which Jasper knew that he as well as Margaret and her son would become inextricably tangled. It was imperative, to safeguard her future and that of her son, that she marry again, and there was no time to be lost. Though the impetus seems to have been Margaret's own, Jasper also appears to have recognised the importance of his sister-in-law taking another husband and played an important role in making arrangements. Margaret was still just thirteen, but on the third occasion on which she would be wedded, she was determined that it be to someone of her own choosing who would consider the interests of her infant son. This time, Margaret would take full responsibility for shaping her own future.

PART TWO

CHAPTER 6

LADY STAFFORD

Margaret spent the first weeks of motherhood bonding with her son—a bond that is likely to have been all the stronger given that, like Henry, she too had never known her father. Having lost her husband, Margaret was her son's sole parent, which may have intensified not only her love for him but also her need to keep him safe. This was undoubtedly a strong consideration when she made her next move. Likewise, the isolation from most of her peers in the early weeks of Henry's life would surely have rendered Margaret's need to keep him close stronger still. Though her brother-in-law Jasper undoubtedly remained at Pembroke in the aftermath of Margaret's ordeal, it is unlikely that he saw much, if anything, of her during this time due to the protocol known as churching, which dictated that a woman could not re-enter society until she had gone through a religious ceremony of purification.

Humphrey Stafford, Duke of Buckingham, was a kinsman and loyal supporter of Henry VI.[1] Buckingham was one of the most powerful noblemen in England, and throughout the political turmoil that came with the king's descent into mental illness, he had attempted to mediate—unsuccessfully—between the Lancastrian court party and the Duke of York. The situation was made all the more uncomfortable for Margaret by Buckingham's family ties: his wife was York's sister-in-law.[2] Still, Buckingham's wealth and unshakeable allegiance to her own house were appealing to Margaret. And so following her churching in March 1457—two months after Henry's birth—she began to consider a match with him. If she were to avoid having another husband thrust upon her, then the matter had to be undertaken as one of urgency.

Once again, there were many who were eager to secure Margaret's hand. Elizabeth Norton has suggested that the obvious choice of husband would have been Margaret's brother-in-law Jasper, who was still unmarried.[3] Yet many at the time would probably have believed her marriage to his brother Edmund rendered them too closely related if indeed the pair ever considered each other as potential spouses. Jasper's support for Margaret's next marriage was nevertheless essential, for his familial ties to her young son, Henry, ensured that their interests would always be closely aligned. It is unthinkable that he and Margaret would not have discussed the matter of her marriage, and it is plausible that an alliance with Buckingham's family came at Jasper's suggestion.

The level of Margaret's own involvement in her marital arrangements is extraordinary, considering her youth and all that she had been through in so short a time period.[4] Henry's birth had had a profound impact on her, imbuing her with a new sense of purpose. The experience of childbirth in a land full of political unrest forced Margaret to grow up quickly, and she emerged a stronger and more determined character who would put her son's interests above all else.

Shortly after she had been churched, Margaret left her infant son in the care of a Welsh nurse by the name of Joan ap Howell.[5] Accompanied by Jasper, Margaret began the journey to Greenfield, the Duke of Buckingham's estate in Newport. The more than one-hundred-mile journey from Pembroke was gruelling, especially for a girl who had so recently given birth. That she chose to undertake it is a testament to her insistence on being involved in negotiations concerning her future—and that of her son. After all, as Margaret already knew, marriage negotiations did not require the person of the woman to be present—or even out of the nursery. Having arrived safely at Greenfield, where she and Jasper were the welcome recipients of Buckingham's hospitality, discussions regarding Margaret's third marriage began.

Henry Stafford was Buckingham's second son, and at around thirty-one years old he was almost two decades Margaret's senior.[6] In spite of this, he had never been married, ironically making Margaret the more experienced of the two in this quarter. This was perhaps because Stafford's father had placed primary importance on arranging the nuptials of Henry's elder brother, Humphrey, who had been wedded to Margaret's cousin—incidentally also named Margaret Beaufort—the daughter of her late uncle Edmund, Duke of Somerset.[7] Thus, the valuable bonds of allegiance that marriages brought had already been forged with Margaret's family. Alternatively, Stafford's accounts reveal that he suffered from ill health at various points in his life, which may also account for his delay in taking a wife.

Although Henry was a second son, his father's powerful position made him a good match for Margaret. Still, the greater advantage was undoubtedly his on account of Margaret's landed wealth. It is unclear from where the impetus for Margaret's choice of a third husband stemmed; though a girl with her inheritance and connections would undoubtedly have had more options, should she have wished, there is no evidence to suggest that she considered any other matches. The couple were related through Henry's mother, Anne Neville, who was a granddaughter of John of Gaunt and Katherine Swynford and so Stafford's noble blood may have made the match more appealing to Margaret.[8] Margaret may also have given consideration to Stafford's age. That a man of Stafford's years and standing had not been married thus far was unusual, but if indeed, as has been speculated, Margaret made a conscious decision not to become pregnant again, she was probably aware that a man in his thirties was considered old by contemporary standards to father his first child. Moreover, as a second son, the need for Henry to produce an heir to continue his line was less pressing than if he had been his father's heir—his elder brother had already produced a son, thereby securing the future of their family for at least another generation. Henry's ill health may also have made the possibility of fatherhood less likely. There is some evidence to suggest that he suffered from a skin complaint known as Saint Anthony's Fire (also called Holy Fire), a relatively common disease in the medieval period.[9] The symptoms resembled those of leprosy, and indeed, not only did Henry and Margaret join the confraternity of the leper hospital at Burton Lazars in Leicestershire, but also Margaret would later show a devotion to Saint Anthony, the patron saint of lepers.[10] Further hints that Stafford may have suffered from the disease come from his accounts indicating that in March 1470, while Stafford was travelling north with the royal army, his chaplain, John Bush, distributed alms to leper colonies.[11]

Although there is no evidence to suggest that Margaret and Stafford's union was not consummated—and by all accounts their marriage was happy—consideration must also be given to the possibility that Stafford was infertile. His accounts show that on several occasions physicians were called for and medicines received from London, and although the nature of his ailments is not known, his health evidently caused concern.[12] In the past, many historians have looked no further than the birth of Henry Tudor when examining Margaret's lack of further children, citing that the physical damage to her body as a result of this experience must have been the cause. Rarely have other causes—such as infertility on the part of Stafford—been considered.

The marriage agreements were settled swiftly, but given their familial ties—Stafford's mother, Anne Neville, being a granddaughter of John of Gaunt and Katherine Swynford—a papal dispensation was required, and it would be Margaret's second. This, too, was applied for promptly, and on 6 April the Bishop of Coventry and Lichfield granted the dispensation so plans for Margaret's marriage could proceed.[13] Yet, it would be some months before the wedding could take place, for Margaret was still in the prescribed year of mourning for Edmund Tudor.

In the space of just four months, Margaret's life had changed unalterably: she had lost her husband, been obliged to abandon her home, given birth to a son in traumatic circumstances, and negotiated a third marriage. It was more than some of her contemporaries would go through in a lifetime, yet Margaret was still just thirteen. That she not only endured all of these changes but also emerged from them with a determination to secure her own future is a testament to her strength of mind and her ability to adapt to the unpredictable circumstances she faced.

MEANWHILE, DISORDER REMAINED RIFE THROUGHOUT the country. To prevent the Duke of York from assuming a role in the council, the king and queen had sent him to Ireland to resume his post as lieutenant. Still, the queen remained fearful of him and his followers. Jasper is likely one of the few people she could trust, and in April—the same month Margaret's dispensation to wed Henry Stafford was issued—he was appointed Constable of Carmarthen Castle, among other titles, thereby replacing York. Given the association of his late brother with Carmarthen, it would have been understandable if this role carried some sad associations for him, but he undertook it admirably. He successfully managed to tame Gruffudd ap Nicholas, once more firmly demonstrating his loyalty to the Lancastrian dynasty. While Jasper was in Carmarthen, Margaret returned to Pembroke Castle to observe her year of mourning for Edmund and to be with her son. Unbeknown to her, these few months were to be the only ones she would spend with her son while he was a baby.

On 3 January 1458, almost a year after Henry's birth, Margaret was married to Henry Stafford. The Duke of Buckingham's favoured red-sandstone residence of Maxstoke Castle in Warwickshire may have served as the setting for the wedding. Given that in later years the couple regularly celebrated their wedding anniversary, often with a sumptuous meal full of delicacies, it must have been a joyful occasion. Unfortunately, there are no clues as to what Stafford looked like, but whatever his appearance, in character at least he was kindly and amiable, if perhaps somewhat weak—he would later actively avoid participating in the conflict that racked the country.

In spite of his father's position, Stafford was not wealthy, and he and Margaret lived primarily off of the revenues that came from her estates. Neither did he have a grand title. Margaret, formerly Countess of Richmond, now became Lady Stafford. Nevertheless, she continued to use the title of Countess of Richmond for the remainder of her life, valuing the prestige associated with it. That Margaret was yet to reach her fifteenth birthday by the time of her third marriage was extraordinary even by fifteenth-century standards. Though their marriage was first and foremost a business arrangement, Margaret and Stafford seem to have genuinely felt some affection for each other. After the tumultuous happenings of Margaret's youth, her third marriage would provide her with exactly the kind of stability that she craved.

According to Norton, on 8 January—five days after Margaret's wedding—Henry VI granted Henry Tudor's wardship to Jasper and the Earl of Shrewsbury.[14] However, the grant issued made no mention of Henry's wardship, and instead stipulated that the men were to have 'the keeping of all possessions in England, Wales and the marches' that had once belonged to Edmund, with the exception of his possessions in Lincolnshire.[15] This was, as Norton indicates, in response to Margaret's marriage to Stafford, but the reason for splitting the lands between Jasper and Shrewsbury remains a mystery. Shrewsbury had been created a Knight of the Garter alongside Margaret's stepfather Lord Welles, so it is certainly possible that he was a friend of the family. Alternatively, he was the king's Lord Treasurer, so the grant might have been a reward for his loyalty.

It is unclear who retained custody of Margaret's son. There is no evidence that Henry remained in his mother's care following her marriage to Henry Stafford. Sometime before her marriage was solemnized, Margaret was probably faced with the heart-wrenching reality of bidding her son farewell. Most likely, it was agreed that Henry would remain in the care of his uncle Jasper at Pembroke. There his safety could be better assured. Margaret would have been left in no doubt that Jasper would safeguard her son's best interests, and indeed for the rest of his life Jasper treated

Henry as his own son. In turn, Margaret, too, remained close to her former brother-in-law, whom she trusted implicitly.

Following her marriage, Margaret and her husband took up residence at Bourne, in the Fens, an estate she had inherited from her father. Bourne had once been a possession of the Holland family, and Edward III had been entertained there in 1330.[16] Set in beautiful parkland with fine rooftop views overlooking the Fens, the house in which Margaret and Stafford lived was of Norman origin—a large motte-and-bailey castle that featured a keep and that was accessed through a medieval gatehouse that may have led into a courtyard. There was ample room to accommodate their household and to entertain visitors in the hall. Margaret's great-grandfather, Thomas Holland, Earl of Kent, lay buried in a nearby abbey. Margaret was evidently fond of Bourne: in the first of her wills, dated 1472, she stipulated her desire to be buried there. Though these plans later changed, she retained her affection for the place until the end of her life, bequeathing a mass book to the abbey in her will.

At first, the separation from her son must have been difficult, and Margaret undoubtedly sought solace in her religion. Her pain would only have been exacerbated by the fact that—as André would later observe—young Henry was 'often sickly at a tender age', and as such was 'tenderly educated by his caretakers, men upright and wise'.[17] Throughout his life, Margaret was eager to retain as much contact with Henry as possible. Stafford also seems to have grown fond of his stepson, though he saw him infrequently. His interest in Henry may have been heightened by the fact that—for whatever reason—in what transpired to be a fourteen-year marriage, Stafford sired no children of his own by Margaret.

Margaret may have been separated from her son, yet in all other respects her domestic arrangements provided her with the security she needed to safeguard both of their futures. Once more, she had married into a family whose head had power and influence matched only by York's. Yet, they were living in uncertain times, and it would not be long before the stability that Margaret's marriage provided was shattered.[18]

THE SAME MONTH AS MARGARET'S marriage in 1458, Henry VI ordered all of his nobles to attend upon him at Westminster. In the interest of a longer-standing peace, the king was eager to reconcile both sides. On 24 March—Lady Day—a reconciliation was staged between the king and queen, on one side, and York and his supporters, on the other: it would become known as Loveday. The queen and York followed the king hand in hand as they processed through London, but few considered this more than a spectacle. Tensions continued to rise, and in anticipation of further violence, both sides continued to recruit men to their cause.

On 23 September 1459, Lord Audley, acting on Queen Margaret's orders, ambushed Yorkist forces at Blore Heath in Staffordshire as they were making their way to Ludlow to join the main army. The result was a Yorkist victory, but the following month, at Ludford Bridge, the tables turned and York, Salisbury and Warwick fled. York managed to evade capture and cross to Ireland, taking his second son, Edmund, Earl of Rutland, with him. Salisbury and Warwick fled to Calais with York's eldest son, Edward, Earl of March. With York and his supporters out of her reach, Queen Margaret took full control of the government. A bill of attainder was drawn up in Parliament against York and his followers, who were found guilty of high treason against the Crown. Their estates were swiftly confiscated and handed out to Lancastrian supporters as rewards for their loyalty. Among the beneficiaries were Owen and Jasper Tudor, as well as Margaret's stepfather Lord Welles, who was granted Salisbury's former lands in Essex.[19]

Meanwhile, across the Irish Sea, York was working tirelessly to drum up support, and sympathy for his cause was growing across the Channel. On 26 June 1460, Warwick, Salisbury and the Earl of March landed in England. They immediately marched to London, where the citizens joyously welcomed them. They nevertheless took care to declare that they had come only to lay their grievances before the king in person and to ensure that good government was restored. Henry VI was in Coventry with the queen and Prince Edward. He swiftly began preparing for an armed confrontation. Thanks to the queen's efforts, Henry now had a sizeable army of around twenty thousand men at his command, and he began to lead his men towards Northampton. The queen, meanwhile, took her son to Eccleshall Castle in Staffordshire, where she waited anxiously for news.[20]

Warwick and March had led their army—double the size of the king's force—towards Northampton and promptly sent a message to Henry in which they pleaded with him to hear their grievances in person. Henry, who was joined by his commander Buckingham—Margaret's father-in-law—steadfastly refused, and in so doing underlined that there was no other choice but to resort to armed conflict. Both he and Buckingham, however, had underestimated Warwick and the Yorkist army.

On the afternoon of 10 July, the two armies came face-to-face. Like the Battle of St Albans, it was to be of short duration and would end with a decisive Yorkist victory 'without a serious fight or much slaughter', as the Milanese ambassador had been told.[21] The Lancastrians suffered heavy losses. Among the dead were Buckingham and the Earl of Shrewsbury. To make matters worse, Henry VI was captured by a Yorkist archer named Henry Mountfort. It was a disastrous outcome for the Lancastrians, and many of those who had survived the battle fled into hiding. But for the king there was to be no escape: the Croyland chronicle reported that Henry was taken 'in solemn procession', with the Earl of Warwick 'bearing the sword before the king, bare-headed and in all humility and respect'.[22] There was to be no repeat of the deference shown in the wake of St Albans. This time, he returned to London as a Yorkist prisoner, and once more the fate of Margaret's family was in the hands of others.

It had been a mere two years since Margaret had married. Now, the death of the Duke of Buckingham meant that the head of Margaret's marital family was gone, and the security that such a powerful magnate had seemingly promised was shown to be as unreliable as that offered by so many of the other men in Margaret's life. Her father-in-law was buried in the Grey Friars in Northampton, which no longer survives. Stafford's elder brother, Humphrey, had died in 1458, meaning that the dukedom of Buckingham passed to Stafford's nephew, Humphrey's son. His name was also Henry Stafford, and the young boy now became the second Duke of Buckingham. The new Buckingham was not only Margaret's nephew by marriage but also her cousin, and in later years the little boy who was then five years old would play an intriguing and pivotal role in her life. Because Buckingham was still a minor, Margaret's husband Stafford temporarily became the figurehead of the family. What was more, his loyalty to the House of Lancaster remained unshaken.

QUEEN MARGARET WAS HORRIFIED WHEN news of the Lancastrian defeat and her husband's capture reached her at Eccleshall Castle. Realizing that flight was her only option, she and her son sailed for Scotland, where she was welcomed by the queen dowager, Mary of Gueldres.[23] Meanwhile, on 8 September York arrived in England from Ireland, where he had been drumming up support since the rout at Ludford Bridge the previous year. Landing in North Wales, he set out for London, but this time he made no pretence of desiring a role as the king's advisor—he was there to claim the throne. On 7 October, Parliament met, but Henry VI, though he attended the opening under the control of York, was otherwise notably absent. Three days later, on 10 October, York reached the capital. He immediately made his way to Westminster, where he marched into Parliament. According to Croyland, in a purposeful gesture, York 'approached the royal throne and claimed the seat as his own'.[24] If he was hoping for an enthusiastic response, though, he was sadly mistaken. Whatever Henry VI's shortcomings, he was still an anointed king, and one to whom most of the nobles had sworn allegiance. Many people, including York's own supporters, felt that York had overreached himself. But York thought otherwise, and on 16 October he staked an official claim to the throne by right of his bloodline, which he believed to be superior to that of Henry VI. Nobody could deny that he had a good claim: he was, after all, descended from two of Edward III's sons—paternally, he was related to Edward's fourth son, but through his mother he claimed kinship with Edward's second son, Lionel of Clarence.

After much debate, it was agreed that Henry VI would remain king but that York would be named his heir—thereby displacing Prince Edward. On 24 October, the Act of Accord by which this became law was drafted, but this did not put an end to York's ambitions. As Alison Weir has highlighted, it was now evident that the divisions between Lancaster and York had escalated into a struggle for the throne itself rather than power between the two rival sides.[25]

When Queen Margaret learned of the Act of Accord, she was outraged. There was worse news to come: on 8 November York was declared not only Henry VI's heir apparent but also Protector of England once more, giving him the right to exercise power in the king's name. The queen and her supporters, among them English nobility thirsting to avenge the deaths of their fathers at St Albans, immediately marched south with a Scottish army provided by Mary of Gueldres. York, accompanied by Salisbury, prepared to journey north to meet her, and the two left London on 9 December. They made it to Sandal Castle, York's impregnable stronghold near Wakefield, where they intended to spend Christmas. By then Lancastrian forces had regained control over the area, and this time it was York's turn to underestimate their strength. It would lead to his undoing.

On 30 December, York, joined by Salisbury, ventured out of the security of Sandal for reasons that are unclear. His forces soon came face-to-face with the Lancastrian army, commanded by the Duke of Somerset. The Milanese ambassador was subsequently told that the Yorkists, 'although they were three times stronger, yet from lack of discipline, because they allowed a large part of the force to go pillaging and searching for victuals, their adversaries, who are desperate, attacked the duke and his followers'.[26] In the ensuing Battle of Wakefield, York and his seventeen-year-old son, Edmund, Earl of Rutland, were slain. Salisbury was captured and later killed. It was a crushing blow for the Yorkists, and the severed heads of all three men were placed on spikes above the Micklegate Bar in the city of York, York's adorned in a paper crown.

Save for his family and the commons, among whom he had been popular, few mourned York's death. Indeed, for Margaret Beaufort and her family, it was cause for much celebration. However, though York was dead—his ambitions for the throne never realized—the wars were by no means over. His eldest son, Edward, Earl of March, now emerged as his father's successor, and he was determined to avenge the savagery and disgrace that had been inflicted upon his father and brother. It was evident that more violence would soon follow, and it was only a matter of time before Margaret's husband, Stafford, would be forced to become involved.

CHAPTER 7

LIKE A FUGITIVE

In January 1461, Margaret and Henry Stafford had been married for three years. Thus far they had remained largely uninvolved in the drama of the Wars of the Roses, bearing the damage from a distance. Still, Jasper Tudor's role ensured that Margaret was in a constant state of anxiety over the welfare of her son.

In January Jasper and his father, Owen, left the young Henry Tudor at Pembroke and moved with their men towards Herefordshire. On 2 February, they met the Yorkist army at Mortimer's Cross, close to the Welsh border. The ensuing battle was one of the most savage of the Wars of the Roses, and the Lancastrian losses were heavy. When it became clear that the Yorkists had the victory, Jasper fled from the battlefield. Owen, however, was not so fortunate. The following day he and several others were taken to the marketplace in Hereford and executed.[1] According to the contemporary author of *Gregory's Chronicle*, it was not until he saw the block and the axe that the realization of impending death set in, causing him to declare, 'That head shall lie on the stock that was wont to lie on Queen Katherine's lap'.[2] His head was set upon the market cross, but *Gregory's Chronicle* claimed that a madwoman took it and 'combed his hair and washed away the blood of his face'.[3] With her father-in-law dead and Jasper a fugitive, Margaret was in a state of panic—her son was still at Pembroke Castle and now he had no protector. What was more, she was utterly helpless to aid him.

In the aftermath of Mortimer's Cross, there was no time to be lost. On 17 February, the two armies once more crossed swords at the Second Battle of St Albans as Warwick and his men attempted to prevent the Lancastrian army from reaching London. Henry VI, who had been in Warwick's train, was 'placed under a tree a mile away, where he laughed and sang' while the battle was fought.[4] This time the Lancastrians were victorious, and Henry was set at liberty. Reunited, the royal couple intended to march to London. However, to Queen Margaret's dismay, she quickly discovered that they were not welcome in the capital. Instead, at the end of February, York's son and heir, Edward of March, entered London to the great elation of the citizens. Shortly afterwards, a meeting took place at Baynard's Castle on the Thames: there, some of the lords agreed that Henry VI had to be deposed; in his place, Edward IV was declared King of England.

The news was largely met with celebrations. Henry's former subjects had grown disenchanted with his rule and lost all patience with his lack of control, to which they attributed the country's economic and political instability. Like his predecessor, Edward had a legitimate claim to the throne, one technically stronger than that of Henry VI. Nevertheless, despite Henry IV's usurpation of the throne in 1399, the deposition of a monarch was still an extraordinary move, one that was not taken lightly by the nobles of the realm. Margaret, who was just seventeen years old and had known no other king than Henry VI, met the news of her kinsman's deposition with horror. But all hope was not yet lost. Henry and his queen were still at liberty, and there was every chance they would continue to fight for their thrones: this was exactly what they intended to do.

Following the Second Battle of St Albans, Henry VI and his men marched towards York. Henry was accompanied by Somerset and those lords who had remained loyal, among them Margaret's stepfather, Lord Welles. This time, Margaret's husband Stafford would also be joining them—perhaps aware that it was of the utmost importance that he should demonstrate his loyalty—leaving behind Margaret, probably at Bourne. The newly established Edward IV, who recognised the need for swift action if he were to crush his rival, pursued them. Within a short time his forces closed in on the Lancastrian army near the Yorkshire village of Towton. Eager to avoid further bloodshed, Henry VI requested a truce, but Edward steadfastly refused: he was determined to destroy his enemies for good.

As dawn broke on the morning of Palm Sunday, 29 March, both armies awoke on the brink of a bitter snowstorm. The treacherous weather conditions did not prevent a battle that was 'great and cruel' from ensuing, during which the crisp white snow was stained with blood.[5] So deadly was the battle that the meadow on which it was fought became known as Bloody Meadow.[6] The atrocities to which Henry Stafford bore witness that day can only be imagined, for the sounds of clashing swords, flying arrows and the screams of the dying were rife. Thousands were mercilessly slaughtered in the ten hours of fighting that ensued, including Lord Welles, Margaret's stepfather.

The appalled Croyland chronicler reported, 'The blood, too, of the slain, mingling with the snow which at this time covered the whole surface of the earth, afterwards ran down in the furrows and ditches along with the melted snow, in a most shocking manner, for a distance of two or three miles'.[7] The Bishop of Salisbury was later told that 'the heralds counted 28,000 slain, a number unheard of in our realm for almost a thousand years, without counting those wounded and drowned'.[8] It eventually became clear that the Yorkists had won the field, but so huge was the slaughter that this was no great victory, despite the Yorkists claiming it as such. Even so, it was enough to establish Edward IV firmly on the throne . . . for now.

With the news of their defeat, Henry VI, Queen Margaret and their son fled across the border into Scotland. Other Lancastrians—including Margaret's cousin Henry Beaufort, Duke of Somerset—soon joined them, but, for some, flight was not an option. Having actively taken up arms against the new king, the life of Margaret's husband Henry Stafford was in danger.

WHEN WORD OF EDWARD IV'S overwhelming victory at Towton reached London, 'all the city were fayne, and thanked God'.[9] Soon after replacing the Yorkist heads on Micklegate Bar with those of his defeated foes, the new king returned to the capital, where he received a rapturous welcome from his subjects. A Milanese observer reported that Edward was welcomed by his subjects 'as if he were their God'.[10] It was little wonder that he was so adored, for he provided a stark contrast to Henry VI.

Edward had been born on 28 April 1442 in Rouen, and by eighteen he was 'young and more handsome than any man then alive', although he would later become very fat.[11] Thomas More, who received his account from one who knew him, described Edward as 'a goodly personage, and very princely to behold', while another contemporary referred to him as being 'tall of stature, elegant in person, of unblemished character, valiant in arms, and a lineal descendant of the illustrious line of king Edward the Third'.[12] Physically, Edward IV had many of the qualities that people expected of a medieval king, but he also possessed other important attributes. He was of 'sharp wit' and 'bountiful to his friends'.[13] He was also 'of heart courageous, politic in counsel, in adversity nothing abashed, in prosperity rather joyful than proud, in peace just and merciful, in war sharp and fierce, in the field bold and hardy'.[14] Like his father he was a natural leader, and unlike Henry VI his very presence commanded respect and admiration. He was certainly popular, and the people had high hopes for his reign. Accordingly, on 28 June a proclamation was issued in the king's name in which Edward promised his people both strong rule and good government. In this he did not disappoint. It seemed that few among the commons were sad to see the back of Margaret's house.

The nobility had more reason to be fearful, especially those who had taken up arms against the new king. Many of their worries proved to be unfounded, for Edward quickly showed that he was eager to heal the wounds of the past. Fortunately for Margaret, his clemency extended to Henry Stafford, who was also his cousin by reason of their mothers being sisters. On 25 June, he issued a pardon to Stafford for 'all offences committed by him'—one that extended to his younger brother, John, who had also fought for Lancaster at Towton.[15] The king's pardon, much to Margaret's relief, ensured that the lands she had inherited from her father would not be confiscated.

Edward IV's victory seems to have been enough to convince Stafford and his younger brother to abandon the Lancastrian cause permanently. From then on, he was a loyal—although often reluctant—adherent of York. It is difficult to comprehend how Margaret felt about her husband's decision, or indeed if she had any hand in it. Her sense of loyalty to her own house is beyond question; though she had just turned eighteen, she still recognised that the balance between expressions of loyalty and the likelihood of survival required a temperate approach. This was to be just the beginning of a period of her life during which she ingratiated herself to her enemies, proving that she knew when a cause was lost—at least for the time being—and that it was necessary to adapt to a new regime. Margaret was a pragmatist. She showed, in the words of her biographers Jones and Underwood, 'political astuteness rather than blindly partisan allegiance'.[16] Whatever her feelings—and given how events unfolded, these must have been strong indeed—she repeatedly mastered them. Her primary motivation over the coming years once again appears to have been the safety of her son and his interests rather than her own preferment.

On 9 May, the news that Margaret had been dreading became a reality. Edward IV issued a commission to his loyal supporter Sir William Herbert and his brothers to 'take into the king's hands the county and lordship of Pembroke', together with all of the other lands belonging to Jasper Tudor.[17] Later, on 10 August, a similar commission was issued, this time declaring Jasper 'a rebel'.[18] This was followed, on 7 September, by a third commission, in which Herbert and his brothers, along with Sir Walter Devereux, were tasked with taking over 'all castles, lordships, manors, lands and possessions late of Humphrey, Duke of Buckingham, in South Wales', on account of the minority of his son, Henry Stafford's nephew.[19]

The Herberts wasted no time in fulfilling all three commissions. Margaret and her family were powerless to prevent them, and on 30 September Sir William Herbert captured Jasper's home of Pembroke Castle just as he had once overtaken Edmund Tudor at Carmarthen. On 4 October, a Paston correspondent reported that 'all the castles and holds in South Wales and in North Wales are given and yielded up into the king's hand. And the Duke of Exeter and the Earl of Pembroke are flown and taken to the mountains, and divers lords with great puissance are after them'.[20] Jasper had fled, leaving his four-year-old nephew Henry Tudor at Pembroke to the mercy of the Yorkists. For Margaret, years of endless agitation agonizing over Henry's welfare had begun.

ON 1 NOVEMBER, EDWARD IV convened his first Parliament. Acts of Attainder were passed against 150 Lancastrians headed by Henry VI and Margaret of Anjou, including Somerset and Margaret's deceased stepfather Lord Welles.[21] Though the king had pardoned her husband, Margaret had good reason to feel concerned, given his treatment of her kinsmen. To her relief, though, a provision was made to secure her lands, presumably as a result of Edward's show of reconciliation towards her husband. It was officially stated that

> no act made or to be made in this present parliament shall extend or be prejudicial to Margaret, countess of Richmond, daughter and heir of John, late duke of Somerset, with regard to any lands, tenements or other possessions, whatever they may be, which she holds in dower, of the endowment of Edmund, late earl of Richmond, her late husband, and by assignment of Henry VI, late in deed and not by right king of England; or to any lands, tenements, rents or other hereditaments which descended or ought to descend to her from the said John, late duke of Somerset, her father.[22]

Margaret was not unique, for in an extension of Edward's attitude of clemency, Parliament secured the lands of other leading noblemen and women, including her mother, the dowager Duchess of Somerset.[23] Still, not everyone was to be so fortunate. The estates of those who had been attainted—whether alive or dead—were now taken from their families. They provided rich rewards, which Edward IV distributed to his faithful supporters. Although Margaret's lands were not affected by the king's redistribution, it would not be long before those of her son were.

Immediately after the capture of Pembroke Castle, young Henry became the king's ward. There is no evidence, though, that he left Pembroke at this time. Nor is there any indication as to who oversaw his care, but Margaret likely petitioned for him to be returned to her or at the very least attempted to communicate with him. Whatever her hopes were, the decision was not hers to make. On 12 February 1462, Edward IV granted to Sir William Herbert 'the custody and marriage of Henry son and heir of Edmund, earl of Richmond, tenant in chief of Henry VI, in the king's hands by reason of his minority'.[24] Henry's wardship was a valuable prize, and in order to secure it, Herbert paid the huge sum of £1,000 (£643,000).

With his uncle branded a traitor, five-year-old Henry now bade farewell to the place of his birth and childhood home and started on the long and arduous journey across the breadth of Wales to the imposing Raglan Castle, his new guardian's main seat. One of the last medieval castles to be built in England and Wales, the site had long been fortified, perhaps as far back as the Norman conquest of Wales. It had only recently become Herbert's home, having been granted to him in 1461.[25] Herbert had a long-standing record of loyalty to the Yorkist cause as well as military experience. Like many magnates, he had fought in France during the Hundred Years' War, during which he had been captured at the Battle of Formigny in 1450.[26] He was knighted two years later and soon became an important figure in Wales, where he kept semi-regal state and wielded great power. He had strong ties to the Duke of York, for whom he had openly declared his support, and then for York's son Edward IV. Having fought bravely for Edward's cause, he would become increasingly powerful in the coming years. For Margaret, losing her son to the man responsible for routing his father at Carmarthen six years earlier must have been bitterly painful, but she had no choice in the matter. Her prudent efforts to position herself in a powerful family so that she could provide her son with a secure future had come to nought, crushed in a battle between kings.

Margaret could at least draw some solace from the knowledge that Henry was comfortable at Raglan Castle. Herbert would spend a vast sum on improvements to the fortress, firmly putting his own stamp on his recently acquired home. These included magnificent suites of new apartments to accommodate his family and an impressive gatehouse that inspired awe in Raglan's visitors. A luxurious setting for Henry's upbringing, it was also the main administrative centre of Herbert's lands and thus would have been a constant hub of hustle and bustle as Herbert and his staff worked to keep these in good order.

To Margaret's relief, Herbert took his role as guardian with great seriousness, and he and his wife proved to be kindly, taking genuine concern in Henry's welfare. In 1449 Herbert had married Anne Devereux, the daughter of Sir Walter Devereux of Weobley, and she was particularly fond of Henry.[27] He in turn formed a close bond with her and years later would not only remember her but also welcome her to his court. At Raglan—for the first time—Henry could enjoy the company of other noble children, for the Herberts had young children of similar ages.[28] In his will Herbert set out his hope that his eldest daughter, Maud, would 'be wedded to the Lord Henry of Richmond'.[29] Whether Herbert ever consulted Margaret about this is unknown. For a time, Henry was able to enjoy some semblance of a normal childhood under the Herberts' supervision, and in later years he would not forget their kindness. Still, he was left in no doubt of his status. He would later recall that 'since the age of five he had been guarded like a fugitive or kept in prison'.[30]

Though she was separated from him, Margaret and her husband still took a keen interest in Henry's welfare. She was able to retain contact with him through letters and messengers and took care to do so regularly, perhaps addressing him as 'my dear heart', as she did when he reached adulthood. Perhaps she even sent gifts on occasion. Given the importance she placed on her own education, she would have been gratified to hear that Henry was doing well in his lessons, which were supervised by the Oxford graduate Andrew Scot. Another former Oxford pupil, Edward Haseley, was later described as 'instructor of the king in grammar in his tender age', while Sir Hugh Johns may have been on hand to assist with some early military training.[31] Unsurprisingly, André was full of praise when it came to young Henry's academic abilities and claimed that Scot told him that 'he had never heard of a boy at that age with such great mental quickness and capacity for learning'.[32] Henry was, André said, 'endowed with such sharp mental powers and such great natural vigour and comprehension' that he grasped his lessons quickly.[33] He apparently 'surpassed his peers' and 'possessed such becoming noble manners, such charmful grace of royal expression, and such great beauty'.[34] He was, in short, a son to be proud of, though to her sorrow, Margaret was not the one to raise him.

On 20 September 1462, it appeared that Henry's lineage and education would be all that he had to commend him, for on that day, to Margaret's horror, the king issued a grant. In it, 'the lordship of Richmond, which Edmund Hadham, late Earl of Richmond, lately had of the grant of Henry VI', which had then passed to his son Henry, was taken from him.[35] Instead, the earldom and the lands that came with it were conferred upon the king's brother, George, Duke of Clarence.[36] In a show of defiance, and demonstrating a resolute determination to acknowledge what she truly believed to be his birthright, Margaret continued to refer to Henry as 'Lord Richmond', as indeed did Lord Herbert. What was more, she was not prepared to give up hope of getting them back, even if it meant humbling herself before her enemies.

NORTH OF THE BORDER, OTHERS of Margaret's family were not so set on appeasement. Having lost his lands, Jasper had almost certainly made his way to Scotland to join Henry VI and his family in exile. He continued to work tirelessly for the Lancastrian cause, though it seemed hopeless. He had already lost several of his family members in active service to Henry VI. In 1462 he joined Queen Margaret as she sailed to her homeland of France to beg for Louis XI's aid in restoring her husband to his throne. On 28 June, Louis signed the Treaty of Tours, a one-hundred-year truce between France and England; both countries agreed that neither party would pledge its support to the other's enemies.[37]

Not all of Henry VI's supporters were as loyal as Jasper Tudor. By 1463, Margaret's cousin Somerset had had enough of exile and decided to throw himself on Edward IV's mercy. As a leading Lancastrian, by submitting himself to Edward, Somerset became a figurehead for those who were willing to accept a monarchy without a Lancastrian king at the head. Edward IV was delighted by this turn of events, and in an attempt to win Somerset's friendship, he made a point of lavishing attention on him: they hunted together, Somerset became captain of Edward's guard, and, in a sign of great favour, he even shared the king's bed.[38] The king evidently recognised the need to broaden his support network, realizing that he could not rely on the Earl of Warwick and his affinity alone.

This reconciliation with the Yorkist regime was advantageous to other members of Margaret's family as well: her aunt, Eleanor, dowager Duchess of Somerset (wife of Margaret's deceased uncle Edmund) was pardoned, and members of the family circle were accepted back into the fold.[39] Margaret may well have deemed this a wise move; it was a similar course of action to that taken by her husband, and in time she too would become a figurehead of Lancastrian submission. On 10 March, Somerset was granted a general pardon, and the king made several gifts of money to him and his family.[40] However, this was not a course that Margaret's cousin would sustain, for at heart he was a true Lancastrian; in December Somerset abandoned Edward IV and joined Queen Margaret in France. Though he had betrayed his house, the queen was relieved to have him once more on her side and was quick to forgive Somerset.

Edward IV was outraged by Somerset's treachery, and Margaret would have been fearful of the potential consequences for her family. She had good reason to be, for the furious king wasted no time in imprisoning Somerset's mother, to whom he had so recently granted a pardon. The dowager duchess was kept in harsh conditions. Somerset's double betrayal meant that Edward IV was in no mood to be merciful or reconcile with the Beaufort family.[41] On 24 April 1464, the duke having returned to England, Somerset's forces were defeated by the Yorkists at Hedgeley Moor. But he was not ready to give up, and on 15 May the two armies met again at Hexham in Northumberland. Once again, the Yorkists were victorious. For Somerset, there were to be no more chances. He was captured and immediately executed.[42]

In the aftermath of Hexham, Henry VI, who had been present, was now a fugitive, and would spend the next year relying on the charity of Lancastrian sympathizers while his wife and son were safe in France. Throughout all of this, Margaret and her husband had remained at Bourne, doing their best to avoid any further involvement in the conflict in the aftermath of Towton. However, they would have been as alarmed as the rest of the country when in the autumn of 1464 some surprising news came to light.

FOR THE FIRST FEW YEARS of his reign, Edward IV devoted himself primarily to enjoying the pleasures of kingship that he had fought so hard to obtain. He loved finery, particularly jewels, in which he indulged heavily. He also took particular pleasure in women, siring several illegitimate children.[43] The chronicler Philippe de Commynes claimed that he 'thought of nothing else but women (far more than is reasonable), hunting and looking after himself'.[44] By 1464, however, the king's lack of a wife had drawn comment among his subjects: his biographer Charles Ross described him as 'Europe's most eligible bachelor'.[45] For months, Warwick, eager to secure an alliance with France and put an end to Louis XI's support of the Lancastrians, had been carefully negotiating a marriage for Edward with Louis's sister-in-law, Bona of Savoy.[46] But, unbeknown to Warwick, Edward had made his own marital arrangements.

In September Warwick was left stunned when the king announced to his councillors that he was already married. Writing about Edward's new wife, the chronicler Dominic Mancini recalled that one of the ways in which Edward 'indulged his appetites was to marry a lady of humble origin, named Elizabeth'.[47] This Elizabeth was no foreign princess who would bring her husband a valuable European alliance, but the daughter of a Northamptonshire knight, Sir Richard Wydeville.[48] Though her mother was Jacquetta of Luxembourg, the widow of John, Duke of Bedford, such a connection did nothing to improve Elizabeth Wydeville's suitability as the wife of a king.[49] To make matters worse, Elizabeth was also 'a widow and the mother of two sons by a former husband'.[50] According to Mancini's account, 'when the king first fell in love with her beauty of person and charm of manner, he could not corrupt her virtue by gifts or menaces'.[51] Determined to have his way with her, 'when Edward placed a dagger at her throat, to make her submit to his passion, she remained unperturbed and determined to die rather than live unchastely with the king'.[52] This display of womanly virtue only served to inflame Edward's passion for her, and as a result he 'judged the lady worthy to be a royal spouse'.[53] Knowing, however, that such a marriage would be unpopular with his supporters, the wedding took place in secret with only the bride's mother, the priest, two gentlewomen and a man who helped the priest to sing in attendance.[54]

News of Edward's secret marriage infuriated the nobles as well as members of his own family. Mancini recorded that the king's mother, the Duchess of York, 'fell into such a frenzy, that she offered to submit to a public inquiry, and asserted that Edward was not the offspring of her husband the Duke of York, but was conceived in adultery, and therefore in no wise worthy of the honour of kingship'.[55] Most significantly, however, Warwick was 'greatly displeased with the king; and after that rose great dissension ever more and more between the king and him'.[56] This would later have serious consequences for their relationship, but for the time being—in public at least—Warwick was forced to put on a display of unity as Queen Elizabeth was presented to the king's nobles for the first time.

Margaret would have been as stunned as the rest of the king's subjects when she learned that the new queen was a commoner, and the Milanese ambassador reported that the marriage 'greatly offended the people of England'.[57] Like the rest of her contemporaries, however, it would not be long before Margaret, too, was forced to bend her knee to Queen Elizabeth.

In July 1465, news reached London that Henry VI had been captured in Lancashire. The deposed king was returned to London 'without all honour like a thief or an outlaw' and paraded through the streets bound to a horse, wearing a straw hat.[58] His former subjects jeered and taunted the fallen man as he was taken to the Tower, where he would spend the next five years as a prisoner. There, Blacman later reported, the conditions in which he was kept were harsh, and 'he patiently endured hunger, thirst, mockings, derisions, abuse, and many other hardships'.[59] His capture was a great blow to Lancastrian morale, yet this did not prevent Queen Margaret, still in France, from continuing her tireless efforts for his restoration. As for Margaret and Stafford, over the next few years they would do all that they could to ingratiate themselves with the Yorkist king.

CHAPTER 8

A LONG GOWN FOR MY LORD

The manor at Woking was idyllic in the summer: its gardens blooming with fragrant flowers, orchards heavy with plump fruits, and fishponds that supplied the household.[1] Located on the banks of the River Wey and surrounded by a moat, it stood in a large deer park that provided excellent hunting and recreation. Nearby stood the ancient church of St Peter's, to which Henry Stafford would later bequeath money in his will.[2] With its easy access to London, the estate provided the ideal setting to enjoy the Surrey countryside. This tranquil spot became Margaret and Stafford's new home in 1467, after Edward IV made them a grant of the former Beaufort property in December 1466. Edward was determined not to treat Margaret—now twenty-three—with the same antipathy he had displayed to other members of her family following the treachery of her cousin Somerset; indeed, Woking had once belonged to the disgraced duke. The grant was a sign that Margaret and Stafford not only were reconciled with the House of York but also had gained favour with the king.

Woking had once been the property of Edward the Confessor, but the first mention of a house on the site comes from 1272.[3] In the fourteenth century, the manor passed into the hands of the Holland family and remained with them until Margaret Holland married Margaret's grandfather John Beaufort, marking the start of its Beaufort ownership.[4] Perhaps because of its resonance with her own family, Woking quickly became Margaret's favourite home and would remain so for many years. It was a grand house that was entered via a gatehouse, which led into a large courtyard. The house boasted a chapel, hall, kitchen quarters that included a bakehouse and a laundry, as well as apartments that both Margaret and Stafford could enjoy. It was sumptuously decorated with beautifully patterned tiles adorning the floors. Archaeological finds from Woking have shown that blue and white glazed tiles originating from Valencia were used—luxury items indeed—and these probably date from the time of Margaret's residence.[5] The couple's steward, Gilbert Gilpyn, who hailed from Westmorland, oversaw life at Woking, and it was his responsibility to ensure that all ran smoothly.[6] He was highly trusted by his employers and often carried out tasks on their behalf, as Stafford's account books testify.[7] Similarly, their receiver general, Reginald Bray (sometimes called Reynold), was an important member of the household; he not only managed Margaret's estates for around twenty years but also became a lifelong friend.[8] Bray would come to play an integral role in some of the most significant events of Margaret's life, risking his own safety in the process. His wife, Katherine, also served in Margaret's household and is referenced at various points in her accounts.[9]

Margaret and her husband were neither important nor regular figures at Edward IV's court, yet at Woking, where they spent a great deal of their time in the late 1460s, they lived a life of luxury and wanted for nothing.[10] They became important magnates in the area and may have on occasion been seen in the local church of St Peter. The couple were rarely apart, and together they visited the nearby towns frequently, including Guildford, from where they regularly obtained household supplies, and Windsor, where they hunted.[11] Hunting appears to have been a favourite pastime, for references to Margaret's participation in this sport appear regularly in Stafford's accounts—on one occasion the couple killed a buck at Henley. Similarly, in later years Margaret's accounts show payments for hawks; clearly, hawking was another sport that she enjoyed.[12]

Despite not having the care of her son, Margaret adored life at her Surrey manor. With a staff of around fifty servants to wait on them, the household consumed meat, fish and red and white wine in large quantities and often sent to London for other luxury items such as salmon.[13] Orders of fruits such as strawberries and cherries also appear in their accounts. They often used Woking as their base from which to travel to the capital, something that as the 1460s progressed they did with increasing regularity. While in London they would frequently purchase clothes, such as fur for 'a long gown for my lord', black velvet for Margaret and material for a kirtle (part of a woman's gown).[14] Contrary to the dour image conveyed in most of her portraits, Margaret was fond of fashion and took a great interest in her appearance. Later in her life, her inventories reveal the extent of her love of clothes and jewels, but earlier evidence also shows that she purchased expensive materials and was conscious of creating an outward impression of splendour as her rank demanded.

On occasion Stafford would travel to London alone. Though he did not have an official role at court, the king sometimes summoned his cousin, clearly eager to keep Stafford on side. Once he travelled to Windsor, and in May 1467 he attended a council meeting at Mortlake Palace.[15] From his infrequent appearances, it is clear that in spite of their familial ties, Stafford was not a part of Edward IV's inner circle and played a minimal role in his affairs. He does not appear to have been an ambitious man, but there is no way of knowing whether the king's failure to promote him rankled Stafford or his wife. It is certainly possible, given that the interests and alliances of the rest of Stafford's family were meanwhile becoming increasingly Yorkist. His Bourchier half-uncles were well favoured by Edward IV: Thomas Bourchier (created a cardinal in 1473) had crowned both Edward IV and his queen; Henry Bourchier had been made Earl of Essex, and his son was married to one of the queen's sisters; and John Bourchier, Lord Berners, was Queen Elizabeth's chamberlain.[16] Stafford had some contact with these relatives, for Thomas is known to have visited his nephew and his wife at Woking, and in July 1470 Stafford dined with Lord Berners in Guildford. By late 1467, Stafford also had a stepfather, Walter Blount, who was the king's Lord High Treasurer.[17]

As the 1460s progressed, Margaret would often join Stafford on his visits to London. In May 1468, for example, the couple travelled to the capital so that Stafford might attend Parliament, where it had been anticipated that Edward IV would announce an expedition to invade France, led by Stafford's stepfather. The announcement was, however, delayed. Margaret and Stafford had arrived in London by boat, taking up lodgings at The Mitre in Cheapside.[18] Cheapside, despite its name, was a wealthy area of medieval London and was one of the main shopping streets, with a market and a vast array of shops and stalls. It was, therefore, the perfect place for Margaret to purchase luxury items. During these trips to London, she may also have socialized with family and friends. On one occasion, a boat was hired when she paid a visit to the Bishop of Chichester, a man who had formerly served as Henry VI's chaplain and confessor.[19]

Stafford's lack of position at court meant that he was in turn able to accompany Margaret on her travels. She showed a genuine interest in the running of her lands and toured some of these estates to check that everything was in good order.[20] In 1467 she and Stafford visited some of her West Country lands in Somerset and Devon, including Langport, where the Beaufort portcullis was proudly carved into the battlements of All Saints Church. This is likely to have been an interest that stemmed from her youth.

It was also during this time that Margaret became close to her husband's family, including Stafford's mother and his brother John, who regularly visited the couple at Woking to hunt and play cards. Margaret was fond of cards, and in later life she once sent a man from Buckden to deputize for her on a pilgrimage while she played.[21] Likewise, she enjoyed both chess and gambling, so much so that she was known to place bets on the results of games of chess. These may have been pastimes that Margaret had in common with her husband, for she and Stafford appear to have been genuinely close, and throughout the course of their marriage they were rarely apart. In spite of the age difference, a picture emerges of a couple who enjoyed one another's company. Given their closeness, Margaret's later decision not to include Stafford's arms on her tomb is a mystery. The Stafford knot does, however, appear on the surviving strip of bronze effigy-plate of the tomb, in a more subtle acknowledgement of their union. Though their marriage is unlikely to have been a love match, it became one of heartfelt companionship.

As a couple, they retained contact not only with Stafford's family members but with Margaret's too. They spent the Christmas of 1466 as the guests of Margaret's mother, the dowager Duchess of Somerset, at Margaret's childhood home of Maxey. Maxey was located at a convenient distance from their home at Bourne, so it is certainly possible that prior to their move to Woking, Margaret saw her mother regularly, spending time together at the duchess's London residence, Le Ryall. They also corresponded regularly.[22] That Christmas they were joined by Margaret's half-sister, Elizabeth St John.[23] Such was the merriment enjoyed by the party during that festive season that they remained at Maxey for six weeks.[24] Mother and daughter had a close relationship—Margaret's mother had, after all, been the only parent she had known—and in 1465 they both joined the confraternity of the Abbey of Crowland (or Croyland) in Lincolnshire.[25] This was a religious community that promoted solidarity through religion and that practised both devotional activities and acts of charity. Bishop Fisher would later recall that Margaret 'so studiously in her life was occupied in good works', and it is wholly possible that this stemmed from this period and before.[26] It was the abbey's chronicler, who had links with Margaret's family, who recorded many of the details of those involved in her story, including the potentially tragic end of her father. It is unknown whether Margaret's son, Henry, was ever given the opportunity to meet his grandmother, but no doubt he would frequently have been the subject of conversation between mother and daughter.

Her son was still a constant in Margaret's thoughts, and in a sign both of her piety and of her concern for Henry's moral welfare, in 1465 she arranged for the two of them, and Stafford, to be admitted to the confraternity of the Order of the Holy Trinity at Knaresborough.[27] The intention may have been to strengthen her family bonds by allying her husband and son in a common interest. Later in life, her piety and religious practices were recorded in greater detail, but it seems highly likely these rituals had begun much earlier. They clearly afforded a great deal of strength during difficult times and may have stemmed from her mother and her links to the various confraternities with which she became involved. It seems plausible that Margaret's piety may have increased as a result of her separation from her son, with prayer helping to sustain her.

In September 1467, twenty-four-year-old Margaret was finally afforded the opportunity to see Henry. It is unclear when she had last seen him, but this was the first recorded occasion in her husband's account books. The previous month she and Stafford had toured her estates, which took them as far as Sampford Peverell in Devon. As they reached Bristol, they paid ten shillings (£321.50) for a ferry to take them to Chepstow, from whence it was a short distance to Raglan Castle.[28] The couple were evidently made welcome by Lord Herbert and his family, and they remained at Raglan as his guests for a week. Thus, Margaret was given a rare chance to spend some time with her son, 'my dearest and only desired joy in this world', who was now ten years old. It may also have been the first occasion on which Stafford met his stepson. The boy was clearly being well cared for. Yet in spite of the Herberts' hospitality, there is also likely to have been a touch of jealousy on account of Margaret being deprived of her son's care. The visit would have been all too short for Margaret, and it would doubtless have come as a huge emotional wrench for her when she was ultimately left with no choice but to bid Henry farewell, not knowing when she would be afforded another opportunity to see him.

'MY LORD OF PEMBROKE, BROTHER of the deposed King Henry of England, with some armed ships has entered the country of Wales', the Milanese ambassador reported in July 1468.[29] Supplied with money and a fleet provided by Louis XI, Jasper took the opportunity to begin raiding the land where he had always been popular. 'The old Lord Jasper', as *Gregory's Chronicle* referred to him, succeeded in capturing Denbigh Castle and was soon holding court 'in King Harry's name', in spite of the fact that Henry VI remained a prisoner in the Tower.[30] Edward IV became convinced that he would have to take control of Harlech Castle, the only Welsh castle to remain in Lancastrian hands. The author of *Gregory's Chronicle* believed that Harlech 'is so strong that men said that it was impossible unto any man to get it'.[31] Sir William Herbert and his brother Richard were sent to secure its fall and were possibly joined by Herbert's ward, Henry Tudor.[32] If Henry did accompany his guardian, he would have witnessed as the garrison surrendered to Herbert's forces on 14 August, forcing his uncle Jasper to flee into exile once more. But there was one final humiliation left for the diehard warrior to endure: on 8 September, Herbert was created Earl of Pembroke—the title previously held by Jasper—in grateful thanks for his loyalty. With Jasper in exile again, Henry Tudor remained in the custody of the newly ennobled Earl of Pembroke.

With every Lancastrian incursion, Margaret's position became even more precarious. Despite her personal feelings, she recognised the necessity of remaining loyal to the king. But Margaret bore Lancastrian blood, and her unwavering submission to Edward's rule was not enough in the king's eyes. In what may have been a test of their loyalty, on 20 December Edward paid the Staffords the honour of a visit at Woking. The couple placed great emphasis on the occasion, and costly preparations were put in place. Every detail was considered, including the pewter dinner service— brought from London—from which the king would eat the five dozen dishes on offer.[33] This is likely to have been Margaret's first meeting with Edward IV, and in honour of the occasion she purchased a sumptuous velvet dress.[34] Brookwood, the hunting lodge that lay next to their home, had been chosen to host the visit. It was there that Margaret remained on the appointed day, busily overseeing the preparations in the hope of making a splendid impression. It was left to Stafford to ride to Guildford to meet the king, and having first enjoyed the hunt together, he escorted his royal guest to Brookwood to indulge in his wife's hospitality.

The chronicler Philippe de Commynes observed that during the hunting season Edward often had 'several tents brought along for the ladies. All in all, he had made a great show of this'.[35] The king would therefore have been pleased at the sight of the elaborate purple tent of sarsenet (a fine fabric) that had been specially erected for the occasion. No expense had been spared when it came to the refreshments the king was to enjoy, and the meal was eaten to the sound of strumming minstrels. There was an assortment of seafood that included hundreds of oysters, as well as eel and lampreys, all of which were washed down with ale. Margaret's impressions of the man who had ousted her family from the throne can only be imagined, but on the surface, at least, she maintained the appearance of the perfect hostess. The king's visit was a success, although it did nothing in terms of improving Stafford's standing.

By the time of the royal visit, Margaret and Stafford would have known of the growing rift between the king and the earl of Warwick. Between Elizabeth Wydeville's rapaciousness and determination to promote the interests of her family and Edward's decision to treat with Burgundy rather than ally with France, by 1469, Warwick had had enough.

In July 1469 the disgruntled earl sailed for Calais with his family and one notable addition: George, Duke of Clarence—the king's brother and recipient of Margaret's son's title of Richmond. On 11 July, Clarence was married to Warwick's eldest daughter, Isabel, in Calais—a match that the king had expressly forbidden. The following day the two men issued a manifesto in which they urged men to rise up and support their attempts to free the king from those around him—chiefly the hated Wydevilles. Warwick also resented the influence of the recently created Earl of Pembroke, Henry Tudor's guardian William Herbert, and he was a direct target in the manifesto. Having laid the groundwork, Warwick and Clarence set sail for England, intending to take up arms against the king.

Unprepared for battle, Edward IV immediately summoned his supporters. Chief among them was William Herbert, who did not hesitate to come to the king's aid. Having gathered a force of men, Herbert left

Raglan and hurried to meet Edward in the north. His brother, Richard, and his twelve-year-old ward, Henry Tudor, joined him. Herbert's reasons for taking Henry with him are unclear, but he may have been fearful lest the boy should be snatched from Raglan during his absence. Whatever the circumstances, Henry was about to witness the devastation wreaked by the Wars of the Roses firsthand.

The Herbert brothers had yet to reach the king when, on 26 July, their heavily outnumbered army engaged with the rebels at Edgecote Moor, northeast of Banbury. The rebels had the victory, and both William Herbert and his brother were taken prisoner. Led before Warwick and Clarence at Northampton, the fate of the two men was a foregone conclusion: the following day they were both executed.[36] In what had been his first taste of warfare, Henry Tudor had lost his guardian. Margaret's son was now in great danger.

CHAPTER 9

DIVINE PROPHECY

Margaret and Stafford were enjoying their favourite pastime of hunting in the forests surrounding Windsor when they received news of Warwick's victory at the Battle of Edgecote.[1] They were told nothing further, for there was no news of either Henry or Herbert—or indeed the king. Evidently aware that Henry had accompanied his guardian, Margaret was frantic with worry: Stafford's accounts provide an insight into Margaret's panic, as a string of payments reflect their urgency to discover Henry's whereabouts.[2] The couple immediately dispatched their servant William Bailey with messages, desperately hoping for positive news.

Though his army had been advancing south from Nottingham, Edward IV had not been present at Edgecote. He was shocked to learn of the defeat of his army and the execution of his staunch ally William Herbert. But the worst had yet to come. Soon, his men began to desert, enabling a jubilant Warwick and Clarence to capture him. Yet their plan was ill thought through. Edward was sent to Warwick's stronghold of Warwick Castle—a prisoner—while the earl attempted to rule in his name, punishing his Wydeville enemies.[3]

Finally, the news that Margaret had been waiting for arrived: though she was horrified to learn of Herbert's execution, her young son was safe. According to the later petition of Sir Richard Corbet, it was he 'that brought your grace out of the danger of your enemies'.[4] Corbet was married to Anne Herbert's niece, and it was to the wife of his deceased guardian, Anne Herbert, that Henry was returned.[5] In the aftermath of Edgecote, she was to be found at Weobley Castle on the Gower Peninsula, the home of her brother Sir Walter Devereux, a significant distance from where the battle had taken place.[6] That Henry was conveyed such a distance shows that his rescuers were eager to ensure that he was as far away from danger as possible. The journey—over a hundred and fifty miles—must have been exhausting for the twelve-year-old boy. But at last, he was safe, and as Margaret digested this welcome news, the immediate concern of her husband seems to have been to ensure that his stepson was kept entertained. Henry was evidently fond of archery, for a payment in Stafford's accounts notes the purchase of bows and arrow shafts 'for his disports' while at Weobley, a touching insight into his stepfather's caring nature.[7] In spite of this attempt at normality, Henry understood that once again he had lost a guardian, and he was old enough to wonder where his future lay.

With Herbert dead and Edward IV seemingly unseated, Margaret had only one thought. On 24 August, she and Stafford travelled to London, intent on gaining an audience with Clarence. Her purpose was to petition for Henry to be returned to her care and to have his title restored. The title currently belonged to Clarence, and with him at the forefront of affairs alongside Warwick, it seemed like the ideal opportunity to negotiate on her son's behalf. Margaret was doubtless hoping to reach some kind of agreement whereby Henry regained an advantage in terms of land and property in the future, but to her disappointment, upon visiting Clarence's London residence alone, she learned that he was at Middleham Castle in the north.[8] Margaret's determination to re-establish Henry's birthright overruled her good sense, for the realm was still greatly unsettled. Yet it is also a sign of her desperation to regain what she felt was her son's due, and throughout her life she demonstrated a fierce resolve to do what she felt to be right, regardless of the obstacles before her. In this instance, however, she made a risky move, one that would prove to be a mistake.

Though Edward IV was in Warwick's custody, ruling England in the king's name was no easy feat, and few were responsive to Warwick's efforts.

On 10 September, Warwick was left with no choice but to release his captive, and the following month Edward was warmly welcomed back to London. Meanwhile, Margaret and Stafford had consulted their lawyers about Henry Tudor's custody, and with the help of the trusted Reginald Bray, a copy of the original wardship document was purchased.[9] However, Herbert had invested an exorbitant sum in Henry's wardship, and his widow was not prepared to simply give this up. On 21 October, The Bell in Fleet Street was chosen as the setting for a meeting between the legal councils of the Staffords and Anne Herbert and her brother. To investigate Margaret's case, the services of a lawyer from London, Humphrey Starkey, had been employed, but in their desire to be kept abreast, characteristically Margaret and her husband also joined the meeting. As the party dined on a meal of cheese, bread, and mutton washed down with ale, Henry's future was discussed. The outcome of the negotiations is unclear, but they were evidently complicated, as a resolution had still not been reached early the following year.[10] During this time, Henry remained with Anne Herbert at Weobley, and once more Margaret was forced to take a back seat in her son's life.

THOUGH BOTH HIS COUSIN AND brother had risen up against him, and he would never again trust them, Warwick and Clarence managed to do enough to convince Edward IV of their renewed loyalty to him. They were family, after all, and in December Edward made sure that the three men were formally reconciled. But it was a superficial peace, and tensions still simmered underneath the surface: it would not be long before they boiled over. Given her swift action on behalf of her son following Edward's imprisonment, Margaret had good reason to be worried by his re-establishment. Although, in a show of loyalty, Stafford had ridden to meet Edward as he returned south, joining his brother and stepfather when the king returned to London, Margaret's rash behaviour in treating with Clarence had not helped matters. Edward was more wary of them than ever, and their disfavour was evident when, on 5 January 1470, Stafford's younger brother John was created Earl of Wiltshire while Stafford was given nothing.[11] It was a clear sign of the king's scepticism towards them.

By February the treacherous Warwick and Clarence were plotting once more, and this time they involved a member of Margaret's own family. Following the slaughter of Margaret's stepfather Lord Welles at Towton, his eldest son Richard inherited his title.[12] Margaret's stepbrother had been a young adult at the time of her mother's marriage to his father, but in spite of their age difference they had almost certainly had some contact as Margaret grew. Like the rest of her family, Richard was a loyal Lancastrian who had fought at Towton, but he had later been reconciled with Edward IV, who pardoned him on 5 February 1462. Furthermore, as a result of Richard's petition in Parliament in 1467, Edward had graciously reversed the attainder of Welles's father that had left him 'so deprived of livelihood that he may not do your highness such good service as his heart particularly desires, nor such as his status requires'.[13] Coupled with the previous grant of his father's goods, this helped Richard steadily rebuild his life.[14]

At the beginning of 1470, however, Welles was summoned before the king to explain his part in a private feud, but was pardoned on 3 March.[15] Unbeknown to Edward, though, Welles was already in league with Warwick and Clarence in a plot to overthrow him and replace him with Clarence. In preparation, Welles's son Robert had already begun to raise troops in Lincolnshire, an action that Warwick and Clarence wholly encouraged. Yet the rising was doomed, and on 12 March Edward's forces defeated the rebels at Stamford. Margaret's stepbrother Richard Welles was executed the same day, and a week later his son Robert was too, bringing further shame on her family.

Stafford and a small force of his men had meanwhile joined the king at Stamford, and as Norton has emphasised, such a demonstration of his loyalty was critical in the aftermath of Margaret's hasty actions during Edward's imprisonment.[16] It was left to him to break the news of her stepson's treachery to Margaret's mother, the dowager Duchess of Somerset, and Stafford rode to nearby Maxey to inform her.[17] Margaret, meanwhile, was at Woking. The duchess had her own reasons to be alarmed, for it seems that she had been involved in the rebellion and had perhaps aided her stepson. Much to her relief—and Margaret's—Edward later chose to pardon his 'kinswoman' for 'all offences committed by her'.[18] Her involvement nevertheless was a reminder of where the loyalties of many of Margaret's family members lay. With the country so unsettled, though, Margaret could not afford to do anything that might put her son or his inheritance at risk.

Following what became known as the Battle of Losecoat Field at Stamford—named so because many of the rebels discarded items of clothing as they fled from the battlefield—letters proving Warwick's and Clarence's involvement in the plot were discovered. Suspicions had already been raised on the battlefield when several of the rebels made cries of 'A Clarence!' 'A Warwick!' but their complicity was then confirmed. Edward IV was furious at this latest betrayal, and having returned from Maxey, Stafford joined the king as they raced towards Exeter, determined to apprehend them.

By the time Stafford and the king reached Exeter, on 14 April, the treacherous duo had gathered up their families and sailed for Calais. Denied entry there, the party sailed for Normandy, where they were able to dock in Honfleur.[19] It was from there that Warwick attempted to seek the support of Louis XI. The French king made his guests most welcome, but Warwick realized that if he were to restore his fortunes, he would have no choice but to reconcile with the House of Lancaster. To this end, Louis XI was keen to heal the rift between the earl and Margaret of Anjou, who was still in France with her son. It was a steep challenge given their background—they had been bitter and implacable enemies for years—and when Louis first approached the subject with Queen Margaret, he found her to be 'very hard and difficult'.[20] It was their mutual ambition that won the day, for the queen was persuaded of the necessity of allying with Warwick if the restoration of her husband were to stand any chance of success.

Three days later, Warwick was gratified when his youngest daughter, fourteen-year-old Anne, was betrothed to sixteen-year-old Prince Edward of Lancaster in Angers Cathedral.

When the extent of Warwick's treachery came to light, Edward IV began canvassing support. In September he was in the north when word arrived that Warwick had landed in the West Country at the head of an invasion fleet supplied by the French king. It had been agreed that Queen Margaret and Prince Edward would remain in France until Warwick had secured the realm. Both Clarence and Jasper Tudor joined him. No sooner had he landed than Warwick began to amass a sizeable militia. Jasper, meanwhile, had set out for Wales to recruit more men. Warwick was so determined that it was reported that 'Warwick has pursued his enterprise with spirit and has practically the whole of the island in his power'.[21] Warwick was gaining men by the day, and his success caused many of Edward's men to desert. The king, whose popularity had waned, partially on account of the greed of the Wydeville family, could no longer command loyalty from his subjects. His only option was to flee. With just a handful of his supporters—including his youngest brother Richard, Duke of Gloucester; Lord Hastings; and Queen Elizabeth's brother Anthony, Earl Rivers— Edward took a boat from King's Lynn to Flanders.[22]

Meanwhile, a confident Warwick made his way to London, 'where he was received in most friendly fashion'.[23] He immediately set the bewildered Henry VI at liberty from the Tower, where he had spent almost five years in quiet imprisonment. Henry was taken to Westminster, where he was once more 'proclaimed through all the town of London with the greatest festivities and pomp as the true king and lord of England'.[24] This period became known as the readeption, and though Henry VI was king once more, it was Warwick who was pulling the strings. Thomas More later wrote that Warwick 'made kings and put down kings almost at his pleasure', earning him the nickname of 'Kingmaker'.[25]

Margaret was delighted at the reversal in her family's fortunes, yet the haste with which she had conducted herself the previous year during

Edward IV's imprisonment had made her all too aware of the swiftness with which fortune's wheel could turn when he was swiftly released. Likewise, she knew that the Wars of the Roses were not over: though Edward IV had fled, he would not give up on his throne.

Having been forced to flee from his realm and his family 'with seven or eight hundred followers who possessed no other clothes than the ones they were fighting in', the fallen Edward IV was a desperate man.[26] The party landed in Flanders, but the exiled king could not even pay the ship's captain; he could offer him only a fur-lined robe with the promise of a better reward in the future. Commynes observed that 'there never was such a beggarly company'.[27]

JASPER TUDOR HAD SPENT MOST of the 1460s as a fugitive in Wales, Scotland and France, and thus had missed out on almost as much of his nephew's life as Margaret. Now, with the House of Lancaster restored to the throne, Henry, once again a member of the royal family, was afforded an opportunity to reconnect with the relatives he barely knew. Parliament was due to convene in November 1470, and having collected his nephew from Hereford, whence he had been delivered by Sir Richard Corbet, Jasper took Henry to London. They arrived at the end of October, and there Margaret was briefly reunited with her son for what was almost certainly the first time in three years. Henry was fast approaching his fourteenth birthday and, according to André, he had been summoned into the presence of his kinsman and king, Henry VI.[28]

Much emphasis was later placed on Henry Tudor's meeting with the newly restored monarch, which took place at Westminster on 27 October. Its significance was perhaps intensified because—unbeknown at the time—it was to be both the first and last occasion on which Margaret's son ever met the man whom he would later go to strenuous efforts to revere. According to André's account, which probably came from Henry Tudor, on his first appearance at court the king held 'a splendid feast with the nobles and best men of the kingdom'.[29] As the king was washing his hands,

Henry was brought before him. It was then, so said André, that 'the king prophesied that some day the boy would undertake the governance of the kingdom and would have all things under his own power'.[30] Given that Henry VI had his own son, it seems unlikely that he would make such a statement, but with his nephew being the posthumous son of his dearly loved half-brother Edmund, it was only natural that he would have been eager to meet Henry. This is, though, unlikely to have stemmed from anything other than a familial interest in the boy, for prior to 1483 nobody considered the prospect of a Beaufort/Tudor claimant to the throne. Nevertheless, in light of later events, it suited the Tudors to relay this tale as one of 'divine prophecy'.[31]

Whatever transpired during Henry's meeting with the king, he later dined with his mother, stepfather, uncle Jasper, and Sir Richard Tunstall, the king's chamberlain.[32] The party were doubtless eager to discuss Henry's impressions, but probably also his future.[33] In the meantime it had been agreed that Jasper would retain custody of his teenage nephew, but not before the boy had first spent some time with his mother.

Before the end of the month, Margaret and Stafford returned to Woking, bringing Henry with them. For nearly two weeks Margaret was given the opportunity to spend time with the son from whom she had been cruelly parted for years, and she was determined to make the most of it. Having spent most of his life in a handful of Welsh castles, Henry was unfamiliar with the Surrey countryside surrounding London. His mother and stepfather took him on a brief tour of some of the towns around their home, including Guildford, which boasted a Norman castle and fourteenth-century guildhall, Maidenhead and the market town of Henley.[34] This afforded Henry a short opportunity to travel that he had hitherto never experienced. His visit also provided Margaret with a chance to get to know her son, who was now at the impressionable age of thirteen. It is not unreasonable to suppose that it was during this time that the strong bonds of trust between mother and son deepened and that Henry's respect for his mother grew—it would later become apparent that he trusted her judgement implicitly. They may also have enjoyed games of cards together, for, like Margaret, Henry also grew to be fond of the pastime.[35] But it was once again over all too soon. On 11 November, Henry bade his mother and stepfather farewell and joined his uncle Jasper. Though neither Margaret nor Henry could have known it, they would not see each other again for almost fifteen years.[36]

On 26 November, Parliament met, and though Henry VI was present, it was Warwick who was in control. He had regained all of his former power, though many loyal Lancastrians were wary of him and distrusted his motives. Jasper Tudor was elated when his attainder was reversed and he was restored to the earldom of Pembroke that had been unceremoniously snatched from him. Margaret also had hopes of recovering her son's inheritance, and she now felt secure enough in the political climate to approach Clarence about the matter. Though Clarence had been afforded a place on Henry VI's council, in other terms his treachery to his brother had not paid off and he had gained little. On 27 November, he agreed to meet with Margaret and her husband at Baynard's Castle—his mother's residence—well aware of what they wanted.[37] Stafford had already approached him about the matter, but he was not obliged to relinquish the Richmond title in spite of Henry VI's restoration. To Margaret's disappointment he would not comply with her wishes. Despite several further visits made by Stafford, there was nothing further Margaret could do: she would have to bide her time.[38]

Across the Channel, Queen Margaret and Warwick's family remained in France. It was there that, on 13 December, a marriage took place between Prince Edward and Warwick's daughter, Anne Neville. Once the wedding celebrations were over, the queen prepared to return to her recently restored husband—and her realm. She was not the only one who was planning a return: in Flanders Edward IV was ready to reclaim his throne. Once more, the Crown—and the future of England—were all to play for.

Chapter 10

HEAVEN PROTECTS HIM
WHO HAS NO BURIAL URN

On 14 March 1471, the deposed Edward IV landed at Ravenspur. With the aid of the Duke of Burgundy, he had managed to assemble a force, hoping to gather more men upon his arrival. He was not to be disappointed, for according to Commynes, 'there were more than two thousand of his supporters' who had gone to ground following his flight, and men soon began rallying to his banner.[1] His brother Clarence, who had been hopeful of acquiring further riches and power, had finally realized that he had nothing to gain by supporting Henry VI and Warwick. He was therefore receptive to attempts to reconcile with his brother, and Edward was only too willing to forgive him. The brothers met at Banbury on 3 April, with Clarence leading his men to join those of Edward. Though Edward was heartened, Warwick, who was in the north when he heard of Edward's landing, was 'greatly distressed' when he discovered that Clarence had abandoned him.[2] He had no choice but to continue raising men, for on 24 March Queen Margaret had at last set sail from France and was on her way to join him.

The forthcoming violence placed Stafford in a predicament. Throughout the Wars of the Roses he had done his utmost to avoid the conflict whenever possible, and this time was no different. However, on 3 March a visitor arrived at Woking. Though it was not Margaret he had come to see, she nevertheless took care to extend her cousin, Edmund Beaufort,

Duke of Somerset, a warm welcome. A younger son of her uncle, the same Edmund Beaufort who had been slain at St Albans, Edmund had upon his brother's death inherited the dukedom of Somerset. He had been raised primarily in France since 1461, and as a result Margaret had not seen him since childhood. Yet now was not the time for a family reunion.

As it was Lent, Margaret sent especially to London for an array of fresh fish for her guest to enjoy as he spoke with her husband.[3] The purpose of Somerset's visit was to persuade Stafford to declare his support for Lancaster—he was aware that Stafford had previously fought for York but was also conscious of his background and connections. Stafford was reluctant and either refused to commit himself or was left to ponder the matter, because on 24 March Somerset returned to Woking—this time for four days. The length of his visit suggests that he was either given some positive sign or was confident of persuading his host. Margaret's feelings on the matter are unknown: Did she urge her husband to take up arms and fight for her own house, or did she advise caution? Whatever she felt, Somerset left Woking without an affirmative answer from Stafford. It would not be long, though, before Margaret's husband was forced to make a choice.

On 11 April, Edward IV arrived in London. Warwick had hoped that the capital would remain loyal to Henry VI, but Edward had always been popular there, and as he entered, he was 'very joyfully received by the whole city'.[4] He immediately went to Old St Paul's, where he declared Henry VI to be deposed. A prisoner once more, Henry was sent to the Tower. Edward then gave orders for his wife and children to be escorted from the sanctuary in Westminster Abbey, where they had remained since his hasty departure abroad. There, the abbot of Westminster, Thomas Milling, who was sympathetic to Queen Elizabeth's plight, had given up his own rooms for her; she had been otherwise wholly dependent on charity, particularly weekly donations of meat by a London butcher named William Gould.[5] It had been 'at Westminster within the Sanctuary' that Queen Elizabeth had given birth on 3 November to a boy.[6] After presenting Edward IV with three daughters, Elizabeth had at last provided her husband with a male heir, but the circumstances surrounding his arrival were a far cry from those of her daughters. Margaret's own half-sister, Elizabeth St John—now Lady Scrope—had been present at the prince's birth, having been sent by a sympathetic Henry VI to assist the deposed queen. She even stood as godmother when the infant—named Edward after his father—was christened 'with little pomp'.[7] Though he had been born in the poorest of circumstances, this was a baby whose existence would have life-changing consequences for Margaret and her son.

Prince Edward was five months old when Edward IV was reunited with his family, an emotional encounter in which the king was at long last afforded the opportunity to meet his baby son. The arrival of his male heir gave Edward IV even greater impetus to turn his attention to crushing the Lancastrians once and for all. It was probably the news of Edward's warm reception in London—so close to Woking—that swayed Stafford to join him. He reluctantly arrived in London on 12 April accompanied by a small group of men, including Gilbert Gilpyn, the steward of Woking. That it was a hesitant decision is clear, for he had made no preparations; the following day, parts of his armour had to be brought to him, and he hastily prepared a will that he ordered to be delivered to Margaret. He evidently feared the outcome.

Edward IV recognised that there was no time to be lost. Taking Henry VI with him, he left London on 13 April, encountering Warwick's forces at Barnet. He was heavily outnumbered, but this did not stop him from engaging with Warwick's army the following morning. It was Easter Sunday, and a 'great mist' had descended over the battlefield, making it difficult to fight. In the confusion, Warwick's men started fighting their own.[8] The battle was 'most bitterly and strenuously fought' and had disastrous consequences for the Lancastrians.[9] Croyland described the battle as 'a terrible conflict', during which 'various nobles fell on both sides'.[10] Among them was Warwick, the Kingmaker. 'The same day after noon, the King came riding through the City and offered at Paul's, and so unto

Westminster; and after him was brought King Henry, riding in a long blue velvet gown; and so to Westminster, and from thence to the Tower, where he remained prisoner as he had done before'.[11] Edward had the bodies of Warwick and his brother, the Marquess of Montagu, returned to the city, too, 'which he caused to be placed in St Paul's Church, so that all the people might see them'.[12]

Though word of Edward's victory had probably reached Margaret at Woking soon after, she had heard nothing of Stafford's welfare—it must have reminded her of those terrible days after Edgecote when she had been forced to endure the agonizing wait for news of her son. She likely sought comfort in religion, and Bishop Fisher later recalled that she often wept 'tears sometimes of devotion sometimes of repentance'. Whatever was going through her mind, it is tempting to wonder, in terms of the latter, for what she may have felt the need to repent. More than five hundred years later, it is impossible to know. By 17 April, Margaret could wait no longer, and she travelled to the capital herself. Though it was only a short distance, it was a dangerous journey, given the political climate and that the countryside was swarming with bedraggled, injured soldiers who were steadily trickling back into the city. Margaret, though, was desperate. To her dismay, upon her arrival there was no news. She immediately sent a rider to Barnet to discover her husband's fate and was relieved to learn that he was alive. However, he had been injured, and to such an extent that he was unable to continue in active military service. The nature of Stafford's injuries is unknown, as are the details of how they were inflicted. But they were serious enough to ensure that he returned to Woking, where Margaret oversaw his care.

Queen Margaret, meanwhile, landed at Weymouth on the day of Edward IV's victory at Barnet, having endured a terrible crossing. She had been delayed by bad weather and was seriously disheartened when she was told of the recent Lancastrian defeat, Warwick's death and her husband's imprisonment. So much so that her first instinct was to return to France. Her supporters, though, including Margaret's cousin Somerset, persuaded her that all hope was not lost. Jasper was raising support in Wales, and if they could meet with his forces, a Lancastrian victory seemed possible. Thus, the queen, accompanied by Prince Edward and his wife Anne Neville, began travelling through the West Country, attempting to rally men to their banner along the way.

When Edward IV learned that Margaret of Anjou had landed in England, he immediately planned to capture her before she had an opportunity to meet up with Jasper in Wales. By 30 April the Lancastrian force had reached Bath and were travelling towards Gloucester, where they planned to cross the River Severn. The queen's army 'grew daily', but Edward was closing in on her.[13] When the Lancastrians arrived at Gloucester, they found the city gates closed against them. The exhausted army had no choice but to head for Tewkesbury. It was unseasonably warm for the time of year, and when they arrived on the afternoon of 3 May, they set up camp. It was there that Edward's army caught up with them, and though both sides were 'too weary of foot and from thirst to march any further', it was clear that a fight would soon ensue.[14]

On the morning of 4 May, a merciless battle took place in Tewkesbury. Supported by his brothers and his loyal friend Lord Hastings, Edward was determined to destroy the Lancastrians and their leaders for good. The battle was fought with great savagery, ending in 'a famous victory' for Edward IV.[15] The triumphant king resolved to show no mercy, and as the Lancastrian forces fled the field, many of them were cut down, among them the eighteen-year-old Prince Edward. Some, including Margaret's cousin Somerset, attempted to take refuge in Tewkesbury Abbey. The Yorkist army took no account of this, forced their way in and dragged Somerset out.[16] Edward ordered his execution in the town marketplace on 6 May. The prince, Somerset and Somerset's brother John were all laid to rest in Tewkesbury Abbey.[17]

While the Battle of Tewkesbury raged, Queen Margaret and her daughter-in-law took refuge nearby, apprehensively awaiting news. She was soon delivered the crushing pronouncement of the disastrous Lancastrian defeat but received no word of her son's fate. The queen's party fled, but they did not get far. On 7 May, Sir William Stanley discovered them hiding at Little Malvern Priory in Worcestershire. It was there that the queen was dealt a devastating blow: when she was told of her son's death, she collapsed in a torment of grief. With Prince Edward 'died the hopes of the House of Lancaster', which now seemed lost.[18] The future of Margaret Beaufort's house had been deprived of its heir, leaving a trail of uncertainty in its wake. Commynes accurately summarized the situation when he stated that 'in eleven days the earl of Warwick had won all of England, or at least got it under his control. In twenty-one days King Edward reconquered it, though there were two desperate and bloody battles'.[19] Margaret's house had been utterly annihilated.

On 21 May, the victorious Edward IV entered London in triumph. With him came the fallen Queen Margaret, who was 'brought to London in a chariot, and after sent home into her own country'.[20] She was subjected to a torrent of abuse from the Londoners as she was carried through the streets of the city that she had once ruled. Her career was at an end, and she would eventually be ransomed to the French king and returned to her homeland. She died in poverty in France in 1482.[21]

For Henry VI there was to be no such outcome. Tradition has it that on the evening of 21 May—the same day that Edward IV returned to London—as Henry knelt at prayer in the small oratory within the Wakefield Tower, he was dealt a heavy blow to the head. Various stories circulated, and Vergil would later write that 'the continual report is, that Richard duke of Gloucester killed him with a sword'.[22] André also laid the blame at Gloucester's door, dramatically claiming that he had been 'thirsty for human blood' and was sent by his brother 'to slaughter King Henry himself'.[23] Writing later, More, too, held Gloucester responsible, reporting, 'He slew with his own hands King Henry the Sixth, being prisoner in the Tower, as men constantly say'.[24] Gloucester is known to have been at the Tower on the evening of Henry's murder, so it is likely that he was present even if he did not slay the deposed king with his own hand. By contrast, the author of the *Arrival of King Edward IV* related that when the news of his son's death was conveyed to Henry, 'he took it so great' that 'of pure displeasure, and melancholy, he died'.[25] Croyland refused to comment but did state that Henry's body was displayed at St Paul's.[26] This took place the morning after his death, and there the chronicler John Warkworth remarked that 'his face was open that every man might see him; and in his lying he bled on the pavement there; and afterward at the Black Friars was brought, and there he bled new and fresh'.[27] Edward IV was taking no chances, and to quell any future unrest it was essential to prove that Henry was dead. The late king's body was taken to Chertsey Abbey for burial, but that would not be an end to Henry's role in Margaret's story.

Margaret was among those who mourned Henry VI's passing. His death, together with those of Prince Edward, Somerset and his brother, meant that the direct male Beaufort line was now extinct: just the female line survived, of which Margaret was the most senior.[28] Though this may have gone unremarked upon by her contemporaries, it was a circumstance that Margaret could not have failed to recognise. She dared not mourn her kinsmen openly, for the House of York reigned victorious. There was no figurehead to challenge Edward IV's authority, and his power seemed unassailable. Though the Lancastrian heirs were dead, Margaret still had reason to be fearful of Edward. Indeed, her son who, like her, possessed Lancastrian blood, was now in the greatest danger of his life.

JASPER TUDOR HAD BEEN UNABLE to reach Margaret of Anjou's army prior to Tewkesbury, and he was at Chepstow with his nephew Henry when he heard of Lancaster's defeat. Though Jasper had not partaken in the fighting, he was aware that his allegiances rendered Edward IV's attitude towards him far from conciliatory. Moreover Edward's behaviour towards those at Tewkesbury had shown that he could be cruel and untrustworthy, determined to crush anyone with Lancastrian blood. Jasper could see that 'matters were past all hope of recovery'.[29] Realizing that neither he nor his nephew was safe, Jasper and Henry hurried west to Pembroke Castle.

Yet, even there Jasper was conscious that his fortress could no longer provide the same level of safety it once had and knew that another plan was needed. The best course of action was to take flight: according to André, the impetus for this came from Margaret. Realizing that her son was in potentially grave danger, she believed that the best course of action was for him to flee. Margaret's 'firm and constant resolve toward him, which demanded more than a woman's frailty, was manifested to several of his most proven counsellors'.[30] Foremost among these was Jasper, and André claimed that as Margaret approached him, she urged him to take her son abroad.

If Henry were to remain, then she feared for his safety:

And unless my imagination or maternal instinct deceives me, the great distance of the sea will help us avoid all perils. I know that the hazards of the sea will be great; yet his life will be safer on the ocean's waves than in this tempest on land. But if it turns out otherwise, heaven protects him who has no burial urn. I would prefer that God keep him from harm rather than see him killed by the bloody sword of a tyrant.[31]

Jasper listened carefully to her worries, answering, 'I shall gladly undertake this office, and shall take as good care of my nephew as if he were my own son'.[32] Henry and Jasper's exile was agreed, and Margaret was left with the realization that she might never see her son again.

Leaving Pembroke Castle behind, Jasper and Henry travelled the short distance to the harbour town of Tenby. It was from there that 'a time and place were arranged and ships provided' with the purpose of aiding their escape.[33] One of the few people who had been entrusted with helping them was the mayor of Tenby, Thomas White. With his aid, on 2 June Henry and his uncle set sail for France. As the Welsh coastline grew more distant, Henry and Jasper had no idea if or when they would see their homeland again: they were exiles. As for Margaret, she was about to embark on almost fifteen years of endless stress and agitation as the ability to keep her son safe seemed beyond her control.

Though the sailing party had been heading for France, 'blustery south winds drove them ashore in Brittany'.[34] Duke Francis II, 'a kind and good prince', ruled the kingdom, and having heard of the fugitives' arrival, he 'welcomed Henry with great joy'.[35] Jasper duly 'submitted himself and his nephew to his protection', and their reception was warm.[36] Duke Francis 'with such honour, courtesy, and favour entertained them as though they had been his brothers, promising them upon his honour that within his dominion they should be from thenceforth far from injury, and pass at their pleasure to and fro without danger'.[37] Jasper and Henry were safe—but were now Francis's prisoners.

Margaret was relieved to learn that her son had succeeded in reaching foreign shores, but she also knew that the danger had far from passed. For the time, though, Margaret had other matters to worry about. The injuries that Henry Stafford had sustained at Barnet had left him in a seriously weakened state, and though initially it was hoped that he would recover, by the beginning of October it was evident that the end was quickly approaching. Stafford had first drafted a hasty will prior to the Battle of Barnet, but on 2 October he made his final will. Two days later, he died. Margaret and her household at Woking were plunged into mourning.

Stafford's death brought Margaret's third marriage—seemingly the most successful in personal terms—to an end, and at the age of twenty-eight she became a widow for the second time. Stafford's feelings towards his wife can be gauged from his final will, in which he referred to Margaret as 'his entirely and best-beloved wife'.[38] Though most of their income had derived from her estates, he nevertheless took care to ensure that she was generously provided for. He also demonstrated his affection for his exiled stepson, to whom he bequeathed a trapper of four new horse harnesses of velvet.[39] Other bequests were made to his brother and to the faithful Reginald Bray, who would continue in Margaret's service. Interestingly, the latter were all horse related, perhaps reflecting a passion of his. Everything else was left to 'my beloved wife Margaret, Countess of Richmond'.[40] In a further testament to his faith in her abilities, Stafford made his young wife the executor of his final wishes. It was left to Bray to make the arrangements for his master's burial, and Margaret's husband was laid to rest in the Church of Holy Trinity at Pleshey in Essex, where other members of his family lay entombed.[41]

Just a year earlier her son had enjoyed his first audience with the king—now, the king was dead and his family destroyed, Margaret's son was in exile and she had lost a husband whom she cared for deeply. The tragedy was almost too much to bear.

CHAPTER 11

GRACE AND FAVOUR
OF THE KING'S HIGHNESS

Following Stafford's death, Margaret, taking three of her ladies with her, briefly joined her mother's household at Le Ryall, the duchess's London residence.[1] It was probably from there that feelers were put out on the subject of her next move: marriage. She was not obliged to remarry, but ever the realist, she recognised her weakness: with no protector, her family allegiances and her son's exile made them both vulnerable. This time it was essential that she choose a husband not only who could offer her protection but also who had strong links to the House of York.

Thomas Stanley was the eldest son of Thomas Stanley, first Baron Stanley, and his wife Joan.[2] The Stanleys hailed from a family whose power base lay largely in Lancashire and Cheshire, where they were powerful magnates. Though the Stanleys had served at Henry VI's court and become embroiled in the wars, it quickly became clear that their priority was to align themselves with the winning side. Like Margaret's third husband, Stafford, Stanley was a cautious man, wary of committing himself, and he did his best to retain some middle ground.

Critically, he had failed to lend his support to Edward IV during the crucial and bloody battles of 1471. Yet, despite his dubious political allegiance, he had managed to retain the favour of Henry VI, and later Edward IV. Keen to promote reconciliation rather than bloodshed, however, the king had forgiven him for his lack of action and that same year appointed him Steward of the King's Household—an integral position within Edward's court that gave him regular access to the king. His position may have been bolstered by the support of his younger brother, William, who had fought for Edward and had probably assured him of his brother's loyalty.

Like Margaret, Stanley was also a pragmatist who was able to put his personal feelings aside, though for largely different reasons than Margaret: he was primarily motivated by self-preservation and a desire to curry favour. That he was a member of the king's council suggests that he was intelligent and politically able. He was slightly older than Margaret and, like her, had been married before. His first wife, Eleanor Neville, had been the daughter of the Earl of Salisbury and sister to the Kingmaker, providing Stanley with prestigious connections.[3]

By the end of 1471, Stanley's position with Edward IV, though more secure, was still not solid. Even so, he was determined to win the king's trust and served him loyally. His place in the royal household meant that he had a strong presence at court, with close access to the king. It was strengthened by his links with those within Edward's circle. His heir George, for example, would later be married to the queen's niece.[4]

Though she was a Lancastrian, for Stanley a marriage with Margaret presented many advantages, not least her wealth. For Margaret, marrying someone closely allied with the Yorkist court had obvious benefits. It effectively helped to neutralise Edward IV's suspicions about her loyalties by aligning her with a man who was integral to his court. It is even possible that the king had a hand in organizing the match, but the arrangements were very much made by Margaret's agents: the trusted Bray played a key role.

Like her previous marriages, the match was clearly one of mutual convenience. The marriage contract made no provision for future children, and this may have been a deliberate strategy on Margaret's behalf: she would present her husband with a prayer book that she had commissioned in 1478, and which is now in the collection at Westminster Abbey, containing prayers that highlighted all of her fears. Within the beautifully illuminated book, on which the badges and coats of arms of both Margaret and Stanley appear, are prayers intended to protect the user against death in battle, from plague, and in pregnancy.[5] Stanley, having sired three sons by his previous wife, had secured his line and had no need to have more children with Margaret.

Love and the production of children were not, therefore, considerations on either side, but this is unlikely to have been a concern for Margaret. She and Stanley seem to have lived harmoniously together, and later remained on good terms when their marriage underwent a dramatic change. Margaret also had good reason to hope that her marriage to Stanley would benefit her son too. Through him, she would gain access to the king and could petition on Henry's behalf. In 1482 this is precisely what she did.

Margaret's fourth wedding took place at one of the Stanley estates in early June 1472—certainly by the twelfth.[6] That she was prepared to marry before undergoing the prescribed year of mourning—before Stafford had even been buried—is a sign of her vulnerability and the urgency with which she perceived her situation. Stanley owned several properties in Lancashire, including Knowsley and Lathom, the latter of which would in time become a grand residence replete with impressive towers and surrounded by moats.[7] Lathom stood around twelve miles north of Liverpool, and in a poem he wrote, Stanley's grandson later claimed that it influenced the building of Henry VII's Richmond Palace: 'King Henry the Seventh, who did lie there eight days, And of all the houses he gave it the most praise, And his haul at Richmond he pulled down all To make it up again after Lathom Hall'.[8] Margaret came to spend time at both of these properties—particularly prior to 1485. Additionally, Stanley had a London residence, later known as Derby House.[9] From the onset of her marriage, Margaret and her husband moved regularly around these properties. At times, they also stayed at Woking, which she had retained after Stafford's death.

In the coming years, though, Margaret is likely to have spent much of her time in the capital. Unlike Stafford, Stanley's presence was often required at court, and as the 1470s progressed, Margaret, too, became an increasing presence. Given her background, it must have been difficult to be surrounded by those who had fought against her own house and those who had reconciled themselves with the king. Likewise, the king's brother Clarence would not have forgotten Margaret's eager petitions to him on her son's behalf just a few years earlier. However, as time passed, Edward's attitude towards her began to thaw. He could afford to be lenient because in the aftermath of Tewkesbury, for the first time in his reign, he had good reason to feel secure on his throne: not only was he in good health, but also he had a male heir. But his goodwill did not extend to everyone.

Having reached the safety of Brittany, as the years passed so too did the conditions of Henry Tudor's exile change. Occasional references to him appear in Duke Francis's accounts, such as in the spring or summer of 1472, when new clothes were purchased for him.[10] Uncle and nephew were moved between palaces until around 1474, when Henry was separated from Jasper and taken to the chateau at Largoët—also known as the Tour d'Elven—away from the coast.[11] There the chateau's owner, Jean IV de Rieux, Marshal of Brittany, who seems to have treated him well, oversaw his custody.[12] Nevertheless, Henry and Jasper's English servants were taken from them and replaced with Breton guards. It had become clear that they were less honoured guests, more prisoners. There is no evidence to suggest that either Henry or Jasper was the victim of poor treatment, for Commynes claimed that Francis 'treated them very gently as prisoners'.[13] Notwithstanding this, it was made plain to them that they were not permitted to leave.

The change in Henry's conditions came as a result of pressure that Francis had received from both France and England and that coincided with Edward IV's desire to invade France in 1475. Margaret and Stanley had celebrated the Christmas of 1474 in London, and she had no doubt learned of the king's plans from her husband, for Stanley was to be actively involved in Edward's pursuit of military glory. The following year, Margaret was among those who gathered in London as Edward made his preparations to invade France. Commynes reported that the king had amassed 'the biggest army with which any king of England had invaded France', and he had good reason to feel confident.[14] In July the English forces crossed to France from Dover, but there was to be no military action on this campaign. Instead, a peace treaty was negotiated with Louis XI, and Stanley was one of those chosen to participate in the discussions, which were concluded at Picquigny on 29 August. Few were pleased with the outcome of the campaign. Rather than achieving a glorious victory in the same manner as that of Henry V, Edward had instead been pensioned off by Louis. As a result, the king became 'so rich no one was able to rival him'.[15] In addition, he had negotiated a seven-year truce between the two countries and agreed to a marriage for his eldest daughter, Elizabeth, with the dauphin.

With the onset of peace between England and France, Edward IV then attempted to lay hands on Henry Tudor. His agents were sent to Brittany in an effort to persuade the duke to hand over his guest, and Edward offered him 'fine promises, bribes, and entreaties'.[16] He even offered Henry the hand in marriage of an English noblewoman, perhaps one of his daughters. However, André reported, Margaret, 'a most cautious woman, saw through the ruse, and through secret addresses by messengers and in letters she continually forbade him to return'.[17] She was right to be wary, for Edward's promises seem to have been nothing more than a ploy to lure Henry to England, and there is no evidence to suggest that they were sincere. Duke Francis, though, was left to ponder.

The situation was precarious for Margaret, who knew that the king had been making efforts to secure her son's return. While Henry's future hung in the balance, all that she could do was attempt to please Edward IV and his unpopular queen. As with her predecessor's, Elizabeth Wydeville's reputation was subjected to a propaganda campaign that has persisted to this day. In personal terms, though, her marriage to Edward IV was both successful and happy, producing ten children—eight of whom survived infancy.[18] Prior to the birth of Prince Edward, born in sanctuary in 1470, the couple's eldest daughter, Elizabeth of York, had been born on 11 February 1466 at the Palace of Westminster. Two further daughters, Mary and Cecily, were born in 1467 and 1469, whilst another son, Richard, was born on 14 August 1473. In addition, Elizabeth had two sons from her first marriage, Thomas Grey, Marquess of Dorset, and Sir Richard Grey.

It is highly likely that Margaret knew many of the royal children well during her time at court: she would certainly have become familiar with Elizabeth of York, and as the princess was of gentle and kindly nature, it is probable that they got along well. There is good evidence from a later period that they had a warm relationship. By the same token, Margaret also became close to Princess Cecily, and it is possible that this stemmed from this time in their lives. Although Margaret left no evidence of how she truly felt about the Yorkist queen, she seems to have been successful in charming her, as by 1476 Elizabeth and Edward afforded Margaret a prominent role in court affairs. The significance of such was to be realized in a highly symbolic ceremony.

In the summer of 1476, the king and queen travelled to Fotheringhay with their court to attend the reburial of the Duke of York and Edmund, Earl of Rutland. The village of Fotheringhay in Northamptonshire had once been the main seat of Edward IV's family, and several of his siblings had been born in the castle where 'there be very fair lodgings'.[19] It was the church, though, that dominated the village, and John Leland declared that 'The glory of it standeth by the parish church of a fair building and collegiate'.[20] It was in this magnificent building that the king had known since childhood that he envisioned building a magnificent tomb for his father and brother, who had been slaughtered at Wakefield. Edward had not forgotten the pain and humiliation that had been caused when the heads of his father and younger brother Edmund had been impaled above the Micklegate Bar in York, before their remains were unceremoniously buried at Pontefract. Indeed, a contemporary chronicler stated that Edward remembered the 'very humble place of his father's burial' and was determined to honour him and his brother with due ceremony.[21]

Margaret and her husband accompanied them, for Margaret had been appointed to wait upon the queen and two of her daughters.[22] The remains of York and Rutland were brought ceremonially from Pontefract, and on 29 July the procession arrived at the church. The following day, funeral masses were celebrated for the souls of the dead, and Margaret joined the princesses in making offerings at the altar rail.[23] She and her husband then watched as the king gave orders and 'translated the bones of his father, as well as those of his brother Edmund, earl of Rutland, to the fine college of Fotheringhay'.[24] A splendid tomb was later erected to York's memory.[25] Following the ceremony, the whole court feasted at Fotheringhay Castle in lavish style on a huge array of dishes that had been prepared especially. Margaret's presence as the closest member of the Lancastrian affinity symbolized not only reconciliation with the past but also her acceptance of Edward IV's rule. It was a public display of Edward's desire for her to be seen within the folds of the Yorkist regime. Edward was righting the wrongs of the past, as he saw them, and Margaret was one of his figureheads. It was a position to which she was happy to humble herself publicly. Privately, though, she would continue to counsel her son to be wary of the king she now knelt before. It was wise counsel, and Henry knew it.

BY NOVEMBER 1476, DUKE FRANCIS had tired of Edward IV's persistent efforts to convince him to hand over Henry Tudor. His treasurer, Pierre Landais, 'a man both of sharp wit and great authority', eventually persuaded him that if he conceded then Edward would treat the young man—now approaching his twentieth birthday—with respect.[26] It was this that finally swayed him.

English envoys wasted no time in conveying the young man to St Malo off the north coast of Brittany, where a ship was waiting to carry him to England. Perhaps he received an urgent message from Margaret, for Henry soon recognised that it was a trap. Claiming to have fallen ill, he sought sanctuary—possibly in the Cathedral at St Malo—but the English envoys were not about to give up their recently won prize easily.[27] They tried to remove Henry from the church, but the townsfolk came to his aid, furious that the envoys would dare to make such an attempt on a church. In the meantime, Jean du Quélennec, the admiral of Brittany, was able to persuade Francis of the danger Henry would face if he were transported back to England. At hearing this, Francis offered Henry his protection once more.

For the time being, Henry was safe. He was escorted to the town of Vannes, and it was there that he was reunited with his uncle Jasper. They were no longer separated but were kept honourably and were also welcome guests at Francis's court. Edward IV's attempts to gain custody of Margaret's son had been thwarted, but he was not about to give up. For now, however, other matters occupied his mind, for it soon became clear that Edward faced greater danger from one much closer to home.

Since their reconciliation prior to the violence of 1471, the relationship between Edward IV and his brother George, Duke of Clarence, had remained strained. The queen also loathed Clarence, for Dominic Mancini claimed that 'she concluded that her offspring by the king would never come to the throne, unless the Duke of Clarence were removed'.[28] Incensed when Edward IV quashed his hopes of marrying Mary of Burgundy following the death of his wife Isabel, Clarence began to plot.[29] At the beginning of 1478 he was put on trial, having been accused of 'conspiring the king's death by means of spells and magicians'.[30] Found guilty of treason, on 18 February Clarence was put to death in the Tower: according to Mancini, Clarence was 'plunged into a jar of sweet wine' and drowned.[31] It was a deed that Edward IV seems to have deeply repented.

The destruction of the king's family by his own hand was an unexpected turn of events, but for Margaret it created an opportunity. The Richmond title that she believed was rightfully her son's was now available. Yet she did not approach Edward right away. Having learned from her haste in her past dealings with Clarence and recognising that she would need more time to assure Edward IV of her loyalty and earn his confidence, Margaret employed caution and chose to wait.

By 1480, it is clear that Margaret had risen in royal favour, for she was that year entrusted with a special task. On 10 November, the queen was at Eltham Palace when she gave birth to her final child. It was a girl, named Bridget, and Margaret was probably at Eltham on the day of the baby's arrival. She was certainly there the following day, as she participated in the princess's christening. In what was a singular honour, Margaret was given the privilege of carrying the newborn baby to the font, where the Bishop of Chichester performed the ceremony. Following this, it was reported that 'the godfather and the godmothers gave great gifts to the said Princess'.[32] The princess's godmothers were her paternal grandmother, the Duchess of York, and her elder sister, Elizabeth of York. It was an occasion of which Margaret once could never have envisioned being a part, but everything had changed. Whether she liked it or not, there was a new royal family, and one that she was not a member of but bound to serve.

SOMETIME BEFORE 3 JUNE 1482, Margaret's mother died. On a personal level, the death of the dowager Duchess of Somerset came as a great blow, for she had been the only parent Margaret had ever known. It had been she who raised Margaret and supervised her early lessons, and she who accompanied her daughter on Margaret's first trip to court. She may also have been responsible for instilling much of Margaret's sense of piety, which Margaret could now turn to for comfort. The duchess was laid to rest beside her second husband—Margaret's father—at Wimborne.[33] Though devastated by the death of her mother, as always, practicality was at the forefront of Margaret's mind. She then attempted to negotiate with the king.

Throughout Henry's exile, Margaret seems to have been a faithful correspondent, keeping her son abreast of affairs in England. Though none of their letters from this period have survived, it is highly probable that they contained sentiments similar to those she expressed in her later letters to him: she often gave him her blessing, and on one occasion, in a reflection of her affection towards him, she assured Henry that 'I trust you shall well perceive I shall deal towards you as a kind, loving mother'. At this time, however, Margaret was clearly considering the possibility of bringing about his return, though she also recognised that this would take time. As her standing with Edward IV improved, so too did her confidence to effect a reconciliation. If she could continue to win the king's trust, Henry's foreign exile could potentially be brought to an end.

By the beginning of June 1482, her efforts appear to have produced some results when Edward agreed that Henry could receive a share of his grandmother the dowager Duchess of Somerset's lands to the value of £400 (£276,500) if he were to return 'to be in the grace and favour of the king's highness'.[34] Edward signed the agreement on 3 June, attaching his official seal. A draft still survives and can be found among Margaret's papers.[35] The groundwork for Henry to return home had been laid. Edward's grip on the reins of power was unchallenged, and with two surviving sons, his dynasty appeared to be assured—Margaret's son was no longer a threat. Thus it was that, on an unknown date, Edward—curiously, using the same piece of paper on which Margaret's second husband had been created Earl of Richmond—drafted a pardon for her son.[36] Margaret began to hope that she and Henry would soon be reunited.

The Christmas season of 1482 was passed with much cheer at court, where it was observed that the king 'very often dressed in a variety of the costliest clothes'.[37] Given her earlier negotiations with Edward IV, Margaret had good grounds to feel hopeful about what 1483 might bring. Yet, the year did not begin well, for early on the king received word that on 23 December Louis XI had signed the Treaty of Arras with Emperor Maximilian. By its terms, the dauphin was to marry Maximilian's daughter, Margaret of Austria, jilting Elizabeth of York in the process.[38] Edward was so outraged that he immediately declared war on France. All thoughts of pardoning Henry Tudor were set aside.

But just as violence was on the horizon, at the beginning of April 1483, Edward suddenly fell ill. His malady was destined to be brief: on 9 April the king, 'who ruled England with great renown', soon 'rendered up his spirit to his Creator' at Westminster.[39] He had been just short of his forty-first birthday, and though Thomas More would relate that in the latter years of his life the king's indulgence had led him to become 'somewhat corpulent and burly, and nevertheless not uncomely', the death of the man who had secured his throne so energetically by right of his sword came as a devastating shock to both his court and his subjects.[40]

Various stories arose about the manner in which Edward met his death: Mancini, who arrived in England at the end of 1482, had heard that he fell into 'the greatest melancholy' over events with the French, or that 'being a very tall man and very fat though not to the point of deformity, allowed the damp cold to strike his vitals, when one day he was taken in a small boat, with those whom he had bidden go fishing, and watched their sport too eagerly'.[41] Whatever the reason, as usual, Margaret's first thoughts were for her son. Henry's return had yet to be finalized, and with Edward dead, who knew if he would still be able to return home?

CHAPTER 12

A BOAR WITH HIS TUSKS

O n 16 April 1483, Edward IV's corpse was conveyed from Westminster with 'all pomp and solemnity' to Windsor Castle.[1] It was there that, in St George's Chapel, which he had 'raised from the foundations' but was yet to complete, the king was laid to rest.[2] More stated that at the time of Edward's death, 'this realm was in quiet and prosperous estate', but within the court the situation was vastly different.[3]

As he lay dying, Edward's thoughts had turned to the future of his kingdom. His heir, Prince Edward, was just twelve years old, meaning that some kind of regency would be necessary until he reached his majority. This task, Edward decided, was to fall upon his younger brother, Richard, Duke of Gloucester, who was to be appointed Lord Protector until the prince was old enough to rule for himself. Gloucester seemed like a solid choice, for he had always been steadfastly loyal to his elder brother and had fought by his side during the decisive battles of 1471. Born on 2 October 1452 at Fotheringhay Castle, Gloucester was an experienced and brave military commander who had led a brief invasion of Scotland in 1482, accompanied by Margaret's husband, Lord Stanley.[4] During the later years of Edward's reign, Gloucester had been responsible for governing the north of England in his brother's name. Since the execution of his brother Clarence, Gloucester only rarely appeared at court and instead 'kept himself within his own lands and set out to acquire the loyalty of his people through favours and justice'.[5]

Though Gloucester was Edward IV's choice of protector, Queen Elizabeth and her family, eager to retain their grip on power, had no intentions of allowing him to rule in the new king's name. They feared, Mancini explained, that 'if Richard took unto himself the crown or even governed alone, they, who bore the blame of Clarence's death, would suffer death or at least be ejected from their high estate'.[6]

At the time of Edward IV's death, his heir was at Ludlow Castle. There, Mancini tells us, 'he devoted himself to horses and dogs and other youthful exercises to invigorate his body'.[7] Edward was a bright child with a special understanding of literature, and Mancini believed that he was clever beyond his years. Queen Elizabeth recognised that in order to secure her own power it was essential that she obtain custody of her son as swiftly as possible. She wasted no time in sending word to her brother, Earl Rivers, her son's guardian, with orders to convey him to London immediately—they set out on 24 April. With the rest of the king's council she then began making plans for the king's coronation; eager for this to take place without delay, the date was set for 4 May.

In a sign of gross discourtesy, she neglected to inform Gloucester, then in the north, of his brother's death. Edward IV's close friend Lord Hastings 'had a friendship of long standing with the duke, and was hostile to the entire kin of the queen'.[8] He was horrified by this disrespect, and as a loyal supporter of Edward IV, disapproved of the queen's plans to cut Gloucester out. Hastings sent word to Gloucester conveying the news of his brother's death and urging him to come to London with a force to 'avenge the insult done him by his enemies'.[9]

According to Croyland, when Gloucester learned that the king was dead and that the queen intended to exclude him, he 'wrote the most pleasant letters' to her in which he assured her of his loyalty to her son.[10] But he recognised that she was eager to exclude him, and in order to prevent his downfall he knew that he had to move quickly. He began journeying south, and when he reached Northampton on 29 April he met with the man who was to be his key ally during the events that followed: the

Duke of Buckingham. As the grandson of Humphrey Stafford, Margaret's one-time father-in-law, Buckingham was Margaret's cousin and former nephew, and she had known him for most of his life. It was to him that Gloucester complained of 'the insult done him by the ignoble family of the queen'.[11] He could not have chosen a better ally, for Buckingham had his own reasons for loathing Elizabeth; in February 1466, when he was still a youth, 'he had been forced', Mancini reported, 'to marry the queen's sister, whom he scorned to wed on account of her humble origin'.[12] Though his marriage to Katherine Wydeville caused him great disgust, it had served to bind Buckingham's allegiances and those of his family to Edward IV.[13] Now, though, he threw in his lot—and his loyalty—with Gloucester.

Shortly after their arrival, the two men were joined in Northampton by Edward V's uncle, Earl Rivers, who had been charged with escorting his nephew to the capital.[14] Leaving the king at Stony Stratford, Rivers had ridden to pay his respects to Gloucester, and before long the queen's son Sir Richard Grey also arrived. Neither Rivers nor Grey had any reason to believe that anything was amiss, but the following morning both were locked in their inns while Gloucester and Buckingham rode to meet the king. Edward V was preparing to leave Stony Stratford when his uncle Gloucester and Buckingham caught up with him. He was shocked when Gloucester informed him that his kinsmen were poor advisors who had been conspiring the duke's death, and issued orders for their imprisonment. The helpless men were 'taken to the North in captivity' and were later executed at Pontefract.[15] The young king was now in Gloucester's control.

In London, when word arrived that Gloucester had intercepted the king and imprisoned the queen's family, 'the unexpectedness of the event horrified every one'.[16] Before long, for the second time in her life the queen gathered her youngest son, Richard, Duke of York, and her five daughters and fled to the sanctuary at Westminster Abbey.

On 4 May—the day scheduled for the coronation—Edward V arrived in London accompanied by Gloucester and Buckingham. Gloucester had already sent word to the council that he had rescued his nephew from the hated Wydevilles and had himself proclaimed Protector of the Realm. There were, nonetheless, already many who feared his motives: Mancini reported that a rumour was circulating that 'the duke had brought his nephew not under his care, but into his power, so as to gain for himself the crown'.[17]

Edward V, meanwhile, was taken to lodge in the Bishop's Palace near St Paul's, but it was agreed that an alternative residence would need to be found. While deliberating the matter in council, claimed Croyland, some suggested 'the Hospital of St John, some Westminster, but the duke of Buckingham suggested the Tower of London and his opinion was accepted verbally by all, even by those who did not wish it'.[18] In the Tudor period, the Tower would gain a terrifying reputation as a place of imprisonment and brutal execution, but it held no such associations in 1483. It was instead a royal palace that had been much favoured by Edward IV and contained luxurious apartments for the king and queen. It was there that Edward V was sent to prepare for his coronation.

MARGARET'S PRECISE WHEREABOUTS AT THE time of Edward IV's death are unknown, but it is certainly likely that she was close to the heart of the events that followed. After all, she and her husband were to be directly involved with what happened next, and the events of spring and early summer 1483 laid the foundations for what would prove to be a turning point in Margaret's life. There is no knowing how she may have felt about Gloucester's wresting of power from the Wydevilles, but perhaps of greater concern to her was the fact that with Edward IV's death, all possible plans for her son to come home had ground to a halt. There was no telling if he would be allowed to return; this cruel twist of fate must have left her feeling frustrated at the very least.

Throughout May the Council met regularly to discuss business and plans for the coronation. As a council member, Stanley was privy to these discussions and probably related some of the happenings to his wife, who was almost certainly with him in London. Margaret would have known the extent of Gloucester's power and Buckingham's unwavering loyalty to the king's protector. She was probably as stunned as many others at the way in which events were transpiring. By the end of May, Gloucester had taken control of the council and set about removing all those who were loyal to Edward IV, including the former king's close friend and ally Hastings. It was clear he planned to take the throne for himself.

On the morning of 13 June, the council met at the Tower. It was not long before Gloucester arrived and 'cried out that an ambush had been prepared for him, and they had come with hidden arms, that they might be first to open the attack'.[19] At Gloucester's command, a group of armed guards stormed the room and began to attack Hastings and his supporters. Having accused the man of plotting against him, Gloucester declared, 'I will not to dinner till I see thy head off'.[20] The helpless Hastings was dragged out and 'brought forth into the green beside the chapel within the Tower, and his head laid down upon a long log of timber, and there stricken off'.[21] His remains were later interred in St George's Chapel, Windsor, near those of his friend and master, Edward IV.[22] His unceremonious execution without trial was seen as an act of tyranny and sent shockwaves through the city: 'Thus fell Hastings, killed not by those enemies he had always feared, but by a friend whom he had never doubted'.[23]

According to More, after suffering from 'so fearful a dream, in which him thought that a boar with his tusks so raced them both by the heads that the blood ran about both their shoulders', Margaret's husband Stanley had suspected that Hastings was in danger—the boar was Gloucester's well-known badge.[24] The dream supposedly had such an effect on him that he attempted to warn Hastings of what was afoot. Sending a 'trusty secret messenger unto him at midnight' the evening before his death, Stanley urged that 'he was thoroughly determined no longer to tarry, but had his horse ready, if the Lord Hastings would go with him to ride so far yet the same night, and they should be out of danger ere day'.[25] Clearly, he was fearful for both of their lives. But Hastings paid Stanley's warning little heed, sending a message assuring him to 'be merry and have no fear'.[26] He would soon discover that his confidence was sorely misplaced in the most brutal manner.

Stanley's life may have been spared, but according to Vergil, as a supporter of Hastings and on Gloucester's orders he was imprisoned.[27] However, he was released 'safe and sound', for Gloucester feared 'lest if he should have done him any wrong George, Lord Strange his son should have stirred up the people to arms somewhere against him'.[28] The shock of the events of 13 June was evidently enough to convince Stanley to declare his allegiance to Gloucester. Margaret would have been left both horrified and fearful as a result of the unexpected brutal treatment that her husband had received and would have become aware of what Gloucester was capable of. She would thus have had good reason to loathe him—and to fear him—as a result.

Though Edward V was in the Tower, his younger brother Richard, Duke of York, had joined their mother in sanctuary. Gloucester had resolved to obtain his custody, and with the support of the Archbishop of Canterbury, managed to coax York away from Elizabeth Wydeville and into the Tower to join his brother. Gloucester now had both of his nephews in his keeping, and 'after that day they never came abroad'.[29] Thomas More disturbingly claimed that 'when the protector had both the children in his hands, he opened himself more boldly, both to certain other men, and also chiefly to the Duke of Buckingham'.[30] These intentions were about to become shockingly clear.

Many of the nobles had arrived in London for Edward V's coronation and were summoned to Westminster by Buckingham on 25 June. There they were informed that Edward V was illegitimate as a result of the supposed invalidity of his parents' marriage, while Clarence's son, the Earl of Warwick, was declared to be unfit to rule on the grounds of his father's attainder.[31] Buckingham therefore claimed that 'the only survivor of the royal stock was Richard, Duke of Gloucester, who was legally entitled to the crown'.[32] It was clear that there was no real choice, and that same day

Edward V was declared illegitimate and deposed: the legacy that Edward IV had fought so hard for had crumbled. The following day, Gloucester was invited to take the throne. After a show of reluctance, he accepted. Thus, on 26 June, the reign of Richard III officially began.

Margaret's feelings about Richard III's usurpation would soon become clear, and she had good reason to be concerned. Richard's treatment of the Wydevilles, his nephews and Hastings—as well as her own husband—demonstrated that he would not scruple to resort to violence if he felt threatened, and this may have made Margaret fearful for her son. She had bent her knee to a Yorkist king in the past, but there was no guarantee that this one would be as willing as his brother had eventually seemed to allow Henry to return home. After all, the circumstances in which Richard had acquired his throne meant that he would not enjoy the same sense of security as Edward IV had done, so he might well have viewed Henry Tudor as more of a threat. However, it would not be long before Margaret was prepared to risk Richard's wrath in order to gain a higher prize.

The coronation of Richard III was set for 6 July, and there was much to be done. Margaret's husband had remained in London throughout the dramatic events of June, and Margaret herself was almost certainly with him. On 4 July, the new king and his queen, Anne, took up residence in the Tower—the same fortress in which their disinherited nephews languished. That same day, Stanley was appointed steward of the household in an attempt to secure his loyalty. The following day, the royal couple rode through the city 'attended by the entire nobility and a display of royal honours', presumably including Margaret and her husband.

At some point that day, Richard granted Margaret and Stanley an audience at Westminster to help settle a dispute that had been lingering since the death of her mother. It was a stark contrast to the ruthless treatment he had meted out to Stanley just three weeks earlier. The matter concerned a long-outstanding debt owed by the Orléans family, and Richard and his chief justice, William Hussey, agreed to lend their support in attempting to secure its repayment. Margaret took the opportunity of her audience with the king to beg for clemency on her son's behalf; Sir Francis Bacon, who referred to Margaret as 'this cunning countess', said that she knew well 'to dissemble great love to the king, to desire and to effect the love of King Richard', so she 'came in all humility and besought him to call home her son and to be gracious to him'.[33] Nothing came of her pleas. Instead, it was agreed that she and her husband were to play a prominent role in the events of the following day.

On 6 July, 'the said Duke was with Queen Anne his wife at and in Westminster Church crowned with great solemnity'.[34] Both the king and queen were magnificently dressed in sumptuous clothes of the most costly materials. Many of the ladies and gentlewomen attending the queen had been delivered beautiful robes, and Margaret had been gifted a crimson velvet as well as a blue velvet gown, both consisting of six yards of white cloth of gold.[35] As Queen Anne processed into Westminster Abbey, 'on her head a rich circlet of gold with many precious pearls and stones set therein', Margaret came bearing her train.[36]

Stanley had also been given an important role, for as the king entered the abbey it was Stanley who walked before him, bearing the mace. The couple looked on as the Archbishop of Canterbury, 'albeit unwillingly, anointed and crowned him king of England'.[37] Afterwards, Margaret and Stanley attended a celebratory banquet at Westminster Hall, for which she was sat next to the Duchess of Norfolk.[38] The royal kitchens had been busy preparing an enormous selection of sumptuous dishes: roast crane and cygnet were followed by courses including peacock, venison, carp, 'fresh sturgeon with fennel' and pike, all of which had been fragranced with spices such as cinnamon, saffron and ginger.[39] These delights were washed down with copious amounts of ale and red and white wine.

Within the space of just a few short months, the entire shape of fifteenth-century England had changed. But behind the masks of loyalty to the new king, many already opposed his rule. None was better than Margaret at masking their true feelings. She had spent Edward IV's reign biding her time and employing all of her pragmatism in order to move closer to the heart of power. All in an attempt to keep her son from harm and achieve the ultimate prize of his restoration. Her goal had been within touching distance when, suddenly, Edward's death cast doubt on Henry's future.

Then Margaret was faced with a new king whose intentions towards Henry were uncertain but whose actions in acquiring his throne had shown that he could be a man without scruple. Margaret once again sought to create an opportunity for her son. Her plan would risk great danger, but having had Henry's restoration so cruelly snatched from her, she was no longer prepared to play the long game—or to wait upon Richard's actions.

CHAPTER 13

THE HEAD OF THAT CONSPIRACY

In the aftermath of Richard III's coronation, life is likely to have resumed much of its normal routine for Margaret. With the celebrations at an end, many of his nobles returned home, but Richard, still wary of Stanley—and possibly Margaret too—was eager to keep him by his side. Stanley had, after all, been an integral member of Edward IV's household, and, together, he and Margaret had much influence in the north. Moreover, Margaret was one of the key surviving members of the House of Lancaster—the most superior in the female line—and her son had spent years in foreign exile as a result of his bloodline. On 22 July, Richard rode out of London on the first stage of his journey north, taking Stanley with him. The events of the spring and summer had thrown the future into a torrent of uncertainty: Richard III's usurpation had been profoundly unpopular throughout the realm.

As he left, London was abuzz with speculation as to the fate of the deposed Edward V and his brother—popularly remembered as the Princes in the Tower. Rumours had begun to circulate that the princes were dead—murdered on the orders of their uncle Richard. When Mancini left England shortly after the coronation, he had learned nothing of Edward's fate but had seen 'many men burst forth into tears and lamentations when mention was made of him after his removal from men's sight; and already there was a suspicion that he had been done away with'.[1] There were, though, some who still believed the princes to be alive, and when the king left his capital, a plan was hatched to set them free. What is more, Margaret may have been involved.

The details of the plot are sketchy and derive largely from the chronicler John Stow, who had access to sources now lost. The plan, led by members of Edward IV's household, appears to have been to set fire to parts of the city, thereby distracting the king's men while the princes were rescued.[2] Margaret's role in the conspiracy is uncertain, but she was probably motivated by a desire to improve her son's prospects, for Jasper and Henry Tudor had been invited to participate.[3] Presumably, she felt that Henry's future would be better assured under Edward V's rule than under that of Richard III. That she was prepared to throw caution to wind and involve herself in such a plot can perhaps be taken as a sign of her desperation and frustration at having any hopes for her son's immediate return thwarted. It was a huge turning point for her, for hitherto she had displayed both patience and caution in her dealings with Edward IV. But there was none of that now. The conspiracy was ill thought out and failed, and on 29 July Richard issued a warrant to his Lord Chancellor referring to 'certain persons of such as of late had taken upon them the fact of an enterprise'. Because Margaret was not punished, it seems likely that the king was unaware of any involvement she may have had. The princes were immediately moved to the inner confines of the Tower. But Richard recognised that his own security could not be assured while the boys lived: it was almost certainly this that prompted him to make a chilling decision.

Thomas More related that while Richard was on progress, he summoned John Green, 'whom he specially trusted'. It was through Green that Richard sent word to the new Constable of the Tower, Sir Robert Brackenbury, that he should 'in any wise put the two children to death'.[4] Although loyal to Richard, Brackenbury was an honourable man and 'plainly answered that he would never put them to death'.[5] In frustration Richard turned elsewhere.

On 30 August, he arrived in the city of York with his wife and son, where the citizens warmly received the royal party. While he was there, Croyland reported, Richard 'arranged splendid and highly expensive feasts and entertainments to attract to himself the affection of many people', but he had always been popular in the north, where he was a major landholder.[6] Having pondered the problem posed by his nephews, Richard's attention, claimed More, was drawn to Sir James Tyrell, a man who was eager for promotion.[7] Approaching him about the possibility of murdering the boys, he 'found him nothing strange', and Tyrell left York for London and the Tower.[8] On Richard's orders, upon his arrival Tyrell was sent to Brackenbury 'with a letter by which he was commanded to deliver Sir James all the keys of the Tower for one night, to the end he might there accomplish the king's pleasure in such thing as he had given him commandment'.[9] Brackenbury must have known what was afoot. It was probably the evening of 3 September when, with the assistance of several accomplices, Tyrell arrived at the Tower.[10] More's account relates that, having entered the chamber where the two princes slept, the men

suddenly lapped them up among the clothes—so bewrapped them and entangled them, keeping down by force the featherbed and pillows hard unto their mouths, that within a while, smored and stifled, their breath failing, they gave up to God their innocent souls into the joys of heaven, leaving to the tormentors their bodies dead in the bed.[11]

Once the deed was complete, the assassins 'laid their bodies naked out upon the bed and fetched Sir James to see them'.[12] The lifeless princes were then buried 'at the stair-foot, meetly deep in the ground, under a great heap of stones'.[13]

Having completed his task, Tyrell returned to Richard in York and 'showed him all the manner of the murder'.[14] He was well rewarded for his services, but later in life his actions may have returned to haunt him: in 1502 he apparently confessed to the princes' murder before his execution for treason.[15] On 8 September, meanwhile, Richard III's young son Edward was formally invested as Prince of Wales in the spectacular York Minster: his line seemed set to continue.

More's account of the murder of the Princes in the Tower was not the only one in circulation, but as Weir has shown in her excellent book on the subject, there are good reasons for believing in its credibility.[16] Following the coronation, nobody had seen the princes, and hopes for their survival faded fast. Many people in England believed them to be dead, and in Europe, too, people were murmuring as to their fate. Numerous stories emerged as to the manner in which the two boys had met their deaths; the *Great Chronicle of London* reported that opinion was divided: 'some said they were murdered between two feather beds, some said they were drowned in Malmsey and some said they were sticked with a venomous poison'.[17] When André wrote that Richard 'cruelly murdered his brother Edward the Fourth's two sons', he said that the king had given orders that 'his unprotected nephews secretly be dispatched with the sword'.[18] The *Grey Friars Chronicle* simply stated that they were 'put to silence', and Commynes confidently declared that it was Richard who was responsible.[19]

Not one contemporary or near contemporary source accused Margaret of complicity in the disappearance or murder of the princes, and her name was never linked with theirs. It was not until the seventeenth century that claims emerged, first by William Cornwallis and then by Sir George Buck, who claimed to have read 'in an old manuscript book' that it was 'held for certain that Dr Morton and a certain countess, conspiring the deaths of the sons of King Edward and some other, resolved that *these* treacheries should be executed by poison and by sorcery'.[20] Buck was often unreliable, and other parts of his story can be proven untrue. There is not a shred of contemporary evidence to connect Margaret with the princes' disappearance—let alone their murder—and this is surely the most definitive indication of her innocence.

Even had Margaret wished to, an opportunity for her to arrange entry for an assassin was highly unlikely to occur; though entry to the Tower would have been possible, it is clear that the princes were extremely well guarded, with even Edward V's physician debarred access.[21] Only one who had the power and authority of the king behind them could have arranged for such a chance. Had Margaret visited or attempted to do so, contemporary chroniclers would certainly have noted it. Practicalities aside, it makes no sense that Margaret would have wished the boys dead when mere months earlier she may have been involved in a plot to free them. Quite simply, she had no motive.

On the other hand, Richard, as the popular phrase goes, had both motive and opportunity. Similarly, it is worth considering Margaret's character. Though she could be politically ruthless, she was a woman of immense religiosity and great kindness who had known and witnessed at least the younger of the boys grow up. Could she realistically have countenanced their death? Would such a thing even have crossed her mind? Her later accounts reveal nothing that could be taken as a show of remorse for such a terrible deed, and with very good reason. Whatever the fate of the princes, the insinuation that Margaret was in any way involved is nothing short of preposterous and an unfair slur on her character.

Though confirmation had not been given, the popular belief in the princes' murder meant that Richard 'lost the hearts of the people', as one London chronicler reported.[22] Given Margaret's subsequent actions, she too clearly believed that they were dead.

Elsewhere, Buckingham, Richard's chief ally, had joined his master on progress but bid him farewell at Gloucester. He returned to his castle of Brecknock in Wales, where he had in his custody Dr John Morton, Bishop of Ely.[23] Following the events that witnessed Lord Hastings's cruel beheading, Morton—himself spared the horrors of execution—had been sent into Buckingham's keeping.

More described Morton as being a man 'of great natural wit, very well learned, and honourable in behaviour, lacking no wise ways to win favour', and much of this transpired to be true.[24] Though his loyalties had always been Lancastrian, following the defeats of 1471 and Henry VI's murder, reconciling with Edward IV seemed to be the only viable option.[25] Before long, Morton had ingratiated himself with his new master, and Edward came to rely on his advice, so much so that Morton was appointed one of the executors of his will. He was one Richard III knew to be loyal to his brother's memory. It was now that Morton supposedly helped to plan Richard's downfall.

The murder of the Princes in the Tower prompted a dramatic change in Margaret's mind-set and ambitions. Though her son Henry was 'a member of the house of Lancaster', Commynes correctly acknowledged that 'he was not the closest claimant to the crown, whatever one may say about it'.[26] Margaret was also aware of this, and prior to 1483 the future of the House of York had appeared secure—Edward IV had been strong and robust with two male heirs, and thus there was no reason to even consider the possibility that Henry Tudor might one day stand a chance of becoming England's ruler. Even after Richard's coup, there were several York boys in line with a possibility of succeeding him, foremost of which was his own son, Prince Edward.[27] Moreover, Margaret's actions in the aftermath of Richard's coronation and the attempt to rescue the princes show that she had not considered her son's claim to be a strong one at this point. Henry's Lancastrian blood was not enough to stake a claim to the throne, particularly as many still considered the Beauforts to be bastards. Margaret, however, had a plan: for Henry to bear the crown once worn by his Lancastrian forebears and to become King of England.

By the time he left Richard at Gloucester, Buckingham had become disaffected. Several reasons for his estrangement have been suggested. Vergil claimed that he was 'partly repenting that hitherto of himself he had not resisted King Richard's evil enterprise' and had thus 'resolved to separate himself from him'.[28] It is certainly plausible that Richard had told Buckingham of his intentions to kill the princes, a step that Buckingham considered to be too far.[29] Having returned to Brecknock by the middle of August, Buckingham spoke with Morton and 'waxed with him familiar'.[30] He told his prisoner that in consideration of his own royal descent he was considering pressing his claim to the throne, which stemmed from Thomas of Woodstock, the youngest son of Edward III. Morton, who had no difficulty in recognising the duke's pride, flattered him. He also perceived an opportunity for Buckingham to join forces, for Margaret, too, was plotting. Vergil claimed that with the duke's consent, Morton summoned Margaret's trusted servant, Reginald Bray, 'to come unto the duke into Wales'.[31] Buckingham had evidently informed Bray of his thoughts in regards to his own claim, and Bray was able to report them to his mistress. For the time, though, Buckingham did nothing further. Intriguingly, however, Margaret already had her own plan in place: 'for she was entered far into them, and none better plunged in them and deeply acquainted with them. And she was a politic and subtle lady'.[32]

In the same manner as his Lancastrian blood was not enough to stake a strong claim to the throne, having spent most of his life in exile, Henry was an unknown entity in England. He needed something—or someone—to strengthen his claim, and Margaret did not have far to look. Elizabeth of York, the eldest of Edward IV's daughters, was beautiful, charming and intelligent. Despite the recent proclamation of her bastardy, in the wake of her brothers' disappearance many were of the opinion that she was the legitimate heir to the throne. What better way, then, to promote Henry's own claim than through a marriage with the Yorkist heiress?

According to Vergil:

After the slaughter of King Edward's children was known, [Margaret] began to hope well of her son's fortune, supposing that that deed would without doubt prove for the profit of the commonwealth, if it might chance the blood of King Henry the Sixth and of King Edward to be intermingled by affinity, and so two most pernicious factions should be at once, by conjoining of both the houses, utterly taken away.[33]

The impetus for Henry's marriage to Elizabeth of York probably did, as Vergil claimed, come from Margaret, and she was certainly the chief maneuverer behind what came next. Margaret trusted her Welsh physician, Dr Lewis of Caerleon, implicitly. Likewise, 'because he was a grave man and of no small experience, she was wont oftentimes to confer freely with all, and with him familiarly to lament her adversity'.[34] It was to him that Margaret suggested the possibility of a marriage between her son and Elizabeth of York, in order that Richard 'might easily be dejected from all honour and bereft the realm'.[35] For such a plan to stand any chance of success, the connivance of Elizabeth Wydeville would be essential. Elizabeth still languished in penury in the sanctuary at Westminster Abbey, and it would have been impossible for Margaret to approach her directly—Richard's men watched the sanctuary closely, and visitors were regarded with suspicion. Margaret needed an intermediary, and Dr Lewis was the ideal candidate.

Conveniently, being 'a very learned physician', Dr Lewis also served Elizabeth Wydeville.[36] It would not appear strange or unusual for him to enter the sanctuary on the pretext of visiting his patient, and on Margaret's orders this was precisely what he did. Elizabeth was incredibly vulnerable, for it was either on an earlier occasion or during the course of Lewis's visit that she had been told that her sons were dead. The news 'drove her into such passion as for fear forthwith she fell in a swoon, and lay lifeless a good while' before descending into hysteria.[37] As Lewis approached the sanctuary, his arrival drew no more than a glance from the guards, and he was able to enter unmolested. When he broached the subject of Margaret's plan with the fallen queen, the response he received was enthusiastic. That Elizabeth agreed to the plan confirms that both she and Margaret believed her sons to be dead, and though, to her sorrow, Elizabeth would never assume the role of the king's mother, she at least had hope of becoming the mother of a queen. She instructed Lewis to return to Margaret with a favourable answer and promised to do all that she could to rally Edward IV's supporters. Thus it was that a new conspiracy was laid between the two women.

Margaret waited anxiously at her husband's London townhouse for news, and when it arrived she tasked Reginald Bray, 'a man most faithful and trusty, to be the chief dealer in this conspiracy'.[38] Bray was to begin recruiting men to Henry's cause, and within a few days he had successfully enlisted a number of gentlemen who had once been members of Edward IV's household, including Giles Daubeney, Richard Guildford, Thomas Ramney, John Cheyney 'and many more'.[39] Elizabeth Wydeville had secured some valuable support from her own family and some of her husband's former allies, and plans were taking shape. It was at this time that Vergil related that Margaret, 'careful for the well doing and glory of her son', charged her chaplain, Christopher Urswick, with travelling to Brittany to inform Henry of what was afoot.[40] But before he could depart, Margaret received word from Buckingham, who had decided that he was intent 'of the same practice'.[41] It was at this point that the two plots— originally separate enterprises—became one.

It is unclear on what basis the two sides agreed to combine forces. Vergil noted that when Margaret received Buckingham's message, she 'altered her intent', and instead of sending Urswick to Brittany she sent her servant, Hugh Conway, 'with a good great sum of money' to deliver to Henry.[42] André later said that Henry had been informed of recent events in England 'through his mother's messengers'—Thomas Ramney was not far behind Conway with a similar purpose—so she had presumably conveyed her belief that the princes were dead.[43] Margaret commanded her son to sail to Wales, where he would find aid awaiting him. Croyland said that Morton urged Buckingham to send a message to Henry 'inviting him to hasten into the kingdom of England as fast as he could reach the shore to take Elizabeth, the dead king's elder daughter, to wife and with her, at the same time, possession of the whole kingdom'.[44] Buckingham never, in fact, made any mention of Henry taking the crown when he wrote to him on 24 September. Jones and Underwood have highlighted the possibility that Margaret recruited Buckingham under false pretences by suggesting that he ought instead to claim the throne for himself.[45] This would explain why Vergil said that Margaret had changed her intent—she was, after all, 'a wise woman'.[46] However, it is equally likely that it was a double bluff, and that Buckingham's intention was to claim the throne while feigning support for Henry's cause.

Margaret, 'commonly called the head of that conspiracy', began to further her plans, and by late September they were almost complete.[47] It had been agreed that all sides would rally their troops in a bid to topple Richard, and they planned to rise on 18 October. Throughout the plotting, Margaret's husband Stanley remained with the king, and though apart from his wife in physical terms it is hard to believe that he had no knowledge of the plans that were being formulated in his own house. It is unlikely that he supported them, though, and he certainly did not join the conspirators. Conveniently, his presence by Richard's side provided him with a watertight alibi. Margaret was aware of the risks that her role as 'the chief spinner of plots' carried.[48] They were risks she was prepared to take, and spurred on by ambition for her son, with Buckingham's support she had high hopes of the plot's success. After all, not only was Richard's former key ally prepared to back the plot, but also Buckingham was a powerful magnate who had both money and men. Coupled with Wydeville support, which had been engineered under Margaret's auspices, there was good reason for her to feel confident that the plan would succeed.

Upon receiving word from his mother, Henry immediately sought the assistance of Duke Francis, who agreed to provide him with 'a large force of men and boats'.[49] Feeling optimistic, Henry sent Conway and Thomas Ramney back to England to prepare his supporters: by 2 October he was ready to sail.

Elsewhere, 'This whole conspiracy was known well enough, through spies, to King Richard', Croyland reported.[50] By 11 October, while in Lincoln he had learned of what was afoot, yet the disaffection of his former ally Buckingham came as a shock. It is unclear whether Richard was aware of Margaret's involvement at this point. Vergil stated that the king believed Buckingham to be 'the head of the conspirators'.[51] Requesting men from his loyal city of York, Richard declared that 'the Duke of Buckingham is traitorously turned upon us contrary to the duty of his allegiance, and in-tends the utter destruction of us'.[52] It soon became clear though that luck was against the duke.

Everything went wrong for the conspirators: In Kent, the Wydeville faction rose too early and was easily suppressed. Meanwhile, in Wales, though Buckingham and his men rose up as planned on 18 October, they found themselves unable to cross the River Severn into England due to relentless rain. Within a short time, most of his army had deserted him, and the duke was forced to flee 'in secret wise unto a servant's place of his' in the Forest of Dean.[53] Immediately, the king issued a reward for his capture. The game was up. Buckingham was betrayed and taken to Salis-bury, where 'the king had arrived with a great army'. He was beheaded on 2 November in the marketplace.

Unaware of what was transpiring, on 3 October Henry Tudor set sail for England. The treacherous weather forced his ships back, and it was not until 18 October that he sailed again. Though aiming for the Devon coast, a storm drove his ships near to Poole in Dorset. Here he came close to landing, for those who had gathered on the shore tried to convince him that they were Buckingham's men and that the rebellion had been a suc-cess. Yet, he was suspicious, and his good judgement soon set in. Turning back, he returned to Brittany once more. For the moment all hope for his cause appeared lost.

It is unclear precisely how or when the king became aware of Margaret's involvement, but it would not remain a secret for long. Her fate then lay in the hands of her enemy. Having committed high treason, she must have been terrified for her life as she awaited the consequences of her plotting— almost certainly in London. When the punishment came, it was remark-ably lenient. Though in the eyes of the law Margaret had committed the most heinous of crimes by conspiring against the king, it was his own vul-nerability that saved her. Richard III was aware of his diminished popular-ity and could not afford to risk alienating Lord Stanley—who had grown in power and prestige over the years since his marriage to Margaret—by ordering the execution of the man's wife. Had he done so, Richard may have left himself vulnerable to potential rebellion, as well as losing a valuable ally. He was therefore left with no option but to spare Margaret the death penalty. However, that did not mean she would go unpunished.

CHAPTER 14

MOTHER OF THE KING'S
GREAT REBEL AND TRAITOR

Henry Tudor returned safely to Brittany, where he took up residence in the medieval walled city of Vannes, but he did not given up on his ambition: with Margaret's support, the seed had been planted in his mind, and Henry was determined to ensure that it was realized. Upon his return, over the course of the next year and more he was joined by a number of those who had been involved in the rebellion, and a steady trickle of exiles continued to arrive—all of whom were disaffected with Richard III. These included Margaret's half-brother John Welles, who had conspired against Richard in August, the Marquess of Dorset, and Elizabeth Wydeville's brothers Richard, Lionel and Edward.[1] Morton, meanwhile, had managed to escape from Brecknock and fled to Flanders. Reginald Bray, Margaret's devoted servant and friend, escaped punishment and on 5 January 1484 was pardoned for his role in the conspiracy.[2]

The conspiracy may have failed, but its very existence permanently altered the political landscape. No longer would Henry Tudor attempt to reconcile with the House of York as his mother had done during the reign of Edward IV; he was a contender for the throne. On Christmas Day, Henry and his supporters gathered in Rheims Cathedral. It was there that he solemnly pledged to overthrow Richard III and marry Elizabeth of York, thereby uniting the Houses of Lancaster and York as his mother had intended. At the same time, his supporters 'swore unto him homage as though he had been already created king'.[3]

Across the Channel, Richard III recognised that the threat posed by Henry had not been vanquished, and Buck later claimed that he 'feared and suspected Jasper, Earl of Pembroke, and his nephew Richmond, and not without good cause, and as was apparent to all the world afterward'.[4] For the time being, they were destined to remain thorns in Richard's side, but he was determined that Margaret would not.

In January 1484 the only Parliament of Richard III's reign convened: it was there that Margaret's fate was decided. Bills of attainder against Henry and Jasper Tudor were passed, as well as against Morton, Dorset and Welles, who were all 'denounced traitors to their country'.[5] Then there was Margaret. Referring to her as 'mother of the king's great rebel and traitor, Henry, Earl of Richmond', it was declared that she had

lately conspired, leagued and committed high treason against our sovereign lord King Richard III in various ways, and in particular by sending messages, writings and tokens to the said Henry, urging, instigating and stirring him by them to come into this realm to make war upon our said sovereign lord; to which urging, instigation and stirring the said Henry applied himself, as experience has recently shown.[6]

Additionally, she had provided her son with great sums of money to support his treasonous activities—with full knowledge of the money's purpose.

The evidence was damning, and Margaret's guilt had been proclaimed in the most public and shameful manner. Yet the king, mindful of the good service shown to him by Margaret's husband Lord Stanley, graciously agreed to spare Margaret the dishonour of attainder. But there were to be other consequences:

The said countess henceforth shall be legally unable to have, inherit or enjoy any manors, lands or tenements, or other hereditaments or possessions whatsoever, and also henceforth shall be unable to bear or have any name of estate or dignity; and that the said countess shall forfeit to our said sovereign lord the king and his heirs all the castles, manors, lordships, lands, tenements, rents, services, reversions and other hereditaments and possessions, whatsoever they may be, of which the said countess, or anyone else to her use, is now seized or possessed of estate of fee-simple, fee-tail, term of life, in dower or otherwise.[7]

AND WITH THAT, ALL OF Margaret's lands and wealth were taken from her and passed to her husband, who was entitled to keep them for the remainder of his life, thence to revert to the Crown. If Stanley died prior to Margaret, there would be no question of them being returned to her. That they were now stripped from her therefore came as a hefty blow, for it was these lands—an integral part of her inheritance—that added to her very identity, for she had always taken a keen interest in their administration. Margaret's lands in her life were of the utmost importance to her, her role as a landowner being one that she took most seriously. Indeed, since the earliest days of her childhood her lands had also added significantly to her marriage prospects. Margaret had become a wealthy heiress—largely in landed terms—upon her father's death, and this had enhanced her appeal to prospective suitors. Later, however, when she began making her own marital arrangements, she was able to use her lands as an attractive incentive when negotiating terms. Margaret would later ensure that nobody would ever take her lands from her again, but this time her punishment did not end there:

> For as much as the working of a woman's wit was thought of small account, the council therefore set down and commanded that Thomas, who proved himself guiltless of the offence, should remove from his wife all her servants, and keep her so straight with himself that she should not be able from thenceforth to send any messenger neither to her son, nor friends, nor practice any thing at all against the king.[8]

With her husband entrusted with the role of jailer, she was to be placed under house imprisonment. Margaret was a traitor.

Margaret's confinement was probably spent at Stanley's northern residences, Lathom and Knowsley. She was no longer permitted to attend court or travel, although her husband treated her leniently. After years of careful political manoeuvring, she had taken the most dangerous gamble of her life only to see it end in bloodshed and dismal failure. She had been publicly disgraced, her wealth had been taken from her and her hopes and ambitions lay in tatters. This can only have intensified her hatred of Richard. Henry Parker, Margaret's servant, wrote, 'Neither prosperity made her proud, nor adversity overthrew her constant mind, for albeit that in king Richard's days, she was often in jeopardy of her life, yet she bare patiently all trouble in such wise, that it is wonder to think it'.[9] It is plausible that she believed that God had kept her safe thus far, and this may also help to explain her numerous religious offerings in later life, by way of thanks.

It was perhaps her faith and the knowledge that her son was safe abroad that gave Margaret the strength to carry on, for, more significantly, the consequences of her actions did not deter her from continuing to support Henry. The fact that they had both survived an episode that could well have ended in their deaths—as it had done for Buckingham—may have been enough to convince Margaret that her son was destined for great things. Perhaps one day Henry would wear the crown, after all. Margaret certainly had no intention of forgoing contact with him, or of lessening her ambitions on his behalf. The Buckingham Rebellion had demonstrated that the English people were prepared to take up arms against Richard, and though it had been unsuccessful, Margaret was not prepared to give up. In her eyes, it was all still to play for.

IN THE SAME PARLIAMENT THAT witnessed Margaret's humiliation, the Act of Settlement—also known as *Titulus Regius*—was passed, establishing Richard III's sovereignty and proclaiming the illegitimacy of Elizabeth of York and her four sisters, who remained in sanctuary. Before long, though, Richard had turned his attention towards their removal, which Vergil believed was an attempt to thwart Henry Tudor's pretensions of marriage with Elizabeth. Croyland claimed that Elizabeth Wydeville had been 'urged by frequent intercessions and dire threats' to release her daughters, until after much persuasion she finally agreed to 'yield herself unto the king'.[10] Much has been made of her decision to do so, with revisionists suggesting that she would never have agreed to this had she believed that Richard was responsible for the murders of her sons. Yet there is no escaping the fact that she did precisely that. Even without the consideration of the princes, Elizabeth knew that Richard had ordered the unlawful execution of her brother, Earl Rivers, and her son Sir Richard Grey, and that she was prepared to come to terms with him was a sign of her desperation. She had been in sanctuary for months and had her daughters' futures and that of her remaining son, the Marquess of Dorset, to consider. Nevertheless, she refused to allow them to leave without Richard first offering some assurance as to their safety. It was with this in mind that on 1 March Richard swore a public oath at Westminster:

> I, Richard, by the Grace of God King of England etc., in the presence of you my lords spiritual and temporal, and you, Mayor and aldermen of my City of London, promise and swear on the word of a king, and upon these holy evangelies of God, by me personally touched, that if the daughters of Dame Elizabeth Grey, late calling herself Queen of England, that is, Elizabeth, Cecily, Anne, Katherine and Bridget, will come unto me out of the Sanctuary of Westminster, and be guided, ruled and demeaned after me, then I shall see that they shall be in surety of their lives, and also not suffer any manner hurt in their body by any manner [of] person or persons to them, or any of them in their bodies and persons by way of ravishment or defouling contrary to their wills, not them or any of them imprison within the Tower of London or other prison.[11]

In light of the imprisonment—and probable murder—of the Princes in the Tower, the reference to the Tower is particularly significant. It was enough to convince Elizabeth, who 'forgetting her faith and promise given to Margaret, Henry's mother', gave up her daughters to Richard.[12] The five princesses emerged from sanctuary, and Vergil reported that they were welcomed at court. It was not until later that year, however, that their mother left Westminster, though she would never attend Richard III's court.[13] Her reconciliation with him, nevertheless, prompted her to send word to her son Dorset—who had joined Henry abroad—'to forsake Earl Henry, and with all speed convenient to return into England'.[14] Though he attempted to do so the following year, he was apprehended and persuaded to return. But Henry would never trust him again.

Following Parliament, Vergil claimed that Richard continued to be 'vexed, wrested, and tormented in mind with fear almost perpetually' of Henry Tudor's return.[15] On account of this, he had 'a miserable life'.[16] His life was about to become worse and his position considerably weakened when on 9 April his son, Prince Edward, died at Middleham Castle 'after a short illness'.[17] The king and queen, who were at Nottingham when they heard the news, were so distraught that they became 'almost out of their minds for a long time when faced with the sudden grief'.[18] Edward had been their only child, and because the queen had experienced no further pregnancies, it was widely believed that she was unable to bear children.[19]

Meanwhile, in Brittany Henry enjoyed considerably more freedom than he had during Edward IV's lifetime. This period of Henry's life is poorly documented, and little is known about his time abroad.[20] As historians Griffiths and Thomas suggest, that he and his supporters were making offerings at Vannes Cathedral indicates that he was no longer under guard.[21] More significantly, Henry was also doing his best to persuade Duke Francis to back a second invasion attempt—an attempt which, in spite of Francis's best intentions, came to nothing. This may partially have been a result of the pressure that Francis was under from England, for in the same manner as his brother, Richard III made several attempts to regain Henry Tudor's custody. Promising Francis 'great gifts', Richard also offered the duke the yearly revenues from the lands confiscated from Henry and those who were with him.[22] Though it may have been an attractive prospect, 'by reason of sore and daily sickness', Francis was too unwell to negotiate.[23] His treasurer, Pierre Landois, however, was far more responsive to Richard's efforts. Landois had greater reason to be tempted by Richard's bribes than his master, for he was motivated by a desire to gain the respect of his countrymen through the conclusion of the negotiations. It was with this in mind that Landois reached an agreement with the English king. Unbeknown to Henry, he was on dangerous ground.

In September, Christopher Urswick arrived in Flanders, bearing news 'from [Henry's] friends out of England'—either Margaret or members of the council—of Richard's plans to lay hands on Henry.[24] The message caught Henry by surprise, and he immediately sent the faithful Urswick to France to discover whether he would be afforded safe passage there. Louis XI had died the previous August and had been succeeded by his thirteen-year-old son, Charles VIII.[25] Given the king's young age, his sister, Anne de Beaujeu, had been named regent of France, and Henry was relieved when he learned that he would be welcomed at their court, safe passage being 'easily obtained'.[26]

Sending his uncle Jasper on ahead, Henry planned to flee Brittany. Few were entrusted with the plans for his escape, and two days after Jasper's departure Henry 'feigned to go unto a friend'.[27] Accompanied by just five servants, he made his way towards the French border. Having changed into 'a serving man's apparel' in some woods, Henry and his men galloped across the border into Anjou.[28] Upon learning that Henry had fled, Landois sent Breton soldiers in pursuit. When Duke Francis recovered and learned what Landois had done, he was outraged. At his own expense, he sent the remainder of Henry's Lancastrian supporters to join him in France.

Having evaded danger once more, Henry travelled to Angers, where the court was in residence. He wasted no time in begging Charles VIII and the regent for assistance in his pursuit of the English crown. André reported that, when he did so, Charles, 'as if advised by a divine oracle, marvelled at Henry's graceful and distinguished countenance, his natural prudence, and his remarkable fluency in French'.[29] His pleas were answered, for 'so much did they abhor the tyranny of king Richard, King Charles promised him aid'.[30]

With French backing, it was probably in November that Henry attempted to canvass greater support for his cause. It may have been then that he wrote to his friends in England, pushing himself forward as a rival candidate to the throne:

Being given to understand your good devoir and entreaty to advance me to the furtherance of my rightful claim, due and lineal inheritance of that crown, and for the just depriving of that homicide and unnatural tyrant, which now unjustly bears dominion over you, I give you to understand that no Christian heart can be more full of joy and gladness than the heart of me your poor exiled friend, who will, upon the instant of your sure advertising what power you will make ready, and what captains and leaders you get to conduct, be prepared to pass over the sea with such force as my friends here are preparing for me.[31]

Nobody was left in any doubt that he was preparing to make another bid for the crown. Richard knew it, too, and on 7 December he issued a proclamation denouncing Henry and his supporters—chief among them Jasper—as 'rebels and traitors'.

THE CHRISTMAS FEAST OF 1484 was celebrated with much merriment at court. Among those who were there to enjoy the revels was the king's niece, Elizabeth of York. At eighteen years old, Elizabeth's beauty was beginning to attract admirers.[32] By January, it was whispered that Richard harboured romantic feelings towards his niece; 'it was said by many that the king was applying his mind in every way to contracting a marriage with Elizabeth', either after his wife died or by means of a divorce.[33] These rumours must have alarmed Margaret, and they certainly unnerved Henry—so much so that he began to consider other potential brides should his plan to marry Elizabeth fail to materialize.[34] It was Margaret, though, who recognised the necessity of a marriage to Elizabeth if his campaign were to stand a chance of success.

Richard was well aware that across the Channel, Henry was planning an invasion, and in an attempt to humiliate and discredit him, he intensified his flirtation with Elizabeth with the aim of 'dispelling the hopes of his rival'.[35] Soon it was widely rumoured that the king would discard his wife, Queen Anne, and replace her with his niece. Elizabeth herself also seems to have harboured some romantic feelings towards her uncle.[36] But as Richard's attentions to his niece grew more apparent, so too did the hostility with which his courtiers viewed it. A startled Croyland reported that the 'people spoke against this and the magnates and prelates were greatly astonished'.[37]

Richard's behaviour caused his wife great distress, and already grief-stricken following the death of their son, Anne became gravely ill. According to Croyland, 'her sickness was then believed to have got worse and worse because the king himself was completely spurning his consort's bed'.[38] She would not have to endure such treatment for much longer. On 16 March, during an eclipse of the sun, Queen Anne died—it would not be long before rumours began to circulate that her husband had had her poisoned.[39] Anne was buried in Westminster Abbey 'with honours no less than befitted the burial of a queen'.[40]

Richard was now at liberty to remarry, but there was great opposition to a match with Elizabeth of York. His councillors, in particular Sir Richard Ratcliffe and William Catesby, informed him that if he were to proceed with such a course 'in order to complete his incestuous association with his near kinswoman', he would lose many of his supporters, particularly in the north, where he had always been popular and where the Nevilles—the family of Richard's deceased queen—held sway.[41] Such was the force of the gossip and the protestations that Richard was compelled to declare that 'such a thing had never entered his mind'.[42] It may have been this that turned a spurned Elizabeth's hopes elsewhere.

According to a contemporary ballad, *The Song of the Lady Bessy*, Elizabeth of York joined Lord Stanley's London household following the death of Queen Anne. Written during the reign of Henry VII by Stanley's esquire, Humphrey Brereton, the historical accuracy of the piece has been questioned. It seems unlikely that Elizabeth would have taken up residence with Stanley, for with Margaret in residence at one of her husband's northern estates, the household would have had no female figurehead. Likewise, in light of the recent scandal, it would have been out of the question for her to do so had Margaret been residing in London, but she was far away in the north. Nevertheless, it seems highly probable that Elizabeth and Stanley were in contact given that they saw one another at court frequently.

Still, it is plausible that the ballad contains elements of truth. Though Elizabeth of York's role in the events of the spring and summer of 1485 is undoubtedly exaggerated, it seems that Elizabeth did in fact urge Stanley to support his stepson's bid for the throne:

> *Good father Stanley, remember thee!*
> *It was my father, that king royal,*
> *He set you in that room so high.*
> *Remember Richmond banished full bare,*
> *Any lieth in Britain behind the sea,*
> *You may recover him of his care,*
> *If your heart and mind to him will gree:*
> *Let him come home and claim his right,*
> *And let us cry him King Henry!*[43]

The ballad continues and claims that Stanley was initially reluctant to support Henry but eventually began to plot with his brother William on Henry's behalf. If this is true—as is certainly plausible, if not likely— then at some point Margaret became aware of it and doubtless encouraged him. If Stanley was planning on supporting his stepson, he must have been partially convinced that he stood some chance of success, but he also knew that he was taking a huge personal risk: if Richard discovered the truth, he would almost certainly be condemned for treason.

Margaret's house imprisonment had not deterred her from continuing to promote her son's claim to the throne, for she was in secret communication with Henry, perhaps discussing plans she may also have shared with her husband, albeit in the utmost secrecy. She must have recognised that, in spite of any suspicions the king may have harboured towards her, he could not risk alienating her husband, and this may have given her the confidence to continue with her plans. Richard III's unpopularity was becoming increasingly apparent, and soon 'man of name passed over daily unto Henry'.[44] However, Margaret, more than most, knew that nothing was certain.

AWARE THAT AN INVASION WOULD soon be upon him, Richard III set up headquarters in Nottingham—the centre of his kingdom—in June. He stepped up his campaign to discredit Henry, issuing another proclamation in which he took care to highlight the latter's dubious lineage, claiming that Henry was 'descended of bastard blood both of father side and of mother side'. Margaret was Henry's route to the throne, so it was she who bore the brunt of the slurs. There is no indication as to how she felt about the insults Richard cast upon her origins, but given that she and her son later went to great lengths to highlight the legitimacy of their ancestors, it seems likely that they hit a nerve and probably served to intensify her animosity towards the king. With her strong family orientations, Margaret was extremely proud of her lineage—in later life she showcased it in every way that she could.

Across the Channel, in France Henry was preparing his forces for invasion. He had been joined by an increasing number of English exiles, including the priest Richard Fox, 'a man of an excellent wit, a man learned', whom Henry immediately admitted to his council.[45] Another important ally was John de Vere, Earl of Oxford, who had hurried to Henry's side, having escaped from Hammes Castle, where he had been imprisoned for ten years.[46] When Henry saw him, 'he was ravished with joy incredible that a man of so great nobility and knowledge in the wars' had joined him.[47] Oxford would remain loyal to him for the rest of his life. Crucially, Henry also had the backing of Charles VIII, for 'an army was immediately provided for, and foot soldiers and mounted knights were levied'.[48] Commynes said that Henry's forces consisted of 'some three thousand of the most unruly men that could be found' in France, a number that he hoped would grow once he landed in England.[49] It seemed, he wrote, that 'God suddenly raised up against King Richard an enemy who had neither money, nor rights [. . .] to the crown of England, nor any reputation except what his own person and honesty brought him.'[50]

Despite the strictures that had been placed upon her, Margaret was exchanging messages with her son during this time, although sadly none have survived. She would later write to Henry that she prayed to 'Almighty God to give you as long, good, and prosperous life as ever had prince, and as hearty blessings as I can ask of God', and there is every reason to believe that her feelings were similar at this time. Her prayers during this period probably carried an increased fervency, because Margaret was painfully conscious of the fact that—unlike Richard III—her son, Henry, had no military experience. It is likely that Stanley also participated in the correspondence with Henry and had probably given his stepson some indication of his support. Husband and wife were both aware that it was only a matter of time before Henry arrived.

On 1 August, Henry and his army set sail from Harfleur. He had left the untrustworthy Dorset behind as surety for his debts and was accompanied by many of the followers who had shown him devoted service. It was 'with a favourable breeze' that the party made their way towards the Welsh coast.[51] From then on, Henry was fighting not only for the throne but also for his life.

CHAPTER 15

THE PRICELESS CROWN

'A little before sunset' on the evening of 7 August, Henry's ship dropped anchor in Milford Haven in Pembrokeshire, an event that Margaret would record in her Book of Hours.[1] For the first time in almost fifteen years, Henry set foot on Welsh soil; the circumstances were a far cry from those in which he had left. The following morning, his army began the first stage of their journey east, making their way 'along wild and twisting tracks'.[2] Henry was delighted when news arrived from Pembroke, the town of his birth, declaring their support for him, but more was needed. One of the first to join him was Sir Richard Corbet, who had once saved Henry from the battlefield at Edgecote.[3] David Owen, the illegitimate son of Henry's grandfather Owen Tudor, also offered his allegiance.[4] They marched through Wales unopposed, but men did not rally to Henry's banner in the numbers that he had hoped. To secure a victory over his enemy, he would need his stepfather's aid.

Shortly before Henry arrived in Wales, knowing what was afoot, Lord Stanley 'received permission to go across to Lancashire, his native county, to see his home and family from whom he had long been away'.[5] The king was greatly concerned about Stanley's loyalties and would permit him to go only on condition that he sent his heir, George, Lord Strange, to him at Nottingham as surety for his good behaviour. Stanley complied, but in so doing he found himself in a predicament.

Since the beginning of her house imprisonment, Margaret had remained in the north, but like Richard III she was well aware that her son's invasion was imminent. When she received word that Henry Tudor had arrived on Welsh soil, she knew what was at stake. For more than two decades, Margaret had played the dutiful subject to a monarchy headed by a rival house, and for the past fourteen years she had sought out every opportunity to bring her son home safely. It all culminated in this moment, but Margaret knew there was no certain outcome. The Wars of the Roses had claimed many Lancastrian lives, whether on the battlefield or the executioner's block. Failure could well mean death for both her and her son. It was their greatest and last chance, and she gave all she had to ensure Henry's success. She seized on the opportunity of her husband's return to speak with him about what lay ahead. Richard 'feared [what in fact happened] that the Earl of Richmond's mother who was the wife of Lord Stanley might induce her husband to support her son's party'.[6] We will never know exactly what passed between Margaret and Stanley on the subject of Henry's invasion, but with his son in Richard's custody, it was clear that Stanley would not openly declare his support for Henry, whatever promises he had made. Margaret knew this.

It was 11 August when word reached Richard III of Henry Tudor's landing. Having carefully prepared his army for the invasion, 'on hearing of their arrival, the king rejoiced', so ready was he to vanquish the threat to his throne.[7] But his elation quickly turned to anger and rage when Stanley, whom he had ordered to appear without delay, answered that he was lying dangerously ill at Lathom with the sweating sickness. Meanwhile, Stanley's heir, Lord Strange, was, so Croyland claimed, apprehended as he 'secretly prepared to escape from the king'.[8] It was then that Strange revealed 'a conspiracy to support the party of the Earl of Richmond' among himself, his uncle Sir William Stanley and Sir John Savage.[9] Both William and Savage were immediately proclaimed traitors, but interestingly Strange did not name his father as a conspirator. On the contrary, having written to Stanley 'announcing the danger he was in together with the urgent need of presenting help of this sort', he begged Richard for mercy, promising 'that his father would come to the king's aid'.[10] Stanley faced a terrible dilemma.

As Henry marched east via Shrewsbury, he was disappointed to find that men were not hurrying to join his ranks. He had sent Christopher Urswick to his mother and stepfather to inform them of his plans and to ask for their aid, and similar messages were sent to Holt Castle, the Wrexham residence of Stanley's brother, William. The response was encouraging, and it is highly likely that Margaret had also sent her son money to help his cause. As Henry approached Stafford, Gilbert Talbot rode to meet him with a small force.[11] He was heartened when, upon arrival in the town, Sir William Stanley greeted him 'with a small retinue'.[12] William's support was of vital importance to Henry's cause, and Vergil later recalled that he had noted William's 'loyalty and devotion'.[13] They did not remain in Stafford for long, but continued on to Lichfield, where they camped outside the city walls. The following day, Henry was 'honourably received' in the city, but he did not linger.[14]

Having recovered from his supposed sickness, Stanley left Lathom—and Margaret—on 15 August. It is unthinkable that the two would not have shared a conversation about his strategy before his departure, and Margaret could only pray that her husband would lend her son the support that he so desperately needed. With his own son as Richard's hostage, though, Stanley was still unable to do so openly. Stanley had reached Lichfield when he first made contact with his stepson, around 20 August. Learning that Henry was not far away, he marched with his five thousand well-armed men the sixteen or so miles to Atherstone to wait for him. Vergil said that he did this 'to avoid suspicion', fearing that if his actions were to become known, then Richard 'might kill his son George'.[15] It was to Atherstone that Henry rode to meet privately with his stepfather and his brother, and according to Vergil, a joyful reunion ensued. Stanley doubtless conveyed messages of support from Margaret, one of which was later imagined by William Shakespeare.

According to Vergil, once pleasantries had been exchanged a discussion of battle tactics followed. What was said will never be known, but Henry is likely to have been left with some assurance that the Stanley brothers were committed to supporting his cause. Neither were they the only ones, for Henry was also fortunate to enjoy the support of the faithful Oxford, Margaret's half-brother John Welles, Urswick, Fox, and numerous others who had supported him during his exile. These men all joined Henry's army at their camp near Merevale Abbey, and it was not long before additional men arrived to swell his numbers. On the evening of 21 August, Henry's men prepared to do battle on the morrow: it would be then that Margaret's fortunes and those of her family would be decided in the most dramatic manner.

MEANWHILE, THE HASTE WITH WHICH Henry was moving necessitated Richard's growing army to leave Nottingham and march south towards Leicester. Richard was confident, and indeed the odds seemed stacked in his favour: in spite of his unpopularity 'there was a greater number of fighting men than there had ever been seen before, on one side, in England'.[16] This is supported by the account of Richard Bygot, who served Richard III and later became Margaret's carver: he claimed that Richard 'had three men for one'.[17] Richard was also the more experienced soldier, for Henry had never before fought a battle. Richard was prepared for war, and on 21 August 'the king left Leicester with great pomp, wearing his diadem on his head' and accompanied by many of the great lords of his realm.[18] Among them were the Duke of Norfolk, Sir Robert Brackenbury and other lords, knights and esquires. But there was one notable absence: Lord Stanley.

Richard's army marched towards the town of Market Bosworth, setting up camp on Ambion Hill close to the village of Sutton Cheney. There, having refreshed his soldiers, the king 'with many words exhorted them to the fight to come'.[19] Yet, in spite of his numbers, he was full of anxiety that evening as the prospect of the battle loomed: this would be the first battle fought on English soil since the bloody scene at Tewkesbury more than a decade earlier, and to secure his crown, it was crucial that Richard should win. But he did not rest easy, for Croyland reported that the king 'had seen that night, in a terrible dream, a multitude of demons apparently surrounding him'.[20] It was an inauspicious start.

To make matters worse, Richard had risen so early on the morning of 22 August that his chaplains were unprepared to celebrate mass. Bygot apparently recalled that when the chaplain had one item ready 'evermore they wanted another; when they had wine they lacked bread, and ever one thing was missing'.[21] Neither was there any breakfast 'to revive the king's flagging spirit'.[22] None knew more than Richard that the day's events would have monumental consequences, and Croyland 'affirmed that the outcome of this day's battle, to whichever side the victory was granted, would totally destroy the kingdom of England'.[23]

The sources for what followed are scant, for there are no surviving eye-witness accounts. When both sides were drawn up in battle order, it became clear that Henry's forces were severely outnumbered. He needed the support of his stepfather, but Stanley's army stood to the north, refusing to take a side. According to Bygot, it was Henry 'coming on apace' who made the first move, thereby ensuring that 'King Richard was constrained to go to the battle'.[24] Within no time, 'there now began a very fierce battle between the two sides'.[25] Henry's French, Welsh and English troops fought valiantly. Still the Stanley brothers would not commit to a side. Richard was furious and ordered that Stanley's son Lord Strange 'should be beheaded on the spot'.[26] But those to whom the task had been entrusted 'failed to carry out that king's cruel command' and instead released him.[27]

With Oxford in charge of Henry's vanguard, within two hours, the tide of the battle turned in Henry's favour. The king refused to flee, declaring his intention to be victorious or die in the field. Even his enemies commended his courage, and the Tudor chronicler John Rous exclaimed that 'he bore himself like a gallant knight'.[28] Placing his crown upon his helmet, Richard prepared to join the battle himself. Spotting Henry with but a 'small force of soldiers about him', he decided to make one final charge in an attempt to bring down his rival.[29] Richard spurred on his horse and pressed himself into the thick of the battle, cutting down Henry's standard bearer, William Brandon, and coming dangerously close to Henry himself.[30] It was then that William Stanley's men rushed to Henry's aid.[31] Richard's men were pushed back, and the king's horse stumbled on the edge of a boggy marsh. Realizing that he had been abandoned by his former allies, he cried out, 'Treason! Treason!'[32] Before long, William Stanley's forces cut Richard down: he 'received many mortal wounds and, like a spirited and most courageous prince, fell in battle on the field and not in flight'.[33] The last Plantagenet king of England had been slain on an English battlefield; it was time for a new dynasty.[34]

IN WHAT SEEMED LIKE A miracle, given his less impressive army, Margaret's son had won the crown: he was King Henry VII of England, and his elated men cried out 'God save King Henry, God save King Henry!'[35] Croyland exclaimed that a 'glorious victory was granted by heaven to the earl of Richmond, now sole king, together with the priceless crown which king Richard had previously worn'.[36] André went so far as to claim that Henry 'liberated the land by divine and human right, with divine power vindicating, willing, and assisting, as from a most brutal enemy'.[37] Commynes, who stated that Henry was crowned on the battlefield with Richard's crown, posed an interesting question that undoubtedly reflected Margaret's own thoughts on the outcome: 'Should one describe this as Fortune? Surely it was God's judgement'.[38]

Following the battle, Henry, 'adorned with the crown which he had so remarkably won', entered the city of Leicester in triumph.[39] It was from there that he issued the first proclamation of his reign, in which he informed his new subjects of Richard III's death and ordered men to return home. Next he gave orders for the executions of Richard's key remaining adherents, including William Catesby.

Following the battle, the body of the dead King Richard was stripped naked and unceremoniously slung over a horse. Croyland attested that, in a shocking display of disrespect, 'many other insults were offered'. The discovery of Richard's corpse confirmed the extent of the humiliating wounds that were inflicted upon him after death. His remains accompanied Henry VII to Leicester in an undignified manner, 'a miserable spectacle in good sooth, but not unworthy for the man's life', as Vergil put it.[40] There he was buried 'without any pomp or solemn' funeral in the church of the Grey-friars.[41] It was not until 1495 that Henry would pay £10 12d (£6,700) for Richard's tomb.[42]

When news of Henry's victory reached Margaret, she was both over-whelmed and elated. It seemed like a miracle and was surely a sign of God's divine intention. Suddenly, the future that neither Margaret nor Henry could ever have envisioned until 1483 had become a reality: her enemy was dead, and her son victorious. With her usual attention to detail, Margaret took care to note in her Book of Hours: 'This day King Henry the VIIth won the field where was slain King Richard the third'.[43] Some of Henry's first thoughts following his triumph were for his mother, and with the news of his success came, too, a very personal gift: the Book of Hours that had once been Richard's own—taken from his tent on the battlefield, and containing his signature.[44] Margaret immediately erased the name of the man whom her son had slain and whose dynasty was at an end—and added her own words:

> For the honour of God and St Edmund
> Pray for Margaret Richmond.[45]

For years Margaret had been forced to serve a rival house and had managed to adapt to the situation. Yet, the reign of Richard III had thrown everything into uncertainty and left her feeling desperate. Her actions throughout his reign could have led to her death, but her experiences highlight her extreme courage and show that she was a survivor. Most significantly, they did not deter her from rallying support for Henry's cause, emphasising that her chief motivation was for the bettering of his future, even if it led to her own peril. Her determination to support her son confirms that she was a strong-minded woman who was prepared to risk her own safety to try to secure his future. The result was that, with Margaret's support, Henry stood victorious on a battlefield as King of England. At the time of Bosworth, though, neither she nor anyone else could have been sure that Henry—a man much changed from the fourteen-year-old boy Margaret had urged into exile—would be successful as a king or even keep hold of his throne. It was in large part thanks to his mother that he went on to establish a dynasty that would become the most famous in English history: the Tudors. In the same manner as she had worked for his rise, she would strive to help her son establish his own bloodline. In so doing, she would pave the way for her own power.

PART THREE

CHAPTER 16

MY LADY THE KING'S MOTHER

On 30 October—two months after Henry's victory at Bosworth— Margaret was full of emotion as all of her ambitions for her son came to fruition in one tangible moment. It was a day that she would cherish for the rest of her life, proudly recording in her Book of Hours that 'this day King Harry the VIIth was crowned at Westminster'.[1] The preparations for the coronation had been undertaken with the utmost care and provided the perfect outlet for Henry to indulge his love for finery. Costly materials, including powdered ermine, rich crimson velvet and decadent crimson cloth of gold, had been specially ordered for the occasion. All of this was intended to make a dazzling impression on the king's subjects, and his tailor George Lovekyn did his utmost to ensure that the king's robes did just that.

Thus it was that Henry VII, bedecked in the most sumptuous of materials, entered Westminster Abbey amid the cheers of his subjects, who had gathered in the thousands to catch a glimpse of him. The abbey was beautifully decorated with symbols of Henry's heritage—the red rose of Lancaster and Welsh dragons proudly proclaimed his descent. Henry's lords carried the coronation regalia, while his stepfather bore the sword of state through the crowds of nobles who had been invited into the abbey. Meanwhile, the ultimate honour of carrying the crown—Saint Edward's Crown, which had been used at the coronation of male monarchs for centuries—was given to Henry's faithful uncle Jasper. The coronation chair, which had been in use since 1308, stood before the high altar in the abbey, and it was there that Henry was officially crowned and anointed.[2]

This was the magnificent sight that Margaret looked on. It was a scene that she could scarcely have imagined would ever be possible. At forty-two, Margaret was no longer the mother of a fugitive: she was the mother of King Henry VII of England. Yet, 'when the king her son was crowned in all great triumph and glory, she wept marvellously'.[3] Her tears were a mixture of the greatest pride and fear, for as Fisher later recalled, 'dare I say of her she never yet was in that prosperity but the greater it was the more always she dread the adversity'.[4] Given the emotional trauma that had overtaken every decade of her life, Margaret's fears were understandable: though Henry had won the crown, the fight to keep it had just begun.

IMMEDIATELY AFTER HIS VICTORY AT Bosworth in August, Henry left Leicester and hastened south. His journey took him through Coventry. There he was presented with a gold cup, a gift of money and the town of Northampton and city of St Albans, where the forces of his uncle, Henry VI, had suffered defeat exactly thirty years earlier. Upon receiving the glorious news of her son's success, a joyful Margaret began making hurried preparations to join him. They had been apart for fifteen years, and she was eager to be reunited. At the beginning of September, the new king, 'accompanied by a great host of nobles, joyfully entered the city of London'.[5] It is unclear whether his mother had already reached him or was yet to do so, but when she did it is sure to have been an emotional reunion.

The son who stood before Margaret was no longer the teenage boy she had last seen during the two weeks they spent together at Woking in 1470, whose future she had agonized over as the Wars of the Roses raged. At twenty-eight, Henry had endured great hardship and uncertainty. In physical terms he was 'remarkably attractive and his face was cheerful, especially when speaking'.[6] Isabella of Castile later referred to him as a 'Prince of great virtue, firmness, and constancy'.[7] He also bore physical similarities to Margaret. Her portraits do not reveal all of the details of her physical appearance, such as her hair colour—Henry had thinning fair hair—but her son certainly inherited her hooded eyes, though his were blue, while hers were dark. Both were also of slender frame. From then on, Margaret took every opportunity she could to be by his side: for much of the next fourteen years, she was an almost constant presence, and Henry in his turn—her 'most humble and loving son'—welcomed it.[8]

Before long more arrived in London, among them Anne Herbert, the wife of Henry's former guardian.[9] More poignant, though, was the arrival of the ten-year-old Earl of Warwick and his cousin, nineteen-year-old Elizabeth of York, 'accompanied with many noblemen and ladies of honour'.[10] While the Battle of Bosworth raged, both had been ensconced in Sheriff Hutton Castle in Yorkshire 'in safe custody', on Richard III's orders.[11] Before leaving Leicester, Henry VII had sent Sir Robert Willoughby north to escort them to the capital. Upon their arrival, Warwick was immediately given into the safekeeping of one whom Henry trusted implicitly: his mother. Despite his young age, he, a male Plantagenet contender for the throne, was a threat to the throne; securing his custody was of the utmost importance. He was not to remain with Margaret for long, though, for in order to safeguard Henry's security, Warwick was soon sent to the Tower, where 'he was shut up close prisoner'.[12] He would never emerge from its walls as a free man. Elizabeth, whom Henry had pledged to marry, and her mother, Elizabeth Wydeville, were also ordered to take up residence with Margaret, who was granted the Thames-side palace of Coldharbour by her son. Henry, though, was in no hurry to marry.

Coldharbour had once been the residence of the mayor of London, Sir John Poultney. It later belonged to John Holland, Duke of Exeter—a paternal relative of Margaret's—who had entertained his half-brother, Richard II, in the house.[13] Margaret of York, Duchess of Burgundy, had stayed in the house during her visit to England in 1480, and Richard III had later given it to the heralds for their college. Henry VII was insistent that his mother have full use of the property, which offered easy access by river to the royal palaces of the capital.[14] Margaret wasted no time in putting her own stamp on Coldharbour, and alterations and improvements took place without delay. All of the principal rooms in the house overlooked the river, including the splendid Great Hall. It was almost certainly there that the new glass with Margaret's arms was displayed, leaving nobody in any doubt of her ownership.[15] The home featured a Little Hall and a Great Chamber containing Dutch glass as well as chambers for Margaret's servants—the room of the devoted Reginald Bray was re-glazed with Normandy glass.[16]

A chamber was also prepared for Elizabeth of York. During her stay with Margaret, Elizabeth would not lack for company, for at Coldharbour she was joined by other royal children—her sisters and probably her cousin Margaret of Clarence, Warwick's sister.[17] Margaret had been granted £200 (£138,260) for the care of these children, and there is every reason to believe that she harboured an affection for them. She had, after all, known these children, as well as the former queen Elizabeth Wydeville, since her days at Edward IV's court. She had schemed for the marriage of Elizabeth of York to her son—a marriage that now appeared to be within touching distance—and thus Elizabeth had every reason to be grateful to her. Rooms were also prepared for the young Duke of Buckingham and his younger brother, Henry, whose wardship she was granted on 3 August 1486.[18] The boys were the sons of her kinsman, and Margaret seems to have had warm feelings for them. Henry Parker later recalled that when Buckingham visited Margaret one Christmas, she gave him a jewel worth £100 (£66,600).[19] Such generosity was not unusual from Margaret, who, as Bishop Fisher remembered, was 'bounteous and liberal to every person of her knowledge or acquaintance'.[20] Perhaps she also felt guilty about the manner in which the boys had lost their father.

Margaret did not spend all of her time in Coldharbour, and in September 1485 she welcomed her son back to Woking, where they had once spent a happy time together before Henry's exile. Henry was clearly attached to the place, so much so that later, in 1503, he would insist that an extremely reluctant Margaret hand it over to him; it was one of the few known occasions on which mother and son clashed, in spite of the fact that, in return, she was granted the use of Hunsdon in Hertfordshire. On this first visit back, Henry remained at Woking for several weeks, almost certainly indulging in his favoured pastime: hunting. For Margaret, too, the return to Woking would have been welcome, for given all that she had endured during Richard III's reign, she is unlikely to have spent much if any time there.

It says much of Henry's relationship with Margaret that he chose to stay with her during these early weeks of his reign. Clearly, the love and affection that Margaret had poured into her son in childhood and that had maintained her through their years of separation were gladly reciprocated. But their partnership was more than a familial bond. Margaret had helped to sow the seed of Henry's ambition for the throne. It was her support, material and emotional, and her counsel that had guided him, kept him safe and ultimately ensured that he attempted to win the English crown. In those pivotal early days of his rule, when much groundwork was needed to stabilize this most unlikely of monarchs, he turned to Margaret once again. It was a role for which Margaret had been in training all her life. Whereas Henry knew only what letters and visitors had told him over the years, Margaret had watched firsthand as kings and queens manoeuvred to claim—and then hold on to—the throne. She had played her hand expertly, and as Henry's reign progressed, her new strategies would prove just as shrewd. Henry was no doubt grateful to have an advisor he could trust implicitly. Misplaced trust had cost his forebears dearly, and he had already experienced the duplicity of men. Though he would continue to rely on faithful supporters such as Jasper, he would never trust anyone more than Margaret.

MARGARET WAS NOT THE ONLY one to benefit as a result of her son's accession. In grateful thanks for their loyalty, Henry soon began to reward his supporters. Margaret's cousin, Charles Beaufort—a bastard son of Henry, Duke of Somerset—was high in the king's favour, and in the first year of Henry's reign his surname was changed to Somerset in a rather interesting twist.[21] Reginald Bray also received generous grants. After his long and loyal (and sometimes perilous) service to Margaret, he would go on to become an integral part of Henry's government and one of the most influential men in the realm. Christopher Urswick, Margaret and Henry's faithful go-between, and Edward Wydeville were also rewarded with lands and positions, as was Dr Lewis of Caerleon, who had aided Margaret's attempts to arrange a marriage between Henry and Elizabeth of York and who would later become her physician.[22] Even Gilbert Gilpyn, Margaret's steward at Woking, was remembered, being granted 'the office of the swans, and master of the game on the Thames and its streams and creeks'.[23] Similarly, David Owen—Henry's illegitimate uncle—was knighted.[24] On 6 March 1486, John Morton was created Chancellor of England and later became Archbishop of Canterbury: he would play a leading role in Henry's government for many years, and thus he and Margaret saw one another regularly. Indeed, many of the men she had trusted, befriended and employed eventually found their way into Henry VII's circle, undoubtedly as a result of Margaret's influence.

The greatest recognitions, though, were reserved for Henry's family. William Stanley, who had come to his rescue on the battlefield, was made the king's chamberlain and the following year would be appointed to the role of 'office of justice' in North Wales.[25] Margaret's husband was well rewarded, too: he already had his fair share of war trophies, for following Bosworth he had been given permission to take the hangings from Richard III's tent. These were put on display at Knowsley in a proud declaration of the role the family had played in Richard's fall. In further recognition of 'his labours and expenses for the king and as in time past and recently in the conflict of England', Thomas Stanley was awarded with grants of land, and 'the king's father' was given the 'offices of master forester and steward of all the king's game north of Trent'.[26] Early the following year he would become Constable of England and Chief Steward of the duchy of Lancaster. And there were greater rewards to come.

While mother and son enjoyed time together at Woking, the pair had almost certainly discussed the king's promise to wed Elizabeth of York and his forthcoming coronation. Before the former could take place, it was essential that *Titulus Regius*—through which Elizabeth had been declared illegitimate—be repealed, and in any case Henry was eager to establish himself firmly as king in his own right first. Many still believed that his claims to the throne were dubious.

On 28 October, Henry took up residence at the Tower in keeping with the custom that a monarch do so prior to their coronation, and it was there that he made some notable elevations to the peerage, the first of which was the ennoblement of 'his most dearly beloved uncle', Jasper Tudor.[27] Beside Margaret, Jasper had been Henry's most loyal companion and had endured as much suffering as Margaret and her son during the uncertain times of the past three decades. He was rewarded with the dukedom of Bedford.[28] Sometime before 7 November, he also took a wife for the first time, marrying Katherine Wydeville, the widow of the executed Duke of Buckingham and mother of two of Margaret's wards. His ennoblement was followed by the creation of Margaret's husband as Earl of Derby, one that allowed Margaret to begin styling herself as the Countess of Richmond and Derby. Two days later, Henry's ultimate moment of triumph arrived, and he was crowned in Westminster Abbey.

ON 7 NOVEMBER, HENRY VII'S first Parliament convened. It was of the utmost significance for Henry, for many of those who had fought at Bosworth and for Margaret, too. *Titulus Regius* was repealed, and the Acts of Attainder that had formerly been passed against Jasper, Henry VI, Margaret of Anjou and their family were all reversed. Elizabeth Wydeville also had her lands restored.

Henry had not been raised as a prince of the blood, and the majority of his youth had been spent in Wales rather than in England. As a result, he was unfamiliar with the layout and affairs of the realm. It was therefore essential that he both secure his claim and strengthen it. Margaret was also acutely aware of this—as it was said of her, echoing the words of Fisher mentioned earlier, 'either she was in sorrow by reason of the present adversities, or else when she was in prosperity she was in dread of the adversity for to come'—and she was resolved to be there to guide her son.[29] By the same token, it may have been at this time that she began to recall how God had guided her towards a union with Edmund Tudor—not only did it reflect well on her piety, it also implied that the union which produced the first Tudor king was ordained by God.

Henry, too, was determined to emphasise his right to rule by establishing that 'his coming to the right and crown of England was as much by lawful title of inheritance as by the true judgment of God in giving him victory over his enemy in battle'.[30] Inaugurating his own—and thus his mother's—legitimacy was a critical part of this. He was Margaret's only heir, and she was directly descended from John of Gaunt. Crucially, therefore, Parliament reaffirmed Richard II's statute of 1397, which removed the stigma of bastardy from the Beauforts. Unsurprisingly, no mention was made of the 1407 clause that barred the Beauforts from claiming the throne—this had never been passed through Parliament, in any case. In a sign of the pride he took in his origins, Henry also adopted the portcullis that had served as an emblem of the Beaufort family. Technically, Margaret had a stronger claim to the throne than her son, but no mention was made of this either. The only other precedent for female rule in England had been that of the Empress Matilda in the twelfth century, and it had not ended well. Margaret not only knew this but also had always prioritized Henry's interests over her own; in any case, to her, they were one and the same thing. Margaret had never considered claiming the throne for herself. But that did not mean she was content to claim nothing.

In the days since Margaret and Henry had been reunited, they had spent much time talking: preparations for the coronation and Henry's marriage were likely important topics of conversation, but Margaret's own position was clearly also a matter she was keen to address. Parliament naturally restored all of her former lands to 'the most noble princess

Margaret', but she wanted more.[31] Her son's accession had already trans-formed her relationship with Stanley. As the king's mother, she was now the superior and he the inferior in their partnership. But this reversal was not enough for Margaret. It was undoubtedly at Margaret's instigation that Parliament declared her to be a *femme sole* (usually, but not always, an unmarried woman, a widow or a divorced woman; also used, as in this case, to mean a married woman who has sole control of her property, es-tates and finances). This extraordinary move gave her full and sole con-trol over her estates, 'which shall be vested and remain in her alone by the same entry, as if she were single and unmarried'.[32] She could act inde-pendently of Stanley. There is no indication as to how Stanley felt about this, but because 'the king wills it', there was nothing he could do.[33] Given that in many ways the couple continued to work together—for example, they later jointly hosted a visit from the king and queen to Lathom and Knowsley—it would seem that whatever reservations he may have had were soon forgotten. The change does, however, highlight that theirs was a marriage of mutual convenience rather than love. Although Margaret was then independent in financial terms, her relationship with Stanley did not deteriorate. Indeed, Stanley appears to have been proud of his wife's status. At Lathom, he even went as far as to have his wife's arms added to the windows, along with the inscription 'our Lady the King's Mother'.[34]

Margaret's bold move was both momentous and unprecedented. That *femme sole* status was usually granted only to unmarried women empha-sises the level of power and independence that Henry was prepared to allow his mother. Up to now, Margaret had been forced to seek security through marriage. Each marriage had been taken with great urgency, hus-bands selected intelligently, always with an eye to her and her son's pro-tection. But the success of each marriage and its consequences had been unpredictable. Margaret had experienced the deaths of two husbands and suffered the ignominy of her lands being handed over to Stanley. Now, as the most powerful woman in England, she would ensure that she held onto those lands.

As the records show, she relished her position. All of her life she had played a supporting role as a wife and mother and had thrown herself wholeheartedly into Henry's attempts to win the throne; she was now eager to establish herself as the leading lady of the realm, and, following a precedent that had formerly been set by Cecily Neville during the reign of Edward IV, she took the title of 'My Lady the King's Mother'.[35] From this moment, she took control of her identity. To accentuate this identity, in 1499 Margaret adopted the signature 'Margaret R', which can be seen in her surviving letters. The meaning of the signature has been a source of controversy. Did she intend for it to represent 'Richmond', or was it supposed to be interpreted as 'Regina'? Her earlier letters were often signed 'Margaret Richmond', and so it seems evident that the R was a deliberate attempt to emphasise her royal status and authority.[36] Likewise, in official documents and accounts she was frequently referred to as 'princess', further emphasising her own royalty.

In 1499 Margaret would further alter the status of her marriage. She 'obtained of him license and promised to live chaste, in the hands of the reverend father my lord of London, which promise she renewed after her husband's death in to my hands again, whereby it may appear ye discipline of her body'.[37] In the presence of Richard FitzJames, Bishop of London, and with her husband's consent, Margaret took a vow of chastity. From then on, she and Stanley maintained separate households, although they continued to visit each other and rooms were reserved in Margaret's homes for Stanley's use. We cannot be sure how long Margaret had been pondering her decision, which was in all likelihood a formality—she and her husband are unlikely to have been living as husband and wife for some time, if at all, and the vow was probably prompted by Margaret's increased independence. Though Stanley gave his consent, in reality it is unlikely that Margaret needed it. Her position as the king's mother gave her the opportunity to mould herself in whichever way she chose, and religion, always an important and decisive factor in Margaret's life, was one of the threads that she chose to emphasise.

ON 10 DECEMBER, PARLIAMENT MADE a final request of Henry. They begged him to fulfil his earlier promise to 'take to himself that illustrious lady Elizabeth, daughter of King Edward IV, as his wife'.[38] With Elizabeth restored to her rightful legitimacy, the following day Henry gave orders for wedding preparations to begin. In so doing, he had taken the first step in healing the breach between Lancaster and York, thereby ensuring that the foundations of the new Tudor dynasty were firmly laid.

As the New Year of 1486 approached, so too did Henry's wedding. It is uncertain when he first met his bride, and given that he and Elizabeth were within the forbidden degrees of consanguinity as a result of their shared descent from Edward III, a papal dispensation was required. This was authorized on 16 January: two days later, the couple were married at Westminster Abbey. In a nice although perhaps not purposeful link with the past, the ceremony was conducted by the elderly Thomas Bourchier, Archbishop of Canterbury, half-uncle of Henry's former stepfather, Henry Stafford. Few details of the wedding survive, but according to André, 'Gifts flowed freely on all sides and were showered on everyone, while feasts, dances, and tournaments were celebrated with liberal generosity to make known and to magnify the joyful occasion and the bounty of gold, silver, rings, and jewels'.[39] In her typical style, Margaret took care to note in her Book of Hours, 'this day king Harry the VIIth wedded the queen Elizabeth'.[40] The result was monumental: as the chronicler John Stow observed, 'the two families of York and Lancaster, which had long been at great division, were united and made one'.[41]

André wrote admiringly of the new queen: 'Marvellous piety and fear of God, remarkable respect toward her parents, almost incredible love toward her brothers and sisters, and noble and singular affection toward the poor and ministers of Christ were instilled in her from childhood.'[42] This seems to have been more than mere flattery, because Elizabeth's surviving accounts bear witness not only to the generosity she displayed to her sisters but also to her extraordinary piety.[43] This would have given her at least one thing in common with her mother-in-law; indeed, less than three weeks after her marriage was solemnized, the king granted his wife and mother, along with Thomas Bourchier, Reginald Bray and several others, a licence to found a perpetual chantry in the church of the Holy Trinity in Guildford.[44] Such chantries were the most common way of showing one's piety, and Margaret was responsible for the endowment of several, including at Wimborne and in Cambridge.[45] Given her fondness for Woking and the frequency with which she had visited nearby Guildford during her marriage to Henry Stafford, it is tempting to speculate that the location may have been selected at Margaret's suggestion.

It has long been said that the relationship between Margaret and her daughter-in-law was strained, primarily as a result of Margaret's relationship with her son and dominance at court. Much of this stems from comments made by the Spanish ambassador in 1498 that 'the King is much influenced by his mother and his followers in affairs of personal interest and in others', which the queen was believed to dislike.[46] The same ambassador also claimed that the queen, 'a very noble woman, and much beloved', was 'kept in subjection by the mother of the King'.[47]

Margaret's anxiety about always being on hand to advise him—and likely Henry's eagerness to accept her advice—may occasionally have caused Elizabeth irritation, but most reports suggest that the two women had a good relationship. From the start, although Elizabeth's role was largely passive and she played little part in politics, Margaret made it clear that she was not prepared to do the same: though she was not the queen, she took care to ensure that she was closely identified as one, and many of Henry's contemporaries rightly believed her to be the most important woman in England. She and Elizabeth were often listed as though they were one person in official reports, and this in turn is reflective of how Margaret was viewed by her contemporaries. She was frequently in her daughter-in-law's company and was reported to walk just half a pace behind her. More often than not her name appeared alongside that of the king and queen on royal ceremonial occasions, leaving nobody in any doubt of her position.

Margaret was small of stature, but she was certainly not lacking in presence. What is more, Margaret certainly took a great interest in her daughter-in-law, speaking warmly of her in her later correspondence with the Earl of Ormond and having a list of all of those in Elizabeth's service in 1501.[48] Had there been true cracks in Margaret's relationship with Elizabeth, then surely these would have become difficult to hide—no other contemporary remarked on any friction between the pair.

It is true that in the decade following her son's accession, Margaret was an almost constant presence at court. Apartments were set aside in each of the royal palaces for her use, and they were always close to those of the king, particularly at Woodstock and the Tower. Given the time that she had spent apart from Henry, her desire to be close to him was understandable. He, in turn, craved her company. Their affection for each other can be seen in one of the rare surviving letters between them, in which he wrote: 'I shall be as glad to please you as your heart can desire it, and I know well, that I am as much bounden to do so, as any creature living for the great and singular motherly love and affection that it hath pleased you at all times to bear towards me'.[49]

Vergil related that Margaret was 'a most worthy woman [whom] no one can extol too much or too often for her sound sense and holiness of life. Henry allotted [her] a share in most of his public and private resources, thus easing her declining years'.[50] This was certainly true, and in 1498 Margaret was listed foremost among those whom the Spanish ambassador believed to have 'the greatest influence in England'.[51] Most of the men who were included in the ambassador's report were Margaret's friends and associates, including Morton and Bray. Given that we do not know to what extent she influenced Henry's decisions, her impact on the politics of Henry's reign can never be fully gauged, but Bacon's statement that 'his mother he reverenced much, heard little' is certainly untrue.[52] The point was that those at court *believed* that she was important. Neither were they alone, for the pope was also of the understanding that she held great sway. On 8 December 1498, Pope Alexander wrote to Margaret on behalf of one Adriano, asking that she do all that she could to encourage the king to promote him.[53] Despite such assumptions, Henry was far from being Margaret's puppet; she could never have gained the power and influence that she did throughout the course of his reign without his consent. That he was willing to give her this is a testament not only to their close bond but also to his recognition of Margaret's abilities.

Equally scrutinized is the relationship between Henry VII and his wife: in the seventeenth century Sir Francis Bacon claimed that the king 'was nothing uxorious; nor scarce indulgent; but companionable and re-spective, and without jealousy'.[54] Henry was faithful to Elizabeth, and in spite of Bacon's statement that he 'showed himself no very indulgent husband towards her though she was beautiful, gentle and fruitful', the marriage was happy.[55] His accounts reveal that he made his wife regular gifts of money: in 1492 there was one for the purchase of gold wire, in 1497 there was £31 10s (£21,000) for jewels, and on other occasions there was cash.[56] The royal couple were frequently together, and there is no evidence that their marriage was anything but harmonious. Henry and Elizabeth may have been sleeping together prior to their marriage; either this or, to the joy of her family and the realm, Elizabeth immediately conceived. The hoped-for birth of a prince through which to secure the Tudor dynasty was eagerly anticipated, and every detail of the queen's confinement was considered.

In the spring, Henry VII set out on a progress across his newly con-quered land, leaving Margaret and his wife in London. As he travelled north, hoping to stamp out disaffection in former Yorkist territories, he was presented with gifts of 'gold, silver, wine, beads'. But not everyone welcomed him.[57] Sir Francis Lovell, Humphrey Stafford and his brother Thomas—loyal supporters of Richard III—had quietly been raising an army. When Henry and his entourage reached York, the king was horri-fied to hear that Lovell and his men were marching towards the city, and he sent his uncle Jasper in an attempt to subdue them. With the offer of a pardon to all men save Lovell, the rebellion faded away. Lovell fled to

Lancashire, and the Stafford brothers sought sanctuary at Culham Abbey. Henry had them forcibly removed, and whereas Thomas was pardoned, Humphrey was executed on 8 July at Grafton. It was not the last of Francis Lovell, though.

IN A DESIRE TO EMULATE the Arthurian legend, Henry VII was determined that his first child should be born in the old city of Winchester. Margaret also believed in the legend of King Arthur, whose kingdom of Camelot was said to have once stood in Winchester, and supported Henry's choice. She accompanied the king and queen when they moved with the court to Winchester for Elizabeth's confinement, probably arriving in the last week of August. The queen, her mother-in-law and the queen's mother, Elizabeth Wydeville, all took up residence in St Swithin's Priory, in the close next to the cathedral. For the first time, the court found itself with a queen and two queen mothers, as well as the elderly Cecily Neville, mother of Edward IV and Richard III.[58] The nature of Margaret's relationship with Elizabeth Wydeville at this time is unclear, but given that Elizabeth had abandoned her support of Henry in the aftermath of the Buckingham Rebellion, Margaret's feelings towards her are unlikely to have been warm. As Fisher recollected, Margaret 'was good in remembrance and of holding memory a ready wit she had also to conceive all things'.[59]

In light of her own harrowing experience of childbirth, Margaret and her son were determined to ensure that Elizabeth of York's was remarkably different. The days that saw Margaret fleeing her home in the depths of winter in terror for her life seemed a far cry from the arrangements put in place for Elizabeth, who was to be surrounded by all of the trappings of royalty. Image meant everything to Henry VII—and indeed to Margaret—and thus everything was conducted against a backdrop of splendour.

The extent to which Margaret was involved in preparations for the birth is unknown. Recently, the extent of Margaret's involvement in the drawing up of the household ordinances, which included the coronation of a king and queen, royal births, christenings and the preparation of food, has been called into question.[60] As Rebecca Olson notes, there is no contemporary evidence that the ordinances were drawn up at her instigation. Rather, her hand in the ordinances was recorded later by the English antiquarian John Leland in his five-volume work *Collectanea*.[61] That is not to say, though, that she had no part in their creation, for she certainly took an interest in the organization of the court. Henry VII, who like his mother placed great emphasis on ceremony and etiquette, gave instructions for the birthing chamber to be hung with rich cloth of arras. There were to be two beds—a royal bed and a pallet bed—and carpets lining the floor. Four cushions made of crimson damask cloth of gold would be needed, alongside items embroidered with the king and queen's arms, and the size of the sheets and their fine material were also to be carefully considered.[62]

As she entered the perilous time of childbirth, Elizabeth's every need was given the greatest attention, and Margaret was probably on hand to ensure that everything ran smoothly. On 20 September, 'in the morning afore one o'clock after midnight', as Margaret proudly recorded in her Book of Hours, the longed-for prince was born.[63] Her first grandson, named Arthur after the legendary king, was 'strong and able', and both Margaret and the infant's parents were elated.[64] The king immediately dispatched messengers to announce the joyous tidings across the realm, and the celebrations that followed were profound: in Winchester, bonfires were set ablaze on the streets as people rejoiced at the arrival of the king's heir. André later claimed that the prince was 'blessed with such great charm, grace, and goodness, that he served as an example of unprecedented happiness to people of all times'.[65] An elaborate christening was planned for Henry's 'first begotten son', in whom all the hopes of the Tudor dynasty were vested: 'Arthur himself enhanced the sweet and shining roses, those red and white flowers blossoming on one and the same branch'.[66]

On Sunday, 24 September, the magnificent Winchester Cathedral was gorgeously decked out in costly fabrics and decorations in anticipation of this most important of christenings. The ceremony had to be delayed for several hours as a result of the late arrival of the prince's godfather, the Earl of Oxford, who had travelled from Lavenham. The baby prince, wrapped in 'a mantle of crimson cloth of gold furred with ermine', was carried to the cathedral in procession by his aunt, the queen's sister Cecily.⁶⁷ Most of the nobility of the realm were present, but in keeping with tradition, neither the king nor the queen attended. Curiously, neither did Margaret, and instead it was the queen's mother, Elizabeth Wydeville, who was chosen to stand as godmother to the young prince. Sir David Owen, the king's uncle, delivered her christening gift of 'a rich cup of gold'.⁶⁸ In what was a great honour, Margaret's husband was also invited to share the role of godfather with Oxford, making his godson a gift of 'a rich salt [cellar] of gold', which Reginald Bray delivered.⁶⁹

Unsurprisingly, Henry VII intended the upbringing of his heir to be vastly different from his own. Prince Arthur's nursery was to be established at the twelfth-century Farnham Palace in Surrey, just nine miles from Woking. There he was to be cared for by Elizabeth Darcy, who had served as a nurse both to his own mother and to her brother Edward V. Margaret naturally took a keen interest in the upbringing of her first grandchild, and given Farnham's proximity to Woking it is not inconceivable that she may have paid the occasional visit there.

When the queen had been churched in mid-October, Margaret accompanied her and Henry as the court moved to Greenwich to celebrate the feast of All Hallows. There they remained for Christmas and New Year, at which time Margaret distributed rewards to the servants of all of those who had brought gifts. The year 1486 had been a triumphant one for her family, and she was now the proud grandmother of a Tudor heir. However, as 1487 dawned, such a propitious start was quickly tinged with insecurity and danger.

CHAPTER 17

PRESERVATION OF YOUR MOST NOBLE AND ROYAL ESTATE

'Your said mother and the said earl shall heartily pray to God for the preservation of your most noble and royal estate, long to endure in felicity'.[1] These were Margaret's words to her son at the end of a petition presented to him in the Parliament of 1485. In 1487 her prayers would be needed, for the New Year's celebrations had barely concluded when news reached Henry VII of the first serious threat to his throne.

In what was to be a continuous theme throughout Henry's reign, from the beginning he was plagued by an array of rumours: the fates of the Princes in the Tower had not been confirmed, for though they were generally believed to be dead no bodies had been found. This left Henry vulnerable, and it was not long before his enemies seized on this as an opportunity to strike. In the summer of 1486, the young son of an Oxford joiner, known as Lambert Simnel—although the *Heralds' Memoir* refers to him as 'John'—came under the tutelage of a priest, Richard Symonds.[2] Symonds, 'a man as cunning as he was corrupt', was also a loyal York-ist.[3] His plan was to overthrow Henry VII and replace him with Simnel, whom he had taught to impersonate Clarence's son, the Earl of Warwick. The real Warwick was incarcerated in the Tower, where he had spent most of his time since Henry's accession. The instigator of the plot was Francis Lovell, who had escaped capture after raising arms against Henry in 1486. Since then, he had gained the support of a valuable ally—one who was not yet known to Henry, and whom he could not have expected: John de la Pole, Earl of Lincoln.

In a strange twist, Lincoln was the eldest son of Margaret's first husband, John de la Pole, Duke of Suffolk. He had been born in around 1460 to Suffolk and his wife Elizabeth Plantagenet, the sister of Edward IV and Richard III, and thus had a trickle of royal blood.[4] Lincoln had been well favoured by his uncle Richard—so well favoured that it is possible that he may have been Richard's intended heir following the death of Richard's son, Prince Edward, in 1484. Though he had been appointed Lord Lieutenant of Ireland and fought bravely for Richard at the Battle of Bosworth, Lincoln had since been reconciled with the Tudor regime.[5] Not only had he attended Prince Arthur's christening, but also he was a trusted member of the king's council: such trust proved to be ill placed. By the end of 1486, Simnel had been taken to Ireland, which was rife with Yorkist sympathizers.

On 2 February 1487, Henry VII's council convened: Vergil reported that by reason of her past agreement with Richard III, it was decided that Elizabeth Wydeville should be deprived of all of her possessions, which were granted to her daughter the queen.[6] On 12 February, having been allotted a small pension, the former queen was removed to Bermondsey Abbey, where she would live out the rest of her days. Was this in response to support that she had shown to the Pretender, or did it merely provide an opportune moment for Henry to remove the burden of supporting a queen dowager in addition to his own wife? Elizabeth's role in the Lambert Simnel conspiracy has been disputed, but it is difficult to imagine that she would have countenanced a rebellion to overthrow not only her daughter but also her grandson. The timing of her removal to Bermondsey is certainly suggestive of something more than coincidence, and if nothing else, she was, as Henry VII's biographer Neville stated, 'a useful figurehead for traitors'.[7] Neither was Henry taking any chances with her son, Dorset, who was safely ensconced in the Tower.

On 29 February, the Earl of Warwick was removed from the Tower and paraded through the streets of London to St Paul's. He was then brought before Henry's courtiers to prove that Lambert Simnel was an imposter. Meanwhile, abandoning all pretence of loyalty to Henry, Lincoln fled England. The king had been unsuspecting of his complicity, but Lincoln 'went into Flanders to the Lord Lovell and accompanied himself with the king's rebels and enemies'.[8] It was a gross betrayal of trust, further highlighted by his father's continuing loyalty to Henry.

Arriving in Flanders, Lincoln travelled to the court of his aunt, Margaret of York, Duchess of Burgundy—the sister of both Edward IV and Richard III—who wholeheartedly offered him her support.[9] Vergil acknowledged that the Duchess Margaret 'pursued Henry with insatiable hatred and with fiery wrath' and 'never desisted from employing every scheme which might harm him'.[10] Her hostility towards him stemmed from her belief that he had usurped the throne from her own house, and Henry himself later wrote of the 'great malice that the Lady Margaret of Burgundy beareth continually against us, as she showed lately in sending hither of a feigned boy, surmising him to have been the son of the Duke of Clarence'.[11]

Shortly after Lincoln's flight it became apparent that an invasion, precipitated by his arrival in Ireland to join the Pretender, Simnel, was forthcoming. On 24 May, the boy was crowned Edward VI in Dublin Cathedral. Yet, it is highly likely that Lincoln's support of Simnel was a front, and that, upon toppling Henry VII, he intended to assume the throne himself. Twelve days later, on 4 June, the rebels set sail for England, landing in Furness in Cumbria on 4 June.

Having been accompanied by 'a great number of knights and esquires', among them Margaret's husband Oxford and Lincoln's father Suffolk, Henry waited at Kenilworth Castle in the Midlands—the former mighty stronghold of Margaret's great-grandfather, John of Gaunt—for news of his enemies. He was greatly concerned for the safety of his family, who remained in the south, and gave orders that Margaret and his wife were to be conveyed to the greater security of Kenilworth. On 13 May, he dispatched a letter to the queen's chamberlain, Thomas Butler, Earl of Ormond, informing him that 'we have sent for our dearest wife and for our dearest mother to come unto us'.[12] Wishing to consult Ormond on how best to deal with the rebels, he continued, 'we pray you that, giving your due attendance upon our said dearest wife and lady mother, ye come with them unto us'.[13] Margaret and her daughter-in-law were thus escorted to Kenilworth. Given how many of the men in Margaret's life had died on the battlefield, her fears may well be imagined. Fisher later recalled the 'perils and dangers innumerable which daily and hourly might have happened unto her whereof this life is full'.[14]

Before long, word reached Kenilworth that Lincoln and 'his enemies were landed in the north parties'.[15] Henry immediately set out to confront the rebels, making his way first to Coventry. As he travelled, 'daily his true servants and subjects drew towards his grace'.[16] The next stop was Leicester, which must have aroused memories of Bosworth less than two years earlier. Having learned that his enemies were approaching Newark, the king's forces marched to meet them, and it was there on the outskirts of the village of Stoke that the two armies met on 16 June. Lincoln's forces were led by a German mercenary named Martin Schwarz, and though 'both sides fought with the bitterest energy', the result was a resounding victory for the king. In what is often considered to be the last battle of the Wars of the Roses, Lincoln was killed alongside 'divers other gentlemen', although the fate of Francis Lovell is uncertain.[17] Lambert Simnel was captured, but Henry was merciful. Rather than ordering the boy's execution, in a sign of extraordinary clemency, he instead set him to work in the royal kitchens. Simnel later became a falconer and continued his royal service into the reign of Margaret's grandson, Henry VIII.[18]

Margaret was overwhelmed with relief when she learned of her son's victory and success. Characteristically, she triumphantly recorded in her Book of Hours the day when 'King Henry VII had victory upon the rebels in [the] battle of Stoke'.[19] In October she was back in London to witness her son's return. As Henry rode through his capital city, all the houses, windows and streets as he passed by were hugely replenished with people in passing great number that made great joy and exaltation to behold his most royal person so prosperously and princely coming into his city after his late triumph and victory against his enemies; and so to behold the fair and goodly sight of his so coming the Queen's grace and my Lady the King's Mother, with other divers ladies and great estates in their company.[20]

But this was Henry's moment, and Margaret and the queen watched discreetly from a house besides St Mary Spital in Bishopsgate. The king, who had until recently been unknown in his realm, revelled in the love of his people in what can have been nothing other than a moment of sheer elation for Margaret: it seemed as though the success of 'my sweet king' was God's divine judgement. However, it would not be long before a more serious threat presented itself.

Following his brief respite from captivity, which had served to reassure Henry's subjects that he was alive, Warwick was sent back to the Tower, where he would remain for the next twelve years. It was at this time that Henry took steps to neutralise others who posed a potential threat to his throne. With some input from Margaret, he arranged for two of the Plantagenet princesses to be married to his own kinsmen. Princess Cecily, Elizabeth of York's younger sister and a favourite of Margaret, was wed to Margaret's half-brother John Welles.[21] Then Margaret, the daughter of the executed Duke of Clarence and another favourite of Margaret, was married off to Margaret's nephew, Richard Pole, the son of her half-sister Edith St John.[22]

The latter marriage has been described as Margaret's 'most serious political misjudgement' for the problems the issue of this marriage caused her grandson, Henry VIII.[23] Opposed to his divorce from Katherine of Aragon, one son was executed, another imprisoned and later pardoned, whereas Reginald Pole stirred up trouble for the king abroad. Margaret

Pole herself met a bloody end on the executioner's block as a consequence of the strife in 1541. The outcome was one that Margaret could not possibly have envisaged and that she would not live to see.

Both of the marriages not only aligned Margaret's family with the royal family but also were intended to unite the Houses of Lancaster and York. The remaining three daughters of Edward IV were too young to be married, and it was not until 1495 that Anne and Katherine would marry members of the nobility.[24]

HAVING ALREADY PRODUCED THE FIRST heir of the Tudor dynasty, in November the moment of Elizabeth of York's triumph arrived—delayed as a result of previous unrest. Margaret took a great interest in the coronation of her daughter-in-law, which was to be conducted on a grander scale than that of her son's in an attempt to emphasise Elizabeth's role in the new Tudor dynasty and the union of the Houses of Lancaster and York.[25] Margaret was listed first among the ladies in attendance.

Leaving Greenwich on 23 November, the Friday before Saint Katherine's Day, 'the Queen's good grace, royally apparelled and accompanied with my Lady the King's Mother and many other great estates, both lords and ladies richly beseen, came forward to the coronation'.[26] They were conveyed by water to the Tower in 'barges freshly furnished with banners and streamers of silk richly beseen'—one of which, *The Bachelor's Barge*, boasted 'a great red dragon spouting flames of fire into [the] Thames' in reference to Henry's Welsh lineage.[27]

It was a magnificent sight, and Margaret must have enjoyed the revelry as they were entertained on the journey by trumpeters and minstrels. When the party landed at Tower Wharf and entered the Tower, the king was waiting to welcome his wife in a manner that was both 'joyous and comfortable to behold'.[28] There followed the customary creation of the Knights of the Bath, undertaken by the king, and among those who were afforded this honour were the queen's chamberlain, the Earl of Ormond, and Hugh Conway, the servant Margaret had once used to convey messages to Henry during his exile. As the banners blew and the music played, those uncertain times must have seemed a world away.

The following day, 'her grace being at the Tower of London after dinner was royally apparelled, having about her a kirtle of white cloth of gold damask and a mantle of the same'.[29] 'Her fair yellow hair hanging down plain behind her back with a calle of pipes over it' was adorned with a 'circlet of gold richly garnished with precious stones upon her head'.[30] Magnificently adorned, the queen left the Tower and rode through the streets of the capital to Westminster. Margaret's name is not mentioned among those who accompanied her, which included her sister Cecily and her aunts the Duchesses of Bedford and Suffolk, so it can be assumed that Margaret did not participate in the spectacle. Presumably she had either decided to let Elizabeth have her moment or was preparing herself for the main event the following day. Margaret understood the power of the common gaze and knew when to concede it to others. She was in any case already well represented. As Elizabeth travelled in great state through London, passing the huge crowds of subjects who had thronged to see her, she was accompanied by Jasper, Stanley, Sir David Owen and Sir Richard Pole.[31] That evening the royal party stayed at the Palace of Westminster, where Margaret probably joined them.

On the morning of Sunday, 25 November, Elizabeth's coronation dawned. The queen was exquisitely dressed in 'a kirtle and mantle of purple velvet furred with ermines', while on her head she wore 'a circlet of gold richly garnished with pearl and precious stones'.[32] Thus apparelled, with her sister Cecily carrying her train, Elizabeth made her way from the palace to Westminster Abbey. The nobles filtered into the abbey ahead of the queen, who was escorted on either side by the Bishop of Winchester and the Bishop of Ely. As with his nephew's coronation, Jasper, who walked ahead of the queen, was given the honour of 'bearing a rich crown of gold'.[33] The majesty of the occasion was only marred by the crowd of people who had gathered to see the queen—no sooner had she stepped upon the carpet than a surge of people attempted to cut it for souvenirs. Such was the crush that in so doing 'certain persons were slain', and the 'the order of the ladies following the queen was broken and disturbed'.[34]

As Archbishop of Canterbury, Morton conducted the ceremony according to the stipulations of the *Liber Regalis*, which set out the protocol for the crowning of monarchs and consorts. Accordingly, the queen was anointed and given the ring, and then the archbishop, having first blessed it, 'set the crown upon her head'.[35] Finally, she was handed her rod and sceptre. Within the abbey, 'on the right side betwixt the pulpit and the high altar, was ordained a goodly stage covered', which offered a perfect view of the proceedings. It was here that the king, 'my lady his mother and a goodly sight of ladies and gentlewomen attending upon her', were able to watch the coronation discreetly.[36] Margaret and her son must have been delighted by the splendour of the occasion and by Elizabeth's evident piety throughout the ceremony.

Once the service was completed, the queen was afforded a brief time to rest while the coronation banquet was prepared. It was left to Jasper, Margaret's husband and the Earl of Nottingham, who joined them, to oversee proceedings and ride their steeds proudly about Westminster Hall before the queen's arrival. As she took her seat in preparation for the banquet, trumpets sounded the entrance of the first course. Elizabeth was presented with the usual assortment of sumptuous dishes: 'kid reversed', crane, swan, and a range of fruit puddings.[37] The second course was equally decadent, consisting of peacock, partridge, quails, and 'castles of jelly in temple wise made'.[38] Once again, neither Margaret nor Henry attended the lavish feast, and instead 'there was made a goodly stage out of a window on the left side of the Hall, richly beseen with Cloth of Arras, and well latticed', where the king and 'the high and mighty princess his mother' could 'privily at their pleasure see that noble feast and service'.[39] When the banquet had come to an end, the queen retired 'to the rejoicing of many a true Englishman's heart'.[40] Such a brilliant piece of spectacle displayed not only the wealth and status of the House of Tudor but also the happy embrace that had been offered to its Yorkist branch. But spectacle it would remain, as the next day's events demonstrated.

On the morning following the coronation, Margaret accompanied her son and daughter-in-law as they heard mass in St Stephen's Chapel. They were joined by around forty 'duchesses, countesses, viscountesses, baronesses, and other ladies and gentlewomen'.[41] The setting must have been bittersweet for Elizabeth, calling to mind memories of her younger brother, Richard, who on 15 January 1478, at the age of four, had been married here to Anne Mowbray.[42] This, though, was a day of thanksgiving, and following mass 'the queen kept her estate in the Parliament Chamber, and my lady the king's mother sat on her right hand', with Princess Cecily and the Duchess of Bedford nearby on the left.[43] Margaret's presence left no doubt of how she wanted to be perceived. Having for years remained in the background, subservient to another royal family, she wanted this moment to serve as a visual reminder of the origins of Henry's royal blood and ancestry.

Another telling reflection of how Margaret wished to be recognised can be seen in her jewellery collection. It seems that her lifelong fondness for clothes may have been equalled by a love of jewels. Certainly, one of the surviving inventories found in the keeping of one of her ladies, Edith Fowler, was crammed full of precious pieces. The historian Maria Hayward has shown that at the time of her death Margaret owned plate and jewels worth a staggering £4,213 4s 3½d (£2,805,820), in addition to numerous household items that were worth another fortune; at her death, the total value of her goods was believed to be an eye-watering £15,000 (£10,000,000).[44]

Outward display meant everything—something that Margaret is likely to have become aware of at a young age through the example of kings and queens. She was particularly conscious of the way that clothes and jewels—as tangible signs of wealth and magnificence—could be used to communicate to those at court and in the streets the security, stability and wealth of a royal house.

In keeping with her piety and her desire to show her religiosity, many of her jewels had a religious theme, such as the cross of gold with a crucifix, enamelled gold images that featured John the Baptist and Saint Jerome, a piece of the Holy Cross set in gold with pearls and precious stones and items that included the Virgin Mary, Saint Katherine and Saint Margaret in their design.[45] In 1505, she would also receive a gift of beads that had been blessed by the pope. Also to be found among the rich assortment of beautiful objects were sapphires and rubies set in gold, a gold chain, gold and silver buttons, pairs of beads, the image of a lady in a ship, numerous pearls and a pomander decorated with marguerite daisies—a symbol adopted by Margaret, because it was a pun on her name.[46] In addition, there were two pieces of unicorn horn, in all likelihood representing Margaret's belief that the substance could be used as a cure for poison. Similarly, payments were made for rings and the setting of them as well as for brooches. Even her glasses—used increasingly later in her life—were made from gold and kept in specially fashioned cases.[47]

Many of these costly pieces adorned Margaret's clothes, which her inventories show were equally lavish and purchased with great regularity. Black was evidently her favoured colour, and given the cost of black dye, this was intended as a sign of her immense wealth. Among her wardrobe were gowns of black velvet edged with ermine, mink and sables, gowns of satin and others that were made of crimson and tawny velvet.[48] There was 'certain apparel of cloth of gold, silks and furs' and petticoats of scarlet furred with both black and white lambs' wool.[49] Other accessories such as slippers, gloves, sleeves, bonnets and frontlets also appear, painting an image of a woman who cared greatly about her appearance.

Aside from the stained glass in the church at Landbeach that depicts a more youthful Margaret wearing an ornate headdress complete with a jewelled daisy (her symbol), the remainder of her surviving portraits— each of which was probably based on a portrait painted during her lifetime, probably dating from around 1500—do not reflect her passion for finery or the richness of her character. All depict Margaret in rich though simple costume which includes a widows barb, though the main focus is her piety: in most of these portraits Margaret is shown either kneeling at prayer, such as in the version in St John's College, Cambridge, or holding an open prayer book. Fisher recalled that 'in favour, in words, in gesture, in every demeanour of herself so great nobleness did appear, that what she spake or did it marvellously became her', yet this does not come across in Margaret's portraits.[50] It is possible that Margaret's image of religiosity was cultivated and highlighted at her own instigation, in light of all of the good works that she was doing. These depictions are, nevertheless, in part responsible for obscuring the far more colourful character of a woman who was certainly pious but who also saw few contradictions between religion and revelry.

For all this wealth and luxury, Margaret was in no way profligate. We are fortunate enough to have access to a relatively complete set of her surviving accounts between 1489 and 1509. Among her payments for silk, rose water, lavender, offerings and rewards, there is a fascinating constant.[51] Throughout hundreds of pages of transactions, one can rarely be found on which her carefully scrawled signature does not appear at the bottom— this was a woman who was in full control of her money and knew where it was going down to the last penny. In an interesting link, her son would do exactly the same. In many respects this is unsurprising, for Margaret had always taken a keen interest in the administration of her estates. Her need to keep track of her money may have become particularly pressing given that during the reign of Richard III all of her assets—and thus control— had been handed over to her husband Stanley, leaving Margaret financially dependent on him. Margaret's determination to manage her own affairs resembles the diligence with which she kept lists (or remembrances, as she referred to them) of those who served her daughter-in-law and Katherine of Aragon. It seems to indicate more than a desire to be kept abreast of affairs, showing rather a woman who liked to be in full control over all aspects not only of her own life, now that she was able to, but also of the lives of those close to her.

This interest in her finances seems to have been one of the factors that has led to Margaret being unfairly misrepresented as more dour than she in fact was. In this, she is not alone. It has been well established that Henry VII was not the miser he was once portrayed as, for his court was often full of revelry and merriment in which Margaret frequently partook. Indeed, Margaret, while having bequeathed to her son her penny-counting ways, appears to have passed on many of her more extravagant habits and hobbies as well.

In December 1487 the royal family celebrated Christmas at Greenwich. It was a joyous occasion for which much of the nobility were present, and 'there were many and divers plays'.[52] Margaret loved to be entertained, and her accounts reveal payments for a range of performers. These included a fool named Skip who wore high-heeled shoes—he was later replaced by a fool named Reginald—and Margaret also employed a poet.[53] The identity of the poet is unknown, but Margaret was certainly responsible for the patronage of John Skelton, who later served as tutor to her grandson Prince Henry. Henry enjoyed clothes and other finery, and his kingship gave him the opportunity to indulge in all of the pleasures that he had hitherto been denied by reason of his exile and near penury.

On Christmas Eve, the king went to mass dressed magnificently in 'a rich gown of purple velvet furred with sables'.[54] The following day, Christmas Day, he sat down to dinner in his Great Chamber next to the Long Gallery, but he did not dine with his family. Instead, Margaret joined the queen and her ladies as they took their dinner in the queen's chamber. The atmosphere was buoyant, and the court remained at Greenwich to celebrate New Year. Since at least the fourteenth century it had been traditional for gifts to be exchanged on New Year's Day as opposed to Christmas Day, and Margaret's accounts are littered with references to such gifts, or more frequently rewards to the servants of those who had brought her gifts. The nature of these gifts is often unspecified, although at New Year 1507, for example, Margaret is known to have made her son an elaborate gift of a rich gold cup.

On the evening of Christmas Day 1487, 'there was a goodly disguising', but in the traditional manner the celebrations did not come to an end until twelfth night.[55] It was then that the king and queen went in procession to evensong. Both wearing their crowns and arrayed in beautiful clothes, they were joined by Margaret, who 'had on a rich coronall'.[56] She often wore her coronet on public ceremonial occasions such as this, doubtless as a way of communicating her power. Nobody would miss her enter 'in like mantle and surcoat as the Queen, with a rich coronall on her head, and walking aside the Queen's half train'.[57] Such was the demeanour of the woman who behaved as though she were an uncrowned queen.

CHAPTER 18

TOO MUCH FOR MY HAND

At Easter 1488, Margaret and her husband joined the court at Windsor. Her surviving accounts show that, as always, she made the traditional offerings that were expected at this time of year and provided Maundy money (money given in alms to the elderly). The court remained at Windsor to celebrate Saint George's Day, which was to be an occasion of the utmost significance for Margaret: she became an honorary Lady of the Garter (a female member of the Order of the Garter), and would be the last woman in England to be so until 1901.[1] The Order of the Garter had been founded by Margaret's ancestor, Edward III, in 1348, and was (and remains) the highest order of chivalry in England. Margaret was not the first woman to be so honoured, for her daughter-in-law Elizabeth of York had also been appointed by her father in 1477, following in a long line of royal and noble ladies.[2] Margaret was, nevertheless, the only woman to be appointed by Henry VII, a testament to their special bond. As she attended matins with the queen, both women wore identical garter gowns. They were treated with equal deference, and throughout the celebration they were seen together, even riding to evensong in a single sumptuous chair covered with costly cloth of gold. This was also reflected in a song that was sung on the occasion:

> O knightly order, clothed in robes with Garter:
> The Queen's grace and thy mother, in the same.[3]

213

Margaret was keen to be seen—and tangibly remembered—as an important part of the dynasty that Henry and Elizabeth were creating, and she was already considering her legacy. This can also be seen in her later inclusion in a window portraying the royal family that was commissioned for the Church of the Friars Observant in Greenwich in 1503. In the image of 'Lady Margaret the King's Mother', she was depicted wearing 'robes like a princess, coronel on head and rod of gold in her hand'.⁴ Sadly, neither the window nor the church survive. Henry VII's subjects evidently recognised that Margaret's position within the royal family was greater than that of the majority of previous kings' mothers, and indeed they seem to have treated her with similar deference as to the queen.

Margaret and her husband joined that court at Windsor for the summer. It was a summer filled with merriment in which the king 'hunted and sported him merrily', activities that Margaret had once taken great pleasure in.⁵ She remained with the court for most of the remainder of the year, celebrating All Hallows at Windsor before returning to Westminster, and going on from there to the Palace of Sheen for Christmas. Likewise, when the court travelled to Hertford for the Easter of 1489, Margaret joined them.⁶ By this time, she would have been aware that her daughter-in-law was to bear another child. The royal family seemed set to blossom.

On All Hallows Eve, the queen took to her carefully prepared chamber at Westminster, 'greatly accompanied with ladies and gentlewomen', at the head of which was Margaret, who was to play a leading role in the ceremony surrounding the birth of her second grandchild.⁷ The queen's chamber had been sumptuously decorated with cloth of blue arras decorated with golden fleurs-de-lis, and a magnificent bed as well as a pallet. As was the custom, the birth of Elizabeth's child was to be an exclusively female process, and Elizabeth Wydeville had also arrived to support her daughter.

At nine o'clock the evening of 28 November, Margaret was overjoyed when the queen was safely delivered of a princess. There was an added reason to be joyful, for the baby was to be 'named Margaret after my Lady the King's Mother'.[8] Margaret would grow to be extremely fond of her firstborn granddaughter and namesake, and on this occasion, there was no question as to who would play the role of godmother. The christening took place the day after the baby's birth and was an unsurprisingly lavish affair. According to the *Heralds' Memoir*, Westminster was 'prepared as of old time been accustomed for kings children'.[9] Lady Berkeley carried the infant princess from the queen's chamber, while the queen's sister Princess Anne bore the chrism. Before her came Margaret's half-brother John Welles, carrying 'a rich salt of gold garnished with precious stones'.[10] When the party arrived at the porch of Westminster, which was 'royally beseen, and had a rich ceiling of embroidery work', they were greeted by John Alcock, Bishop of Ely.[11] It was he who was to conduct the ceremony. Joining 'the high and excellent princess my lady the King's Mother' at the font in the role of godmother was the Duchess of Norfolk. The princess's godfather was Margaret's friend John Morton, Archbishop of Canterbury.[12] Once the ceremony was complete, John Welles presented Margaret's christening gift to her granddaughter and goddaughter on her behalf: 'a chest of silver and gilt full of gold'.[13]

Princess Margaret's christening was not the only celebration to be staged that day, for Margaret's grandson also enjoyed a moment in the limelight. On 21 November, three-year-old Prince Arthur had arrived in London from Farnham. Though Margaret was fond of him, she had seen little of him during his early years, and neither was she to be a part of the ceremony that necessitated his visit. On the same day as his sister's christening, in another part of Westminster, having first been made a Knight of the Bath, Arthur was created Prince of Wales and Earl of Chester, following in the footsteps of heirs apparent since 1301.[14]

With the new addition to the royal family and Arthur's ennoblement, Margaret and her family had extra cause for celebration as the court began the Christmas festivities at Westminster. However, 'that season there were the measles so strong, and in especial amongst the ladies and the gentlewomen, that some died of that sickness'.[15] Soon afterwards, the court removed to Greenwich to celebrate Christmas Day and New Year. Perhaps as a result of the outbreak, there were no disguisings and few plays that season, but there was 'an abbot of misrule that made much sport and did right well his office'.[16] On New Year's Day, the king rewarded his officers of arms, as did the queen and Margaret. The sickness did not affect their spirits, for the royal family was flourishing.

Moreover, Henry was also making progress in a political capacity. On 11 September 1490, Henry and his council gathered at Woking. There they met the ambassadors of the Emperor Maximilian to sign a treaty. By its terms, the two monarchs and their countries would unite against France—indeed, with financial support from Margaret to the tune of a thousand marks (£300,000), in October 1492 Henry set sail across the Channel, although he soon came to terms with Charles VIII.[17] At the same time, the Treaty of Medina del Campo, which had been signed the previous March by the joint Spanish sovereigns Ferdinand of Aragon and Isabella of Castile, was ratified. The treaty not only sued for peace between England and Spain but also arranged for the marriage of Prince Arthur with the youngest of the Spanish *infantas*, Katherine.[18] This topic would dominate English politics for the next decade and would be shaped by events that threatened the security of Margaret's whole family.

MARGARET'S DAUGHTER-IN-LAW, Elizabeth of York, proved to be a fertile bride, and by the autumn of 1490 she was pregnant once more. The following summer her mother, Elizabeth Wydeville, made a brief appearance from Bermondsey in order to attend the birth, and naturally Margaret was also present. On 28 June 1491, the queen gave birth to a prince at Greenwich. He was named Henry after his father, and though, as usual, Margaret recorded his arrival, she did so with none of the meticulous detail with which she had recorded Prince Arthur's—just the date, rather than the time, in Henry's case.[19] Neither was it just the baby's grandmother who omitted the details, for none of the contemporary chroniclers made more than a passing reference to his birth—a clear sign of Henry's status as the spare rather than the heir.

Even so, when the baby prince was christened at the Church of the Friars Observant in Greenwich, it was with all of the pomp that would have been expected, the ceremony being performed by Bishop Fox.[20] The infant Henry joined his elder sister, Margaret, in the nursery; unlike Arthur, these royal children were to be raised in the Thames-side palaces rather than in the Surrey countryside. The nursery was established primarily at Eltham, which provided convenient access for their parents—and grandmother—to visit them. Eltham was one of only six royal palaces large enough to accommodate and feed the entire Tudor court.[21] The swans that glided across the moat wore around their necks enamelled badges displaying the Beaufort portcullis. Eltham was a former favourite of both Henry VI and Edward IV, who had built the splendid Great Hall in the 1470s. It was one of the largest in medieval England, boasting an impressive oak hammerbeam roof that can still be seen, and was to be the setting for the visit of the humanist scholar Desiderius Erasmus in 1499, when he came with Thomas More to see the royal children.[22]

By the end of 1491, the queen was pregnant once more, but her confinement was marred by sadness when news arrived that her mother had died on 8 June 1492 at Bermondsey, at the age of about fifty-five. A recently discovered letter in the National Archives, dating from 1511 and written by the Venetian ambassador, claimed that the late queen had died of the plague.[23] This is the only near contemporary source to make such a claim, but by 10 April Elizabeth Wydeville had made her will, suggesting that her health was fragile. In this, her straitened circumstances became clear: pointedly omitting any reference to the king or his mother, she claimed that 'I have no worldly goods to do the Queen's Grace, my dearest daughter, a pleasure with, neither to reward any of my children, according to my heart and mind, I beseech Almighty God to bless her Grace'.[24] She asked to be laid to rest beside her royal husband at Windsor. It is impossible to envisage how Margaret reacted to the death of the woman whose court she had once attended—with whom she had once plotted—and with whom she now shared a family. She did not attend the late queen's funeral, although her half-brother John Welles was present, almost certainly representing his wife Cecily, who was also absent. Less than a month after Elizabeth Wydeville's death, on 2 July the queen gave birth to a daughter at Sheen. Princess Elizabeth joined Margaret and Henry in the royal nursery.

The following year, it was decided that Prince Arthur—like his late uncle, Edward V, before him—should take up residence at Ludlow Castle to continue his education and be schooled in the art of government. Arthur was a serious and studious boy; unsurprisingly, André, who also tutored him, praised his understanding of literature and grammar and flatteringly described him as 'that noblest and most liberally educated prince of Wales'.[25] He was an heir to be proud of, and the king invested in him all of his hopes for the future.

Margaret was particularly fond of her firstborn grandchild, who was tall and fair, resembling his mother in looks, and on occasion she sent messages to 'my lord prince' and received them in return. In around 1495 she made him the gift of a copy of Cicero's De Officiis—a book on the best way to live fulfilling one's moral obligations—which was beautifully illuminated with his arms and is now in Emmanuel College, Cambridge.[26] Arthur's biographer, Sean Cunningham, has suggested that after 1493 Margaret and her husband were likely regular visitors to Ludlow, though he acknowledges that this is hard to prove.[27] It is, nevertheless, plausible that Margaret visited when travelling from London or Woking to her husband's estates in the north. Given that Arthur was seldom at court with his family and thus saw his grandmother infrequently, such visits would have provided Margaret with a rare opportunity to spend time with her grandson. Cunningham has also emphasised her influence on Arthur's household, with her nephew Sir Richard Pole fulfilling the role of Chamberlain, to which he was appointed in 1493, a post undoubtedly obtained with Margaret's support. Margaret was always eager to show favour to her family in whichever quarter she was able, in so doing binding them closer both to herself and to the royal family.

Margaret took an interest in all of her grandchildren, in whom she took great pride. Given that she was strongly family oriented, this is unsurprising, and her accounts provide touching glimpses into her relationships with them. On one occasion, for example, she sent gifts of brooches to the Princess Margaret and Prince Henry; on another, clothes were purchased for the two boys.[28] Similarly, her husband appears to have shared a good relationship with the royal children, for an inventory of Prince Henry's jewels shows that he was once given 'a George of gold' by his step-grandfather.[29] The royal family was close-knit, and Bacon remarks that Henry VII cared deeply for his children, being 'full of paternal affection, careful of their education, aspiring to their high advancement, regular to see that they should not want of any due honour and respect'.[30] Her grandchildren provided Margaret and her daughter-in-law with another shared interest, for Elizabeth was a devoted mother. As will later become apparent, they would eventually work together to safeguard their welfare.

MUCH OF THE 1490S WAS occupied with other, more distressing matters. In the autumn of 1491, another pretender to the throne emerged, this time in Cork: he claimed to be Richard, Duke of York—the younger of the Princes in the Tower. In Ireland many diehard Yorkists seized upon his close physical resemblance to the duke, and there could be no denying that his manners, bearing, and knowledge of court affairs were convincing. Yet, like Lambert Simnel, this boy was no prince. His name was Perkin Warbeck, and he was the son of a boatman who hailed from Tournai in Flanders. In spite of his fraudulent claims, Warbeck would plague Henry VII for many years, causing the royal family a great deal of distress.

It was not long before it became apparent that the Pretender had enlisted the support of the Duchess of Burgundy, at whose court he arrived in November 1492. The duchess publicly declared that she recognised

Warbeck as her long-lost nephew, a claim that is particularly dubious given that she had only met York once, on a visit to England in 1480 when he was not yet seven years old. Her grudge against Henry had not lessened with time; indeed, as André declared, 'a woman's wrath is eternal'.[31] Her support of Warbeck was cause for alarm. Henry would later write to Gilbert Talbot of 'the perseverance of the same her malice, by the untrue contriving eftsoon of another feigned lad called Perkin Warbeck'.[32]

In an attempt to convince other European rulers of his credibility, Warbeck wrote to Isabella of Castile conveying the story of his escape from the Tower and the murder of his elder brother, Edward V—yet he would never be drawn on the details. The Spanish queen was not taken in, although she was concerned about where this latest threat left her daughter Katherine, who was to marry Prince Arthur. Others seemingly were duped by Warbeck's trickery, and Vergil later claimed that these included some of Henry's own courtiers. Some felt compelled to join him, being 'moved partly by resentment and partly by greed'.[33] Henry was understandably anxious about the latest threat to his throne, and Vergil declared that 'unless the deception was quickly recognised as such by all, some great upheaval would occur'.[34]

It was the appearance of the Pretender that prompted a very deliberate decision from Henry. On 27 October 1494, Margaret accompanied the king and queen as they sailed down the Thames from Sheen to Westminster. They were soon joined by the youngest of Henry's sons, Prince Henry, who had been summoned from the nursery at Eltham. On 30 October, the three-year-old prince—who would grow to resemble his grandfather, Edward IV, in looks—was created a Knight of the Bath, just as his elder brother had once been.[35] The following day, Margaret watched with her daughter-in-law as her grandson took part in the ceremony that witnessed his creation as Duke of York. Given that the dukedom of York had once been held by the younger of the Princes in the Tower, Henry's creation served to reinforce the idea that the real York was dead and that Warbeck was an imposter.

Following the ceremony, a procession formed, which Margaret and the queen joined—the former wearing her coronet, and the latter her crown. In celebration of the occasion, three days of jousts were held, with Henry VII's daughter the Princess Margaret distributing many of the prizes. On the second day, though, the competitors wore Margaret's own livery, and it was she who distributed the prizes. When the festivities ended, Margaret joined the court as they moved to Greenwich to celebrate Christmas. While they enjoyed the customary revelries, however, they were on the brink of receiving news that shook Margaret to the core.

Sir William Stanley, Margaret's brother-in-law, had been well rewarded for his loyalty to her son, with one London chronicler reporting that 'this was a man of great might in his country'.[36] He had grown wealthy in the king's service, and André believed that he 'possessed great stores of riches'.[37] None of this, it seemed, was enough for him. On 6 January 1495, the king travelled to the Tower. Grave news had reached him concerning William Stanley: he had joined Warbeck's conspiracy.

Vergil claimed that Sir Robert Clifford—a Yorkist—had been 'sent by the king as a spy into Flanders to find out whether the popular rumours about the youth were true or not' and whether he had the support of any of the English nobility.[38] When the king questioned Clifford upon his return, he apparently revealed a number of names, including that of Sir William Stanley. On learning of William's involvement, initially Henry refused to believe it. But having been presented with proof, Vergil reported that he 'grievously mourned that William was in the plot, since he was Chamberlain and Henry entrusted him with all his affairs'.[39] He was shocked and in a state of disbelief but soon gave the order for William's arrest.

Margaret and her husband were equally shocked by the news. Suspicion of William's involvement in the conspiracy seems to have been based purely on words. Vergil claimed that William had said of Warbeck that 'if he were sure that the man was Edward's son he would never take up arms against him'. Such sentiments indicated lukewarmness towards King Henry rather than treason.[40]

In spite of William's words, initially the king seemed bent on sparing his life. Understandably, he was concerned about disaffecting his stepfather, Stanley, 'of whose most zealous loyalty he was well aware'.[41] Ultimately, however, Henry became fearful of the consequences of letting William live. On the morning of 16 February, William was taken from the Tower to nearby Tower Hill and executed. Vergil, who said that William was 'proud-spirited and frankly confessed to being in some degree an offender', also acknowledged that he was 'beyond doubt a valiant soldier and had been brought low (as they say) through the very loftiness of his pride'.[42] In spite of his treason, the king paid the sum of £15 19s (£10,700) for William's burial at Syon.[43] Four years later he also paid off some of William's debts, perhaps in respect of the support William had once given him in 1485.[44]

The fall of Sir William Stanley shocked his contemporaries, many of whom—perhaps Margaret too—believed that he would be spared. His involvement with the Pretender must have been difficult for both Margaret and her husband to comprehend, but there is no evidence that either of them intervened. Stanley's family were now tainted with treason, but the death of his brother does not seem to have caused a rift with his stepson. Stanley continued to appear in Henry's accounts for the rest of his life, and André was quick to emphasise that the 'faithfulness, constancy, and integrity of the rest of his family shone more brightly at that time'.[45]

The scandal surrounding Sir William Stanley's execution had settled down by the summer, when Margaret and her husband jointly hosted a visit from the king and queen at Lathom and Knowsley. On 1 July, the royal couple left the capital, and by 27 July they had reached Lathom after a leisurely progress. They were there 'to comfort [the king's] mother, whom he did always tenderly love and revere', and during their time with Margaret, they seemingly enjoyed themselves; the king's accounts note a payment at Knowsley to 'the women that sang before the King and Queen'.[46] That same month, Warbeck made another attempt to invade England, but after finding the people off the coast of Deal 'determined to resist the royal foes', he sailed to Scotland.[47] There James IV, who even arranged for Warbeck's marriage to his cousin, Lady Katherine Gordon, enthusiastically welcomed him.[48] For the time being, Warbeck was destined to remain a thorn in Henry's side.

The year was to be one of loss, for on 14 September 1495 the three-year-old Princess Elizabeth, a beautiful child, died at Eltham. Her family were devastated, and it was left to Morton to arrange the funeral. The body of the little princess was conveyed in state to Westminster Abbey, where a tomb of black marble was erected to her memory.[49] Then on 21 December Margaret and her son were dealt yet another crushing blow when Jasper Tudor died at Thornbury Castle.[50] Jasper had been an almost constant presence in Henry's life and had faithfully supported Margaret throughout some of the most testing moments. Henry had given them a common purpose: ensuring his well-being and security. They had willingly placed their lives in jeopardy in order to do so, while Jasper had striven to fill the void that had been left by the death of the father that Henry had never known. His own death, therefore, left an unfillable gap. In a final show of love and respect to his dearly beloved uncle, the king and queen travelled to Keynsham to witness his interment in the abbey of his choice.[51] They were accompanied by many nobles, but there is no record of Margaret joining the party.[52]

By the time of the Princess Elizabeth's death in September, the queen was already pregnant with her fifth child. The arrival of another daughter at Sheen on 18 March 1496, named Mary, probably brought some much-needed comfort and joy into the lives of the royal family. Yet, in the background, the problem of Perkin Warbeck lurked.

It was the month following Princess Mary's birth that Margaret wrote to the Earl of Ormond, the queen's chamberlain, from Sheen to 'thank you heartily that ye list so soon remember me with my gloves the which were right good save they were too much for my hand'. She continued, 'I think the ladies in that parts be great ladies all, and according to their great estates they have great personages'. This portrays something of her sense of humour, for the 'great ladies' to whom she referred was intended as a jibe against the Duchess of Burgundy, who was clearly larger than Margaret! In February a treaty had been agreed whereby trading relations—suspended by Henry in light of the duchess's support of Warbeck—were restored, but in so doing the duchess was unable to continue her support of the Pretender. Nevertheless, Margaret's feelings about the woman who harboured such a vendetta against her son had evidently not thawed. By the same token, though Warbeck had been deprived of Burgundian support, the threat of invasion still loomed.

On a lighter note, the rest of Margaret's letter to Ormond conveyed much of her affection for her family as well as her relief at the queen's recovery, presumably from Princess Mary's birth:

> As for news here I am sure ye shall have more cert then I can send you, blessed be God the King the Queen and all our sweet children be in good health the Queen hath been a little crased [unwell] but now she is well God be thanked. Her sickness is so good as I would but I trust hastily it shall with good grace whom I pray give you god sped in your great matters and bring you well and soon home.[53]

In the summer, Margaret joined the king and queen on progress, where she was afforded the opportunity to tour her estates in Dorset. Travelling via Hampshire and the Isle of Wight, the royal party visited Christchurch, where the king made several offerings, and Poole.[54] At the end of July, Margaret was given the chance to view the progress of Corfe Castle, a property that her son had granted to her in 1487. In personal terms, Corfe held immense importance because it was a former Beaufort property that had once been owned by her father—it may even have been where he died. Upon acquiring the castle, Margaret had immediately begun a lavish programme of rebuilding, and through her efforts, Corfe once more became a resplendent palace.[55] During the course of their visit, Margaret and her son had a chance to enjoy some leisure time, and the mood was full of revelry. The king's accounts note payments to 'Dick, the fool's master', as well as money for cards and goshawks.[56] There was also an opportunity to visit Wimborne Minster, where Margaret's parents lay entombed, and here, too, the king made an offering.[57] The following year, he would grant Margaret a licence to found a chantry dedicated to the Annunciation of the Virgin Mary in the Minster; Margaret likely chose this spot to celebrate and exhibit the success and continuation of her house.[58] The party then made their way through Wiltshire, Bath and Bristol, before arriving at Woodstock at the end of August.

THE PRESENCE OF WARBECK REMAINED a constant cause for alarm, but in the summer of 1497 Henry was faced with another threat. The men of Cornwall had grown disenchanted with Henry on account of the king's heightened taxes—raised to retaliate against the Scots for their support of Warbeck—and soon word arrived that the rebels were marching on London. The royal family were at Sheen when the news reached them, and they immediately sought the greater protection of London. They were evidently fearful of the threat posed by the rebels, so much so that in June 'the Queen with my lord of York' travelled to Coldharbour to join Margaret.[59] After six days, however, Elizabeth and her son Henry travelled to the greater security of the Tower upon hearing alarming reports of the rebels' advance. It is unclear whether Margaret joined them. As the rebels continued to approach the city, they met with no resistance, and it was left to the Earl of Oxford to take control of the royal army. The two sides met at Blackheath on 17 June, and to Margaret's great relief, Oxford defeated the rebels: a thousand Cornishmen were killed, and a jubilant Margaret noted the success in her Book of Hours.[60]

In August the royal family moved to Woodstock, there to celebrate the betrothal of Margaret's grandson, ten-year-old Prince Arthur, to the eleven-year-old Spanish *infanta* Katherine of Aragon. It was left to the

Spanish ambassador, Roderigo de Puebla, to stand in for the *infanta*, and the following February, the marriage was ratified. It would be several years before it was solemnized.

The family were still at Woodstock in September when the Venetian ambassador visited, and he was extremely impressed by what he saw. Henry received him in a small, tapestry-hung hall. As he leaned across a gilt chair covered with cloth of gold, the ambassador was struck by the king's magnificent clothes: he wore 'a violet coloured gown, lined with cloth of gold, and a collar of many jewels, and on his cap was a large diamond and a most beautiful pearl'.[61] During the course of the visit, the ambassador was given the opportunity to meet the queen, who was 'dressed in cloth of gold'.[62] As was her custom, Margaret stood to one side of the queen and Prince Arthur. The Venetian ambassador did not note his impressions of Margaret, although he did report that 'the Queen is a handsome woman'.[63] Underneath this show of outward splendour, however, the royal family were feeling the strain.

Though the Cornish threat had been vanquished, Warbeck remained at large. By the autumn, however, James IV had grown tired of his guest and was wearier still of the drain Warbeck placed on his financial resources. He urged him to action, and Warbeck finally left Scotland for Ireland. The response he received was cold, for the formerly rebellious Irish lords had now made peace with Henry VII. In a final attempt to win support, on 7 September Warbeck landed in Cornwall in what was to be the beginning of the second rebellion of the year originating in the county. On 17 September, he laid siege to Exeter, but though he burnt two of the city gates, he found little support and was soon driven off. He made it as far as Taunton before he learned that the royal army was approaching. Losing his nerve, Warbeck abandoned his supporters and fled to the New Forest, where he took sanctuary at Beaulieu Abbey. It was not long before Henry's men caught up with him, and having been 'promised pardon he thereupon put his trust in Henry's official clemency'.[64] He surrendered on 5 October and before long had made a full confession about his true identity.

Henry finally had the Pretender in his custody, and he 'returned to London in triumphal style', bringing Warbeck with him.[65] The king was 'greeted by all his subjects with the profoundest respect and affection, because with so rapid and fortunate a campaign he had disposed of a dangerous conspiracy and because he brought back with him as a captive the leader of it'.[66] Crowds gathered to catch a glimpse of the Pretender as he passed, 'for most accounted it miraculous that a man of such humble origins should have been bold enough to seek to acquire by guile so great a kingdom'.[67] Warbeck was immediately placed in the Tower, but displaying the same leniency that he had once shown to Lambert Simnel, Henry was merciful. Unlike Simnel, it soon became clear that Warbeck would not heed the mercy he had been shown.

Warbeck was not held in the Tower for long, and in a similar manner to Simnel before him, he was brought to join the court in London. Unlike Simnel, Warbeck was not set to work but was instead treated as a guest—although he was closely watched. He was also reunited with his wife, who had been treated honourably by the king on account of her royal lineage, and came under the protection of the queen. In November the Venetian ambassador reported that 'he is a well favoured young man, 23 years old, and his wife a very handsome woman; the King treats them well, but did not allow them to sleep together'.[68] In December, however, the Milanese ambassador related that 'Perkin has been made a spectacle for everybody and every day he is led through London, in order that everyone may perceive his past error. In my opinion he bears his fortune bravely'.[69] It is unclear how Margaret felt about her son's attitude towards the Pretender, but after all of the emotional trauma she had been forced to endure by his hand, she is certainly likely to have been wary. Unbeknown to her, there was further anxiety around the corner.

At Christmas the royal family and the court were celebrating at Sheen. It was here that 'upon St Thomas day at night in the Christmas week about 9 of the clock, began a great fire within the King's lodging, and so continued unto 12 of the night and more'.[70] The fire ravished the palace with such 'violence whereof much and great part of the old building was burned', and much of the interior was destroyed.[71] The royal family escaped unharmed, and miraculously nobody died, 'which was to the King's singular comfort'.[72] Shortly afterwards, however, Henry paid £20 (£13,400) in reward to 'them that found the King's jewels at Sheen', presumably among the rubble.[73] In spite of the devastation, Henry was determined to rebuild his palace and spent a vast sum. By 1501, much of the work was complete, and it was indeed a marvel to behold, highly influenced by ideas of Burgundian architecture. The new palace was renamed Richmond, in honour of the king's previous earldom and the title that his mother still bore—perhaps also in a touching reminder of Henry's father.[74] It was a splendid place indeed, boasting a library, a chapel and a hall decorated with the statues of mighty warrior kings. There were also magnificent grounds in which the royal family could enjoy recreation, and it quickly became the king's favoured residence. Given how fraught the last few years of Henry's reign had been, it must have offered some much-needed respite.

As had become the usual pattern, Margaret remained a constant presence by her son's side in the following year of 1498. Although at the end of May she turned fifty-five, that summer she continued to travel throughout the realm. She joined the king as they travelled to the Thames-side palaces, and she was with him and the queen when they journeyed through East Anglia. Their tour took them to, among other places, Castle Hedingham, Bury St Edmunds, Walsingham and Norwich, where they arrived in August. By 7 September, they had reached Margaret's Northamptonshire residence, Collyweston. The main topic of conversation there is likely to have been Prince Arthur's marriage to Katherine of Aragon, for which plans were well under way. As usual, Margaret was determined to have her say.

CHAPTER 19

THE RIGHT NOBLE PUISSANT AND EXCELLENT PRINCESS

I n July 1498 the Spanish ambassador de Puebla relayed to his sovereigns the eager involvement of Margaret and the queen in the plans for the arrival of Katherine of Aragon. This included their desire that Katherine speak French with her sister-in-law, Margaret of Austria, in order 'to be able to converse in it when she comes to England'. This would be a necessity, he explained, because neither Margaret nor her daughter-in-law understood Latin, 'and much less, Spanish'.[1] But it was not just the language barrier that concerned Margaret. De Puebla also expressed the women's wish that 'the Princess of Wales should accustom herself to drink wine. The water of England is not drinkable, and even if it were, the climate would not allow the drinking of it'.[2] Margaret and the queen were clearly eager for Katherine to be prepared for what lay ahead of her.

Once the arrangements had been concluded, Elizabeth wrote to Queen Isabella, assuring her that she was keen to do all that she could to accommodate her future daughter-in-law, who 'we think of and esteem as our own daughter'.[3] There is no record of Margaret writing in a similar manner, though she is likely to have shared the queen's sentiments towards the newest member of their family. In the same way as she had for her daughter-in-law, no doubt in an indication of her interest, she later had a list of Katherine's attendants drawn up.[4] This may also, perhaps, reveal a desire to be kept well informed—and in control—of court management and of the way in which the princess's household was organized. Always fond of detail, Margaret invariably seems to have been eager to know as much as possible about the lives of those close to her and her family.

At this time, the king and Margaret probably pondered the problem of Warbeck, who had remained a thorn in Henry's side. Disregarding the leniency with which he had been treated, on 9 June he had escaped from Westminster and begun making his way towards the Charterhouse at Sheen. It was not long, however, before the king's men caught up with him. There is some indication that Henry's servants deliberately encouraged his escape in order to provide the king with an excuse to move against him, and indeed it seems to have been all too easy for Perkin to slip past his guards.[5] Given that Henry was embroiled in negotiations for the marriage of Prince Arthur and Katherine of Aragon, this is certainly plausible; the Spanish sovereigns were always eager for news of him, for they viewed his presence in England as an obstacle to Katherine's marriage—they did not want to send their daughter into a realm where her father-in-law might be toppled by a pretender, and Perkin's presence was becoming an embarrassment.

This time, his treatment was to be less gentle. De Puebla reported that Warbeck spent two days in the pillory, and he was subsequently 'secured in such a manner, and in such a prison, that, with the help of God, he will never be able to play such a trick again'.[6] Imprisoned in a windowless cell in the Tower where 'he sees neither sun nor moon', those who saw him soon afterwards were shocked by the change in him. De Puebla reported that his appearance had altered so much that it was his belief that 'his life will be very short'.[7] For the time being, though, in his determination to be merciful, Henry remained intent on sparing Warbeck's life.

FEBRUARY 1499 WAS MINGLED WITH sorrow and joy. On 9 February, John Welles, 'the king's uncle', died.[8] He had joined his nephew in exile during the uncertain days of Richard III's reign and had offered him his support at Bosworth. In his will he left instructions that he was to be buried 'as the King and Queen, and the Lady Margaret Countess of Richmond and Derby', as well as his own wife Cecily, should choose.[9] It is unknown from where the impetus for his choice of burial location came, though in all likelihood it was either Margaret or Henry, but he was interred in the old Lady Chapel in Westminster Abbey.

Almost two weeks later, on 21 February, Elizabeth of York gave birth to a son at Greenwich. The Spanish ambassador, Don Pedro de Ayala, revealed that 'there had been much fear that the life of the Queen would be in danger, but the delivery, contrary to expectation, has been easy'.[10] This child was one for whom Margaret had a special affection—perhaps on account of his close association to her—and she duly rewarded the queen's midwife in thanks for his safe delivery. Named Edmund after Henry's father, the infant was also given Margaret's father's title of Duke of Somerset. Once more, Margaret was called upon to fulfil the role of godmother when the christening, which was, naturally, 'very splendid', took place. Verily, as the Spanish ambassador observed, 'the festivities [were] such as though an heir to the Crown had been born'.[11] As he had done for the births of all of his children, Henry gave orders that the font from Canterbury was to be borrowed for the occasion.[12] In her usual manner, Margaret took the responsibility of being a godparent seriously, outlaying £100 (£67,000) as a christening gift for the little boy. Meanwhile, Prince Edmund joined his brother and sisters at Eltham.

IN 1475 EDWARD IV HAD commissioned Henry Janyns to redesign the old medieval chapel at Windsor, and he was later buried there, in the new St George's Chapel, one of this master mason's many great creations. Yet the work was incomplete at his death and was continued by Henry VII. In 1492 Margaret had accompanied her son to Windsor to view the chapel's progress and to make offerings at the tomb of their kinsman Henry VI. Henry's remains had been moved to Windsor from Chertsey by Richard III in 1484 at a cost of £5 10s 2d (£3,800), and his tomb had become a place of pilgrimage.[13]

The memory of Henry VI played an important part in early Tudor court ritual, and later, in 1494, Henry VII—eager to revere his uncle's life—would petition the pope for his canonization. The king intended to build a magnificent tomb for himself within the chapel and a shrine to Henry VI. It was with this in mind that Margaret followed suit, contributing money to the chapel and planning her own memorial there. On 1 March 1497, the king granted his mother a licence to 'found a chantry for four chaplains, with power to increase the number' in St George's Chapel, 'to be called the chantry of the Blessed Jesus and St Mary the Virgin'.[14] On 18 July, Margaret's former chaplain Christopher Urswick, now the Dean of Windsor, granted consent for the chantry.[15]

The following year, however, the plans changed when it became known that Henry VI had in fact wished to be buried in Westminster Abbey. Thus, Henry VII agreed that his uncle's remains should be moved there, where he planned to build a shrine behind the main altar and a magnificent new Lady Chapel in the abbey.[16] The king's attempts to have his uncle canonized never materialized, however, nor were his remains ever moved from Windsor—it transpired to be a long and complicated process that eventually ground to a halt following Henry VIII's separation from the Church of Rome. Predictably, when her son's intentions became known, Margaret's plans changed. On 28 April 1499, she asked for her chantry request at Windsor to be cancelled: from then on, her efforts, too, would be centred on Westminster.[17]

Following the demolition of the old chapel, on 24 January 1503 the foundation stone of the new Lady Chapel at Westminster was laid. By this time Henry had decided that he, too, would be buried in the new chapel of his creation, and he had probably appointed Henry Janyns to oversee some of the work. Though it was incomplete at the time of Henry's death, the result when it was finished in 1512 was a spectacular, fan-vaulted chapel containing statues of saints in wall niches, the red rose of Lancaster, the Beaufort portcullis, the Welsh dragon, the Richmond greyhound and the daisy or marguerite that Margaret adopted as one of her symbols. It was a dramatic and breath-taking expression both of Henry's magnificence and that of his dynasty. In 1506 Margaret saw to it that two priests were to offer up prayers for

> Margaret and the king her son during their lives and thereafter for their souls and also for the souls of her late husband Edmund, Earl of Richmond father of the king, her parents John duke of Somerset and Margaret his wife and all her other progenitors and ancestors, her late husbands Thomas, Earl of Derby and Henry, Lord Stafford, Elizabeth late queen of England late wife to the king and their issue deceased and all the souls that Margaret will have prayed for and all Christian souls.[18]

Ensuring that the souls of those with whom she had spent her life were well cared for was important to her, particularly at Westminster, where she and her son intended to be laid to rest. Her wealth also meant that she had the ability to ensure that this was done to the highest order and at regular intervals both within her lifetime and after.

Bishop Fisher remarked that Margaret was 'to God and to the church full obedient and tractable searching his honour and pleasure', and this can be seen in her accounts, which are full of offerings and payments to religious foundations.[19] Indeed, Margaret's outward displays of piety and the care she took to demonstrate this to society were essential parts of her core identity. Among the institutions to which she gave her patronage were John's Hospital in Rome and Syon, the first Bridgettine monastery in England.[20] Located in Isleworth on the outskirts of London, the monastery had been founded by Henry V in 1415. The patronage of her grandmother Margaret Holland, who had also purchased several expensive books for the monastery, likely was the inspiration for Margaret's support. Margaret's accounts in the 1500s show a steady stream of payments for boat hire to convey her to and from Syon, where she visited her goddaughter, Margaret Windsor, and Margaret Pole, who had moved to the monastery following the death of her husband in 1504.[21] Syon lay a very short distance from the Charterhouse at Sheen, another institution that earned both Margaret's and her son's interest. In her will, Margaret bequeathed money to both monasteries. Margaret's religious activities included the regular distribution of alms. At Westminster she established an almshouse for thirteen women, and almshouses could be found at her own properties. Fisher explained:

> poor folks to ye number of 12 she daily and nightly kept in her house, giving them lodging, meat and drink and clothing, visiting them as often as she conveniently might. And in their sickness visiting them and comforting them, and ministering unto them with her own hands. And when it pleased God to call one of them out of this wretched world she would be present to see them depart and to learn to die.[22]

Charity was an expected part of fifteenth-century life, but it is clear that Margaret's contribution was both heartfelt and above and beyond the call of duty. Her accounts contain numerous examples of money she gave for the relief of the poor. But it was not only the poor whom Margaret helped; on one occasion she provided money for an imprisoned priest, though further details of this are unknown. Margaret felt compelled to help those less fortunate, and Fisher was not exaggerating when he said, 'Merciful also and piteous she was unto such as was grieved and wrongfully troubled and to them that were in poverty or sickness or any other misery'.[23]

Margaret's wealth and position enabled her to extend her patronage in other quarters. She had always cherished a fondness for books, and her chapel contained numerous fine mass books, all beautifully bound.[24] As Fisher said, 'She had divers books in French wherewith she would occupy herself when she was weary of prayer', as well as translate them.[25] She was doubtless gratified when Henry appointed the first royal librarian: Quintin Poulet, who hailed from Lille.[26] She made regular payments for books, but with her position she also perceived a greater opportunity to bestow her own patronage.[27] In so doing, she was able to wield power through an altogether different medium, one that had the ability to extend beyond the realms of her son's kingdom, too.

Margaret's patronage began with the London printer William Caxton. In 1472 Caxton had established his own printing press in Westminster and had been fortunate enough to enjoy the patronage of Margaret of York, Duchess of Burgundy, Edward IV and Elizabeth Wydeville, among others.[28] Shortly after Henry VII's accession, Margaret, too, threw her patronage behind the printer, and by way of thanks he dedicated two books to her; he would also dedicate one to her eldest grandson, Prince Arthur.[29] As the king's mother, Margaret wielded a huge level of power and influence, and her backing had an enormous impact on Caxton's business, immediately bringing him to the notice of those at court, including the king.

The queen also supported the printer, and together she and Margaret jointly commissioned Caxton for a copy of *The Fifteen O's*. The book was reputedly written by Saint Bridget of Sweden, to whom Margaret had a special devotion, presumably for her widespread acts of charity, and who was founder of the Bridgettine order.[30] As the title suggests, all fifteen prayers of which the book was composed began with 'O Blessed Jesu'. In 1483 Margaret had also purchased a copy of the French romance *Blanchardyn and Eglantine* from the printer. Much has been made of the parallels between the story of the couple it portrays and that of Henry VII and Elizabeth of York in the perilous days of Richard III's reign.[31] Margaret was discernibly fond of the book, for in 1489 Caxton related that it was through her 'good grace, and her commandment' that he had been ordered to 'reduce and translate it unto our maternal and English tongue'. In his dedication, though, he mixed up Margaret's title with that of her mother, referring to her as 'the right noble puissant and excellent princess, my redoubted lady, my lady Margaret Duchess of Somerset'. Though Caxton himself described the romance as 'honest and joyful to all virtuous young noble gentlemen and women', the subject matter shows that not all of the books enjoyed by Margaret were of a serious nature.[32]

Caxton was not the only printer to receive Margaret's support. In 1494, at her request, Wynkyn de Worde printed Walter Hilton's *Scala Perfectionis*, or *The Ladder of Perfection*. It came complete with a glowing dedication:

> This heavenly book more precious than gold
> Was late direct with great humility
> For godly pleasure. Thereon to behold
> Unto the right noble Margaret as ye see
> The king's mother of excellent bounty
> Henry the seventh that Jesus him preserve
> This mighty princess hath commanded me
> To emprint this book her grace for to deserve.[33]

The book was a work of mystic theology that described the soul's journey of contemplation and provided spiritual exercises that were centred around the soul. It is likely to have been this interest in cleansing one's soul of sin that attracted Margaret to it. She was in the happy position of being able to choose texts that appealed to her, and, given that she purchased a further copy in 1507, *The Ladder* evidently did so. She was also happy to distribute it, and, together with her daughter-in-law, she gave a copy to Lady Mary Roos, one of the queen's ladies.[34] Both women had taken the time to personalize the gift, adding inscriptions, of which Margaret's read: 'Mistress Roos, I trust in your prayers, the which I pray you I may be partner of. Margaret R, the King's Mother'.

Margaret was the chosen dedicatee of ten books, five of which came from Wynkyn de Worde. Authors often selected their dedicatee with a mind to acquiring support from a wealthy patron, and this is likely to have been the thinking behind a dedication that Margaret received from Inghelbert Hague in Rouen (whom she had never met). Dedications were sometimes also an acknowledgement of a dedicatee's intellect or interest or a token of thanks for support already given. Two came from another fortunate recipient of her patronage, Richard Pynson.[35] Pynson's name first appeared in relation to Margaret in the early 1500s, and it was doubtless through her influence that he came to the attention of the king. In 1503 the first payments to Pynson appear in Henry VII's accounts, and it was clear that he was a regular customer.[36] But it was from Margaret that the highest orders stemmed. In 1505 she paid Pynson for a hundred books that were delivered to Syon on her orders.[37] The following year, a further fifty were bought from him, which were of her own translation.[38] On another occasion, she rewarded a monk of the Charterhouse for books that he had given to her.[39]

Literature was an important part of Margaret's life and would remain so until her final days. Though she regularly purchased books, unfortunately the subject matter is frequently unrecorded. She is, however, known to have owned a copy of Geoffrey Chaucer's *The Canterbury Tales* as well as of Froissart's *Chronicles*, among other texts. By the time of her death, she had amassed an impressive library and took great pleasure in its many pages.

Several of Margaret's books survive, including the beautifully decorated and illuminated prayer book that she had commissioned for her husband Stanley.[40] She often used books as gifts, presenting a Book of Hours that had once belonged to her father to Lady Anne Shirley, the wife of Sir Ralph Shirley. The book, in St John's College, Cambridge, contains a personal message from Margaret to the recipient: 'my good Lady Shirley pray for me that giveth you this book, I heartily pray you. Margaret, mother to the king'.[41] It is also possible that she passed a book that had once been owned by her grandmother, Margaret Holland, to her daughter-in-law the queen, who was likewise fond of books.[42] Another of these very personal mementoes was given to Lady Scrope.

ON 19 MAY 1499, THE marriage by proxy of Prince Arthur and Katherine of Aragon was conducted at Bewdley in Worcestershire. Once again, de Puebla stood in for the *infanta*; it would be more than two years before she would set foot on English soil. Arthur's marriage had dominated the political arena for more than a decade, and Henry was eager to consolidate his alliance with the most powerful sovereigns in Europe as soon as possible. The continuing presence of the Earl of Warwick and Warbeck, however—though both were ensconced in the Tower—left the Spanish reluctant to send their *infanta* to England. From Henry's perspective, it was vital that England ally itself with Spain, even if it meant bloodshed. He now perceived an opportunity to rid himself of Warbeck—and Warwick—for good.

The Earl of Warwick's existence had been a sad one; as well as him enduring years in captivity, it is possible that he suffered from some kind of disability—Vergil later claimed that he could not tell a goose from a capon. It is no coincidence that the earl's cell in the Tower lay close to that of Warbeck's in the summer of 1499; within a short space of time, the two young men reportedly had begun to plot together. By 3 August the king had been made aware of it, and in November both men were put on trial for their lives. They were inevitably found guilty and condemned for treason. It is possible that Margaret felt some sympathy for the young earl over the hand that fate had dealt him, for his only real crime had been his blood. Still, while he lived, his presence as a Plantagenet heir made him a continual target for dissenters, and her concern for her family's safety would have overruled any sentiment. With their removal, there was no reason why plans for Katherine of Aragon's journey to England could not proceed.

On 23 November, Warbeck was 'drawn from the Tower of London to Tyburn, and there hanged and beheaded'.[43] Before his execution, he once more confessed that he was not the son of Edward IV. His body was taken to the priory of the Austin Friars in the city for burial, and in a gruesome example to the king's subjects of the fate of traitors, his head was set upon London Bridge. His widow, Lady Katherine Gordon, remained at court, where the king continued to show her great favour and paid her servants' wages.[44] She remarried three times before her death in 1537.[45]

Five days after Warbeck's demise, on 28 November, the twenty-four-year-old Earl of Warwick was executed on Tower Hill. Vergil wrote that 'the entire population mourned the death of the handsome youth', and, indeed, Margaret and her son may have been regretful of what had come to pass.[46] Nevertheless, at the stroke of the axe another candidate for Henry's throne had been removed. As with many of his ancestors, Warwick's remains were interred at Bisham Abbey at the king's charge.[47]

It was not for nothing that Katherine of Aragon would later claim that her marriage was made in blood. Yet with both Warbeck and Warwick definitively dealt with, Henry was finally able to make arrangements for Prince Arthur's wedding. Ferdinand and Isabella were pleased with the developments—two potential threats to their daughter's future security had been removed—and the following year the Spanish ambassador was able to report to them cheerfully that 'England has never before been so tranquil and obedient as at present'.[48] He continued, 'Now that Perkin and the son of the Duke of Clarence have been executed, there does not remain "a drop of doubtful Royal blood," the only Royal blood being the true blood of the King, the Queen, and, above all, of the Prince of Wales'.[49] In the eyes of both Margaret and her son, this was all that mattered. With everything seemingly safe, there was no reason why the marriage of Margaret's eldest grandson could not go ahead.

In May 1500, the king and queen travelled to Calais, primarily on matters of diplomacy. There is no record of Margaret accompanying them, so she probably remained at home. The royal couple landed back in England on 16 June, and almost immediately, tragedy struck. Three days after their arrival, their youngest son Edmund, who had reached his first birthday in February, succumbed to an unknown illness at Hatfield. His death devastated Margaret and her family, and in accordance with custom it was left to the Duke of Buckingham to assume the role of chief mourner at the youngster's funeral. The little prince's body was conveyed 'honourably' to Westminster Abbey, where he was buried close to the Shrine of St Edward.[50]

Three months later, on 15 September, Margaret's ally Cardinal Morton died at Knole, and he was interred in Canterbury Cathedral.[51] Margaret had known him for years, and he had proved a willing ally and conspirator when she had plotted with Buckingham in 1483 to overthrow Richard III. From then on, it would be Richard Fox, Bishop of Durham—a man with whom Margaret was on excellent terms—who was foremost in the king's favour.[52] By this time, however, Margaret was spending an increasing amount of time away from court: indeed, she was establishing a court of her own elsewhere.

CHAPTER 20

MY GODLY MISTRESS, THE LADY MARGARET

In 1487 Henry VII had granted his mother a sizeable amount of property, including Tattershall Castle, Maxstoke Castle and Collyweston. Beginning in 1499, Collyweston, a handsome manor house that lay around three miles southwest of Stamford, became Margaret's principal residence.[1] The house had originally been built by Sir William Porter in the early fifteenth century. In 1441 Ralph, Lord Cromwell, who was responsible for enlarging it, purchased the house, and following his death in 1455, it passed first to Warwick the 'Kingmaker' and then to George, Duke of Clarence. When Clarence was executed in 1478, Collyweston became Crown property. Under Margaret's ownership, Collyweston was gradually transformed into a palace, rendering it unrecognisable from its humble beginnings. John Leland later acknowledged that the house 'for the most part is of a new building by the Lady Margaret, mother to Henry VII'.[2] Featured prominently in the work undertaken by Margaret was glass that proudly proclaimed her Beaufort heritage.[3] She spent staggering sums on the property, ensuring that the magnificence of Collyweston would inspire awe in those who visited. It was a home that was as comfortable as it was luxurious. There she was a queen in all but name and mistress of her own household.

The exterior of Collyweston was built to impress and boasted two splendid clock houses. The interior was equally splendid, with a presence chamber, a chapel, a library, magnificent apartments for Margaret and her family and a jewel house. The jewel house fell under the keepership of Edward Bothe, who was employed to ensure that his mistress's treasures were securely kept. In an indication of Margaret's love of money, there was also a counting house.

Margaret seems to have paid particular attention to her gardens— another interest she had in common with her daughter-in-law—and delighted in the planning of them with the help of William Love. Colly- weston featured beautiful pleasure gardens, as well as orchards, herb gar- dens, fishponds and a deer park.

All of Margaret's homes were lavishly furnished, and this was partic- ularly true of Collyweston. The amount of material wealth that she ac- quired was staggering, as we can see from the inventories of her chapel and household plate. In a reflection of the importance that religion played not only in Margaret's life but also in that of her household, there were numerous copes (ecclesiastical vestments) in blue, crimson, purple and green, many of which were embroidered with her arms and symbols; one featured Margaret's arms with a coronal, while another contained the Beaufort portcullis and a coronal.[4] Her chapel contained numerous beau- tiful objects, including decorative altar cloths. One magnificent pair were made of crimson velvet embroidered with marguerites.[5] Another, made of red velvet—later given to Christ's College—was embroidered with mar- guerites and an image of Saint Margaret.[6] There were also splendid gold cups featuring a number of designs: those that contained Margaret's arms, another fashioned like a serpentine, gold salts (salt cellars) containing pre- cious stones and plate featuring Saint Anthony, Saint George, Saint Anne and Saint Margaret with a green dragon.[7] Margaret had a special devotion to these saints, and this is reflected in the design of these pieces found in her magnificent chapel trove. In a further indication of the importance she placed upon the plate in her chapel, on one occasion a goldsmith was paid to make a container to hold holy water; evidently, Margaret believed that something sumptuous was required to store something so sacred.[8]

Many of the objects Margaret owned provide a window into her piety as well as her magnificence as the king's mother. Her chapel plate was one such example, but her domestic plate also showed signs of this. Margaret's pride in her role can be seen by her adoption of Henry VII's arms on items such as gilt pots, while other pieces emphasised her own origins—carving knives, for example, decorated with marguerites and portcullises. Other items, such as gilt spoons shaped like strawberries—believed to be the fruit of righteousness and sometimes symbolic of the fruitfulness of the Virgin Mary—were also reflective of Margaret's piety.[9]

Thanks largely to the thoroughness of Margaret's accounts, we know a fair deal about those who made up her household, all of whom wore the blue and silver livery of the Beaufort family, which featured the portcullis from the family crest. Between two hundred and four hundred people were employed at Collyweston (the latter figure comes from Henry Parker and is almost certainly an exaggeration)—a huge number, particularly when one considers that Margaret's household at Woking in the 1460s had been made up of around fifty people and had been considerably smaller in the brief interlude between Stafford's death and her marriage to Stanley. There were clearly enough to attend to her every need. Reginald Bray was, of course, a trusted and integral member of the household, while Hugh Oldham, appointed as her receiver in 1492, was responsible for overseeing all of her estates in the West Country. Margaret thought highly of him, and in 1501 he became her receiver general.[10] Roger Ormeston was her chamberlain until his death in 1504, when the role was taken over by Margaret's nephew, John St John. Her secretary was Henry Hornby, who was also the dean of her chapel, and there were several cofferers (treasurers), including Miles Worsley. She also employed three gentlewomen: Edith Fowler, Elizabeth Massey and Alice Parker and the chamberer, Elizabeth Collins, who would later serve Katherine of Aragon and be remembered after Margaret's death with a financial reward of 26s 8d (£900).[11]

There can be no doubt that Margaret was a woman who inspired great loyalty and whose kindness and generosity improved the lives of many. All of those who knew her were genuinely fond of her, and she was beloved by her household, who were well treated and had the utmost respect for their mistress. Fisher remarked that 'full courtesy answer she would make to all that came unto her', going so far as to state that 'of marvellous gentleness she was unto all folks, but specially unto her own, whom she trusted and loved right tenderly. Unkind she would not be unto no creature, or forgetful of any kindness or service done to her before'.[12] Her household was run 'with marvellous diligence and wisdom', and in her usual desire to observe etiquette, she ordered 'reasonable statutes and ordinances for them, which by her officers she commanded to be read four times a year. And oftentimes by herself she would so lovingly courage every of them to do well'.[13]

Fisher painted a flattering picture, but so too did Henry Parker.[14] Though written later, his account reveals a great deal of what life in Margaret's household was like. Referring to her as 'my godly mistress the Lady Margaret', Parker was highly complimentary.[15] He explained, 'I was ever one by her special commandment, and bout her person, either in that room to be her carver, or her cup-bearer'.[16] He both admired and had a good relationship with her, and she in turn appears to have been fond of him. It is from Parker that we get a glimpse of Margaret in her everyday life, for he painted a vivid picture of the regularities and habits of her household. Much of this was dominated by her religious observances:

Her grace was every morning in the chapel betwixt six and seven of the clock, and daily said matins of the day with one of her chaplains. And that said from seven til it was eleven of the clock, as soon as one priest had said mass in her sight another began. One time in a day she was confessed, then going to her dinner how honourably she was served I think few kings better, her condition always at the beginning of her dinner was to be joyous, and to hear those tales that were honest to make her merry. The midst of her dinner either her amner or I, read some virtuous tale unto her of the life of Christ, or such like, the latter end of her dinner again she was disposed to talk with the bishop or with her chancellor which sat at her board end of some godly matter.[17]

Parker's account is similar to that given by Fisher. The latter claimed that Margaret often rose at five o'clock each morning, and so devout was she that following her morning prayers she heard 'with one of her gentlewomen ye matins of our lady, which kept her to then she came in to her closet, where then with her chaplain she said also matins of ye day. And after that daily heard four or five masses upon her knees, so continuing in her prayers and devotions unto ye hour of dinner'.[18] In spite of the break for dinner—usually served at around eleven o'clock in the morning—Margaret never indulged. Fisher was adamant that her modest eating habits were known to all who encountered her. In fact, she fasted regularly, and continued to do so until the end of her life. Although 'for age and feebleness albeit she were not bound yet those days by ye church were appointed she kept them diligently and seriously, and in especial ye holy lent throughout yet she restrained her appetite til one meal and til one fish on ye day, beside her other peculiar fasts of devotion'.[19]

Margaret took her devotion further than this, for underneath her beautiful clothes she often wore a hair shirt that left her skin raw and painful. In the same way that it began, Margaret's day would end with prayers, which were frequently said on her knees. Later in life this would be troublesome for her when her arthritis caused her great pain in her back. Nevertheless, 'divine service which daily was kept in her chapel with great number of priests, clerks and children to her great charge and cost, her tongue occupied in prayer much part of the day'.[20] Her chapel and the staff that it encompassed were a vital part of her everyday life, and at Collyweston its importance is highlighted by the fact that it rivalled that of the royal household in terms of its size and the way in which it was organized.[21] The children who formed a part of Margaret's chapel staff were an active part of life at Collyweston and educated at Margaret's expense.[22] They sat at desks in a chamber in the palace where they were taught grammar, and there are frequent references to them in Margaret's accounts.[23] On one occasion, for example, they were rewarded for singing two songs for her pleasure.

The structure at Collyweston was only marginally smaller than that of the royal court, with Margaret, rather than the king or queen, at the top. There she was the sole mistress, and it was she who dictated how life was run. Hers was the deciding voice when it came to organizing the important festivities of the year, which were frequently celebrated according to her status with great pomp. Christmas, for example, was often joyous. Parker described one such occasion:

> In Christmas time she kept so honourable a house, that upon one new year's day I being her sewer of the age of fifteen years, had five and twenty knights following me of whom mine own father was one, and sitting at her table the Earl of Derby her husband, the Viscount Welles, the old Lord Hastings, the Bishop of Lincoln, and by her person under her cloth of estate the Lady Cecily King Edward's daughter your aunt.[24]

Margaret often had noble company at this time of year and doubtless played the role of hostess to perfection, as she had always done. This occasion was not a one-off, for at Christmas 1505 Margaret had engaged an abbot of misrule to oversee the celebrations, which in a reflection of her own pleasure included morris dancers and players.[25] Neither was her hospitality restricted to members of her family and the nobility who deigned to visit and enjoy her hospitality. For,

> no poor man was denied at that said feast of Christmas if he were of any honesty, but that he might come to the buttery, or to the cellar to drink at his pleasure, her liberality was such that there came no man of honour or worship to her as there came many of the greatest of the realm, but that they were well rewarded.[26]

It is clear that Collyweston offered an impressive backdrop for Margaret to hold sway over her household and provided a luxurious setting for the visits of friends, family and nobles. None could fail to admire the lavish interiors and furnishings or complain of the generous hospitality that was offered. But there was more to Margaret's Midlands palace than that.

Behind its impressive façade, Collyweston served a practical purpose. It was there that Margaret set up her administrative headquarters as she assumed the unofficial role of the king's lieutenant, her authority extending from the Midlands into Northern England. It was with this in mind that during the reconstruction of Collyweston Margaret included among the buildings a counting house and even a jail. At her own charge, to assist her, she 'provided men learned for the same purpose evenly and indifferently to hear all causes, and administer right and justice to every party'.[27] Thus, with the support of her own council, Margaret was authorized to settle disputes and administer justice on the king's behalf; in so doing, she 'broke new ground', for never before had a woman been entrusted with such a role.[28] She heard numerous depositions, including one against John Stokesley, who was accused of several offences, including the baptism of a cat and another concerning slanders made about her son's dubious ancestry, which emanated from a Colchester tavern.[29] Other petitioners, such as Isabel El-mes, who wrote to 'the right excellent princess and her good lady's grace the king's mother' to ask for help in settling a property dispute, begged for her intervention.[30] Margaret's involvement in all of these cases shows the level of power and influence she wielded in her son's name. None recognised this better than Margaret. More significantly, such a prominent role was completely unprecedented and therefore extraordinary; never before had a queen, let alone a queen mother, been so active in the administration of justice in the king's name. Margaret, with her son's support and approval, had carved a new post for herself within the Tudor regime.

Margaret's letters during this period reveal another, more assertive side of her character. They differ entirely in tone from those she wrote to her son and demonstrate the commanding approach that she took to business matters. This can be seen in a letter written to the mayor of Coventry, headed authoritatively 'By the King's Mother'. The letter was in response to a complaint made by a burgher of the city named Owen, and Margaret commanded the mayor 'to call afore you the parties comprised in the same complaint'. She encouraged him to resolve the issue 'so as no complaint be made unto us hereafter in that behalf. Endeavouring you thus to do, as ye tend the King's pleasure and ours, and the due ministration of justice'.[31]

Margaret attended to business with tenacity; she was vigilant and could even be ruthless. Indeed, as she had demonstrated when pursuing her son's title and lands when they were stripped from him, if she believed something to be right, she pursued it with dogged conviction. And this commitment to what Margaret saw as justice appears to have characterized her role as law enforcer. Indeed, Fisher commented, 'It is not unknown how studiously she procured justice to be administered by a long season so long as she was suffered'.[32] She did not shirk from taking action, and though Fisher claimed that Margaret 'was not vengeful, or cruel, but ready anon to forget and to forgive injuries done unto her', she was eager to ensure that justice was done.[33]

AS THE AUTUMN OF 1501 approached, anticipation of the arrival of Prince Arthur's bride began to build. In September Arthur had turned fourteen, and having been born in December 1485, Katherine of Aragon was just under a year older. Lavish preparations for the coming wedding had begun to take shape the previous year, and the king had spent the enormous sum of £14,000 (£9,323,400) on jewels for the occasion.[34] The marriage of an heir to the throne during his father's lifetime had not occurred in England since 1361, when the Black Prince married Joan of Kent.[35] In recent years Margaret had spent much of her time at Collyweston, but there was no question of her avoiding the capital on this momentous occasion—the greatest of Henry VII's reign: Margaret was determined to play her part.

CHAPTER 21

RIGHT ROYAL AND
PLEASANTLY BESEEN

In an indication of its importance, Margaret recorded Katherine of Aragon's journey to England in her Book of Hours. The Spanish princess had set sail from the port of Corunna on 17 August, but storms had driven the ships back to Spain and they were forced to wait for better conditions. At last, on 2 October Margaret was able to note the princess's arrival at Plymouth, where 'a large retinue of Spanish nobles' accompanied her.[1] Katherine soon began making her way towards the capital, drawing awe from the English people along the way. By 4 November, she had made it as far as Dogmersfield in Hampshire, and it was there that she would meet her future husband and father-in-law for the first time. Having spent years negotiating for the Spanish princess's hand, Henry VII was naturally eager to meet the girl who would be England's future queen. Upon his arrival, however, the king was told that Katherine 'was in her rest', but he responded that he would see the princess even 'if she were in her bed'.[2] He was not to be disappointed, for in spite of the protests of the Spanish ambassador, when Katherine appeared, 'the most goodly words' were exchanged 'to as great joy and gladness' of all those present.[3] Katherine's ladies and minstrels soon joined them, and 'with right goodly behaviour and manner they solaced themselves with the disports of dancing', to everyone's great delight.[4]

Arriving back at Richmond on 9 November, the king was reunited with his wife, to whom he 'made privy of the acts and demeanour between himself, the Prince, and the Princess, and how he liked her person and behaviour'.[5] Margaret may also have been present, but if not, she would soon have learned of her son's satisfaction.

Three days later, Katherine arrived in London, having journeyed through Hampshire and Surrey to the capital. To ensure she received a welcome fit for a future queen, the city had spent a fortune on preparations, and the splendour of the festivities delighted those who observed them. A number of elaborate pageants were staged across the city, and among the imagery that featured were red dragons, red roses, and 'a white hart with a crown of gold about his neck and a chain of golden links coming from the crown'.[6] No contemporary was left in any doubt of the wealth and prestige of Henry VII's dynasty. The royal family had also gathered in Cheapside to witness the pageants—albeit in secret: the king and Prince Arthur, who were joined by Oxford, Stanley and others, watched from one chamber, while Margaret, the queen, Margaret's two granddaughters and 'many other ladies of the land' watched from another.[7] Meanwhile, Margaret's youngest grandson, Prince Henry, had joined Katherine as she rode through the city 'upon a great mule richly trapped after the manner of Spain'.[8] She was gorgeously bedecked in 'rich apparel on her body after the manner of her country', with her fair auburn hair hanging about her shoulders, topped by a hat.[9] The crowds cheered endlessly as she passed.

Following Katherine's joyous entry into London, she was taken to meet the king and queen at Baynard's Castle. This was the first occasion on which Elizabeth met her future daughter-in-law, and Katherine took great pleasure in the 'goodly visiting and sight of the Queen' and the king.[10] She in turn was welcomed into the folds of her new family 'with pleasure and goodly communication, dancing, and disports'.[11] Margaret's name is not mentioned, so it is unclear whether she met Katherine at this time. If she did not, then she would not have long to wait.

The magnificent Old St Paul's Cathedral in the eastern part of the capital had been chosen as the setting for Arthur and Katherine's wedding on 14 November. In preparation for the royal nuptials, the cathedral had been sumptuously decked out with 'plates, jewels, and relics of wonderful riches and preciousness'.[12] No expense had been spared for the celebrations of this momentous occasion that signalled the cementing of a powerful alliance between England and Spain.

Margaret watched the nuptials privately. Arthur and Katherine were to be the centre of attention, and as Katherine arrived at the cathedral, her white satin train borne by the queen's sister Cecily, 'after her followed a hundred ladies and gentlewomen', all sumptuously dressed.[13] A London chronicler recorded that 'wonderful it was to behold the riches of garments and chains of gold, that that day were worn' by the lords in attendance.[14] Arthur was magnificently adorned in white satin, and the young couple were married by Henry Deane, Archbishop of Canterbury, 'where was present in secret manner the King, the Queen, my Lady the King's Mother', all of whom 'stood secretly in a closet'.[15] The royal minstrels 'struck up and made such melodies and mirth as they could, the which was comfortable and joyful to hear'.[16] For Henry VII and Margaret, the marriage was the culmination of all their hopes, for a union with the powerful Spanish sovereigns signified an acknowledgement of the legitimacy—and continuity—of the Tudor dynasty. So happy was Margaret at this moment, Fisher later recalled, she wept with joy 'at the great triumph'.[17]

As Katherine and Arthur were put to bed that evening, there followed one of the most controversial wedding nights in English history. According to later depositions, the following morning it was Margaret's nephew, Maurice St John—a member of the prince's household—who asked his master how he had fared, to which Arthur replied that he had that night been in the midst of Spain. By contrast, Katherine would later swear that her marriage was never consummated. But that was all in the future, and in November 1501, the mood was nothing other than celebratory.

Margaret's feelings about her grandson's bride are unclear, though it is wholly possible that she felt the same warmth and enthusiasm towards Katherine as her son did—she would later take care to bequeath her a magnificent girdle and a gold cup that was bettered only by those she left to her grandson Henry. Several members of Margaret's household would later transfer their service to Katherine's household, including Margaret's nephew John St John. Margaret would also undoubtedly have been impressed by Katherine's education: the Spanish princess was skilled at both music and dancing and would later earn praise from Erasmus for her scholarly abilities. Margaret had certainly shown a great interest in Katherine, demonstrated in her earlier requests—coupled with those of Elizabeth of York—to ensure that the Spanish princess was adequately prepared for her arrival in her new land. Such concern was typical of Margaret, and there is every reason to believe that she was as eager as the rest of her family to make the princess feel welcome. She also recognised Katherine's prestigious connections and the benefits that this brought to her own family, and she would have seen her as the means through which the next generation of the Tudor dynasty would stem. It was to Katherine whom all of England—including Margaret—looked for the arrival of a male heir, in the same manner as they had once done to Elizabeth of York. Elizabeth had amply succeeded in fulfilling this role, and Margaret would have been both hopeful and expectant that Katherine would do the same.

Arthur and Katherine's wedding celebrations were set to continue for several days, and Margaret had decided earlier that she should take up the baton. Coldharbour was to be the setting for the next stage of the revelries, and Margaret had employed William Bolton to carry out improvements in preparation. She was pleased with the new ovens, the glazing, the painting of the stairs and the improvements to the gardens. A coppersmith by the name of William Horn had been paid for making two dozen portcullis badges; how they were used is unclear, but Margaret was evidently eager to take the opportunity to proclaim her Beaufort origins to the Spanish princess. She had even given orders for the 'making and writing of a play'.[18]

Additionally, many costly materials had been purchased, doubtless in an attempt to show Coldharbour at its best.

The day after the wedding, 'the reverent and most worshipful my Lady the King's Mother' hosted a dinner 'at her lodging within the City of London called the Coldharbour, for whom that place was right royal and pleasantly beseen and addressed, enhanged with rich cloth of Arras, and in the hall a goodly cupboard made and erect with great plentieth of plate, both silver and gilt'.[19] Margaret had ordered her cooks to prepare a sumptuous feast, and those in attendance were served with 'divers wines abundant and plenteous'.[20] Numerous entertainments had also been arranged, including music from the queen's minstrels, those of the Earl of Northumberland and the prince's trumpeters, as well as a juggler, named Matthew, who was in the employ of the Earl of Oxford. Katherine could not fail to have been impressed with her host's hospitality. But that was only the beginning, and that same evening the party left Coldharbour and travelled the short distance to Derby House, where Margaret's husband hosted a supper. There, they celebrated with 'right worshipful cheer and parleyance as my Lady the King's Mother did unto them at their dinner'.[21] Margaret had played her part to perfection.

Other celebrations ensued, including a mass at St Paul's for which Margaret was plausibly present—her husband certainly was. An elaborate joust was staged at Westminster, at which Margaret joined the queen, Katherine and her granddaughters, 'with many other ladies and gentlewomen of honour'.[22] There was a great feast at Westminster Hall, which was 'furnished and filled with as goodly and rich treasure of plate as ever could lightly be seen'.[23] This was followed by 'a good disguising', which Margaret doubtless enjoyed.[24] It was her youngest grandson, Prince Henry, who stole the show, for while dancing with his sister Margaret, 'perceiving himself to be encumbered with his clothes, suddenly cast off his gown and danced in his jacket' with his sister.[25] This was so joyous that 'it was to the King and Queen right great and singular pleasure', and Margaret—always eager to embrace such merriment—probably felt the same warmth.[26]

When the festivities finally ceased, the serious business of Arthur's marriage began. Princess Katherine was afforded no time to get to know her new family, for in December the newlyweds bade farewell. Leaving London behind, they travelled more than a hundred and fifty miles to Shropshire, there to take up residence at Ludlow Castle. Arriving in mid-December during a bitter winter, Arthur and Katherine set up court and prepared to celebrate Christmas.

AS NEW YEAR PASSED AND 1502 dawned, Margaret had much to occupy her time. With the marital prospects of his eldest son now settled, Henry VII immediately turned his attention to his eldest daughter. In January, twelve-year-old Princess Margaret was betrothed to James IV of Scotland, the ceremony taking place in the queen's chamber at Richmond. Talks for the marriage had been staged over the course of several years, and in 1498 Henry had expressed his concerns that his daughter was 'so delicate and weak that she must be married much later than other young ladies'.[27] It seems that the princess was, like her grandmother, a slow developer. In echoes of her own experience, Margaret had doubtless influenced Henry, for he continued, 'the Queen and my mother are very much against this marriage. They say if the marriage were concluded we should be obliged to send the Princess directly to Scotland, in which case they fear the King of Scots would not wait'.[28] In their concern for the princess's welfare, Margaret had combined forces with the queen, and Henry had evidently paid them heed. They were probably also aware that James IV, although 'as handsome in complexion and shape as a man can be', was a notorious womanizer with a string of mistresses and bastards.[29]

But at the beginning of 1502, Princess Margaret was three years older, and though her grandmother is not listed among those who attended the betrothal, the level of ceremony would surely have gratified her. The celebrations lasted several days, and immediately the young Queen of Scots was treated with an increased level of ceremony. Her parents, and probably Margaret, too, took a great deal of care in preparing the youngster for her new role, and though she was not to leave for Scotland immediately, costly new garments for her wedding trousseau were ordered. In 1503 Henry would outlay the exorbitant sum of £16,000 (£10,655,300) for jewels 'for the Queen of Scots as for the King's own use'.[30]

Margaret's absence from her granddaughter's betrothal ceremony can be easily explained, for at this time she had business of her own. Fisher later claimed that Margaret 'most hated' avarice, yet she was never afraid to pursue what she believed to be rightfully hers.[31] At the beginning of 1502, following in her son's footsteps, Margaret made her own visit to Calais.[32] This was rather remarkable given that she was fifty-seven—old by contemporary standards—and the journey cannot have been comfortable. Nevertheless, she had a very important matter of business to attend to, chiefly pursuing a debt that had been owed to her family since before her birth and which she was determined to settle.[33] The debt had been inherited by the French king Louis XII, and with her strong sense of obligation, Margaret was determined to obtain what was owed.[34]

It was probably three years earlier, on 14 January 1499, that Margaret had written to her son in a tone of optimism about the affair:

My own sweet and most dear King and all my worldly joy, in as humble manner as I can think I recommend me to your Grace, and most heartily beseech our lord to bless you; and my good heart where that you say that the French King hath at this time given me courteous answer and written letters of favour to his court of Parliament for the treve expedition of my matter which so long hath hanged, the which I well know he doth especially for your sake.[35]

She continued by expressing her thanks to Morton, who had evidently been of assistance, and by assuring Henry that if she were successful in obtaining the debt, it would be his. In a final demonstration of her maternal affection, she ended her letter with a blessing: 'Our Lord give you as long good life, health, and joy, as your most noble heart can desire, with as hearty blessings as our Lord hath given me power to give you. At Colly-weston, the 14th day of January, by your faithful true bedwoman, and humble mother, Margaret R'.[36]

By 1502, however, the issue continued to drag on. That Margaret was prepared to travel to France in an attempt to settle the matter personally is a testament to how seriously she took it, but the debt, despite Margaret's best efforts, was never fully repaid during her lifetime. In 1504, she formally handed it over to her son, for which, in his own words, 'in my most hearty and humble wise I thank you'.[37]

MARGARET WAS BACK IN ENGLAND when the royal family were struck with a devastating tragedy. In April, news reached London that an attack of a fearful sickness had descended on Ludlow, with which the Princess of Wales may have been infected. Katherine would recover from her illness, but for her groom it was to prove fatal. Arthur's health appears to have been fragile for some time, and though it has been suggested that he was infected with the sweating sickness, it is more probable that he had contracted a form of consumption (tuberculosis).[38] On 2 April—less than five months after his marriage—Margaret recorded the death of her beloved grandson in her Book of Hours.[39] There is no record of whether she was with the court at Greenwich when a messenger arrived bearing letters from Sir Richard Pole, the prince's chamberlain. It was left to the king's chaplain to deliver the crushing news that Henry's 'dearest son was departed to God'.[40]

The effect was devastating. Though the king and queen attempted to comfort each other, their grief was profound. They now had just one son on whom the future of their dynasty lay. In spite of her heartbreak, the queen tried to remind her husband that 'my Lady his mother had never no more children but him only, and that God by His Grace had ever preserved him and brought him where that he was'.[41] She assured him that they still had a 'fair, goodly and towardly young Prince and two fair Princesses, and over that, God is where He was, and we both young enough'.[42] Though

Margaret's reaction to Arthur's death is not recorded, the behaviour of his parents allows us to surmise some of the grief she felt. Arthur was not the first of his siblings to succumb to death, but he was the one upon whom the greatest emphasis had been placed.

At Ludlow the prince's body had lain in state in his chamber, 'under a table covered with rich cloth of gold, having a rich cross over him', but on the king's orders the funeral cortège then made its way to Worcester.[43] Among those in attendance were Arthur's faithful servants, Sir Richard Pole and Maurice St John, who had begun his career as a member of Henry VII's bodyguard. The heartbroken king paid £666 16d (£444,000) for the prince's burial in Worcester Cathedral, where his tomb can still be seen.[44] His widow, meanwhile, returned to London.

Henry VII was painfully aware that only one life now stood between the future succession of his family and disaster. Within weeks of Arthur's death, the queen was pregnant. As Margaret grieved for her grandson, it remained to be seen whether the arrival of her unborn grandchild could help to heal the wounds that Arthur's death had inflicted. Suddenly, the Tudor dynasty, whose future had looked so bright in September 1486, now hung by a thread.

CHAPTER 22

IN EVERYTHING
LIKE TO THE QUEEN

As the queen's pregnancy progressed, it became clear that her health was delicate. It had been three years since she had borne a child, and Margaret may therefore have been concerned when Elizabeth began a progress that took her far from home. One of her stops was at Raglan Castle, where Margaret's son had spent some of his childhood and where her host was Margaret's cousin Sir Charles Somerset.[1] She returned to London in time for Christmas, which the court spent at Richmond. At New Year, Elizabeth rewarded Margaret's servant Richard Bygot for conveying her mother-in-law's gift—perhaps in an indication of Elizabeth's affection and gratitude towards her mother-in-law, the reward he received was larger than that of any other servant.[2] Towards the end of January 1503, Elizabeth prepared for her confinement.[3]

The queen took to her chamber in the royal apartments at the Tower. With her favourite midwife, Alice Massy, in attendance, it was there that on 2 February, Candlemas Day, she gave birth prematurely. Her child was not the hoped-for son who would have strengthened the male continuance of her dynasty, but a daughter, named Katherine. Furthermore, it quickly became clear that all was not well, as the queen's health began to decline at an alarming rate. Puerperal fever may have set in, but iron-deficiency anaemia has also been suggested.[4] Whatever the cause, on 11 February— her thirty-seventh birthday—Elizabeth of York died.[5] Seven days later, on 18 February, baby Katherine followed her mother to the grave. She was buried in Westminster Abbey. It was a tragic outcome and the culmination of a terrible two years for Margaret's family. Her three surviving young grandchildren were motherless, with only their grieving father and grandmother to turn to for comfort. Margaret was now the royal children's closest female relative. It was on the orders of 'the right high, mighty and excellent Princess Margaret, Countess of Richmond' that a set of ordinances for the court mourning of ladies was drawn up, almost certainly as a result of the queen's death.[6] These stipulated precisely the apparel that all rank of women were expected to wear following a death; interestingly, the king's mother was 'to wear in everything like to the queen', which consisted of an elaborate mantle and train.[7]

On 23 February, the queen was given a stately funeral at Westminster Abbey, the ceremony being performed by Richard FitzJames, Bishop of London. No expense was spared, and Elizabeth's funeral effigy was bedecked in the full regalia of a queen of England.[8] She was laid to rest in the abbey, where a splendid memorial would later be erected to her memory, although neither Margaret nor her son would live to see it. In spite of his grief, Henry VII considered remarrying, with his widowed daughter-in-law Katherine of Aragon and Joanna of Naples—the niece of Ferdinand of Aragon—put forward as candidates. Yet neither of these materialized, and Henry remained a widower for the rest of his life, leaving Margaret the most powerful and influential woman in the kingdom. She was believed by her contemporaries to wield power comparable to that of many of the men in the king's inner circle. This may very well have been the case, for given the constancy with which Margaret sent messengers to her son and received them in return, it is difficult to believe that they would not have consulted each other about matters of business and affairs of state, even if only on occasion.

Following the death of the queen, Margaret seems to have assumed a greater degree of responsibility for the care of her grandchildren, although there is no evidence that she played a role in their education.[9] She was certainly eager to ensure that a high level of ceremony was employed for the departure of her granddaughter the Queen of Scots in the summer, and extra plate was brought from Coldharbour for the occasion. On 27 June, Henry VII and his daughter left Richmond and London behind. It would transpire to be a forty-one-day progress for the young queen as she journeyed north to meet her new husband, James IV of Scotland. The first stop on their travels was to 'a place of the right high and mighty Princess my Lady his Mother', with Margaret noting carefully in her Book of Hours that on 5 July 'King Henry the VIIth and the Queen of Scots his daughter, with a great multitude of lords and other noble persons, came to Collyweston unto my lady his mother'.[10] This was intended to be a huge progress—one of the most important of Henry's reign. According to the *Great Chronicle of London*, when the king and his daughter arrived at Collyweston, having been escorted by John St John, 'they were joyously received'.[11] The importance Margaret placed on the visit can be seen in the preparations and building work that she had ordered, which included the glazing of the windows, constructing new chimneys, putting lead on the roof and borrowing hangings from Fox, now Bishop of Winchester.[12] It was the need to ensure that it provided a fitting setting for the visit that, as Jones asserted, 'marked the transformation of Collyweston into a palace'.[13] In her usual style, Margaret was the perfect hostess.

The royal visit to Collyweston was full of the splendours and entertainments that would be expected, but it was over all too soon. Having 'tarried a certain season after their pleasure, the which season expired', it was time for the young Queen of Scots to leave her family.[14] Margaret's granddaughter, who was 'richly dressed', bade a tender farewell to her father and grandmother.[15] As she rode out of Collyweston 'with an honourable company of lords and ladies' that had been appointed by her father, the young queen proceeded to make her stately journey towards her new land.[16] She was formally married to James IV on 8 August in the chapel at the Palace of Holyroodhouse. Margaret would never see her granddaughter again, but her accounts, particularly in the months following the princess's departure, show that Margaret and her granddaughter exchanged messages. Margaret would have been delighted when the Queen of Scots gave birth to her first child, Margaret's first great-grandchild—a son named James—on 21 February 1507. Tragically, the boy died the following February, by which time his mother was once again pregnant.[17]

Margaret had formerly expressed her disapproval and concern at her granddaughter being married too young, but as the Queen of Scots was approaching her fourteenth birthday—generally considered to be a more acceptable age for consummation—there is no evidence that she was unhappy at the king's decision to send his daughter north at this time. Whereas Margaret had claimed for herself a role of great independence, she still recognised the advantages of marriage and took a proactive role in arranging matches for her family and friends. Given her influence and proximity to the king, having some kind of connection with Margaret was believed to be advantageous by many of her contemporaries.[18] She was therefore granted the wardship of many noble children throughout the course of Henry VII's reign and saw to it that these children were all raised well and often married well.[19]

Just days after her granddaughter's departure from Collyweston, on 16 July Margaret hosted the wedding of her niece, Elizabeth St John. The king was evidently fond of Elizabeth, for it was he who paid for the festivities. Yet, there is no doubt that it was Margaret who was the instigator of the marriage, assuredly in an attempt to ensure the future security of another member of her family. The groom was Gerald Fitzgerald, the heir of the Earl of Kildare, who had been raised 'in his youth and tender age' at the king's court.[20] By contrast, Elizabeth had been raised in Margaret's household along with her sister Eleanor, which would have been viewed as a significant honour by their parents.

WITHIN A SHORT SPACE OF time, by the end of 1503 Margaret's family had become considerably smaller: with her eldest granddaughter gone, she now had just one grandson and one granddaughter left to occupy her time. Though she remained in contact with them, Margaret's appearances in London and at court grew increasingly less frequent.[21] Instead, much of her time was spent at Collyweston; although she was sixty years old, her energy seemed boundless. She continued to work tirelessly on her son's behalf, displaying no signs of slowing down.

She was left greatly saddened when, on 5 August, her trusted servant Reginald Bray died. Bray had been a constant presence in Margaret's life for the past four decades: she had first met him during her marriage to Henry Stafford, and he had offered her years of faithful and devoted service, risking his life during the reign of Richard III while in her service. Bray had been more than a faithful servant; he had become a dear friend whom Margaret had relied upon. His death signified a further broken link with Margaret's past and came amid a painful period of loss. Though Bray had been married, he did not leave behind any children. At his request, he was buried at St George's Chapel, Windsor, in whose construction he had assisted.[22] This explains why his arms can be seen scattered at various points on the chapel's roof; in his lifetime he had contributed significant sums towards the building of the chapel, which is surely his greatest legacy.

The opening years of the 1500s were a time of great upheaval for Margaret. On 29 July 1504, her husband Stanley died. Margaret was not with him when he breathed his last, though at New Year they had exchanged gifts in the same manner as they had always done.[23] Nevertheless, she is likely to have been saddened by his death. Though their marriage had not been based on love, it had been mutually advantageous and friendly. When the news of Stanley's death reached Collyweston, Margaret and her household assumed full mourning. In his will, of which his sons were the executors, Stanley left instructions that 'my Lady my wife shall peaceably enjoy all the lordships, manors, etc, assigned for her jointure'.[24] He left Margaret no personal bequests, but neither did he leave any to his other family members, perhaps an indication that the writing of the will was undertaken in haste. However, he was also aware that Margaret's personal wealth meant that she lacked for nothing and that she was able to provide for herself. Notwithstanding this, he did leave his stepson the king a gold cup, entreating him to be good to his family and to ensure that Stanley's final wishes were carried out, for 'I have been a true servant'.[25] Stanley left instructions that he was to be buried in the church of his ancestors at Burscough near Lathom. It was where 'the bodies of my father, mother, and other of my ancestors lay buried, having provided a tomb to be there placed, with the personages of myself and both my wives'.[26] Despite his hopes, Margaret never joined him there.

There was no question of Margaret remarrying—it was neither desirable nor necessary—and instead she chose to renew her vow of chastity, promising Bishop Fisher 'with full purpose and good deliberation for the weal of my sinful soul with all my heart promise from henceforth the chastity of my body, that is never to use my body having actual knowledge of man after the common usage in matrimony'.[27] As a result of Stanley's death, which freed up her jointure and parts of her inheritance, Margaret's landed income was boosted by £3,000 (£2,000,000) a year, and it was not long before she put the extra money to good use.

FOLLOWING THE DEATH OF PRINCE Arthur in 1502, his widow Katherine of Aragon had remained in England. Her parents had been vehemently opposed to Henry VII's brief consideration of marrying her himself, with Queen Isabella describing the notion as 'a very evil thing'.[28] Instead, plans were put in place for her marriage to Margaret's youngest grandson—the king's only surviving male heir—Prince Henry. On 23 June 1503, a formal marriage treaty was drawn up and ratified by Katherine's parents. Because the prince was just short of his eleventh birthday at this time, plans for the wedding were put on hold, and in early 1504 Henry was formally created Prince of Wales.

But everything changed following the death of Katherine's mother on 26 November 1504. Katherine was rendered significantly less valuable due to complications in the Spanish succession, which meant that her father was now King of Aragon only rather than wielding power over Castile in the same manner as he had done during his wife's lifetime, and Henry VII therefore dithered over what to do with her. She took up residence at Durham House on the Strand, but at the instigation of the king, on 27 June 1505 Prince Henry repudiated their betrothal in front of Bishop Fox and others. Katherine had no idea, and within months the king stopped paying her pitiful allowance. This forced her to return to the court at Richmond, but her circumstances remained dire: she was unable to pay her servants and even resorted to pawning some of her jewels and plate in order to buy food. It was a far cry from the welcome she had been afforded in 1501.

Margaret's feelings about her son's cruel treatment of Katherine are unknown. Her accounts offer little insight into her relationship with the Spanish princess. She had once taken as great an interest in the young woman's arrival as had the king, but following Prince Arthur's death, it seems unlikely that she had much to do with Katherine. For one thing, the language barrier between the two women presented a major problem. Still, if contemporary reports of Margaret's kind nature are to be believed, she must have felt some sympathy for Katherine's plight. At this time, however, Margaret's mind was very much occupied with her own affairs, for she was busy embarking upon an enterprise of the utmost importance: her legacy.

CHAPTER 23

NOS MARGARETA

With its close associations with her family, it was little wonder that the town of Wimborne had always held a special place in Margaret's heart. It was there that she chose to found a grammar school, complete with schoolmaster, a decision that was only natural given her commitment to scholarship. And what better place to endow a school than in the town where her parents lay entombed? By reason of the death of Elizabeth of York and the departure of Margaret, Queen of Scots, the demands of her family had lessened, ensuring that Margaret had an opportunity to pursue this interest. Margaret was part of a circle that had strong ties to both Oxford and Cambridge. Reginald Bray, her former servant, had been appointed Steward of the University of Oxford in 1496.

In 1494 the court was at Greenwich when Margaret first met John Fisher, from whom many of the details of her life are sourced. Born in 1469, Fisher was more than twenty years Margaret's junior and hailed from Beverley in Yorkshire. Though he was the son of a merchant, in 1484 he was fortunate enough to attain a place at Cambridge, where his mother supported him.[1] Fisher was exceptionally intelligent and excelled at university, earning not only a degree but also a master's. Upon completing his studies, he took orders to become a priest and returned to the north, where he took up a post as the vicar of Northallerton. It was not long, though, before he returned to Cambridge, for in 1494 he was offered a position as senior proctor of Cambridge. It was at this time that he came to the notice of the king's mother, for

> at length his name grew so famous, that, passing the bonds of the university, it spread over all the realm, in so much as the noble and virtuous lady, Margaret, Countess of Richmond and Derby, mother to the wise and sage prince King Henry the VIIth, hearing of his great virtue and learning, ceased not till she had procured him out of the university to her service.[2]

So impressed was she with Fisher that Margaret determined he should join her household, and after just a few years in his role, he became her chaplain and confessor. More importantly, though, the two immediately struck up a friendship, and Margaret seems to have spoken highly of him to her son, for in 1504 he was created Bishop of Rochester. Fisher's position in Margaret's household ensured that he was perfectly placed to encourage his mistress's educational patronage.

Margaret was by no means the first high-ranking lady to take an interest in this quarter, for the precedent had long since been set. In 1341, for example, Robert de Eglesfield had founded Queen's College, Oxford, in honour of Margaret's ancestress, Queen Philippa.[3] Similarly, six years later, Marie de St Pol, the widowed Countess of Pembroke, had been granted a licence to found Pembroke College, Cambridge.[4] Margaret's family also had strong ties to Cambridge. Her kinsman, Henry VI, had been responsible for the patronage of many educational institutes, including Eton College close to Windsor Castle in 1440, King's College, Cambridge, and All Souls College, Oxford. He had also taken an interest in God's House, another Cambridge foundation begun by the priest William Byngham in 1439. Henry had been passionate about his scholarly pursuits, and it was an interest that his wife, Queen Margaret, shared. It was she who founded Queen's College, Cambridge, in 1448, and sent her chamberlain, Sir John Wenlock, to lay the foundation stone on her behalf.[5] Though Margaret herself was just a small child at this time, she is likely to have admired the examples set by the king and queen. Elizabeth Wydeville had also shown an interest in Queen's College, and it was refounded under her patronage in 1465. In turn, Anne Neville became the college's patron, though Elizabeth of York did not follow suit. Margaret had visited Cambridge before, and in September 1489 refreshments, including a roast buck and pike, had been prepared for her.[6] On 1 and 2 September 1498, she had accompanied the king and queen during their visit to the city.

At the end of 1504, the king granted Margaret a licence to 'found a perpetual chantry of one preacher of God's Word, to be called the chantry in honour of the name of Jesus and of the Annunciation of St Mary the Virgin, in the University of Cambridge'.[7] But Margaret had greater plans for educational patronage. She was eager not only to emulate the example of those before her but also to surpass it. In so doing she accentuated her own power in another, more tangible way that few before her had attempted, using her passion for education and scholarship and her love of books as the catalyst. She succeeded, earning herself a reputation as a great benefactress and philanthropist whose legacy continues to educate scholars today.

Margaret originally planned to split her patronage between Oxford and Cambridge; on 1 March 1497, the king had granted her a licence to 'found a perpetual lectureship of sacred theology' in both universities.[8] Both were to be called 'the lectureship of Margaret, mother of King Henry VII'.[9] In grateful thanks, Oxford had written to express their gratitude: 'Those most respected kings, prelates, and generals, and men of almost every rank of society have been solicitous for our welfare and the progress of education; but it has remained for one princess, of rank most exalted and of character divine, to do that which none have done before'.[10]

Although, with Fisher's encouragement, Margaret directed most of her energies towards Cambridge, she nevertheless maintained a good relationship with Oxford and helped them when she was able. Three of her letters to the university survive—two of which were written from Buckden in the summer of 1500—and her goodwill is evident. By the same token, when it suited her to do so, she was prepared to ask the university to fulfil her requests, on one occasion asking them to find a position for a man recommended to her by Richard FitzJames. Given its proximity to Collyweston, however, Cambridge suited Margaret, and her representatives were also regular visitors to the city. Following the death of Elizabeth of York, Margaret's patronage began with Queen's College, but she also took an interest in Jesus College, which had been founded by Bishop John Alcock, the former tutor of Edward V, in 1496. In May 1503 she gave £26 towards the building work.[11] This was not enough for Margaret, and it was not long before she turned her attentions towards creating her own foundations. With Fisher's encouragement, Margaret cast her eye on God's House, which had been founded in 1439 by William Byngham but which was greatly impoverished. Henry VI had also shown an interest in God's House, and this unquestionably had occurred to Margaret. On 1 May 1505, she was granted a license to expand and rename Christ's College.[12] In 1508 Pope Julius II issued a bull confirming its foundation. The bull survives in the National Archives, beautifully decorated with Margaret's arms, the arms of England and the Tudor rose in pen and ink.[13] Christ's was fully established at the time of Margaret's death.

Modern visitors to Christ's College are left in no doubt as to who was responsible for its establishment, for Margaret's coat of arms displaying the mythical yales—adopted by Margaret after 1485—and the Beaufort portcullis proudly adorn the gatehouse underneath a statue of the college's patroness. Much evidence of Margaret's involvement at Christ's College can still be seen, including the window on the north wall of the chapel and the Beaufort arms and motto *Souvent me Souvient* (I often remember) above the entrance to the master's lodge. The glass, probably dating from 1510, shows her wearing a coronet and kneeling at a desk in front of a Book of Hours. Her symbols are stamped all over the college, and when, from 1505, she began to visit the city on a regular basis, a suite of four rooms for her use was reserved there. These can still be seen, exquisitely decorated with the badges of both the Beauforts and the Tudors. One of the rooms contained an oratory that overlooked the chapel, where Margaret could pray in private. She would later bequeath the college 'the Beaufort Cup'—a silver-gilt cup dating from 1507, exquisitely engraved with roses and marguerites, portcullises and fleurs-de-lis, proudly displaying Margaret's heritage.[14] Neither was this the only piece she left to the college, for she also bequeathed to it much of her plate and library. Payments for the building of the college, overseen by James Morice, clerk of the works at Collyweston, litter her accounts. On one occasion, she even paid for 'the making of a seal for Christ's College'.[15] To support her new foundation, on 14 July 1507 the king granted Margaret the abbey of St Mary de Pratis in Norfolk, with a licence to pass it over to the master of Christ's, 'first begun by Henry VI and by her increased, finished and established'.[16]

For both the city of Cambridge and the university, Margaret's patronage was of crucial importance, creating public awareness. When she arrived in the city in 1505, she was greeted with almost royal ceremony. The bells of the city churches were rung out in celebration. Margaret was eager to show that the Tudors were avid supporters of the city's educational foundations, and her arrival amid such pomp served to underline their presence and therefore her patronage. The following year, the king visited, joined by his mother, and through Fisher's persuasions he donated money towards the completion of King's College Chapel; the chest in which the money was sent can still be seen in the chapel today. Though the work would not be complete by the time of his death, the chapel is full of the symbols of the Tudor dynasty.

Margaret was eager for as many people as possible to be given access to her foundation, but she also expected her scholars to work hard. It was with this in mind that a series of statutes were put in place to ensure the smooth running and good order of the college. On 3 October 1506, Margaret's statutes were delivered on her behalf to the master of Christ's. The statutes, written on vellum and decorated with Margaret's arms, the badges of the marguerite, rose and portcullis, open with the words *Nos Margareta* (We Margaret), written in Margaret's own hand.[17] They include stipulations concerning punishments and rewards for those who excelled, and from these we are able to glean further insights into what Margaret expected of a Cambridge scholar: First and foremost, they were to devote themselves to 'the worship of God, the increase of the faith, and probity of morals'.[18] When visiting Christ's on one occasion, peering outside, Margaret saw the dean punishing one of his students. Leaning out of the window, Margaret exclaimed: 'Lente, lente!' (Gently, gently!) Scholars were also expected to pray for her soul, and those of her son and grandchildren, in this world and the next. Prayers were also to be said for the souls of Edmund Tudor, 'my husband and father of the King my Son'; her parents; Elizabeth of York; Henry VI, his wife and son; William Byngham and John Broklee, another significant benefactor.[19]

Margaret treated her patronage with the utmost seriousness. Fisher would later record that she 'builded a college royal to ye honour of ye name of Christ Jesus, and left to her executors another to be built to maintain his faith and doctrine'.[20] In truth, in 1508 it was Fisher who informed Margaret of the poor state of the Hospital of St John the Evangelist in Cambridge. She, in turn, intended to transform the hospital into a college that would be able to support fifty scholars, but this was no easy feat. To refound a religious house as another institution, the permission of the Bishop of Ely was necessary. Given that the bishop was Margaret's stepson, James Stanley, this did not appear to present too great a problem, and he readily agreed. However, because of a series of delays, the matter would not be settled in Margaret's lifetime, and it was only after her death that St John's College was founded in 1511—pushed through by Fisher, who retained the utmost admiration for Margaret, as we have seen, extolling her many virtues and remaining loyal to her memory. The college later attracted the interest of Katherine of Aragon, who had perhaps been inspired by her grandmother-in-law. As at Christ's, symbols of Margaret's patronage can be seen all over St John's. Her passion and energy for her foundations is evident throughout her accounts, as is her generous nature. Margaret's determination to create a lasting legacy for herself as a patroness of learning was built into the very fabric of Cambridge—in the bricks and mortar of Christ's and St John's.

AFTER 1505, AS HER SON'S health began to decline, Margaret spent less time at Collyweston and more at Hatfield and Croydon, which lay closer to London.[21] She even borrowed the former Yorkist stronghold of Fotheringhay Castle for a brief time. The red-brick palace at Hatfield had been built by Morton in 1480 and was to become the home of the bishops of Ely: in 1505 Richard Redman held this office, and Margaret's stepson, James Stanley, later owned it upon his appointment in 1506. Croydon, built between 1443 and 1452, was a residence of the archbishops of Canterbury. There, Morton had also made various improvements, and much of his work can still be seen today. Following his death, the property came into the hands of William Warham, who became Archbishop of Canterbury in 1504.

Clearly, Margaret felt at home in properties that were owned by churchmen. During her residences in Hatfield and Croydon, Margaret took care to ensure that both houses were filled with all of her luxurious home comforts, and she paid for various improvements, including, at Croydon, glazing and the installation of plumbing. At Hatfield, items featuring her portcullis were scattered throughout the house, along with cloths of estate made of purple velvet, black velvet and cloth of gold. There was also a sumptuous crimson satin bed embroidered with gold portcullises and another of white damask.[22] Many pieces from her tapestry collection, depicting biblical and mythological scenes, such as the history of Paris and Helen of Troy, were on display. The closet next to her bedchamber contained powder boxes and a purse with cramp rings used for the relief of ailments, two pairs of gold spectacles, an image of the Salutation of our Lady, a pair of Spanish gloves and an indenture containing the details of Margaret's jointure from Stanley.[23] As was the case in all of her residences, life was conducted on a luxurious scale, and copious amounts of food and wine were ordered for consumption. It would not be long before

Margaret's skills as a hostess were called upon once more, and in a most important capacity.

In January 1506, Philip of Castile and his wife, Juana—sister of Katherine of Aragon—were sailing to Spain to take possession of the Castilian throne when they were caught in a storm.[24] They were shipwrecked off the Dorset coast, leaving them with no choice but to accept the hospitality of Henry VII. Henry's accounts note a reward given to a man who 'brought the King word of the landing of strangers in the West Country', and when he heard of Philip's arrival, Henry immediately gave orders for a lavish welcome to be prepared for his guests.[25] Henry saw this as an opportunity to negotiate a diplomatic advantage. In her usual desire to be kept abreast of affairs, Margaret had a report prepared describing Philip's reception.[26]

Philip began making his way towards Windsor, where the king rode to meet him a mile outside of the town. As the party approached the castle, Henry ensured that there was a due level of ceremony, and Margaret's step-grandson the Earl of Derby—who had succeeded her late husband to the title—carried the sword of state before the king. Henry's guest was then treated to an opulent display of hospitality, and the entertainments included a dance performed by Princess Mary and the court ladies. But the king was determined to turn the unexpected visit to his advantage. In July 1501, Edmund de la Pole, Earl of Suffolk—brother of the Earl of Lincoln who had been killed at Stoke in 1487—had left England with his younger brother, Richard.[27] The brothers had travelled to Flanders, where Suffolk had hoped to enlist the support of the Emperor Maximilian to make a bid for the throne. By 1506, Suffolk and Richard had become guests of Philip of Castile, and with the king now effectively his prisoner, Henry seized on an opportunity to neutralise Suffolk.

On 9 February, the two monarchs signed a treaty under the terms of which Philip agreed to extradite Suffolk and his brother back to England. Philip was also created a Knight of the Garter, for which the king paid a London goldsmith for providing an elaborate collar.[28] The following day, Philip's wife, Juana, who had travelled separately from her husband and at a slower pace, reached Windsor. Having achieved what he had sought, Henry could afford to be hospitable, and soon the party travelled to Richmond. This provided Henry with a chance to dazzle his guests with his splendid new palace, and every courtesy was extended to them. Determined not to exclude his mother from his show of magnificence and geniality, he issued orders for Margaret to arrange a sumptuous entertainment for his visitors at Croydon.[29]

In her usual consummate manner, Margaret prepared to play her role. In April she summoned her ten-year-old granddaughter Princess Mary—already growing into a beauty—from Richmond. When the royal party, which included her grandson Prince Henry, arrived, Margaret had prepared a lavish feast. The entertainment, though, was actually provided by Philip's entourage. A performance by his musicians ensued, perhaps in the magnificent Great Hall that had been built around 1452. There was also time for Margaret to present her grandson with a generous gift of a new horse, which had been dressed with a magnificent new saddle made of cloth of gold.

What Margaret's impressions of Philip and Juana were can only be imagined, but Katherine of Aragon would no doubt have appreciated the opportunity to be reunited with her sister. In a deliberate ploy to prevent her from complaining to Juana about her treatment, however, there was little time for this. Likewise, the visit of her sister and brother-in-law placed her future in jeopardy, for Philip discussed the possibility of several marriages with Henry. One of these was between Prince Henry—to whom Katherine had been betrothed in June 1503—and Philip's daughter, Eleanor, while another was suggested with Princess Mary and Philip's son, Charles.[30] This was probably an arrangement of which Margaret heartily approved, for marriage to the leading European dynasties provided an effective way of strengthening and securing the future of her own family.

Soon after their visit to Croydon, Philip and Juana sailed for Spain on 16 April. Philip had been true to his word, Suffolk having arrived back on English soil the previous month—an occasion Margaret noted in her

Book of Hours. He was immediately taken to the Tower, where—as with Simnel, Warbeck and Warwick before him—Henry intended to show him leniency. He was not executed but would remain locked up for the remainder of Henry's reign. Unfortunately for Suffolk, Margaret's grandson felt differently, and in 1513 the earl met his end on the executioner's block.[31] His younger brother, Richard, meanwhile, remained at large and was killed at the Battle of Pavia in 1525.[32]

IN THE LATER YEARS OF Henry's reign, as he grew older, he exhibited an increasing desire for privacy and began to seclude himself in his apartments as much as possible. He had grown increasingly suspicious, and with good cause, given that he had spent the entirety of his reign deflecting the threat posed by rival contenders to the throne. Both he and Margaret employed spies freely. The death of both Prince Arthur and Elizabeth of York in swift succession had served to highlight the fragility of the royal family, and Margaret was just as eager to secure the Tudor dynasty as Henry was. This was even more pertinent given that Henry's health was becoming progressively fragile.

At New Year 1507, Margaret became aware that her son's health was in decline; it had in fact been failing for some time. As early as 1504, Henry had complained to Margaret of problems with his eyesight, but early in 1507 he became so unwell that it was feared he would not live. For six days he was so sick with quinsy that he was unable to eat or drink. Margaret's role as a mother was always her foremost priority, and she immediately moved to Richmond to nurse him. There she ordered medical supplies and took charge of paying the king's servants—she even went as far as purchasing black materials in preparation for mourning. So she was greatly relieved, although perhaps somewhat surprised, when he rallied. By the autumn, indeed, so good was his recovery, Henry had resumed the pastimes of which he was so fond, including hunting.

Henry's recovery was only temporary, for by then he was suffering from what was probably consumption. In 1508 he fell sick once more, and at that time the emphasis was firmly on the next generation, in particular, Margaret's grandson Prince Henry, who had become the shining star of the Tudor court. In June 1507, the prince reached his sixteenth birthday, and that month Margaret watched proudly as he participated in his first joust. It was she who ordered his first saddle and harness to mark the occasion, and she was doubtless delighted—although anxious—to see him take such pleasure in the sport.[33] The following year she would also send him a gift after he had been 'running at the ring'.[34] Prince Henry brought a young and vibrant energy to the court of his ailing father and was well-liked by all. With the future of his dynasty hinging on the life of just one son, however, the king kept his son on a tight lead and in close proximity. This inevitably led to friction between father and son, who yearned to break free. He would not have long to wait.

By Christmas 1508, marriage negotiations appeared to be moving towards a happy conclusion. Though Philip of Castile had died in the autumn of 1506, months after his visit to England, negotiations for the marriage of his heir, Charles, to Princess Mary had continued.[35] On 17 December, the marriage by proxy was staged: from then on, Mary was to be addressed as the Princess of Castile.

In February 1509, while at Hanworth, the king once more lapsed into illness. Preparations were put in place for him to return to Richmond as swiftly as possible. Because his condition deteriorated quickly, word was sent to his mother at Coldharbour.[36] Margaret, herself in fragile health, once again rushed to Richmond to be by his side, arranging for her belongings, which included her favourite bed, to follow her. She may have been aware that the end was approaching, for the king was suffering from tuberculosis. The realization that her son was going to die before she did must have been difficult to bear. There was just thirteen years between them, but all of his life she had striven to protect him, supporting him in adversity and revelling later in his glory. She had missed out on most of his childhood and adolescence; now, for the second time, he was about to be taken from her—this time permanently. In a sermon preached after his death,

Fisher wrote of the piety that Henry displayed in his final days. Margaret, who would almost certainly have witnessed this firsthand, would have been proud and probably overwhelmed with emotion. As Fisher recalled at one point in the sermon, 'all that stood about him scarcely might contain them from tears and weeping'.

On 21 April, the king heard mass for the last time. Later that day, he slipped from life into death at the age of fifty-two. Margaret was left utterly devastated.

CHAPTER 24

A WOMAN MOST OUTSTANDING

By the end of March 1509, Henry had known that he was dying. While he was still able, the ailing king had dictated his final will, a characteristically detailed document. Unsurprisingly, Henry requested that he be laid to rest in the spectacular new Lady Chapel that he was building in Westminster Abbey. He wanted to be buried among his relatives and made particular reference to his royal grandmother, Katherine of Valois, who lay close to the Lady Chapel with Henry V. He left thorough instructions for the creation of his tomb, which he was to share with his deceased wife, Elizabeth of York. It was intended to be a celebration of the Tudor dynasty that they had created together, but it was not begun until 1512.

When it came to overseeing his wishes, there was one person Henry could be sure would fulfil all of his requests to the best of her ability. At the top of the king's list of executors was 'our dearest and most entirely beloved mother Margaret Countess of Richmond', who was to be assisted by the Archbishop of York, the Bishop of Winchester, John Fisher and many others.[1] One last time, Henry put his trust in Margaret, relying on her to honour his memory even after his death. It was a task that Margaret—as with everything relating to her son—would do her utmost to fulfil.

Henry VII's achievements, though often overlooked, are not to be underestimated. Through his marriage to Elizabeth of York, he largely succeeded in uniting a country that was torn and divided by war and faction. Together they had created a new dynasty, and England began to prosper.

The royal coffers were full, and at Henry's death a Venetian envoy reported that he had 'accumulated more gold than that possessed by all the other Christian kings'.² All of this passed into the hands of his heir, Margaret's grandson, who succeeded his father as Henry VIII. To organize matters and ensure his smooth succession, the late king's death was initially kept a secret. But there was little to fear. Henry VIII would become the most famous monarch of the Tudor dynasty, and he was from the start exceptionally popular. Vergil wrote that 'everybody loved him', and in appearance he was very like his grandfather Edward IV, being both tall and comely.³ A Venetian envoy concurred, declaring that the new king was 'liberal and handsome', as opposed to his father, whom he described as being 'a most miserly man but of great genius'.⁴ This was, of course, not quite true, but there was no denying the heartfelt enthusiasm expressed for young Henry.

At the time of his accession, Henry VIII was just a couple of months short of his eighteenth birthday. Though many would have considered him old enough to reign by himself, he was legally still a minor: he would have to wait a few short weeks more. It was therefore left to his formidable grandmother, Margaret, to take up the reins of government and act as regent on Henry's behalf. This was never an official post, but nevertheless Margaret was determined to ensure that her grandson's accession was as smooth as possible: she need not have worried. In spite of her sex, Margaret had earned the utmost respect and admiration of those who had served on her son's council and at court. Everyone was aware of her abilities and of Henry VII's implacable faith in her, and for a brief time she held sway over her grandson's realm: for the first time, Margaret was officially recognised in her role of uncrowned queen.

In the aftermath of her son's death, as her body continued to weaken, Margaret knew that she would not be around to support her grandson for long. Her foremost concern was therefore to ensure that he was surrounded by men he could trust, who would act in the best interests of England and her family. Unsurprisingly, most of these were men upon whom Margaret and her son had relied: John Fisher, her illegitimate cousin

Charles Somerset (formerly Beaufort and now also Baron Herbert) and Richard Fox, Bishop of Winchester. Margaret was careful to confirm that these men knew what was expected of them. One of the council's first acts was to order the arrest of the king's hated tax collectors, Richard Empson and Edmund Dudley. Their methods had been harsh, and Henry's subjects had loathed them as a result. Margaret may have actively encouraged their arrest, for Dudley had once crossed her in a deal over property.[5] They were executed on 17 August 1510.

Much of Margaret's time, however, was spent in arranging her son's funeral: the bill, settled in July, amounted to an exorbitant £8,474 4s 6d (£5,640,000). The late king's executors signed the warrants, at the head of which was Margaret, who, in her usual style, signed herself 'Margaret R.' It was recorded that the king's embalmed body was brought 'out of the privy chamber to the great chamber and rested there three days, on each day three masses and dirges being sung by a mitred prelate; then carried to the hall for three days with like services; then to the chapel for three days'.[6] Among the expenses were hangings of black cloth, many of which were allotted for the use of the king's servants and Margaret's ladies, including Margaret's chamberer, 'Perrot the French woman', Perrot Doryn.[7] Money was set aside for alms and livery provided for the mourners. The funeral procession was elaborate. The late king's coffin was moved from Richmond to St Paul's, where Bishop Fisher preached a mass and a sermon on 10 May, 'which sermon was printed at the special request of the right excellent princess Margaret, mother unto the said noble prince'.[8] The following day, the coffin was removed to Westminster, where the funeral service and burial were to take place. There, the king's household broke their staves of office and cast them into the grave before departing for 'a great and sumptuous feast'.[9]

Though the contract for Henry's tomb was not signed until 26 October 1512, the result following its completion in 1518 was, as he had anticipated, magnificent. A splendid black marble tomb-chest adorned with the bronze-gilt effigies of Henry and Elizabeth of York dominates the Lady

Chapel, surrounded by a brass screen.[10] A fitting monument to the first king and queen of the new dynasty.

AT THE BEGINNING OF MAY, Margaret travelled by water from Richmond to the Tower, where her grandson was in residence. She was delighted when, on 19 May, he granted his grandmother her former palace of Woking, which is likely to have been at her own request.[11] As she returned to the home she had loved so dearly though, it would be for the last time.

Within a matter of weeks after his accession, the young king had resolved to wed, declaring his intention to marry his brother Arthur's widow, Katherine of Aragon—five years his senior. There is no reason to believe that Henry's decision met with anything other than Margaret's approval. Whether she had any influence in her grandson's choice is unclear, but the decision was certainly popular. Henry would later claim that his father, on his deathbed, had ordered him to marry Katherine. For the Spanish princess, it brought all of the uncertainty of the last few years to a welcome end. In stark contrast to the celebrations that had marked Katherine's marriage to Arthur, the wedding was to be a small and private affair. On 11 June, Henry and Katherine were married at Greenwich, and preparations were put in place for their joint coronation. It is unclear whether Margaret was present to witness her grandson take his marriage vows—she had been at Greenwich three days earlier, so it is possible—but she was certainly there to see what came next, much of which had been arranged at her command.

On 24 June, the crowds were out in force to celebrate the coronation of Henry VIII and Katherine of Aragon. It was a magnificent affair for which huge sums had been outlaid, and the people of London cheered rapturously as the royal couple passed through the streets of the city. The royal couple were bedecked in the costly materials that Margaret's son and daughter-in-law had worn when they celebrated their marriage years earlier, and Margaret had also outlaid a substantial sum on new garments.[12] For the occasion, she and her ladies wore tawny velvet, satin and silk, as well as black bonnets, which had been specially purchased.[13] In spite of her magnificent new clothes, Margaret, as she had done on previous occasions, once again watched the coronation celebrations in private. Joined by her granddaughter Princess Mary, she paid for the use of a house in Cheapside to watch as the royal couple processed from the Tower to Westminster.[14] By the same token, she privately observed the ceremony in Westminster Abbey, which was conducted by William Warham, Archbishop of Canterbury. Though she 'had full great joy' at her grandson's triumph, Fisher noted, not unsurprisingly given what we know of Margaret's character, 'she let not to say that some adversity would follow'.[15] Henry's coronation was the third that Margaret had attended in the last three decades, and she had lived through the reigns of five monarchs prior to her grandson's accession. The usual celebrations and revelries ensued, and for several days afterwards, there were 'tournaments and many sorts of games'.[16] Though Margaret partook in the traditional coronation banquet in Westminster Hall, she no longer had the energy for such entertainments; indeed, the coronation turned out to be the last occasion on which she would see her grandson.

In May, Margaret had reached her sixty-sixth birthday, and her health was extremely fragile. Fisher explained that she was fearful that, had she lived longer,

> her body daily should have waxen more unwieldy, her sight should have been darked, and her hearing should have dulled more and more, her legs should have failed her by and by. And all the other parts of her body waxed more crased every day, which things should have been matter to her of great discomfort.[17]

Margaret's poor health had probably been exacerbated by the death of her beloved son, but Vergil's claim that 'while all were revelling in joy and light-heartedness' she was 'seized by a sudden illness' is untrue.[18] The reality is that she had been ailing for some time. It may have been some form of food poisoning or similar that worsened Margaret's condition, for when recollecting the end of his mistress, Henry Parker claimed that during the recent coronation banquet she 'took her infirmity, with eating of a cygnet', which immediately made her sick.[19] Following her grandson's coronation, she retired to the abbot's house within Westminster Abbey.[20] Aware that she faced imminent death, the location was almost certainly a deliberate choice, reflecting both her desire to be buried close to her son, and her own connection with the abbey. She had striven for control in all aspects of her life; why should death be any different?

On 28 June, Henry VIII reached his eighteenth birthday and, with it, his majority. It was clear that Margaret would not live to see him reign. In the same way that she had organized her life, so too had she long prepared for her death. Fisher recalled that there were many present to witness how with 'her heart and soul she raised her body to make answer thereunto' as her end approached.[21] Margaret's great-nephew Reginald Pole, son of Lady Margaret Pole, would later claim that, as death drew close, Margaret was fearful for her grandson. She was, he said, worried that Henry would turn away from God, a comment that Pole probably made in light of subsequent events. But she could do no more to safeguard her grandson's future and his realm. Realizing that death was swiftly approaching, on 29 June she summoned

> her ghostly father, being shriven and receiving the blessed sacrament of the alter, the bishop said mass before her, and as he lift up the precious host this worthy Lady expired, and so as she had honoured the blessed sacrament, even so the last thing that ever she saw as I do think was God.[22]

If Margaret really died as the bishop lifted the host, it was an appropriate end for the woman who had set so much store by her faith. As a result, Henry Parker believed that she 'is now joyful in that celestial court of heaven, where she shall be in eternal felicity for ever'.[23]

The reaction of Margaret's three surviving grandchildren to her death is unrecorded, but coming in such close proximity to that of their father, it is likely to have hit them hard. Certainly, for others who had known her it came as a great tragedy, and she was deeply mourned. Those in her household regretted that they

should forego so gentle a mistress, so tender a lady then wept they marvellously, wept her ladies and kinswomen to whom she was full kind, wept her poor gentlewomen whom she had loved so tenderly before, wept her chamberers to whom she was full dear, wept her chaplains and priests, wept her other true and faithful servants.[24]

Fisher, in the sermon preached shortly after her death, went as far as to claim that

all England for her death had cause of weeping. The poor creatures that were wont to receive her alms, to whom she was always piteous and merciful. The students of both the universities to whom she was as a mother. All the learned men of England to whom she was a very patroness. All the virtuous and devout persons to whom she was as a loving sister, all ye good religious men and women whom she so often was wont to visit and comfort. All good priests and clerks to whom she was a true defenderess. All the noble men and women to whom she was a mirror and example of honour.[25]

Similarly, Vergil praised Margaret as being 'a woman most outstanding both in her pious love of God and charity to all men, and whose countless virtues each one of us may find it easier to admire than to analyse'.[26]

Margaret had taken great care when it came to composing her will, working on it over the course of many years. She had appointed John St John, the son of her half-brother who had served as her chamberlain

since 1504, Bishop Fox and former members of her household as its exe-
cuters. But it was John Fisher, Margaret's trusted friend and chaplain, who
had been tasked with the role of chief executor. He took the responsibility
seriously and would go to a great deal of trouble to ensure that Margaret's
final wishes were met.

Fascinatingly, throughout her will she refers to herself as 'Princess': a final statement to the world about how she saw herself and how she wished
to be remembered. She may not have worn a crown, but Margaret would
ensure that she was remembered as royalty.

Unsurprisingly, Margaret's first thoughts were for the welfare of her
soul. She also took great care to lay out her wishes for her Cambridge
foundations: 'the said Princess willed, that all her plate, jewels, vestments,
altar cloths, books, hangings, and other necessaries belonging to her chapel
in the time of her decease, and not otherwise bequeathed, should be divided between her said colleges of Christ and St John'. It was the responsibility of Edward Bothe, her master of the jewel house, to ensure that
these goods were handed over to Dr Thomson, the master of Christ's.
The pieces bequeathed were rich indeed, and included crucifixes, a gold
chalice, candlesticks, altar cloths and mass books.[27] Other religious foundations were also left various items, including Wimborne Minster, Syon,
the Charterhouse at Sheen and the parish church at Collyweston.[28] Interestingly, Fisher, Henry Hornby and Lord Mountjoy purchased items such
as carpets, pieces of tapestry and cloths of estate from Margaret's former
collection, which were carefully noted in her inventories.[29] Additionally,
Fisher had also been left various other pieces of plate by his former friend.

All of Margaret's bequests serve as testimony both to her generosity
and to her staggering wealth. Even at the end, she had thought of others,
stipulating that on the day of her death alms to the sum of £133 6s 8d
(£88,800) were to be distributed to the poor.[30] Her family were also to
receive generous bequests, chiefly of jewels. The highest value of goods was
naturally left to her grandson, the king, and included several gold cups, as
well as books from her treasured library. Katherine of Aragon, Margaret,

Queen of Scots, and Princess Mary were also included, the latter of whom was bequeathed a gold cup garnished with precious stones and pearls decorated with white harts, on the horns of which were a long sapphire.[31] Neither were Margaret's friends and servants forgotten; many were left personal bequests that served perhaps to highlight the relationship that they had once shared with this extraordinary woman.

On 3 July, Margaret's body was moved from the abbot's house into Westminster Abbey, where it lay in state within the abbey refectory until it could be buried. She had left detailed instructions in her will for her funeral, which was conducted with all of the pomp and ceremony that she had planned; black satin was provided for covering her coffin, and the total cost of the funeral came to £1,021 (£680,000).[32] Fisher composed and read the 'mourning remembrance' for 'the noble princess Margaret, Countess of Richmond and Derby, mother unto King Henry VII, granddame to our sovereign lord that now is, upon whose soul almighty God have mercy', extolling the manner in which Margaret had met her death and comparing her to a scriptural Martha.[33] Fittingly, it was published by Wynkyn de Worde, whom Margaret had supported for the greater part of his career.

Margaret had left instructions for her burial in the magnificent Lady Chapel within Westminster Abbey, 'which is now begun by the said our most dear son'. On 23 November 1511, more than two years after her death, the contract for her tomb was signed. It was to be created by the Florentine sculptor Pietro Torrigiano, whose work would have an instrumental effect on Renaissance tombs and who was later responsible for the tomb of Henry VII and Elizabeth of York.[34] The commission was carried out with painstaking detail, as can be seen in the surviving accounts. In 1513 the Flemish painter Meynnart Wewyck was paid 'for making the picture and image of the said lady', and many other payments were made besides.[35] Though it would take many years to complete the work, the result was stupendous: Margaret's intricately sculpted face was almost certainly modelled on a death mask, her features appearing unmistakeably lifelike. The Beaufort and Tudor family arms are proudly displayed on the tomb, an indication of those with whom Margaret wished to be associated: Edmund Tudor and Thomas Stanley, Henry VII and Elizabeth of York, along with the Royal Arms, Henry VIII and Katherine of Aragon, and Margaret's parents; there was also a shield—now lost—probably depicting the arms of her grandparents. On 27 December 1511, a payment of 20s (£650) was made to Erasmus for 'the epitaph about my lady's tomb', which was composed in Latin.[36] The Bilbao iron grill that surrounds her tomb was provided by St John's College, Cambridge, in grateful thanks to their patroness, and was completed in 1529 by the English smith Cornelius Symondson. It was once beautifully painted, featuring coats of arms and other embellishments that were personal to Margaret. Today, the tomb of the uncrowned queen is one of the masterpieces of Westminster Abbey and one of the most splendid examples of a Renaissance monument. It is a memorial that Margaret would have been proud of.

Margaret's legacy is enduring and worthy of celebration. She worked to subsidize education, established religious foundations and supported writers. She had been well loved and was well mourned by those who knew her: the poor to whom she had given alms and sustenance, the children of her chapel whose education she had paid for, her household who had served her devotedly and her family, whose interests she had always placed before her own. Such a legacy had been hard won indeed.

Margaret had not only survived all of the obstacles that life had thrown at her—she had thrived. The intelligent young woman who grew up in Bletsoe's tranquil security had remained generous and conscientious through it all. Many of her qualities—her intelligence, in particular—enabled her to adapt to the unpredictable political climate in which she found herself, setting aside pride and family loyalty, both of which had felled many of her kin. She had learned quickly the need to be flexible and had emerged as a woman of extraordinary determination and self-possession, capable of raising her son to be a king. Early life had taught her the perils of being a pawn, and she had worked hard to exercise control whenever she could.

Setting aside matters of the heart, she chose husbands carefully, based on the protection they could offer her.

Having always found strength in her faith—likely instilled in her during the earliest days of her youth—it must have seemed as though God had blessed Margaret and her family, who had always been her primary consideration. She left behind a dynasty that would be the most talked of in British history, whose foundations she had striven to instil, risking her life in the process. Yet Margaret, it would appear, never felt truly secure, being wracked throughout her life by anxiety, which in turn appears to have lent her boundless energy in pursuing security and stability for herself and her family. That energy was always tied to her deep love for her son, her 'dear heart', and the love of life. It is little wonder, therefore, that when Henry met his end, Margaret too—long plagued by ill health—drifted into death. But for all her worry and tragedy, she had emerged victorious, and so, as Bishop Fisher said upon her death: 'Therefore we put aside all weeping and tears, and be not sad and heavy as men without hope. But rather we be glad and joyous'.[37]

THE TUDOR LEGACY

At the time of Margaret's death, the world in which she had lived began to change rapidly. Many of these changes came at the instigation of her beloved grandson Henry VIII and would have profound consequences for Margaret's family and many of those to whom she had been close. Not all of these changes would have been welcome to Margaret.

The accession of Henry VIII signified the beginning of a lively period at court, where entertainment and revelry revolved around the dazzling royal couple. In February 1510, Queen Katherine gave birth to a stillborn girl, but just months later—less than a year after Margaret's death—the queen became pregnant once more. The realm erupted into celebrations when a son was born on New Year's Day 1511, immediately christened Henry in honour of his father. The Tudor dynasty begun by Margaret's son seemed set to continue. But such confidence was short-lived. For the infant Prince Henry died just a month after his birth, becoming one of five infants born to the royal couple who would not survive and leaving the future of the dynasty uncertain. The sole survivor of Henry and Katherine's marriage was a girl, Mary, born in 1516.

In Scotland, meanwhile, the life of Margaret's eldest granddaughter and namesake was destined to be turbulent. In 1513 the country found itself at war with England, and having led his army south to invade, Margaret's husband James IV was slain on 9 September at the Battle of Flodden, his forces defeated by her brother's army. Katherine of Aragon, who was acting as regent while her husband was in France, gave orders that the Scottish king's bloodied coat be sent to Henry VIII as a war trophy, and she even contemplated sending the dead king's body. With his father's death, Margaret's one-year-old great-grandson succeeded to the Scottish throne as James V, leaving his mother at the head of a regency for as long as she remained a widow.[1] Yet, Queen Margaret's life quickly spiralled out of control. The following year, she remarried on 6 August, taking as her second husband Archibald Douglas, Earl of Angus. This marriage not only alienated the Scottish nobles but also ensured that Margaret lost her position as regent. Having fled across the English border, in October 1515 she gave birth to a daughter at Harbottle Castle in Northumberland. The infant was called Margaret and was raised largely at her uncle Henry VIII's court, where the fallen queen took refuge after recovering from her daughter's birth.

When Queen Margaret arrived in London, she was reunited not only with her brother but also with her younger sister, Mary, too. Mary's earlier betrothal to Charles of Castile had been dissolved in 1513, when Henry VIII believed that he had found a better match for his sister. Thus it was that, on 9 October 1514, Mary was married to Louis XII of France. The marriage was hugely unappealing to the English princess, who at eighteen was described as 'a nymph from heaven' with a lively and passionate nature. Her groom, by contrast, was 'a gouty old man' of fifty-two.[2] But it was not a match she would have to endure for long, for after just three months of marriage, Louis died on 15 January 1515. It was probably in the middle of the following month that Mary took her future into her own hands. Eager to avoid another husband being thrust upon her, she was secretly married to Charles Brandon, Duke of Suffolk, a close friend and jousting companion of her brother. When the news was broken to Henry VIII, he was furious, but eventually, having agreed to pay a large fine, the couple were welcomed back to England in May. Mary was now Duchess of Suffolk and spent much of her time at her brother's court.

Having spent more than a year in England, Queen Margaret was allowed in 1517—after a reconciliation had been achieved with her son's regent, the Duke of Albany—to return to Scotland.[3] Over the next few years, however, matters ran far from smoothly, and in 1527 she divorced her husband and married for a third time the following year. Her groom was Henry Stewart, Lord Methven, but in time Margaret tired of him and sought another divorce. Although on this occasion her wishes were not granted, she set a precedent that her brother would seek to follow.

By 1526, long-standing cracks in Henry VIII's marriage were magnified when the king fell in love. The object of his desire was Anne Boleyn, the daughter of an English knight and one of Katherine's ladies. The following year it became apparent that Henry's marriage was damaged beyond repair. Claiming that his lack of a legitimate son was God's judgement that his union with Katherine was unlawful, he began proceedings to have his marriage annulled on the basis that Katherine's marriage to his brother Arthur had been consummated. His intention was to marry Anne Boleyn instead, by whom he felt confident he could sire sons. Yet it was to be no simple process, and the events of the following six years would not only cause strife within the king's—and therefore Margaret's—own family but also divide the country. In so doing, the entire course of the monarchy changed permanently.

Henry VIII's desire to be rid of Katherine of Aragon, combined with the pope's refusal to comply with Henry's demands, sparked the English Reformation, as Henry separated from the Catholic Church, declaring himself Head of the English Church. His actions were too much for many of his subjects, including some of Margaret's friends, to stomach. Margaret herself would have been horrified. So too would she have been appalled by the Dissolution of the Monasteries, many of which she had helped to support and which were close to her heart.

In May 1533, Henry's Archbishop of Canterbury, Thomas Cranmer, declared his marriage to Katherine of Aragon to be null and void. Henry had already married Anne Boleyn, who was also pregnant with what her husband confidently believed to be a son. Margaret's youngest grand-daughter, Mary, Duchess of Suffolk, made no secret of her sympathy for the plight of her sister-in-law. She was reported to have used 'opprobri-ous language' about Anne Boleyn, but this does not seem to have caused a permanent rift in her relationship with her brother. Notwithstanding this, her support for Katherine was destined to be tragically short-lived, for Mary's health was fragile. In June 1533, she died at Westhorpe Hall in East Anglia at the age of thirty-seven. She left behind two daughters, Frances and Eleanor, the former of whom became mother to the ill-fated Grey sisters.[4] They would later endure their own bitter tragedy at the hands of Margaret's great-granddaughters, the future Tudor queens Mary and Elizabeth. After a brief thirteen-day reign, Lady Jane Grey met a bloody end on the executioner's block on 12 February 1554. Her two younger sisters became victims of Elizabeth's wrath when they dared to marry without her consent; both were imprisoned. Those who refused to accept the king's new authority as Head of the English Church met similar ends. Margaret's good friend Bishop Fisher was beheaded on Tower Hill on 22 June 1535. He was canonized in 1935.

Until her end, Katherine of Aragon refused to accept Archbishop Cranmer's judgement on her marriage. Having been banished from court, she lived out the rest of her days in a series of uncomfortable houses. She died on 7 January 1536 at the age of fifty-one. Meanwhile, fate was about to deal Anne Boleyn a cruel hand. Despite Henry's hopes, she failed to provide him with a son, and of four pregnancies just one daughter sur-vived. She was named Elizabeth. By the spring of 1536, Henry had tired of Anne, and having been accused of trumped-up charges of adultery and incest with her own brother, she met her end at the hand of an expert French swordsman on 19 May at the Tower.

It was not until 12 October 1537 that Henry was at last provided with a legitimate male heir. But it came at a price, for the experience cost his third wife, Jane Seymour, her life. He married three more times but produced no further children. As with his father before him, the future of his dynasty rested on the life of a sole male heir.

Henry's dynasty, though, was better secured than that of James V, son of Margaret, Queen of Scots. James's first marriage to Madeleine of Valois produced no children, and though he sired two sons by his second wife, Marie de Guise, tragically both died within a day of one another in April 1541.[5] His mother would not live to see the birth of his sole surviving heir, for on 18 October 1541 Queen Margaret died at Methven Castle in Perthshire.[6] On 8 December the following year, Marie de Guise gave birth to a daughter, Mary. Six days later, her father died, leaving the infant Queen of Scots born in the midst of decades of strife between England and Scotland. Things would not be fully settled until 1603.

On 28 January 1547, Henry VIII died, the latter part of his reign by no means mirroring the glory of the first. Henry had torn his country— and his family—apart as a result of his decision to split from the Catholic Church in Rome and establish the Church of England with himself at its head. Of his six marriages, two had ended in divorce, two in execution, and one by death in childbirth—just three legitimate children had been produced as a result, only one of them male. Henry's nine-year-old son, Edward, succeeded him. Though a minor, Edward was a zealous Protestant and continued the religious changes started by his father. But there was no time to ensure that their foundations were truly secure.

When Edward died unmarried and childless at the age of fifteen in 1553, a brief power struggle saw Lady Jane Grey—appointed the king's Protestant successor—eventually lose her head for treason at the hands of another of Margaret's great-granddaughters, Mary I. The sole surviving child of Henry VIII's union with Katherine of Aragon, Mary, like her great-grandmother Margaret before her, was exceptionally pious. She immediately took steps to restore Catholicism in England, but her desire to produce a Catholic heir to succeed her did not bear fruit. Her marriage to Philip of Spain was childless and unhappy. She died unpopular and alone on 17 November 1558.

Succeeded by her half-sister Elizabeth, it was through this daughter of Anne Boleyn that Margaret's dynasty arguably reached its zenith, somewhat fittingly, under the leadership of a woman. Elizabeth would die childless, for like Margaret before her she had decided that her fate would not be dictated by powerful men—she would be mistress of her own destiny. A royal *femme sole*, she in many ways emulated the earlier example of her great-grandmother, choosing in her case to do so without the support of a husband. It is Elizabeth who is remembered by history as one of the Tudor dynasty's most celebrated monarchs, often revered as 'the Virgin Queen'.

Elizabeth's death in March 1603 brought the Tudor dynasty—begun by Margaret's son in 1485—to an end. But Margaret's family continued to reign, for the man who succeeded to the English throne was Margaret's great-great-great-grandson: James VI of Scotland and I of England.[7] For the first time, the two kingdoms were united, and they remain so to this day: as a result, Margaret's bloodline endures. Every English monarch since Henry VIII—meaning every British monarch since 1603, including Queen Elizabeth II—has been able to trace their descent from Margaret, as could her grandson, James V, across the border in Scotland.[8] It is a fitting and enduring legacy for the woman who had striven so hard to achieve a crown for her family.

So too is the elegy written in Margaret's memory by John Skelton on 16 August 1516:

> Inspire my elegy, ye sacred nine,
> For pious Marg'ret mix your tears with mine.
> Within this pile a King's fam'd mother lies;
> Henry, who in yon stately edifice
> In splendour lives with many a noble peer,
> 'Tis his grand parent lies inhumed here.
> Queen Tanaquil's exalted mind and birth,
> (Whom Livy's pen extolls 'bove all on earth)

Fall short of Marg'rets; ev'n Penelope
Was less renowned for chastity, than she;
Prudent as Abigail, King David's wife;
As Hester bold, in hazarding her life
To plead her people's cause; resembling three
The noblest Princesses in history.
Reader, I pray, whoe'er thou art, thy tears
For such a Princess offer, and thy prayers.
Grief forbids more; To write I listless try,
Since our great benefactress here doth lie,
And all regard is lost for probity.
For now to sing of death it scarce avails;
Even death itself to startle sinners fails.
D'you ask, what modern honour means? 'Tis this,
Instead of virtue, 'tis lasciviousness.
The virtuous die, it's true, but they shall rise
Again to praise, and Charon's power despise.
Men now live, as they lift; nothing can dart,
Or make the least impression on their heart;
No sepulchres of Dukes, no monuments
Of Kings or Senators, no precedents
Of past or frequent funerals, have the power
T'affright the present age from sinning more.
To write what none will ever regard 'tis vain,
As Juvenal avers; so I'll refrain.
He that defaces, spoils, or takes away
This script, may Satan snatch him as his prey
Forthwith, and on him all his rage display.
Thou great illustrious ruler of the sky,
Who made the world and reigned eternally;
Gracious admit this Princess to thy throne,
Renowned for several virtues, like thy own.[9]

AUTHOR'S NOTE

I HAVE SPENT MONTHS PAINSTAKINGLY transcribing hundreds—if not thousands—of pages of fifteenth- and sixteenth-century material for this book. Although this is always an invaluable part of the research and writing process for me, the sheer volume of material has obliged me to seek the services of the excellent team at Transcription Services Limited on occasion. I am extremely grateful for their help. As always, I have modernized all of the spelling and punctuation from contemporary books and documents in order to create a clearer narrative.

All monetary values have been presented with the contemporary amount, followed by the modern-day equivalent in parentheses. All conversions were done according to the National Archives Currency Convertor (www.nationalarchives.gov.uk/currency) and are approximate values. Please also be aware that they may be subject to change.

Finally, for clarity, all dates have been calculated using the modern-day Gregorian calendar, under which the year turns on 1 January.

NOTES ON SOURCES

THE SOURCES FOR MARGARET'S LIFE are both varied and plentiful, providing us with a wealth of information about this extraordinary woman. One of the most abundant supplies of documents is stored in the archives of St John's College, Cambridge. There can be found many of her surviving household accounts and inventories, all of which provide compelling details of Margaret's life and the luxury in which she lived. Some of her personal papers are also extant, including copies of her will in which she painstakingly recorded her final wishes over the course of many years. Household accounts belonging to Margaret's third husband, Henry Stafford, survive in the Westminster Abbey Muniments, along with other documents that provide further insights into her life.

Further sources of information come from those who knew her. The account of Henry Parker, Lord Morley, was later presented to Margaret's great-granddaughter, Mary I. Having been a member of Margaret's household during his youth, Parker knew her well, and it was probably by her arrangement that he was married to her great-niece, Alice St John.[1] His account provides some charming details of the sort that can only be gleaned from sources of this personal nature. It must be remembered, though, that it was written many years after his service to Margaret had come to an end. Of equal importance is the account of John Fisher, Bishop of Rochester, who became Margaret's chaplain and close confidant. He knew his mistress well and preached a sermon in her honour at her funeral. Unsurprisingly, both Morley and Fisher painted highly flattering pictures of Margaret, praising her achievements and her generosity. Fisher did, though, claim that 'my purpose is not vainly to extol or to magnify above her merits', but to use her as an example for the bettering of others.[2] Even so, the praise of those who knew Margaret is not unjustified in many quarters, for these accounts are often supported by other sources. They are most useful for their ability to provide personal details from people who actually knew Margaret, thereby offering glimpses into her personality in a way that other sources are unable to.

The sources covering the dramatic and dangerous events of both the Wars of the Roses and Richard III's coup of 1483 are plentiful, for they were relatively well documented by contemporary chroniclers. Margaret features in some of these too, yet, as with all historical sources, they need to be carefully scrutinized to establish their reliability. The account of the Croyland Chronicler, for example, is one of the most superior sources for this period, and much of the information it provides can be shown to be accurate.[3] Though its author is anonymous, it is likely to have been John Russell, Bishop of Lincoln, a member of the royal council. Margaret and her family had close links with Croyland Abbey in Lincolnshire, which was one of the richest religious houses in England, and she also knew Russell. Dominic Mancini, an Italian visitor to England in the summer of 1483, is a useful source, whose account was only discovered in 1936.[4] Although he has been heavily criticized and had doubts cast upon his reliability, it is clear that he spoke to a number of people who were involved in the mysterious happenings of the spring and summer of 1483, including Dr John Argentine, physician to Edward V. Mancini left England after Richard III's coronation on 6 July and wrote his account in December—just months after the events that he had witnessed took place. The Italian-born Polydore Vergil was responsible for writing an official history of England, the *Anglica Historia*, which Henry VII commissioned from him in 1507.[5] Vergil claimed to have consulted a wide range of sources when composing his history, and though his work can often be shown to be accurate, it must be remembered that he had to employ tact when writing about his patron. Similarly, Bernard André, a blind French poet, penned an official account of the life of Henry VII, 'the most prosperous and victorious of the kings of England and France', producing a work that was highly flattering not only of Henry but also of Margaret.[6] He did, however, experience first-hand many of the events about which he wrote, and he gleaned much of his information not only from Henry but also from Margaret.

What we lack is an account from Margaret herself, who, of course, was an eyewitness to many of the events that saw Richard III's usurpation and the disappearance of his two royal nephews in the summer of 1483. From her days at court, she knew both Edward IV and Richard III personally, as well as at least one of the two boys—Prince Richard, the younger of the pair—who have become known to history as the Princes in the Tower. She herself heard the rumours that the princes had been murdered, and, keeping in mind the events of the autumn of 1483, it is almost certain that she believed them to be dead, although she had no way of confirming this. Contrary, though, to several suggestions that emerged in the seventeenth century and that have inspired some modern interpretations, there is not a shred of contemporary evidence that even hints at Margaret's involvement in the princes' disappearance. This is the strongest evidence of her innocence, and that she has been mooted as a potential murderer demonstrates the extent to which her reputation has been blackened over time. This, in turn, provides a compelling reason for a fresh appraisal of her life.

Documentary sources are not unique in their ability to fill in the jigsaw pieces of Margaret's life, and there are other clues for those who seek to find them. Westminster Abbey, the splendid Gothic monument so long associated with royal authority, houses the magnificent tomb that was raised to Margaret's memory after her death. This provides the most tangible and lifelike depiction of the woman who was determined to be remembered by history as an integral part of the Tudor dynasty. Likewise, fragments of several of the places that Margaret would have known still survive, including Woking Palace, one of her favourite homes, and archaeological digs are currently under way at the site of her once-magnificent palace of Collyweston in Northamptonshire. The tomb of Margaret's parents, created at her own commission, can be seen in Wimborne Minster, and the two Cambridge colleges of her foundation, Christ's and St John's, are still active.

ABBREVIATIONS

Add MS   Additional manuscript
BL   British Library
CCR   *Calendar of Close Rolls*
CPR   *Calendar of the Patent Rolls Preserved in the Public Record Office, 1476–1509*, 3 vols. (London, 1901–1916)
CSPS   *Calendar of State Papers, Spain*, ed. G. A. Bergenroth et al., 13 vols. (London, 1862–1954)
CSPV   *Calendar of State Papers, Venice*, ed. R. Brown et al., 38 vols. (London, 1864–1947)
L & P   *Letters and Papers, Foreign and Domestic, of the Reign of Henry VIII, 1509–1547*, ed. J. Brewer et al., 21 vols. (London, 1862–1932)
SJLM   St John's College Archives, University of Cambridge
TNA   The National Archives
WAM   Westminster Abbey Muniments

SELECT BIBLIOGRAPHY

MANUSCRIPT SOURCES

BRITISH LIBRARY

Additional Manuscripts	4712, 7099, 12060, 21480, 29976, 35814, 45133, 59899, 88965
Egerton Manuscripts	2341
Royal Manuscripts	2 A XVIII
Seals	C VIII 84
Sloane Manuscripts	403
Stowe Manuscripts	1047

LAMBETH PALACE LIBRARY

MS 474	Book of Hours

NATIONAL ARCHIVES

Chancery

C1	Early Chancery Proceedings
C47	Miscellanea
C139	Inquisitions Post Mortem, Series I, Henry VI
C140	Inquisitions Post Mortem, Series I, Edward IV

Court of Wards and Liveries

WARD 2	Deeds and Evidence

Duchy of Lancaster

DL 29	Accounts of Auditors, Receivers, Feodaries and Ministers
DL 41	Miscellanea

Exchequer

E 36	Treasury of Receipt, Miscellaneous Books
E 40	Treasury of Receipt: Ancient Deeds, Series A
E 101	King's Remembrancer, Various Accounts
E 135	Miscellaneous Ecclesiastical Documents
E 154	King's Remembrancer and Treasury of Receipt, Inventories of Goods and Chattels
E 327	Augmentation Office: Ancient Deeds, Series BX
E 404	Warrants for Issue

Lord Chamberlain's Department

LC 9	Accounts and Miscellanea

Prerogative Court of Canterbury

PROB 11	Registered Copy Wills

Court of Requests

REQ	Pleadings

Special Collections

SC	Ancient Petitions

ST GEORGE'S CHAPEL, WINDSOR

SJC XV.58.C.13	Consent for Lady Margaret to found a Chantry in the Chapel, 1497

ST JOHN'S COLLEGE, CAMBRIDGE

SJLM/1	Accounts of Lady Margaret Beaufort
SJLM/2	Inventories
SJLM/3	Wills and Bequests
SJLM/4	The Inheritance of Lady Margaret Beaufort
SJLM/7	Executors of Lady Margaret Beaufort
SJLM/9	Extended Family, Heirs and Assigns
St John's College, MS N.24	Prayer Book

WESTMINSTER ABBEY MUNIMENTS

Westminster Abbey MS 39	Prayer Book commissioned by Lady Margaret Beaufort for Sir Thomas Stanley
WAM 12181–90	Household Accounts of Sir Henry Stafford at Bourne and Woking, 1466–1471
WAM 22830	Bill of Prests by Lady Margaret's Cofferer, 1493–1494
WAM 5472	Miscellaneous Receipts and Expenses of Sir Reginald Bray, 1468–1469
WAM 5479	Miscellaneous Receipts of Sir Reginald Bray, 1469–1472
WAM 32348	Account of Lands of Edward Stafford, 1495–1496
WAM 32377	Account of Sir Reginald Bray for Receipts and Charges on Lady Margaret's Lands
WAM 32378	Draft of a Pardon from Edward IV to Henry Tudor
WAM 32407	Miscellaneous Receipts and Expenses of Sir Reginald Bray, 1473–1474
WAM 6658	Admission of Lady Margaret, Henry Stafford and Henry Tudor to Confraternity of the Order of the Holy Trinity, Knaresborough, 1465
WAM 6660	Admission of Henry Stafford and Lady Margaret to Confraternity of Burton Lazars, 1466

PRINTED PRIMARY SOURCES

Allen, P. S., and H. M. Allen (eds.). *Letters of Richard Fox 1486–1527* (Oxford: Clarendon Press, 1929).

André, B. *The Life of Henry VII*, trans. D. Hobbins (New York: Italica Press, 2011).

Anstey, H. (ed.). *Epistolae Academicae Oxon*, Part II (Oxford: University of Oxford, 1898).

Astle, T. (ed.). *The Will of Henry VII* (London: T. Payne & B. White, 1775).

Bayne, R. (ed.). *The Life of Fisher MS. Harleian 6382* (London, 1921).

Bentley, S. (ed.). *Excerpta Historica or illustrations of English history* (London, 1831).

Bergenroth, G. A. (ed.). *Calendar of State Papers, Spain, Volume 1, 1485–1509* (London, 1862).

Bliss, W. H. (ed.). *Calendar of Papal Registers relating to Great Britain and Ireland* (London, 1893).

Brewer, J. S. (ed.). *Letters and Papers, Foreign and Domestic, of the Reign of Henry VIII, 1509–47*. 21 vols. and addenda (London, 1862–1932).

Brown, R. (ed.). *Calendar of State Papers, Venice. Volume 1, 1202–1509* (London, 1864).

Calendar of Ancient Deeds in the Public Record Office. Vol. I (London, 1890).

Calendar of Close Rolls: Edward IV, Edward V, Richard III. 3 vols. British History Online. www.british-history.ac.uk/catalogue/guides-and-calendars.

Calendar of Close Rolls: Henry VII. 2 vols. British History Online. www.british-history.ac.uk/catalogue/guides-and-calendars.

Calendar of Patent Rolls: Henry VII: 1485–1509. 2 vols. (London: HMSO, 1914–1916).

Campbell, W. (ed.). *Materials for a History of the Reign of Henry VII*. 2 vols. (London, 1873).

Cavell, E. (ed.). *The Heralds' Memoir 1486–1490: Court Ceremony, Royal Progress and Rebellion* (Donington: Shaun Tyas, 2009).

Caxton, W. *The Game and Playe of the Chesse*, ed. J. Adams (Kalamazoo: Western Michigan University Press, 2009).

Commynes, P. *Memoirs: The Reign of Louis XI 1461–83*, trans. M. Jones (London: Penguin Books, 1972).

Crawford, A. (ed.). *Letters of Medieval Women* (Stroud: Sutton, 2002).

———. (ed.). *Letters of the Queens of England 1100–1547* (Stroud: Sutton, 1994).

Dalton, J. N. (ed.). *The Manuscripts of St George's Chapel, Windsor Castle* (Windsor: Dean and canons of St. George's Chapel, 1957).

Davies, J. S. (ed.). *An English Chronicle of the Reigns of Richard II, Henry IV, Henry V, and Henry VI* (London: Camden Society, 1856).

Davis, N. (ed.). *The Paston Letters* (Oxford: Oxford University Press, 2008).

Dockray, K. (ed.). *Edward IV: A Source Book* (Stroud: Sutton, 1999).

———. *Richard III: A Source Book* (Stroud: Sutton, 1997).

———. (ed.). *Three Chronicles of the Reign of Edward IV* (Gloucester: Sutton, 1988).

Ellis, H. (ed.). *Hall's Chronicle* (London, 1809).

———. (ed.). *Original Letters Illustrative of English History*. 3 vols. (London, 1825).

———. (ed.). *Three Books of Polydore Vergil's English History* (London: Camden Society, 1844).

Fenn, J. (ed.). *The Paston Letters*. 5 vols. (London, 1787–1823).

Fisher, J. 'Mornynge Remembraunce had at the moneth mynde of the Noble Prynces Margarete Countesse of Rychemonde and Darbye'. Early English Books Online. https://quod.lib.umich.edu/e/eebo/A00766.0001.001?view=toc.

Gairdner, J. (ed.). *Gregory's Chronicle, or the Historical Collections of a Citizen of London in the Fifteenth Century* (London: Camden Society, 1876).

———. (ed.). *Letters and Papers Illustrative of the Reigns of Richard III and Henry VII*. 2 vols. (London: Longman, Green, Longman, and Roberts, 1861–1863).

Given-Wilson, C., P. Brand, S. Phillips, M. Ormrod, G. Martin, A. Curry, and R. Horrox (eds.). *Parliament Rolls of Medieval England* (Woodbridge: Boydell Press, 2005).

Gough Nichols, J., and J. Bruce (eds.). *Wills from Doctors' Commons: A Selection from the Wills of Eminent Persons Proved in the Prerogative Court of Canterbury, 1495–1695* (London: Camden Society, 1863).

Hall, E. *Chronicle*, ed. C. Whibley (London, 1809).

Halliwell, J. O. (ed.). *A Chronicle of the First Thirteen Years of the Reign of King Edward the Fourth, by John Warkworth* (London: Camden Society, 1839).

———. (ed.). *Letters of the Kings of England*. 2 vols. (London: H. Colburn, 1848).

———. (ed.). *The Most Pleasant Song of Lady Bessy* (London: Percy Society, 1847).

Hanham, A. *John Benet's Chronicle, 1399–1462* (Basingstoke: Palgrave Macmillan, 2016).

Harriss, G., and M. Harriss. 'III John Benet's Chronicle for the Years 1400 to 1462', *Camden Fourth Series* 9 (1972): 151–233. doi:10.1017/S0068690500002877.

Hay, D. (ed.). *The Anglica Historia of Polydore Vergil* (London: Office of the Royal Historical Society, 1950).

Hayward, M. (ed.). *The Great Wardrobe Accounts of Henry VII and Henry VIII* (London: London Record Society, 2012).

Heseltine, G. C. (ed.). *The Shepherd's Calendar* (London: Peter Davis, 1930).

Hinds, A. B. (ed.). *Calendar of State Papers, Milan, Volume 1, 1385–1618* (London: HMSO, 1912).

Hymers, J. (ed.). *The Funeral Sermon of Margaret, Countess of Richmond and Derby* (Cambridge, 1840).

Ingrams, J. K. (ed.). *De Imitatione Christi* (London: Kegan Paul, 1893).

James, M. R. (trans.). *Henry the Sixth: A Reprint of John Blacman's Memoir* (Cambridge: Cambridge University Press, 1919).

Kellner, L. (ed.). *Blanchardin and Eglantine* (London, 1890).

Kingsford, C. L. (ed.). *Chronicles of London* (Oxford: Clarendon Press, 1905).

———. (ed.). *English Historical Literature in the Fifteenth Century* (Oxford: Clarendon Press, 1913).

Kipling, G. (ed.). *The Receyt of the Ladie Kateryne* (Oxford: Oxford University Press, 1990).

Legg, L. G. W. *English Coronation Records* (London: Archibald Constable, 1901).

Leland, J. *Antiquarii de Rebus Britannicis Collectanea*, ed. T. Hearne. 6 vols. (London: Benjamin White, 1774).

Mancini, D. *De Occupatione Regni Anglie per Riccardum Tercium* (*The Usurpation of Richard III*), 2nd ed., ed. and trans. C. A. J. Armstrong (Oxford: Clarendon, 1969).

Mayor, J. E. B. (ed.). *Early Statutes of St John's College, Cambridge* (London, 1859).

———. (ed.). *The English Works of John Fisher* (London: Early English Text Society, 1876).

———. *The Mirroure of Golde for the Synfull Soule* (London, 1522).

More, T. *The History of King Richard III*, ed. G. M. Logan (Indiana: Indiana University Press, 2005).

Myers, A. R. (ed.). *The Household of Edward IV: The Black Book and the Ordinance of 1478* (Manchester: Manchester University Press, 1959).

Nichols, F. M. (ed. and trans.). *The Epistles of Erasmus*. 2 vols. (London: Longman, 1904).

Nichols, J. (ed.). *A Collection of all the Wills, now known to be extant, of the Kings and Queens of England* (London: Society of Antiquaries, 1780).

Nichols, J. (ed.), and Society of Antiquaries. *A Collection of ordinances and regulations for the government of the royal household, made in divers reigns: from King Edward III to King William and Queen Mary, also receipts in ancient cookery* (London: Society of Antiquaries, 1790).

Nichols, J. G. (ed.). *The Chronicle of Calais* (London: Camden Society, 1846).

———. (ed.). *Chronicle of the Grey Friars of London* (London: Camden Society, 1851).

———. (ed.). *Inventories of the wardrobe, plate, chapel stuff, etc. of Henry Fitzroy, Duke of Richmond, and of the wardrobe stuff at Baynard's Castle of Katherine, Princess Dowager* (London: Camden Society, 1855).

Nichols, N. H. (ed.). *Testamenta Vetusta.* 2 vols. (London, 1826).

———. (ed.). *Privy Purse Expenses of Elizabeth of York* (London: W. Pickering, 1830).

———. (ed.). *Proceedings and Ordinances of the Privy Council of England.* 7 vols. (London: G. Eyre & A. Spottiswoode, 1834–1837).

Palgrave, F. *The Antient Kalendars and Inventories of the Treasury of His Majesty's Exchequer,* I (London: G. Eyre & A. Spottiswoode, 1836).

Pollard, A. F. (ed.). *Reign of Henry VII from Contemporary Sources.* 3 vols. (London: Longman, 1913–1914).

Pronay, N., and J. Cox (eds.). *The Crowland Chronicle Continuations: 1459–1486* (London: Sutton, 1986).

Raine, A. (ed.). *York Civic Records.* 2 vols. (Leeds: Yorkshire Archaeological Society, 1939–1941).

Riley, H. T. (ed.). *Ingulph's Chronicle of the History of Croyland* (London: Bohn, 1854).

Rymer, T. (ed.). *Rymer's Foedera.* 16 vols. (London, 1739–1745).

Sandford, F. *A Genealogical history of the kings and queens of England, and monarchs of Great Britain, &c. from the conquest, anno 1066, to the year 1677* (London, 1677).

Searle, W. G. (ed.). *The Chronicle of John Stone, Monk of Christ Church 1415–1471* (Cambridge: Cambridge Antiquarian Society, 1902).

———. (ed.). *The Narrative of the Marriage of Richard, Duke of York with Anne of Norfolk, 1477* (Cambridge, 1867).

Shakespeare, W. *Henry VI, Part One,* ed. M. Taylor (Oxford: Oxford University Press, 2003).

———. *Henry VI, Part Two,* ed. R. Warren (Oxford: Oxford University Press, 2002).

———. *Henry VI, Part Three,* ed. R. Martin (Oxford: Oxford University Press, 2001).

———. *Richard III,* ed. M. Taylor (London: Penguin, 2015).

Sitwell, G. (ed.). *The Scale of Perfection* (London: Burns Oates, 1953).

Smith, G. (ed.). *The Coronation of Elizabeth Wydeville* (London: Ellis, 1935).

Starkey, D. (ed.). *The Inventory of King Henry VIII,* trans. P. Ward (London: Society of Antiquaries, 1998).

Stow, J. *The Annales or Generall Chronicle of England* (London, 1615).

Strachey, J., et al. (eds.). *Rotuli Parliamentorum.* 6 vols. (London, 1767–1777).

Sutton, A. F., and P. W. Hammond (eds.). *The Coronation of Richard III: The Extant Documents* (Gloucester: Alan Sutton, 1983).

Sutton, A. F., L. Visser-Fuchs, and P. W. Hammond (eds.). *The Reburial of Richard, Duke of York, 21–30 July 1476* (London: The Richard III Society, 1996).

Thomas, A. H., and I. D. Thornley (eds.). *The Great Chronicle of London* (London: Corporation of the City of London, 1983).

Toulmin Smith, L. (ed.). *John Leland's Itinerary in England and Wales in or about the Years 1535–43*. 5 vols. (London: G. Bell, 1964).

Ullmann, W. (ed.). *Liber Regie Capelle* (London: Henry Bradshaw Society, 1961).

Williams, C. H. (ed.). *English Historical Documents, Vol. V: 1485–1558* (London: Eyre & Spottiswoode, 1967).

Wriothesley, C. *A Chronicle of England during the reigns of the Tudors from 1485 to 1559*, Vol. I, ed. W. D. Hamilton (London: Camden Society, 1875).

SECONDARY SOURCES

Alcock, N. W. 'Maxstoke Castle, Warwickshire'. *Archaeological Journal* 135 (1978).

Amin, N. *The House of Beaufort: The Bastard Line That Captured the Crown* (Stroud: Amberley, 2017).

———. *Tudor Wales* (Stroud: Amberley, 2014).

Anglo, S. 'The Foundation of the Tudor Dynasty: The Coronation and Marriage of Henry VII'. *Guildhall Miscellany* II (1960): 3–11.

———. *The Great Tournament Roll of Westminster: Historical Introduction* (Oxford: Clarendon, 1968).

———. 'Ill of the Dead: The Posthumous Reputation of Henry VII'. *Renaissance Studies* 1 (1987): 27–47.

———. *Images of Tudor Kingship* (London: Trafalgar Square, 1992).

———. 'The London Pageants for the Reception of Katharine of Aragon: November 1501'. *Journal of the Warburg and Courtauld Institutes* 26 (1963): 53–89.

———. *Spectacle Pageantry, and Early Tudor Policy* (Oxford: Clarendon, 1969).

Archbold, W. A. J. 'Sir William Stanley and Perkin Warbeck'. *English Historical Review* 14 (1899): 529–534.

Archer, I. W. 'City and Court Connected: The Material Dimensions of Royal Ceremonial, ca. 1480–1625'. *Huntingdon Library Quarterly* 71 (2008): 157–179.

Armitage Smith, S. *John of Gaunt* (London: Constable & Company Ltd., 1904).

Arnold, P., and R. Savage. *Woking Palace: Henry VIII's Royal Palace* (Woking: Friends of Woking Palace, 2011).

Arthurson, I. *The Perkin Warbeck Conspiracy 1491–1499* (Stroud: Sutton, 1994).

Ashdown-Hill, J. *The Last Days of Richard III* (Stroud: History Press, 2010).

Axon, W. E. 'The Lady Margaret as a Lover of Literature'. *The Library* 8 (1907): 34–41.

Bacon, F. *The History of the Reign of King Henry VII*, ed. B. Vickers (Cambridge: Cambridge University Press, 1998).

Bagley, J. J. *The Earls of Derby 1485–1985* (London: Sidgwick & Jackson, 1985).

———. *Margaret of Anjou* (London: Herbert Jenkins, 1948).

Bak, J. M. (ed.). *Coronations: Medieval and Early Modern Monarchic Ritual* (Oxford: University of California, 1990).

Baldwin, D. *Elizabeth Woodville: Mother of the Princes in the Tower* (Stroud: Sutton, 2002).

———. *Richard III* (Stroud: Amberley, 2012).

Ballard, G. *Memoirs of Several Ladies of Great Britain* (London, 1775).

Barron, C. M. 'The "Golden Age" of Women in Medieval London'. *Reading Medieval Studies* 15 (1989).

Beaumont James, T. *The Palaces of Medieval England 1050–1550: Royalty, Nobility, the Episcopate and Their Residences from Edward the Confessor to Henry VIII* (London: Seaby, 1990).

Becker, L. M. *Death and the Early Modern Englishwoman* (Aldershot: Routledge, 2003).

Beer, M. L. 'Practices and Performances of Queenship: Catherine of Aragon and Margaret Tudor, 1503–1533' (unpublished PhD thesis, University of Illinois, 2014).

Bennett, H. S. *English Books and Readers 1475 to 1557* (Cambridge: Cambridge University Press, 1969).

Bennett, M. *The Battle of Bosworth* (Gloucester: Sutton, 1985).

———. *Lambert Simnel and the Battle of Stoke* (Gloucester: Sutton, 1987).

Bennett, M. J. 'Henry VII and the Northern Rising of 1489'. *English Historical Review* 105 (1990): 34–59.

Blaauw, W. H. 'On the Effigy of Sir David Owen in Easeborne Church, near Midhurst'. *Sussex Archaeological Collections* 7 (1854): 22–43.

Blair, C. 'A Drawing of an English Medieval Royal Gold Cup'. *Burlington Magazine* 121 (1979): 370, 372–373.

Bolland, C., and T. Cooper. *The Real Tudors: Kings and Queens Rediscovered* (London: National Portrait Gallery, 2014).

Borman, T. *Henry VIII and the Men Who Made Him* (London: Hodder & Stoughton, 2018).

———. *The Private Lives of the Tudors* (London: Hodder & Stoughton, 2016).

Bramley, P. *A Companion and Guide to the Wars of the Roses* (Stroud: Sutton, 2007).

Bromley, J. 'The Heraldry of Ormskirk Church'. *Historic Society of Lancashire and Cheshire* 58 (1906): 64–90.

Brooke, C. N. L. *The Medieval Idea of Marriage* (Oxford: Oxford University Press, 1989).

Buck, Sir G. *The History of King Richard III*, ed. A. N. Kincaid (Gloucester: Sutton, 1982).

Burton, E. *The Pageant of Early Tudor England* (New York: Scribner, 1976).

Campbell, L. *Renaissance Portraits: European Portrait-Painting in the 14th, 15th and 16th Centuries* (New Haven, CT: Yale University Press, 1990).

Campbell, M. *Medieval Jewellery in Europe 1100–1500* (London: V & A, 2009).

Carlson, D. R. 'The Latin Writings of John Skelton'. *Studies in Philology*, 88 (1991): 1–125.

Carson, A. *Richard III: The Maligned King* (Stroud: History Press, 2008).

Castor, H. *Blood and Roses: The Paston Family and the Wars of the Roses* (London: Faber and Faber, 2004).

———. *The King, the Crown, and the Duchy of Lancaster: Public Authority and Private Power, 1399–1461* (Oxford: Oxford University Press, 2000).

———. *She Wolves: The Women Who Ruled England Before Elizabeth* (London: Faber and Faber, 2010).

Cecil, Lord D. *Hatfield House* (London: St George's Press, 1973).

Cherry, J. 'Healing Through Faith: The Continuation of Medieval Attitudes to Jewellery into the Renaissance'. *Renaissance Studies* 15 (2001): 154–171.

———. *The Middleham Jewel and Ring* (York: Yorkshire Museum, 1994).

Chrimes, S. B. *Henry VII* (London: Eyre Methuen, 1972).

Clark, J. W. *Endowments of the University of Cambridge* (Cambridge: Cambridge University Press, 1904).

Clarke, P. D. 'English Royal Marriages and the Papal Penitentiary in the Fifteenth Century'. *English Historical Review* 120 (2005): 1014–1029.

Cobban, A. B. *The Medieval Universities: Their Development and Organization* (London: Methuen, 1975).

Cocke, T. '"The Repository of Our English Kings": The Henry VII Chapel as Royal Mausoleum'. *Architectural History* 44 (2001): 212–220.

Cokayne, G. E. *The Complete Peerage of England, Scotland, Ireland, Great Britain and the United Kingdom*, ed. W. Gibbs et al., 12 vols. (London, 1910–1959).

Collinson, P., R. Rex, and G. Stanton. *Lady Margaret Beaufort and Her Professors of Divinity at Cambridge 1502 to 1649* (Cambridge: Cambridge University Press, 2003).

Colvin, H. M., D. R. Ransome, and J. Summerson (eds.). *The History of the King's Works*. 6 vols. (London: Ministry of Public Building and Works, 1963–1982).

Conway, A. *Henry VII's Relations with Scotland and Ireland 1485–98* (Cambridge: Cambridge University Press, 1932).

Cooper, C. H. *The Lady Margaret: A Memoir of Margaret, Countess of Richmond and Derby*, ed. J. E. B. Mayor (Cambridge, 1874).

Coulstock, P. H. *The Collegiate Church of Wimborne Minster* (Woodbridge: Boydell, 1993).

Coward, B. *The Stanleys, Lords Stanley and Earls of Derby 1385–1672: The Origins, Wealth and Power of a Landowning Family* (Manchester: Manchester University Press, 1983).

Crawford, A. 'The Queen's Council in the Middle Ages'. *English Historical Review* 116 (2001): 1193–1211.

Cressy, D. *Birth, Marriage and Death: Ritual, Religion and the Life-Cycle in Tudor and Stuart England* (Oxford: Oxford University Press, 1997).

Cunningham, S. *Prince Arthur: The Tudor King Who Never Was* (Stroud: Amberley, 2016).

Davies, C. S. L. 'Bishop John Morton, the Holy See, and the Accession of Henry VII'. *English Historical Review* 102 (1987): 2–30.

———. 'Tudor: What's in a Name?' *History* 97 (2012): 24–42.

Dean, K. *The World of Richard III* (Stroud: Amberley, 2015).

De Lisle, L. *Tudor: The Family Story* (London: Chatto and Windus, 2013).

Delman, R. M. 'Gendered Viewing, Childbirth and Female Authority in the Residence of Alice Chaucer, Duchess of Suffolk, at Ewelme, Oxfordshire'. *Journal of Medieval History* (2019).

Demers, P. '"God may open more than man maye vnderstande": Lady Margaret Beaufort's Translation of the De "Imitatione Christi"'. *Renaissance and Reformation* 35 (2012): 45–61.

Dickinson, J. C. *The Shrine of Our Lady of Walsingham* (Cambridge: Cambridge University Press, 1956).

Dodson, A. *The Royal Tombs of Great Britain: An Illustrated History* (London: Duckworth, 2004).

Domvile, Lady M. *The King's Mother: Memoir of Margaret Beaufort, Countess of Richmond and Derby* (London: Burns and Oates Ltd., 1899).

Drimmer, S. 'Beyond Private Matter: A Prayer Roll for Queen Margaret of Anjou'. *Gesta* 53 (2014): 95–120.

Duffy, E. *Marking the Hours: English People and Their Prayers, 1240–1570* (New Haven, CT: Yale University Press, 2006).

Duffy, M. *Royal Tombs of Medieval England* (Stroud: Tempus, 2011).

Eales, J. *Women in Early Modern England, 1500–1700* (London: UCL, 1998).

Earle, P. *The Life and Times of Henry V* (London: Weidenfeld and Nicolson, 1972).

Edwards, A. S. G. 'Northern Magnates and Their Books'. *Textual Cultures* 7 (2012): 176–186.

Elton, G. R. *The Tudor Revolution in Government: Administrative Changes in the Reign of Henry VIII* (Cambridge: Cambridge University Press, 1953).

Emery, A. *Greater Medieval Houses of England and Wales, 1300–1500: Volume 3, Southern England* (Cambridge: Cambridge University Press, 2006).

Erlanger, P. *Margaret of Anjou* (London: Elek, 1970).

Evans, J. *A History of Jewellery 1100–1870* (New York: Faber and Faber, 1953).

———. *Magical Jewels of the Middle Ages and the Renaissance* (New York: Dover Publications, 1976).

Fahy, C. 'The Marriage of Edward IV and Elizabeth Woodville: A New Italian Source'. *English Historical Review* 76 (1961): 660–672.

Fetherston-Dilke, M. C. *Maxstoke Castle* (Bidford-on-Avon, 2008).

Fisher, S. '"Margaret R": Lady Margaret Beaufort's Self-Fashioning and Female Ambition'. In *Virtuous or Villainess? The Image of the Royal Mother from the Early Medieval to the Early Modern Era*, ed. C. Fleiner and E. Woodacre (Basingstoke: Palgrave Macmillan, 2016).

Flood, A. '"White Queen" Died of Plague, Claims Letter Found in National Archives'. *The Guardian*, April 25, 2019. www.theguardian.com/books/2019/apr/25/white-queen-died-of-plague-claims-letter-found-in-national-archives.

Foister, S. 'Paintings and Other Works of Art in Sixteenth-Century English Inventories'. *Burlington Magazine* 123 (1981): 273–282.

Fraser, A. *The Six Wives of Henry VIII* (London: Weidenfeld & Nicolson, 1992).

Galvin, C., and P. Lindley. 'Pietro Torrigiano's Portrait Bust of King Henry VII'. *Burlington Magazine* 130 (1988): 892–902.

Gill, L. 'William Caxton and the Rebellion of 1483'. *English Historical Review* 112 (1997): 105–118.

Gillespie, V. 'Syon and the English Market for Continental Printed Books: The Incunable Phase'. *Religion and Literature* 37 (2005): 27–49.

Girouard, M. *Life in the English Country House* (Harmondsworth: Penguin, 1980).

Given-Wilson, C. 'The Court and Household of Edward III, 1360–1377' (unpublished PhD thesis, University of St Andrews, 1976).

Given-Wilson, C., and A. Curteis (eds.). *The Royal Bastards of Medieval England* (London: Routledge and Kegan Paul, 1984).

Goodwin-Austen, R. A. C. 'Woking Manor'. *Surrey Archaeological Collections* 7 (1874).

Gray, A., and F. Brittain. *A History of Jesus College Cambridge* (London: Heinemann Educational, 1979).

Green, R. F. 'Historical Notes of a London Citizen, 1483–1488'. *English Historical Review* 96 (1981): 585–590.

Gregory, P., D. Baldwin, and M. Jones. *The Women of the Cousins' War* (London: Simon & Schuster, 2011).

Griffiths, R. A. 'Henry Tudor: The Training of a King'. *Huntingdon Library Quarterly* 49 (1986): 197–218.

———. *The Reign of Henry VI* (London: Benn, 1981).

Griffiths, R. A., and R. S. Thomas (eds.). *The Making of the Tudor Dynasty* (Gloucester: Sutton, 1985).

Gristwood, S. *Blood Sisters: The Hidden Lives of the Women Behind the Wars of the Roses* (London: HarperPress, 2012).

Gunn, S. 'Henry VII in Context: Problems and Possibilities'. *History* 92 (2007): 301–317.

———. *Henry VII's New Men and the Making of Tudor England* (Oxford: Oxford University Press, 2016).

Gunn, S., and L. Monckton (eds.). *Arthur Tudor, Prince of Wales: Life, Death and Commemoration* (Woodbridge: Boydell & Brewer, 2009), 20–30.

Gunn, S. J. 'The Courtiers of Henry VII'. *English Historical Review* 108 (1993): 23–49.

Haggard, D. J. 'The Ruins of Old Woking Palace'. *Surrey Archaeological Society Collections* 55 (1958).

Halsted, C. A. *Life of Margaret Beaufort, Countess of Richmond and Derby* (London: Smith, Elder & Co, 1839).

Hampton, W. E. *Memorials of the Wars of the Roses* (Gloucester: The Richard III Society, 1979).

Hanham, A. *Richard III and His Early Historians 1483–1535* (Oxford: Oxford University Press, 1975).

Harper, S. P. 'London and the Crown in the Reign of Henry VII' (unpublished PhD thesis, University of London, 2015).

Harris, B. J. *English Aristocratic Women 1450–1550* (Oxford: Oxford University Press, 2002).

———. 'The Fabric of Piety: Aristocratic Women and Care of the Dead, 1450–1550'. *Journal of British Studies* 48 (2009): 308–335.

———. 'A New Look at the Reformation: Aristocratic Women and Nunneries, 1450–1540'. *Journal of British Studies* 32 (1993): 89–113.

———. 'Power and Personal Relations: Elite Mothers and Sons in Yorkist and Early Tudor England'. *Signs* 15 (1990): 606–632.

———. 'The View from My Lady's Chamber: New Perspectives on the Early Tudor Monarchy'. *Huntingdon Library Quarterly* 60 (1997): 215–247.

———. 'Women and Politics in Early Tudor England'. *Historical Journal* 33 (1990): 259–281.

Hart-Davis, A. *What the Tudors and Stuarts Did for Us* (London: Boxtree, 1996).

Harvey, A., and R. Mortimer (eds.). *The Funeral Effigies of Westminster Abbey* (Woodbridge: Boydell, 1994).

Harvey, B. *Westminster Abbey and its Estates in the Middle Ages* (Oxford: Clarendon, 1977).

Hayward, M. *Dress at the Court of King Henry VIII* (Leeds: Maney, 2007).

Heinze, R. W. *The Proclamations of the Tudor Kings* (Cambridge: Cambridge University Press, 1976).

Hepburn, F. *Portraits of the Later Plantagenets* (Woodbridge: Boydell, 1986).

———. 'The Portraiture of Lady Margaret Beaufort'. *Antiquaries Journal* 72 (1992): 118–140.

Hicks, M. *Anne Neville: Queen to Richard III* (Stroud: Tempus, 2007).

———. 'Crowland's World: A Westminster View of the Yorkist Age'. *History* 90 (2005): 172–190.

———. *False, Fleeting, Perjur'd Clarence: George, Duke of Clarence, 1449–78* (Gloucester: A. Sutton, 1980).

———. 'The Piety of Margaret Lady Hungerford'. *Journal of Ecclesiastical History* 38 (1987): 19–38.

———. *Richard III* (Stroud: Tempus, 1991).

Hilton, L. *Queens Consort: England's Medieval Queens* (London: Phoenix, 2008).

Hochstetler Meyer, B. 'The First Tomb of Henry VII of England'. *Art Bulletin* 58 (1976): 358–367.

Hogrefe, P. 'Legal Rights of Tudor Women and the Circumvention by Men and Women'. *Sixteenth Century Journal* 3 (1972): 97–105.

Hooker, J. R. 'Some Cautionary Notes on Henry VII's Household and Chamber "System"'. *Speculum* 33 (1958): 69–75.

Horrox, R. *Richard III: A Study of Service* (Cambridge: Cambridge University Press, 1989).

Hoult, J. *The Vill, Manor and Township of Knowsley* (Liverpool: Northern Publishing Co, 1930).

Howard, M. *The Early Tudor Country House: Architecture and Politics 1490–1550* (London: George Philip, 1987).

Hutchinson, R. *Young Henry: The Rise of Henry VIII* (London: Weidenfeld & Nicolson, 2011).

Impey, E., and G. Parnell. *The Tower of London: The Official Illustrated History* (London: Merrell, 2000).

James, S. E. *Women's Voices in Tudor Wills, 1485–1603: Authority, Influence and Material Culture* (Farnham: Ashgate, 2015).

Jansen, S. L. *The Monstrous Regiment of Women: Female Rulers in Early Modern Europe* (Basingstoke: Palgrave Macmillan, 2002).

Jones, D. *The Hollow Crown: The Wars of the Roses and the Rise of the Tudors* (London: Faber and Faber, 2014).

Jones, M. '"For My Lord of Richmond, a *pourpoint* . . . and a palfrey": Brief Remarks on the Financial Evidence for Henry Tudor's Exile in Brittany 1471–1484'. In *The Ricardian*, Vol. XIII, ed. L. Visser-Fuchs (2002), 283–293.

———. 'Henry VII, Lady Margaret Beaufort and the Orléans Ransom'. In *Kings and Nobles in the Later Middle Ages*, ed. R. A. Griffiths and J. Sherborne (Gloucester: Sutton, 1986).

———. 'John Beaufort, Duke of Somerset and the French Expedition of 1443'. In *Patronage, the Crown and the Provinces*, ed. R. A. Griffiths (Gloucester: Sutton, 1981).

———. 'Margaret Beaufort: Mother of the Tudors'. *BBC History Magazine*, January 2017, 50–55.

Jones, M., and M. Underwood. 'Lady Margaret Beaufort'. *History Today* 35 (1985).

Jones, M. K. 'The Beaufort Family and the War in France, 1421–1450' (unpublished PhD thesis, University of Bristol, 1982).

———. *Bosworth 1485: Psychology of a Battle* (Stroud: Tempus, 2002).

———. 'Richard III and Lady Margaret Beaufort: A Re-assessment'. In *Richard III: Loyalty, Lordship and Law*, ed. P. W. Hammond (London: Richard III and Yorkist History Trust, 1986).

———. 'Sir William Stanley of Holt: Politics and Family Allegiance in the Late Fifteenth Century'. *Welsh History Review* 14 (1988).

———. 'Somerset, York and the Wars of the Roses'. *English Historical Review* 104 (1989): 285–307.

Jones, M. K., and M. G. Underwood. *The King's Mother: Lady Margaret Beaufort, Countess of Richmond and Derby* (Cambridge: Cambridge University Press, 1992).

Kaufman, P. I. 'Polydore Vergil and the Strange Disappearance of Christopher Urswick'. *Sixteenth Century Journal* 17 (1986): 69–85.

Keiser, G. 'Patronage and Piety in Fifteenth-Century England: Margaret Duchess of Clarence, Symon Wynter, and Beinecke MS. 317'. *Yale University Library Gazette* 60 (1985): 32–46.

Kibre, P. 'Lewis of Caerleon, Doctor of Medicine, Astronomer, and Mathematician (d. 1494?)'. *University of Chicago Press on behalf of The History of Science Society* 43 (1952): 100–108.

Kingsford, C. L. *English Historical Literature in the Fifteenth Century* (Oxford: Clarendon, 1913).

———. 'On Some London Houses of the Early Tudor Period'. *Archaeologica* 71 (1920–1921).

Kipling, G. *The Triumph of Honour: Burgundian Origins of the Elizabethan Renaissance* (The Hague: Leiden University Press, 1977).

Kisby, F. 'A Mirror of Monarchy: Music and Musicians in the Household Chapel of the Lady Margaret Beaufort, Mother of Henry VII'. *Early Music History* 16 (1997): 203–234.

———. 'Officers and Office-Holding at the English Court: A Study of the Chapel Royal, 1485–1547'. *Royal Musical Association Research Chronicle* 32 (1999): 1–61.

———. 'The Royal Household Chapel in Early-Tudor London, 1485–1547' (unpublished PhD thesis, University of London, 1996).

Lander, J. R. 'The Crown and the Aristocracy in England, 1450–1509'. *Albion: A Quarterly Journal Concerned with British Studies* 8 (1976): 203–218.

Lawson, S. (ed.). *Eltham Palace* (London, 2011).

Laynesmith, J. L. *Cecily Duchess of York* (London: Bloomsbury Academic, 2017).

———. *The Last Medieval Queens* (Oxford: Oxford University Press, 2004).

Lee, P.-A. 'Reflections of Power: Margaret of Anjou and the Dark Side of Queenship'. *Renaissance Quarterly* 39 (1986): 183–217.

Legg, P. *Winchester: History You Can See* (Stroud: History Press, 2011).

Levine, M. *Tudor Dynastic Problems, 1460–1571* (London: Allen and Unwin, 1973).

Lewis, J. 'Lathom House: The Northern Court'. *Journal of the British Archaeological Association* 152 (1999): 150–171.

Lewis, J. E. *London: The Autobiography* (London: Constable, 2008).

Lewis, M. *The Survival of the Princes in the Tower* (Stroud: History Press, 2017).

Leyser, H. *Medieval Women: A Social History of Women in England 450–1500* (London: Phoenix Giant, 1995).

Licence, A. *Cecily Neville: Mother of Kings* (Stroud: Amberley, 2014).

———. *Red Roses: Blanche of Gaunt to Margaret Beaufort* (Stroud: History Press, 2016).

Lloyd, A. H. *The Early History of Christ's College Cambridge* (Cambridge: Cambridge University Press, 1934).

———. 'Two Monumental Brasses in the Chapel of Christ's College'. *Proceedings of the Cambridge Antiquarian Society* 33 (1933).

Loades, D. *Mary Rose: Tudor Princess, Queen of France, the Extraordinary Life of Henry VIII's Sister* (Stroud: Amberley, 2012).

———. *The Tudor Court* (London: Batsford Ltd, 1986).

Lodge, E. *Portraits of Illustrious Personages of Great Britain*. 4 vols. (London: London Printing and Publishing Company, 1821–1834).

Lowry, M. J. C. 'Caxton, St Winifred and the Lady Margaret Beaufort'. *The Library* 6 (1983): 101–117.

Lucraft, J. *Katherine Swynford: The History of a Medieval Mistress* (Stroud: History Press, 2006).

Ludlow, N. *Pembroke Castle: Birthplace of the Tudor Dynasty* (Pembroke: Pembroke Castle Trust, 2001).

Lynn, E. *Tudor Fashion* (New Haven, CT: Yale University Press, 2017).

MacGibbon, D. *Elizabeth Woodville: A Life* (London: Arthur Barker, 1938).

Matthews, C. P. *The Story of the Abbey Church Bourne* (Gloucester: British Publishing Co, 1962).

Mattingly, G. *Catherine of Aragon* (London: Jonathan Cape, 1942).

Maurer, H. 'Whodunit: The Suspects in the Case'. *Ricardian Register* 18 (1983): 4–27.

Maurer, H. E. *Margaret of Anjou: Queenship and Power in Late Medieval England* (Woodbridge: Boydell, 2003).

McFarlane, K. B. *Lancastrian Kings and Lollard Knights* (Oxford: Clarendon Press, 1972).

———. *The Nobility of Later Medieval England* (Oxford: Clarendon Press, 1973).

McIntosh, M. K. 'The Benefits and Drawbacks of *Femme Sole* Status in England, 1300–1630'. *Journal of British Studies* 44 (2005): 410–438.

Mertes, K. *The English Noble Household 1250–1600: Good Governance and Politic Rule* (Oxford: Basil Blackwell, 1988).

Mitchell, A. *Kingston Lacy* (Swindon: National Trust, 1994).

Murray Kendall, P. *Richard the Third* (London: Allen & Unwin, 1968).

Myers, A. R. 'The Household of Queen Elizabeth Woodville, 1466–7'. *Bulletin of the John Rylands Library* 50 (1967–1968): 207–215.

———. 'The Household of Queen Margaret of Anjou, 1452–3'. *Bulletin of the John Rylands Library* 40 (1958): 79–113.

———. 'The Jewels of Queen Margaret of Anjou'. *Bulletin of the John Rylands Library* 42 (1959): 113–131.

Norton, E. *The Lives of Tudor Women* (London: Head of Zeus, 2016).

———. *Margaret Beaufort: Mother of the Tudor Dynasty* (Stroud: Amberley, 2010).

Okerlund, A. *Elizabeth: England's Slandered Queen* (Stroud: Tempus, 2009).

———. *Elizabeth of York* (New York: Palgrave Macmillan, 2009).

Oliver, C. *A Guide to the Minster Church of St Cuthburga* (Christchurch, 2016).

Olson, R. 'Margaret Beaufort, Royal Tapestries, and Confinement at the Tudor Court'. *Textile History* 48 (2017): 233–247.

Orme, N. *English Schools in the Middle Ages* (London: Methuen, 1973).

Ormrod, W. M. 'The Royal Nursery: A Household for the Younger Children of Edward III'. *English Historical Review* 120 (2005): 398–415.

Owen, H., and J. B. Blakeway. *A History of Shrewsbury*. 2 vols. (London: Simpkin, Marshall and Co, 1825).

Painter, G. D. *William Caxton* (London: Chatto and Windus, 1976).

Penn, T. *Winter King: The Dawn of Tudor England* (London: Penguin, 2011).

Perry, M. *Sisters to the King: The Tumultuous Lives of Henry VIII's Sisters— Margaret of Scotland and Mary of France* (London: Andre Deutsch, 1998).

Pierce, H. *Margaret Pole, Countess of Salisbury 1473–1541: Loyalty, Lineage and Leadership* (Cardiff: University of Wales Press, 2003).

Plomer, H. *Wynkyn de Worde and his Contemporaries* (London: Grafton & Co, 1925).

Pollard, A. J. *The Wars of the Roses* (Basingstoke: Macmillan Education, 1988).

———. *The Worlds of Richard III* (Stroud: Tempus, 2001).

Poulton, R., and G. Pattison. *Woking Palace* (Woking, 2017).

Powell, S. *The Birgittines of Syon Abbey: Preaching and Print* (Turnhout: Brepols, 2017).

———. 'Lady Margaret Beaufort and Her Books'. *The Library* 3 (1998): 197–240.

———. 'Margaret Pole and Syon Abbey'. *Historical Research* 78 (2005): 563–567.

Rackham, H. (ed.). *Christ's College in Former Days* (Cambridge: Cambridge University Press, 1939).

———. *Early Statutes of Christ's College, Cambridge* (Cambridge: Fabb & Tyler, 1927).

Rawcliffe, C. *The Staffords, Earls of Stafford and Dukes of Buckingham 1394–1521* (Cambridge: Cambridge University Press, 1978).

Reid, R. R. *The King's Council in the North* (London: Longmans and Co, 1921).

Reynolds, A. *In Fine Style: The Art of Tudor and Stuart Fashion* (London: Royal Collection Trust, 2013).

Rickert, M. 'The So-Called Beaufort Hours and York Psalter'. *Burlington Magazine* 104 (1962): 238–246.

Roberts, S. E. *Jasper: The Tudor Kingmaker* (Croydon: Fonthill Media Limited, 2015).

Robinson, J. M. *Windsor Castle: The Official Illustrated History* (London: Royal Collection, 2011).

Rosenthal, J. T. *Nobles and the Noble Life 1295–1500* (London: Allen and Unwin, 1976).

———. *The Purchase of Paradise: The Social Function of Aristocratic Benevolence, 1307–1485* (London: Routledge and Kegan Paul, 1972).

Ross, C. (ed.). *Patronage, Pedigree and Power in Later Medieval England* (Gloucester: A. Sutton, 1979).

Ross, C. D. *Edward IV* (London: Book Club Associates, 1975).

Ross, J. *Henry VI: A Good, Simple and Innocent Man* (London: Allen Lane, 2016).

Routh, E. M. G. *A Memoir of Lady Margaret Beaufort, Countess of Richmond and Derby, Mother of Henry VII* (Oxford: Oxford University Press, 1924).

Sadlack, E. A. *The French Queen's Letters: Mary Tudor Brandon and the Politics of Marriage in Sixteenth-Century Europe* (New York: Palgrave Macmillan, 2011).

Saul, N. *The Three Richards: Richard I, Richard II and Richard III* (London: Hambledon Continuum, 2005).

Scarisbrick, D. *Rings: Jewelry of Power, Love and Loyalty* (London: Thames & Hudson, 2007).

———. *Tudor and Jacobean Jewellery* (London: Tate Publishing, 1995).

Schroder, T. 'A Royal Tudor Rock-Crystal and Silver-Gilt Vase'. *Burlington Magazine* 137 (1995): 356–366.

Schutte, V. 'Royal Tudor Women as Patrons and Curators'. *Early Modern Women* 9 (2014): 79–88.

Scofield, C. L. 'Henry, Duke of Somerset, and Edward IV'. *English Historical Review* 21 (1906): 300–302.

———. *The Life and Reign of Edward the Fourth.* 2 vols. (London: Longmans & Co, 1923).

Scott, R. F. 'On the Contracts for the Tomb of the Lady Margaret Beaufort, Countess of Richmond and Derby, Mother of King Henry VII, and Foundress of the Colleges of Christ and St John in Cambridge'. *Archaeologica* 66 (1915).

Seward, D. *A Brief History of the Hundred Years War* (London: Robinson, 1978).

———. *A Brief History of the Wars of the Roses: The Bloody Rivalry for the Throne of England* (London: Robinson, 1995).

———. *The Last White Rose: The Secret Wars of the Tudors* (London: Constable, 2010).

Shoesmith, R., and A. Johnson (eds.). *Ludlow Castle: Its History and Buildings* (Almeley: Logaston Press, 2006).

Sicca, C. M., and L. A. Waldman (eds.). *The Anglo-Florentine Renaissance: Art for the Early Tudors* (New Haven, CT: Yale University Press, 2012).

Simon, L. *Of Virtue Rare: Margaret Beaufort, Matriarch of the House of Tudor* (Boston: Houghton Mifflin Company, 1982).

Sinclair, A. (ed.). *The Beauchamp Pageant* (Donington: Richard III and Yorkist History Trust, 2003).

Skidmore, C. *Bosworth: The Birth of the Tudors* (London: Weidenfeld and Nicolson, 2013).

———. *Richard III: Brother, Protector, King* (London: Weidenfeld and Nicolson, 2017).

Stanley, A. P. *Historical Memorials of Westminster Abbey* (London, 1868).

Starkey, D. *Henry: Virtuous Prince* (London: W.F. Howes, 2008).

———. 'Intimacy and Innovation: The Rise of the Privy Chamber, 1485–1547'. In *The English Court: From the Wars of the Roses to the Civil War*, ed. D. Starkey, D. A. L. Morgan, J. Murphy, P. Wright, N. Cuddy, and K. Sharpe (London: Longman, 1987), 71–118.

———. (ed.). *Rivals in Power: Lives and Letters of the Great Tudor Dynasties* (London: Macmillan, 1990).

———. *Six Wives: The Queens of Henry VIII* (London: Chatto and Windus, 2004).

St John Hope, W. H. *Windsor Castle: An Architectural History* (London: Country Life, 1913).

St John's College. *Collegium Divi Johannis Evangelistae, 1511–1911*. Quatercentenary publication. (Cambridge: Cambridge University Press, 1911).

———. 'Painting of Mother of King Henry VII Revealed as Oldest Large-Scale Portrait of an English Woman'. University of Cambridge, March 29, 2019. www.joh.cam.ac.uk/painting-mother-king-henry-vii-revealed-oldest-large-scale-portrait-english-woman.

Struthers, J. *Royal Palaces of Britain* (London: New Holland, 2004).

Sutton, A., and L. Visser-Fuchs. 'A "*Most Benevolent Queen*": Queen Elizabeth Woodville's Reputation, Her Piety and Her Books'. *The Ricardian* 10 (1995): 214–245.

———. *Richard III's Books* (Stroud: Sutton, 1997).

Swanson, R. N. *Church and Society in Late Medieval England* (Oxford: Basil Blackwell, 1989).

Tallis, N. L. 'All the Queen's Jewels, 1445–1548' (unpublished PhD thesis, University of Winchester, 2019).

Thomas, D. H. *The Herberts of Raglan and the Battle of Edgecote 1469* (Enfield: Freezywater Publications, 1994).

Thompson, B. (ed.). *The Reign of Henry VII*, Vol. V (Stamford: Paul Watkins, 1995).

Thornton, T. 'Lancastrian Rule and the Resources of the Prince of Wales, 1456–61'. *Journal of Medieval History* 42, no. 3 (2016): 382–404.

Thurley, S. *The Royal Palaces of Tudor England: Architecture and Court Life 1460–1547* (New Haven, CT: Yale University Press, 1993).

Trapp, J. B. 'Christopher Urswick and His Books: The Reading of Henry VII's Almoner'. *Renaissance Studies* 1 (1987): 48–70.

Tremlett, G. *Catherine of Aragon: Henry's Spanish Queen* (London: Faber and Faber, 2010).

———. *Isabella of Castile: Europe's First Great Queen* (London: Bloomsbury, 2017).

Tuck, A. *Richard II and the English Nobility* (London: Edward Arnold, 1973).

Twigg, J. *A History of Queens' College, Cambridge 1448–1986* (Woodbridge: Boydell, 1987).

Underwood, M. G. 'The Lady Margaret and Her Cambridge Connections'. *Sixteenth Century Journal* 13 (1982): 67–82.

———. 'Politics and Piety in the Household of Lady Margaret Beaufort'. *Journal of Ecclesiastical History* 38 (1987): 39–52.

Venables, E. 'Bourne: Its Abbey and Castle'. *Associated Architectural Societies, Reports and Papers* 20 (1889).

Visser-Fuchs, L. 'The Casualty List of the Battle of Barnet'. *The Ricardian* 8 (1988).

Ward, J. C. *English Noblewomen in the Later Middle Ages* (London: Longman, 1992).

Warnicke, R. M. *Elizabeth of York and Her Six Daughters-in-Law: Fashioning Tudor Queenship, 1485–1547* (Basingstoke: Palgrave Macmillan, 2017).

———. 'The Lady Margaret, Countess of Richmond; a Noblewoman of Independent Wealth and Status'. *Fifteenth Century Studies* 9 (1984).

———. 'The Lady Margaret Beaufort, Countess of Richmond (d. 1509) as Seen by John Fisher and by Lord Morley'. *Moreana* 19 (1982).

———. 'Sir Ralph Bigod: A Loyal Servant to King Richard III'. *The Ricardian* 6 (1984).

Warrior, J. *A Guide to King's College Chapel Cambridge* (Cambridge, 1994).

Weightman, C. *Margaret of York: The Diabolical Duchess* (Stroud: Amberley, 2009).

Weir, A. *Britain's Royal Families: The Complete Genealogy* (London: Pimlico, 1989).

———. *Elizabeth of York: The First Tudor Queen* (London: Jonathan Cape, 2013).

———. *Henry VIII: King and Court* (London: Pimlico, 2001).

———. *Katherine Swynford: The Story of John of Gaunt and His Scandalous Duchess* (London: Jonathan Cape, 2007).

———. *Lancaster and York: The Wars of the Roses* (London: Jonathan Cape, 1995).

———. *The Princes in the Tower* (London: Pimlico, 1992).

———. 'A Tudor of Rare Talent'. *BBC History Magazine* (2013).

Westlake, H. F. *Westminster Abbey* (London: A.R. Mowbray and Co, 1923).

Wilkinson, J. *Henry VII's Lady Chapel in Westminster Abbey* (London: Scala, 2007).

Williams, D. (ed.). *England in the Fifteenth Century* (Woodbridge: Boydell Press, 1987).

Williams, D. M. (ed.). *Raglan Castle* (Cardiff, 1998).

Williams, N. *The Life and Times of Henry VII* (London: Weidenfeld and Nicolson, 1973).

Wolffe, B. P. *Henry VI* (London: Methuen, 1981).

Woodman, F. *The Architectural History of Canterbury Cathedral* (London: Routledge, 1981).

Wroe, A. *Perkin: A Story of Deception* (London: Vintage, 2003).

NOTES AND REFERENCES

INTRODUCTION

1. Lander, 'The Crown and the Aristocracy in England, 1450–1509', 213.

2. Williams, *Life and Times of Henry VII*, 110.

3. In 1965 Margaret formed the subject of Betty King's novel *The Lady Margaret*, which focused on the relationship between Margaret and her second husband, Edmund Tudor. It was portrayed as a great love story that resulted in the birth of Henry Tudor. *The King's Mother* followed this in 1969, continuing Margaret's story after Edmund's death. In the 1972 BBC series *The Shadow of the Tower*, Marigold Sharman plays the role of Margaret. The series was extremely well received and showcases Margaret's relationship with her son. She is also portrayed as ambitious, and even ruthless when it comes to the safety of her son and family. For example, in the penultimate episode, Margaret can be seen urging her son to execute the Earl of Warwick in order to secure his own safety. Though it is possible that she did so, there is no contemporary evidence to support this.

4. S. Gristwood, *Blood Sisters*, 6.

CHAPTER 1: NOBLE BLOOD

1. In 1327 Bletsoe's owner, John de Patishull, received a licence to crenellate the house. The medieval Bletsoe Castle no longer survives, and instead a Grade II listed building now stands on the site it once occupied. Following the death of Margaret's mother, it came into the hands of John St John, Margaret's half-brother. It passed through several generations of the St John family.

2. See Jones and Underwood, *King's Mother*, 32, for the history of the book.

3. Fisher, 'Mornynge Remembraunce', 2.

4. The eldest of Edward III and Philippa's sons was Edward, the Black Prince. When Edward predeceased his father on 8 June 1376, his son, Richard, became the king's heir. The births of Lionel, Duke of Clarence; John of Gaunt; Edmund,

Duke of York; and Thomas, Duke of Gloucester, followed that of the Black Prince. Additionally, four surviving daughters were born of the marriage.

5. Blanche was the younger daughter of Henry, first Duke of Lancaster, and Isabel de Beaumont. She was married to Gaunt on 19 May 1359 at Reading Abbey. The couple also had two other sons who died in infancy.

6. Blanche died on 12 September 1368 at Tutbury Castle, possibly as a result of the Black Death that raged through Europe in the mid-fourteenth century. Gaunt was heartbroken, and it was not until 21 September 1371—three years after Blanche's death—that he remarried Constance. Constance's mother was María de Padilla, a Castilian noblewoman who had been Pedro's mistress before she became his wife.

7. The couple still managed to produce two children of which one, a daughter named Catherine, survived infancy.

8. Weir, *Katherine Swynford*, 103. Alison Weir confirms that it is uncertain when the affair began, but it was certainly taking place by late spring 1372. Katherine was the daughter of Sir Paon de Roët, although the identity of her mother is uncertain. Paon was a faithful servant of Queen Philippa, into whose household his daughter Katherine seems to have been placed at an early age. See Weir, *Katherine Swynford*, 2–6. Philippa became Queen of Portugal through her marriage to João I in 1387, and Elizabeth was later Duchess of Exeter.

9. Katherine's first husband, Hugh Swynford, a knight hailing from the small Lincolnshire estate of Kettlethorpe, died while campaigning with Gaunt in Aquitaine, leaving Katherine with two young children to support.

10. Weir highlights that every English monarch since 1461 is descended from Katherine, as well as no fewer than five American presidents. Weir, *Katherine Swynford*, 2.

11. Beaufort had been lost to the French in 1369. See Weir, *Katherine Swynford*, 111.

12. Constance was buried at great expense in the Church of St Mary in Leicester, where Blanche's father also lay entombed. Mary de Bohun, first wife of Gaunt's son Henry, who died within a few months of Constance, was also buried there. The church no longer survives. After an unsuccessful military campaign, Gaunt also renounced his claim to the Castilian throne on condition that his daughter, Catherine, be married to the Trastámaran heir, Henry. In 1390 the couple became king and queen of Castile, and thus Gaunt's hopes for the throne were finally realized, albeit in a different form than he had originally anticipated. Catherine's marriage to Henry III produced three surviving children, including John II, King of Castile. Among John's children from his second marriage were Isabella, mother of Queen Katherine of Aragon.

13. Given-Wilson et al., *Parliament Rolls of Medieval England*, Richard II: January 1397.

14. Henry became a cardinal and one of the most powerful men in England, Joan became Countess of Westmorland and produced a number of children who became involved in Margaret's story, and Thomas was a distinguished military commander.

15. Ellis, *Original Letters*, I:164.

16. Gaunt was laid to rest beside his first wife, Blanche, in Old St Paul's Cathedral. Katherine Swynford outlived him, dying on 10 May 1403. She was buried in Lincoln Cathedral, where her tomb and that of her daughter, Joan, still survive.

17. Contemporary chroniclers provided conflicting reports as to the manner in which Richard met his death: some suggested that he was deliberately starved to death; others, that he refused all food; and some, that he died by different means altogether. He was buried first at Kings Langley, but in 1413 his remains were moved to the tomb he had commissioned for himself in Westminster Abbey.

18. Margaret was the daughter of Thomas Holland, Earl of Kent, who was in turn the son of Richard II's mother, Princess Joan of Kent, from her first marriage.

19. CPR 1405–1408, 284.

20. The hospital had been founded in 1147 by Queen Matilda, consort of King Stephen. Other medieval queens had also shown an interest in it, notably Philippa of Hainault.

21. The eldest daughter, Joan Beaufort, married James I of Scotland on 12 February 1424. When her husband was murdered in 1437, Joan attempted to assert her authority in the name of her son, James II. She was unsuccessful. The youngest Beaufort daughter, Margaret, married the Earl of Devon.

22. Henry Beaufort died during the siege of Rouen.

23. Henry IV died on 20 March 1413 in the Jerusalem Chamber at Westminster Abbey. He was buried in Canterbury Cathedral.

24. CPR 1436–1441, 515.

25. Like his father, Thomas was buried in Canterbury Cathedral.

26. The Château de Vincennes still survives, as does the donjon in which Henry V died.

27. Kingsford, *Chronicles of London*, 74.

28. Riley, *Ingulph's Chronicle*, 391.

29. Ibid., 398; CPR 1436–1441, 515.

30. CPR 1436–1441, 515.

31. Jones and Underwood, *King's Mother*, 27.

32. The identity of Tacyn's mother is unknown.

33. Fisher, 'Mornynge Remembraunce', 2.

34. Tombs of members of the Stourton family can still be seen in the church at Mere, Wiltshire.

35. Oliver St John was the heir of John St John by his wife, Isabel Paveley.

36. Jones, 'Beaufort Family and the War in France', 9.

37. TNA, C 1/24/230.

38. Jones states that his position as the heir of the first earl, and his closeness in blood to the Crown, made him a natural choice. See Jones, 'John Beaufort, Duke of Somerset', 80.

39. Riley, *Ingulph's Chronicle*, 399.

40. Nicholas, *Proceedings and Ordinances of the Privy Council of England*, V:252.

41. Ibid.

42. Harriss and Harriss, 'III John Benet's Chronicle for the Years 1400 to 1462', 21.

43. Riley, *Ingulph's Chronicle*, 399.

44. Somerset returned either to Corfe Castle, the main family home, or to Kingston Lacy. The ruins of Corfe can still be seen, the castle having been largely destroyed during the English Civil War. It was there that Edward the Martyr was murdered in 978. Kingston Lacy became a part of the royal Duchy of Lancaster in the fourteenth century and was visited by John of Gaunt. There is still a house at Kingston Lacy, now the property of the National Trust, but it is the product of a later age.

45. Riley, *Ingulph's Chronicle*, 399.

46. See Davies, *English Chronicle of the Reigns*, 60.

47. The royal peculiar was abolished in 1846.

48. The Tudor traveller John Leland would later declare that Somerset 'lieth buried in a goodly tomb with his wife in the south side of the prebestry'.

49. I am indebted to Alison Weir for bringing this to my attention and for sending me some beautiful images of the likeness. See Fen Edge Archaeology Group website, www.feag.co.uk.

50. See TNA, E 135/3/21.

51. CPR 1441–1446, 283.

CHAPTER 2: OF SINGULAR WISDOM

1. Bentley, *Excerpta Historica or illustrations of English history*, 4.

2. Fisher, 'Mornynge Remembraunce', 2.

3. Ibid.

4. Suffolk had been injured during the siege of Harfleur in 1415; his father died of dysentery. Just weeks later, Suffolk's brother—their father's heir—was killed at the Battle of Agincourt. In 1429 Suffolk was captured during the siege of Orléans, but he was ransomed the following year.

5. Chaucer had been married to Katherine Swynford's sister, Philippa, making their daughter a relative of Margaret's. At the time of her marriage to Suffolk, Alice had already been widowed twice. She had been married at the age of eleven to Sir John Philip, who died in 1415 while campaigning in France with Henry V.

She later married Thomas Montacute, Earl of Salisbury. Neither of these marriages produced any children. Alice's magnificent tomb can still be seen in the church at Ewelme, Oxfordshire.

6. Fisher, 'Mornynge Remembraunce', 2.

7. CPR 1446–1452, 1. Letters Patent dating from 16 September 1446 refer to the fact that Suffolk 'bought of late the keeping of Anne'. Anne was also the niece of Eleanor Beauchamp, the wife of Margaret Beaufort's uncle Edmund.

8. Jones and Underwood, *King's Mother*, 38.

9. CPR 1441–1446, 283.

10. Suffolk's great-grandfather was a wool merchant who had lent Edward III money. He rose in prominence and was knighted in 1339. Richard II later created his son Earl of Suffolk in 1385.

11. James, *Henry the Sixth*, 27.

12. Margaret's mother was Isabella, the daughter of Charles, Duke of Lorraine.

13. Myers, 'Household of Queen Margaret of Anjou', 86.

14. Henry VIII dissolved Titchfield Abbey, and although it was transformed into a grand Tudor mansion by Thomas Wriothesley, it is now in ruins. Both Richard II and Henry V visited.

15. Hinds, *Calendar of State Papers, Milan*, I:26.

16. Images of Margaret survive in two contemporary manuscripts, a medal and a prayer roll.

17. Cardinal Beaufort died at Wolvesey Castle on 11 April and was buried in Winchester Cathedral, where his tomb can be seen.

18. Halsted, *Life of Margaret Beaufort*, 18. The duchess's lifestyle can be inferred from an epitaph that once adorned the tomb of Ralph Lannoy in Bletsoe Church, in which he was styled 'Cofferer and Keeper of the Wardrobe to the most noble Margaret, Duchess of Somerset'. Jones and Underwood have also drawn attention to the fact that the duchess had a swan farmer by the name of David Philip, giving a further indication as to her lifestyle.

19. Tacyn married Reginald Grey, seventh Baron Grey of Wilton. The family resided in Bletchley in Buckinghamshire, where the tomb of Tacyn's father-in-law, Richard Grey, can still be seen in St Mary's Church. She died in 1494.

20. SJLM/1/1/2/1, f. 19; Jones and Underwood, *King's Mother*, 31. James I visited Bletsoe on several occasions as the guest of Lord St John. Domvile reported that on one such visit, when James was hunting nearby, he asked to see the embroidery, hearing that his ancestress had created it. See Domvile, *King's Mother: Memoir of Margaret Beaufort*, 8.

21. Fisher, 'Mornynge Remembraunce', 2.

22. Ibid.

23. WAM 5472, f. 33. On Margaret's orders, William Bailey was sent to return the books to the duchess.

24. Ballard, *Memoirs of Several Ladies of Great Britain*, 13.

25. Bliss, *Calendar of Papal Registers*, X:245.

26. See Jones and Underwood, *King's Mother*, 184.

27. Fisher, 'Mornynge Remembraunce', 2.

28. William Thorpe had built Maxey Castle in the 1370s.

29. The precise identity of John Neville has been difficult to pinpoint owing to the fact that there were several of that name during this period, but it is probable that he was a son of Ralph Neville, Earl of Westmorland, and his second wife, Joan Beaufort—daughter of John of Gaunt and Katherine Swynford. He would therefore have been a cousin of Margaret's father.

30. Bliss, *Calendar of Papal Registers*, IX:579.

31. Ibid.

32. CPR 1446–1452, 44.

33. Lord Welles was later buried beside Joan Waterton in St Oswald's Church, Methley. His eldest daughter, Cecily Welles, married Sir Robert Willoughby and produced a son, Christopher Willoughby, Baron Willoughby de Eresby.

34. Riley, *Ingulph's Chronicle*, 400.

35. Given-Wilson et al., *Parliament Rolls of Medieval England*, Henry VI: November 1449.

36. Ibid.

37. Ibid.

38. Ibid.

39. Fenn, *Paston Letters*, I:39.

40. Davis, *Paston Letters*, 28.

41. Ibid.

42. There is no memorial to Suffolk, although the splendid tomb of his son John and his wife Elizabeth Plantagenet lies in the church.

43. Bliss, *Calendar of Papal Registers*, X:471–474.

44. Ibid.

45. Ibid.

46. Seward, *Brief History of the Wars of the Roses*, 7.

CHAPTER 3: A MARVELLOUS THING

1. Starkey, *Inventory of King Henry VIII*, 238. A portrait of Henry V is also listed.

2. TNA, E 36/84; Blacman, *Memoir*, p. 36.

3. James, *Henry the Sixth*, 36.

4. Ibid.

5. Fisher, 'Mornynge Remembraunce', 2.

6. Ibid.

7. Ibid.

8. Ibid.

9. Ibid.

10. Ibid.

11. Ibid.

12. Given-Wilson et al., *Parliament Rolls of Medieval England*, Henry VI: October 1427.

13. Ibid.

14. Ellis, *Three Books*, 62.

15. Dating from 1385, the tomb that Gronw Fychan ap Tudur shares with his wife, Myfanwy, survives in St Gredifael's Church, Penmynydd. It originally stood in Llanfaes Friary but was moved to St Gredifael's following the Dissolution of the Monasteries. The church also contains a window displaying the symbols of the Tudor family. The Welsh inscription translates as 'Unity is like a rose on a river bank, and like a House of Steel on the top of a mountain'. Part of the original fifteenth-century glass was destroyed by vandals in 2007 but has since been restored.

16. Given-Wilson et al., *Parliament Rolls of Medieval England*, Henry VI: March 1453.

17. Ibid.

18. CPR 1452–1461, 78.

19. TNA, E 404/69/145.

20. Clarendon is now a ruin and lies in the grounds of Clarendon Park.

21. Harriss and Harriss, 'III John Benet's Chronicle', 35.

22. Kingsford, *Chronicles of London*, 163.

23. Somerset was also the prince's godfather, as was the Archbishop of Canterbury, and the Duchess of Buckingham was his godmother.

24. Griffiths and Thomas, *Making of the Tudor Dynasty*, 41.

25. Fenn, *Paston Letters*, I:81. His secretary was also sent to the shrine of St Edward the Confessor at Westminster Abbey to offer on his master's behalf.

26. Fenn, *Paston Letters*, I:83.

27. The order for his release was dated 5 February 1455 from Westminster. CCR 1454–1461, 9.

28. The Parliamentarians largely destroyed Sandal Castle following a siege during the English Civil War in 1645. It now lies in ruins.

29. Hinds, *Calendar of State Papers, Milan*, I:23.

30. Ibid.

31. Harriss and Harriss, 'III John Benet's Chronicle', 38.

32. Ellis, *Three Books*, 96.

33. Hinds, *Calendar of State Papers, Milan*, I:23.

34. The abbey is the modern-day St Albans Cathedral.

35. Gairdner, *Gregory's Chronicle*, 198.
36. Hinds, *Calendar of State Papers, Milan*, I:23.

CHAPTER 4: AT WAR TOGETHER IN WALES

1. This child was the future Henry V, born on 16 September 1386.
2. Jones and Underwood, *King's Mother*, 95.
3. SJLM/3/2/1.
4. In the seventeenth century, Oliver Cromwell's army desecrated St David's Cathedral, and in so doing caused damage to Edmund's tomb. It was not until 1873 that Thomas Waller restored the brass, which was originally created on the orders of Henry VII.
5. Given-Wilson et al., *Parliament Rolls of Medieval England*, Henry VI: July 1455.
6. Hinds, *Calendar of State Papers, Milan*, I:23.
7. Griffiths and Thomas, *Making of the Tudor Dynasty*, 43.
8. Given-Wilson et al., *Parliament Rolls of Medieval England*, Henry VI: July 1455.
9. Fenn, *Paston Letters*, I:137.
10. Some parts of the ruins of Carmarthen Castle can still be seen, most substantially the gatehouse.
11. Although Caldicot Castle is a ruin, having been largely destroyed by the Parliamentarians in the seventeenth century, significant parts survive.

CHAPTER 5: MY GOOD AND GRACIOUS PRINCE, KING AND ONLY-BELOVED SON

1. The inscription on the tomb is as follows: 'Under this marble stone here enclosed resteth the bones of the noble Lord, Edmund Earl of Richmond, father and brother to kings; the which departed out of this world in the year of our Lord God, 1456, the third day of the month of November; on whose soul Almighty Jesu have mercy. Amen'.
2. Nichols, *Testamenta Vetusta*, I:431.
3. André, *Life of Henry VII*, 10.
4. The keep still survives, although, like the rest of Pembroke Castle, it is now a ruin.
5. At least one person, John Whithorn, was incarcerated in the dungeon and starved to death over a land dispute in the fourteenth century.
6. The oriel window has not survived, although it is possible to see where it once was.

7. Although in the fifteenth century the new year did not officially begin until March, for the purposes of clarity and ease of use, I have deemed it to start on 1 January in keeping with the Julian calendar.

8. André, *Life of Henry VII*, 10.

9. Westminster Abbey MS 39. Viscount Dillon presented the prayer book in 1923.

10. The Henry VII Tower still survives, and today contains a wax tableau depicting the scene of Henry Tudor's birth.

11. Williams, *Life and Times of Henry VII*, 12.

12. André, *Life of Henry VII*, 6.

13. Ibid., 8–9.

14. Cited in Cooper, *Lady Margaret*, 67.

15. I am extremely grateful to Suzanne Schuld, an experienced nurse, and her medical colleagues, for taking the time to share their thoughts on this matter. Similarly, to my mother, Sylvia Howard, a midwife with over thirty years' experience.

16. M. Jones, 'Margaret Beaufort'. In *The Women of the Cousins' War*, ed. P. Gregory, D. Baldwin and M. Jones (London: Simon & Schuster, 2011), 256–257.

17. André, *Life of Henry VII*, 11.

CHAPTER 6: LADY STAFFORD

1. Buckingham's royal blood stemmed from his mother, Anne of Gloucester, who was the daughter of Edward III's youngest son, Thomas of Woodstock. Buckingham's father, Edmund Stafford, was killed fighting for Henry IV at the Battle of Shrewsbury in 1403.

2. Anne, Duchess of Buckingham, and York's wife, Cecily Neville, were sisters.

3. Norton, *Margaret Beaufort*, 49.

4. Jones and Underwood, *King's Mother*, 40.

5. CPR 1485–1494, 95. Joan's husband, Philip, was described as the king's servant and was also rewarded. Husband and wife may have been members of Jasper Tudor's household.

6. Henry Stafford is believed to have been born in around 1425, but his precise date of birth is unknown.

7. Margaret was the fourth of Edmund Beaufort's surviving daughters. When her husband Humphrey died in 1458, Margaret later remarried Sir Richard Dayrell. Together they had a daughter, also named Margaret. The younger Margaret married James Tuchet, Baron Audley, who was later executed by Henry VII for his involvement in the Cornish Rebellion of 1497.

8. Anne was the daughter of Ralph Neville and Joan Beaufort.

9. See Jones and Underwood, *King's Mother*, 143–144.

10. WAM 6660.

11. Jones and Underwood, *King's Mother*, 143–144.

12. WAM 5472, f. 45.

13. Ralph Griffiths as referenced in Jones and Underwood, *King's Mother*, 41.

14. Norton, *Margaret Beaufort*, 53.

15. CPR 1452–1461, 433.

16. Venables, 'Bourne: Its Abbey and Castle', 5.

17. André, *Life of Henry VII*, 10.

18. Jones and Underwood, *King's Mother*, 40.

19. CPR 1452–1461, 545.

20. Eccleshall Castle was largely destroyed during the English Civil War but was rebuilt at the end of the seventeenth century. It is now a private residence.

21. Hinds, *Calendar of State Papers, Milan*, I:38.

22. Pronay and Cox, *Crowland Chronicle Continuations*, 111.

23. Mary had been married to James II of Scotland, who died on 3 August 1460 following the explosion of a piece of artillery during the siege of Roxburgh Castle. Mary acted as regent on behalf of the couple's son, James III, until 1463.

24. Pronay and Cox, *Crowland Chronicle Continuations*, 111.

25. Weir, *Lancaster and York*, 252.

26. Hinds, *Calendar of State Papers, Milan*, I:54.

CHAPTER 7: LIKE A FUGITIVE

1. He was buried in the Grey Friars in Hereford, which no longer stands.

2. Gairdner, *Gregory's Chronicle*, 211.

3. Ibid. Leanda De Lisle has suggested that the madwoman could actually be the mother of Owen's illegitimate son, David. See De Lisle, *Tudor: The Family Story*, 25.

4. Hinds, *Calendar of State Papers, Milan*, I:71.

5. Ibid., I:91.

6. Weir, *Lancaster and York*, 284.

7. Riley, *Ingulph's Chronicle*, 426.

8. Hinds, *Calendar of State Papers, Milan*, I:79.

9. Gairdner, *Gregory's Chronicle*, 215.

10. Hinds, *Calendar of State Papers, Milan*, I:69.

11. Commynes, *Memoirs*, 188.

12. More, *History of King Richard III*, 5; Riley, *Ingulph's Chronicle*, 424.

13. Ellis, *Three Books*, 172.

14. More, *History of King Richard*, 5.

15. CPR 1461–1467, 12. John married Constance Green, who was the daughter of Sir Henry Green. Little is known of their marriage, but they sired a son, Edward.

16. Jones and Underwood, 'Lady Margaret Beaufort', 24.

17. CPR 1461–1467, 30.

18. Ibid., 99.

19. Ibid., 100.

20. Henry Windsor to John Paston, cited in K. Dockray, *Edward IV*, 28.

21. Weir, *Lancaster and York*, 308.

22. Given-Wilson et al., *Parliament Rolls of Medieval England*, Edward IV: November 1461.

23. Margaret, Countess of Shrewsbury, is another notable example.

24. CPR 1461–1467, 114.

25. Raglan Castle is now a spectacular ruin.

26. The outcome of Formigny was a French victory, during which many of the English were taken prisoner.

27. Anne was born in around 1430 and had three other siblings. Her family's lands were largely in Herefordshire.

28. They would sire at least ten children, many of whom made prestigious marriages. Herbert also had several illegitimate children, from one of whom the line of the current earls of Pembroke are descended; William would marry Mary Wydeville, sister of Queen Elizabeth Wydeville, and later Richard III's illegitimate daughter, Katherine. He also served in the household of Richard's son, Prince Edward. Walter was wed to Anne Stafford, the daughter of Henry Stafford's nephew, Henry, Duke of Buckingham.

29. Nichols, *Testamenta Vetusta*, I:305.

30. Commynes, *Memoirs*, 354.

31. CPR 1485–1494, 332.

32. André, *Life of Henry VII*, 11.

33. Ibid., 10.

34. Ibid., 10–11.

35. CPR 1461–1467, 212–213.

36. In the seventeenth century, Sir George Buck would claim that the title of Richmond was conferred upon Clarence because the king 'was in great mislike of the young Earl of Richmond, Henry Tudor', but there is no evidence to confirm this. See Buck, *History of King Richard III*, 18.

37. Griffiths and Thomas, *Making of the Tudor Dynasty*, 61.

38. Ross, *Edward IV*, 65.

39. Jones and Underwood, *King's Mother*, 45.

40. Scofield, 'Henry, Duke of Somerset', 300.

41. Ibid., 301–302.

42. Somerset was buried in Hexham Abbey, which, though dissolved in 1537, still stands.

43. Among them were Arthur Plantagenet and Grace, who later attended Elizabeth Wydeville's funeral.

44. Commynes, *Memoirs*, 188.

45. Ross, *Edward IV*, 84.

46. Bona's sister, Charlotte, was Louis's second wife. They were both daughters of Louis, Duke of Savoy, and his Cyprian wife, Anne.

47. Mancini, *Usurpation of Richard III*, 61.

48. The name Wydeville is variously spelt and commonly appears as Woodville.

49. Jacquetta was the daughter of the Count of St Pol, and had been married to Bedford in 1433. She had married Richard Wydeville in secret in early 1437.

50. Mancini, *Usurpation of Richard III*, 61. This former husband was Sir John Grey, who had been killed fighting for Margaret's own House of Lancaster at the Second Battle of St Albans in 1461.

51. Ibid.

52. Ibid.

53. Ibid.

54. Halliwell, *Chronicle of the First Thirteen Years*, 3–4; cited in Dockray, *Edward IV*, 47.

55. Mancini, *Usurpation of Richard III*, 61–63.

56. Halliwell, *Chronicle of the First Thirteen Years*, 3–4.

57. Hinds, *Calendar of State Papers, Milan*, I:138.

58. James, *Henry the Sixth*, 43.

59. Ibid., 41.

CHAPTER 8: A LONG GOWN FOR MY LORD

1. The fishponds can still be seen today.

2. SJLM/4/2/2; TNA, PROB 11/7/2.

3. Poulton and Pattison, *Woking Palace*, 1.

4. Arnold and Savage, *Woking Palace*, 7.

5. Ibid., 20.

6. Gilpyn remained at Woking until his death in 1500. He was buried in St Peter's Church, although the plate that once adorned his tomb no longer survives.

7. See WAM 5472, f. 5r, for example.

8. Bray was born in around 1440, the son of a surgeon from Worcester; see WAM 5472 and WAM 5479 for numerous receipts and expenses kept by Bray; WAM 32377 for Bray's later receipts and charges on Margaret's lands.

9. Katherine later joined the household of Elizabeth of York. She died in 1508 and was buried with her husband in St George's Chapel, Windsor.

10. WAM 5472, f. 45r.

11. Ibid., f. 43r.

12. SJLM/1/1/3/2, f. 107.

13. WAM 5472, f. 40r–v.

14. Ibid., ff. 5r–6r.

15. WAM 12185, f. 104. Mortlake Palace was owned by the Archbishops of Canterbury and was visited by monarchs frequently in the medieval period. It no longer survives.

16. Henry Bourchier was created Earl of Essex soon after Towton. His heir, William, married Anne Wydeville. John Bourchier also served as Constable of Windsor Castle.

17. Walter Blount came from a family of Derbyshire origin. As a result of his first marriage to Helena Byron, Blount had six children. He was made a Knight of the Garter in 1472, and his stall plate can be seen in St George's Chapel, Windsor. He also stood as godfather to Elizabeth of York.

18. WAM 5472, f. 5r. The Mitre was a famous London inn, mentioned in Samuel Pepys's diary.

19. WAM 5472, f. 5r. This was John Arundel, who had become Bishop of Chichester in 1459. He died in 1477 and was buried in Chichester Cathedral. Other entries in Stafford's accounts show that they were both rowed to Lambeth on one occasion, while on another Margaret was conveyed to Westminster. WAM 5472, f. 5v.

20. Jones and Underwood, *King's Mother*, 141.

21. Ibid., 157–158.

22. Prior to the move, the duchess's servants are known to have visited Woking.

23. At this time Elizabeth was the widow of William, Baron Zouche, who had died in 1462. Before the end of 1471, Elizabeth had remarried, taking as her second husband John Scrope, Baron Scrope of Bolton.

24. WAM 12181, f. 52.

25. The ruins of Crowland Abbey can still be visited.

26. Fisher, 'Mornynge Remembraunce', 7.

27. WAM 6658.

28. WAM 12185, f. 39.

29. Hinds, *Calendar of State Papers, Milan*, I:162.

30. The ruins of Denbigh Castle are extant; Gairdner, *Gregory's Chronicle*, 237.

31. Ibid.

32. Jones and Underwood, *King's Mother*, 48.

33. Ibid., 140.

34. WAM 12186, f. 42; Jones and Underwood, *King's Mother*, 47.

35. Commynes, *Memoirs*, 188.

36. In his will Pembroke requested that he be buried in Abergavenny, but he was instead interred in Tintern Abbey. He also reminded his wife to 'take the said order that ye promised me as ye had in my life, my heart and love'. TNA, PROB 11/5/430.

CHAPTER 9: DIVINE PROPHECY

1. WAM 5472, f. 43r.

2. Ibid., f. 41v.

3. Queen Elizabeth's father, Earl Rivers, and her younger brother, Sir John Wydeville, had gone to ground after hearing of the Yorkist defeat at Edgecote, but Warwick's men caught up with them at Chepstow. There was to be no mercy, and on 12 August both men were executed at Kenilworth Castle.

4. Owen and Blakeway, *History of Shrewsbury*, I:248.

5. Corbet's wife was Elizabeth Devereux, daughter of Sir Walter Devereux, Anne Herbert's brother.

6. Walter was loyal to the House of York and—in spite of his sister's connection to Henry Tudor—fought for Richard III at the Battle of Bosworth in 1485. He was killed during the battle and was attainted soon after. The ruins of Weobley Castle can still be visited. Following Henry VII's accession, it became the property of Sir Rhys ap Thomas, who spent heavily on improvements.

7. WAM 5472, f. 44v.

8. Ibid., f. 43v.

9. Ibid., ff. 46r–47v. See also Hicks, *False, Fleeting, Perjur'd Clarence*, 45.

10. See Jones, 'Richard III and Lady Margaret Beaufort', 34.

11. Having fought for Edward at Hexham, John was already a recipient of his favour. In 1472 he was made a Knight of the Garter.

12. Richard Welles had been married first to Joan, a niece of Thomas, Earl of Salisbury, which explains their inclusion in the Salisbury Roll. He later married Margery Ingelby.

13. Given-Wilson et al., *Parliament Rolls of Medieval England*, Edward IV: June 1467.

14. CPR 1461–1467, 357.

15. The private feud was with Sir Thomas Burgh, during the course of which Burgh's house was destroyed.

16. Norton, *Margaret Beaufort*, 88.

17. WAM 12184, f. 48r.

18. CPR 1467–1477, 294.

19. As the party approached Calais, Lord Wenlock, who was in command, received orders to refuse them entry. Commynes reported, 'Instead of welcoming

him they fired several cannon shots at him'. Their ship was therefore forced to remain out of port, and before long the Duchess of Clarence went into labour. The birth was riddled with complications, and though the duchess survived, her baby son did not. Commynes, *Memoirs*, 182.

20. Hinds, *Calendar of State Papers, Milan*, I:189.

21. Ibid., I:196.

22. Hastings was unswervingly loyal to Edward IV, but he was also married to Warwick's sister, Katherine.

23. Hinds, *Calendar of State Papers, Milan*, I:197.

24. Ibid.

25. More, *History of King Richard III*, 76.

26. Commynes, *Memoirs*, 187.

27. Ibid., 189.

28. André, *Life of Henry VII*, 11.

29. Ibid.

30. Ibid.

31. Ibid., 12.

32. WAM 12183, f. 19r–v; Tunstall had remained with Henry VI during his exile in Scotland and had been attainted in 1461.

33. André later recalled that Henry VI had counselled his nephew to flee abroad 'so that he might escape the fierce hand of the enemy', but André's chronology had probably become confused with a later point. See André, *Life of Henry VII*, 12.

34. Expenses incurred throughout this short trip included firewood for Henry's chamber at Maidenhead, new horseshoes and horses. Four were needed for Margaret to complete the last leg of the journey.

35. Following his accession to the throne, there are a number of references in Henry's accounts to the playing of cards. In 1494, for example, forty shillings were outlaid for the king's losses at Windsor. See BL, Add MS 7099, f. 14.

36. Griffiths and Thomas surmise—almost certainly correctly—that this is likely to have been the last occasion on which Margaret saw Henry before he fled abroad in 1471. See Griffiths and Thomas, *Making of the Tudor Dynasty*, 69.

37. WAM 12183, f. 25r.

38. Hicks, *False, Fleeting, Perjur'd Clarence*, 84–85.

CHAPTER 10: HEAVEN PROTECTS HIM WHO HAS NO BURIAL URN

1. Commynes, *Memoirs*, 195.

2. Ibid.

3. WAM 12189, f. 58r.

4. Commynes, *Memoirs*, 194.

5. Ellis, *Original Letters*, I:140–141.

6. Kingsford, *Chronicles of London*, 183.

7. Thomas and Thornley, *Great Chronicle of London*, 213. On 21 April 1471, Edward IV granted Lady Scrope a pardon on account of her Lancastrian sympathies. This was doubtless in grateful thanks for her services to his wife. CPR 1467–1477, 258.

8. Halliwell, *Chronicle of the First Thirteen Years*, 16.

9. Commynes, *Memoirs*, 195.

10. Pronay and Cox, *Crowland Chronicle Continuations*, 125.

11. Kingsford, *Chronicles of London*, 184.

12. Hinds, *Calendar of State Papers, Milan*, I:213; both men were later taken to Bisham Priory for burial.

13. Pronay and Cox, *Crowland Chronicle Continuations*, 127.

14. Ibid.

15. Ibid.

16. Today the sacristy door in Tewkesbury Abbey is covered with the plates of armour from slaughtered Lancastrians.

17. The Beaufort brothers were both ceremonially reinterred in Tewkesbury in December 1488.

18. Weir, *Lancaster and York*, 408.

19. Commynes, *Memoirs*, 196.

20. Kingsford, *Chronicles of London*, 184–185.

21. She was buried in Angers Cathedral, although there is no monument.

22. Ellis, *Three Books*, 156.

23. André, *Life of Henry VII*, 19.

24. More, *History of King Richard III*, 12.

25. Dockray, *Three Chronicles*, 38.

26. Pronay and Cox, *Crowland Chronicle Continuations*, 131.

27. Halliwell, *Chronicle of the First Thirteen Years*, 21.

28. Weir, *Lancaster and York*, 409.

29. Ellis, *Three Books*, 154.

30. Ibid.

31. Ibid.

32. Ibid.

33. Ibid., 14.

34. André, *Life of Henry VII*, 14.

35. Ibid. Francis was the son of Richard of Brittany and Margaret of Orléans. Richard was the youngest son of Duke John IV of Brittany, and though both his elder brothers succeeded their father, neither had a living male heir at the time of their deaths. Thus, in 1458, Francis succeeded his uncle.

36. Ellis, *Three Books*, 155.
37. Ibid.
38. TNA, PROB 11/7/2.
39. Cited in Domvile, *King's Mother*, 11.
40. Nichols, *Testamenta Vetusta*, I:324.

41. No monument survives, but in the church today there are two altar tombs, one of which may have belonged to Stafford's parents.

CHAPTER 11: GRACE AND FAVOUR OF THE KING'S HIGHNESS

1. Le Ryall once stood on the site now occupied by the College of Arms; Jones and Underwood, *King's Mother*, 144. These three ladies were Elizabeth Johnson, Jane Atkins and Elizabeth Denman.

2. Joan was the daughter of Sir Robert Goushill. Henry IV had knighted Robert for his bravery following the Battle of Shrewsbury in 1403. The tomb he shares with his wife, Elizabeth Fitzalan, can be seen in St Michael's Church in Hoveringham, Nottinghamshire.

3. The wedding took place in 1451 at Middleham Castle. The marriage was successful in personal terms, producing eleven children, although eight of these died young. The three that survived were all sons: George, Edward and James. George was well favoured by both Edward IV and Henry VII; Edward was a soldier who played a prominent role at the Battle of Flodden; James became Bishop of Ely.

4. This was Joan Strange, whose mother, Jacquetta Wydeville, was the queen's sister.

5. Jones and Underwood, *King's Mother*, 40; Westminster Abbey MS 39. This object is the only surviving artefact relating to Margaret and one of her husbands.

6. Jones and Underwood suggest that this may have been Knowsley, one of Stanley's main residences near Liverpool. They also clarify that the marriage took place between the creation of Margaret's first will on 2 June and the arrangement of the marriage settlement, which was staged on 12 June. See Jones and Underwood, *King's Mother*, 59; Knowsley still stands but is the product of the eighteenth century.

7. Lewis, 'Lathom House', 150. A fireback from Knowsley emblazoned with Margaret's arms still survives. See Hoult, *Vill, Manor and Township of Knowsley*, 32.

8. Cited in Lewis, 'Lathom House', 150.

9. Derby House was destroyed during the Great Fire of London.

10. See Skidmore, *Bosworth*, 98.

11. In around October 1472, the two had been taken to Suscinio, a chateau at Sarzeau that was used as a summer palace by the dukes of Brittany. After about a year, they were moved to Nantes. Following their separation, Jasper was taken to Josselin, which still stands, as does Largoët.

12. Griffiths and Thomas, *Making of the Tudor Dynasty*, 90.

13. Commynes, *Memoirs*, 354.

14. Ibid., 237.

15. Ibid., 353.

16. André, *Life of Henry VII*, 20.

17. Ibid.

18. Princess Mary was fourteen when she died in 1482. The two who died in infancy were Margaret, who was born and died in 1472, and George. He was born in 1477 and died in 1479.

19. Toulin Smith, *John Leland's Itinerary*, 5. One piece of stonework and a mound are all that survive of Fotheringhay Castle, which is best known as the place where Mary, Queen of Scots, was executed in 1587. Anne was the first of Edward's siblings to be born at Fotheringhay, as were Margaret and Richard.

20. Ibid., 4.

21. Riley, *Ingulph's Chronicle*, 475.

22. Though the princesses are unnamed, they are likely to have been the two eldest, Elizabeth and Mary.

23. Sutton, Visser-Fuchs and Hammond, *Reburial of Richard*.

24. Riley, *Ingulph's Chronicle*, 475.

25. The York tombs were destroyed during the Reformation, but new ones were created around the altar on the orders of Elizabeth I.

26. Ellis, *Three Books*, 205.

27. Griffiths and Thomas, *Making of the Tudor Dynasty*, 83.

28. Mancini, *Usurpation of Richard III*, 63.

29. Isabel's child, Richard, died within months of his birth. Isabel was buried in Tewkesbury Abbey.

30. The suggestion to marry Mary had come from Clarence's sister, Margaret of Burgundy, who was her stepmother. Mary later married Maximilian, future Holy Roman Emperor. She was tragically killed at the age of twenty-five when she was thrown from a horse and broke her back; Mancini, *Usurpation of Richard III*, 63.

31. Mancini, *Usurpation of Richard III*, 63.

32. BL, Stowe MS 1047, f. 204v.

33. Duffy points out that there is no record of the duchess's burial at Wimborne, and that in the nineteenth century it was claimed that she was buried in the

church at Lydiard Tregoze. It was Margaret who was responsible for commissioning her parents' tomb at Wimborne, so there is no reason to believe that her mother was not interred there alongside her father. See Duffy, *Royal Tombs of Medieval England*, 233.

34. Cited in Jones and Underwood, *King's Mother*, 60.

35. SJLM/4/4/2.

36. WAM 32378.

37. Pronay and Cox, *Crowland Chronicle Continuations*, 149.

38. Margaret was the daughter of Mary of Burgundy, the lady whose hand the Duke of Clarence had previously coveted.

39. Mancini, *Usurpation of Richard III*, 59; Riley, *Ingulph's Chronicle*, 483.

40. More, *History of King Richard III*, 5.

41. Mancini, *Usurpation of Richard III*, 59.

CHAPTER 12: A BOAR WITH HIS TUSKS

1. Ellis, *Three Books*, 172.

2. Pronay and Cox, *Crowland Chronicle Continuations*, 155.

3. More, *History of King Richard III*, 5.

4. Stanley laid siege to the border town of Berwick and succeeded in taking it.

5. Mancini, *Usurpation of Richard III*, 63.

6. Ibid., 71.

7. Ibid.

8. Ibid.

9. Ibid., 73.

10. Pronay and Cox, *Crowland Chronicle Continuations*, 155.

11. Ibid., 75.

12. Mancini, *Usurpation of Richard III*, 75.

13. Buckingham and Katherine had two sons and two daughters. The eldest son, Edward, became the third Duke of Buckingham but was executed in 1521; the second son, Henry, became Earl of Wiltshire and died in 1523. Elizabeth married the Earl of Sussex, and Anne married the Earl of Huntingdon.

14. Described by More as 'a right honourable man', Rivers had been supervising his nephew's education at Ludlow. More, *History of King Richard III*, 18.

15. Pronay and Cox, *Crowland Chronicle Continuations*, 157.

16. Ibid., 79.

17. Ibid., 81.

18. Ibid., 157.

19. Mancini, *Usurpation of Richard III*, 91.

20. Ibid., 57.

21. Ibid.

22. Hastings was buried in the chantry chapel that he himself had founded, which still survives. There is no effigy.

23. Mancini, *Usurpation of Richard III*, 91.

24. More, *History of King Richard III*, 57.

25. Ibid.

26. Ibid., 58.

27. Ellis, *Three Books*, 181.

28. Ibid., 182.

29. More, *History of King Richard III*, 48.

30. Ibid., 48–49.

31. Edward, Earl of Warwick, had been born in February 1475 at Warwick Castle. Mancini says that Gloucester had summoned the ten-year-old boy to London and 'commanded that the lad should be kept in confinement in the household of his wife'. See Mancini, *Usurpation of Richard III*, 89.

32. Ibid., 97.

33. Bacon, *History of the Reign of King Henry VII*, 64. The Tudor chronicler Edward Hall also claimed that Margaret sought an alliance with Richard on her son's behalf. See Ellis, *Hall's Chronicle*, 388–389.

34. Kingsford, *Chronicles of London*, 191.

35. Sutton and Hammond, *Coronation of Richard III*, 169. Other ladies included the duchesses of Suffolk and Norfolk and the countesses of Surrey and Nottingham.

36. Ibid., 276.

37. Mancini, *Usurpation of Richard III*, 101.

38. Sutton and Hammond, *Coronation of Richard III*, 169.

39. Ibid., 294–297.

CHAPTER 13: THE HEAD OF THAT CONSPIRACY

1. Mancini, *Usurpation of Richard III*, 93.

2. Stow, *Annales or Generall Chronicle of England*, 460.

3. Ibid.

4. More, *History of King Richard III*, 98; Brackenbury had been appointed to this post on 17 July.

5. Ibid.

6. Pronay and Cox, *Crowland Chronicle Continuations*, 161.

7. Tyrell's father had been executed in 1462 for his part in an alleged plot to kill Edward IV. He nevertheless remained a Yorkist and was knighted at the Battle of Tewkesbury.

8. More, *History of King Richard III*, 99.

9. Ibid.

10. Weir, *Elizabeth of York*, 99.

11. More, *History of King Richard III*, 100.

12. Ibid.

13. Ibid. The skeletons of two children were discovered in the White Tower by workmen in 1674 and were widely believed to be those of the princes. They were buried with full honours in Westminster Abbey.

14. Ibid., 100.

15. He was executed on 6 May 1502 for aiding a Yorkist claimant to the throne, Edmund de la Pole, Duke of Suffolk.

16. See Weir, *Princes in the Tower*.

17. Thomas and Thornley, *Great Chronicle of London*, 236–237.

18. André, *Life of Henry VII*, 8, 20.

19. Nichols, *Chronicle of the Grey Friars*, 23; Commynes, *Memoirs*, 354.

20. Buck, *History of King Richard III*, 163.

21. Croyland describes them as having 'a specially appointed guard'. See Pronay and Cox, *Crowland Chronicle Continuations*, 163.

22. Kingsford, *Chronicles of London*, 191.

23. The ruins of Brecknock can still be seen, but most of the castle was pulled down during the English Civil War.

24. More, *History of King Richard III*, 105.

25. Following the Lancastrian defeat at Towton, he had been captured while attempting to flee to Scotland and was imprisoned in the Tower. Incredibly, he managed to escape and he hurried to join Queen Margaret in France. There he remained until the Readeption.

26. Commynes, *Memoirs*, 354.

27. Edward, Earl of Warwick, the son of the attainted Duke of Clarence, was a popular candidate. Likewise, John de la Pole, Earl of Lincoln, was the son of Richard III's sister, Elizabeth.

28. Ellis, *Three Books*, 194. See also Weir, *Princes in the Tower*, 148.

29. Weir, *Princes in the Tower*, 148.

30. More, *History of King Richard III*, 105.

31. Ellis, *Three Books*, 195.

32. Buck, *History of King Richard III*, 63–64.

33. Ellis, *Three Books*, 195.

34. Ibid.

35. Ibid., 196.

36. Ibid.

37. Ibid., 189.

38. Ibid., 196.

39. Ibid. Thomas Ramney was later executed on Richard III's orders.

40. The Stanley family had supported Urswick through his education at Cambridge, and it is likely to have been through them that he met Margaret, whose household he joined in 1482. He would enjoy both her patronage and that of her son for the rest of his life. He died in 1522, and a drawing of the brass that once adorned his tomb in Hackney Church still survives.

41. Ellis, *Three Books*, 197.

42. Ibid.

43. André, *Life of Henry VII*, 20.

44. Pronay and Cox, *Crowland Chronicle Continuations*, 163.

45. Jones and Underwood, *King's Mother*, 64.

46. Ellis, *Three Books*, 195.

47. Ibid., 204.

48. Chrimes, *Henry VII*, 21.

49. Commynes, *Memoirs*, 354.

50. Pronay and Cox, *Crowland Chronicle Continuations*, 163.

51. Ellis, *Three Books*, 198.

52. Raine, *York Civic Records*, I:83–84.

53. Kingsford, *Chronicles of London*, 191.

CHAPTER 14: MOTHER OF THE KING'S GREAT REBEL AND TRAITOR

1. Welles had fled England in August when his property—Maxey—was seized; Richard succeeded to the title of Earl Rivers following the execution of his brother in 1483; Lionel was Bishop of Salisbury but died in around 1484; Edward had been appointed Admiral of the Fleet in the aftermath of Edward IV's death.

2. CPR 1476–1485, 411.

3. Ellis, *Three Books*, 203.

4. Buck, *History of King Richard III*, 30.

5. Ellis, *Three Books*, 204.

6. Given-Wilson et al., *Parliament Rolls of Medieval England*, Richard III: January 1484.

7. Ibid.

8. Ellis, *Three Books*, 204.

9. BL, Add MS 12060, f. 22v.

10. Pronay and Cox, *Crowland Chronicle Continuations*, 171; Ellis, *Three Books*, 210.

11. Ellis, *Original Letters*, I:149.

12. Ellis, *Three Books*, 210.

13. Precisely when Elizabeth Wydeville left sanctuary is unknown, as are her whereabouts.

14. Ellis, *Three Books*, 210.

15. Ibid., 205.

16. Ibid.

17. Pronay and Cox, *Crowland Chronicle Continuations*, 171. It was long thought that Edward was buried in the church at Sheriff Hutton, but the tomb once assumed to belong to him is now believed to represent another. His place of burial therefore remains uncertain, and the church at Middleham has also been suggested.

18. Ibid.

19. Richard did, however, have two illegitimate children: John of Gloucester and a daughter named Katherine.

20. M. Jones, "'For My Lord of Richmond, a *pourpoint* . . . and a palfrey", 283.

21. Griffiths and Thomas, *Making of the Tudor Dynasty*, 117.

22. Ellis, *Three Books*, 205.

23. Ibid.

24. Ibid., 206.

25. In 1498 Charles died and was succeeded by his cousin, Louis XII. Louis married Margaret's granddaughter Princess Mary in 1514. He died three months later.

26. Anne would rule as regent until 1491, sharing power with her husband, Peter of Bourbon; Ellis, *Three Books*, 206.

27. Ibid.

28. Ibid., 207.

29. André, *Life of Henry VII*, 21.

30. Ellis, *Three Books*, 208.

31. Halliwell, *Letters of the Kings of England*, I:161–162.

32. Pronay and Cox, *Crowland Chronicle Continuations*, 175.

33. Ibid.

34. Henry had not forgotten that his former guardian, William Herbert, had wished to marry him to his daughter Maud. At some time in the 1470s, however, Maud had married Henry Percy, fourth Earl of Northumberland. At this time, she did have younger unmarried sisters, although Katherine, Anne, Isabel and Margaret all later wed.

35. Ibid.

36. See Weir, *Elizabeth of York*, 121–142.

37. Pronay and Cox, *Crowland Chronicle Continuations*, 175.

38. Ibid.

39. Anne was twenty-eight at the time of her death. In spite of the rumours, she almost certainly died of natural causes.

40. Pronay and Cox, *Crowland Chronicle Continuations*, 175. No tomb was ever raised to her memory, but she was buried on the southern side of the High Altar.

41. Ibid.

42. Ibid.

43. Halliwell, *Most Pleasant Song of Lady Bessy*, 2.

44. Ellis, *Three Books*, 212.

45. Ibid., 209.

46. Oxford came from a strong Lancastrian background, and though Edward IV had initially treated him well, Oxford had repaid him by becoming embroiled in Lancastrian plots. In September 1473 he had taken control of St Michael's Mount in Cornwall, but he was forced to surrender the following February. He was imprisoned in Hammes Castle and attainted in 1475.

47. Ellis, *Three Books*, 208.

48. André, *Life of Henry VII*, 22.

49. Commynes, *Memoirs*, 397.

50. Ibid.

51. Ibid.

CHAPTER 15: THE PRICELESS CROWN

1. Ellis, *Three Books*, 216.

2. Pronay and Cox, *Crowland Chronicle Continuations*, 179.

3. Incidentally, Corbet was also the stepson of Stanley's brother, William. Corbet had been the result of his father's marriage to Elizabeth Hopton. Elizabeth was William Stanley's second wife, and they had wedded sometime around 1471. The couple had a daughter, Jane.

4. David Owen had been born at Pembroke Castle in 1459, so it is plausible that Henry may have spent some time with him in the earliest days of his childhood.

5. Pronay and Cox, *Crowland Chronicle Continuations*, 179.

6. Ibid.

7. Riley, *Ingulph's Chronicle*, 501.

8. Pronay and Cox, *Crowland Chronicle Continuations*, 179.

9. Ibid. Savage continued in his support of Henry, but though he survived Bosworth, he was killed during the siege of Boulogne in 1492.

10. Ibid.

11. Gilbert Talbot was a younger son of the second Earl of Shrewsbury, who had been slain at the Battle of Northampton.

12. Ellis, *Three Books*, 218.

13. Hay, *Anglica Historia*, 75.

14. Ellis, *Three Books*, 218.

15. Ibid.

16. Pronay and Cox, *Crowland Chronicle Continuations*, 179.

17. BL, Add MS 12060, f. 20r. Bygot had previously served Queen Anne Neville.

18. Pronay and Cox, *Crowland Chronicle Continuations*, 179.

19. Ellis, *Three Books*, 221.

20. Pronay and Cox, *Crowland Chronicle Continuations*, 181.

21. BL, Add MS 12060, f. 20r.

22. Pronay and Cox, *Crowland Chronicle Continuations*, 181.

23. Ibid.

24. BL, Add MS 12060, f. 20r.

25. Pronay and Cox, *Crowland Chronicle Continuations*, 181.

26. Ibid.

27. Ibid.

28. Cited in Dockray, *Richard III*, 123.

29. Ellis, *Three Books*, 224.

30. William was the father of Charles Brandon, Duke of Suffolk, later a close confidant of Margaret's grandson, Henry VIII. He also married Margaret's granddaughter, Princess Mary, following her marriage to Louis XII. Their granddaughters were the ill-fated Grey sisters.

31. Ellis, *Three Books*, 224.

32. Cited in Dockray, *Richard III*, 123.

33. Pronay and Cox, *Crowland Chronicle Continuations*, 183.

34. Richard was also the last King of England to be killed in battle.

35. Ellis, *Three Books*, 226.

36. Pronay and Cox, *Crowland Chronicle Continuations*, 181–183.

37. André, *Life of Henry VII*, 8.

38. Commynes, *Memoirs*, 355.

39. Pronay and Cox, *Crowland Chronicle Continuations*, 183.

40. Ellis, *Three Books*, 226.

41. Ibid. Richard's remains were discovered in September 2012 following excavations at the site of the Greyfriars church in Leicester. In March 2015 they were reinterred at Leicester Cathedral.

42. BL, Add MS 7099, f. 30.

43. BL, Royal MS 2 A XVIII, f. 31v.

44. The Book of Hours is now in Lambeth Palace Library, MS 474. Richard also added his birthdate, 2 October, to the book.

45. Ibid.

CHAPTER 16: MY LADY THE KING'S MOTHER

1. BL, Royal 2 A XVIII, f. 32.

2. The Coronation Chair had been made for Edward I and has been used at the coronation of every monarch since 1308. It is still on display in Westminster Abbey.

3. Fisher, 'Mornynge Remembraunce', 6.

4. Ibid.

5. André, *Life of Henry VII*, 31.

6. Hay, *Anglica Historia*, 145–146.

7. CSPS, I, 123.

8. Cited in Cooper, *Lady Margaret*, 210.

9. She died on 25 June 1486.

10. André, *Life of Henry VII*, 33.

11. Bacon, *History of the Reign of King Henry VII*, 32.

12. Ibid.

13. John Holland's brother, Thomas Holland, was the father of Margaret's grandmother Margaret Holland.

14. Coldharbour once stood to the east of Cannon Street Station but was destroyed during the Great Fire of London. An office block at 89 Upper Thames Street now stands on the site it once occupied.

15. See Kingsford, 'On Some London Houses of the Early Tudor Period', 26.

16. Ibid., 24.

17. TNA, E 404/79; Margaret was born on 14 August 1473 at Farleigh Hungerford Castle in Somerset.

18. CPR 1485–1494, 113; SJLM/9/1/1; Buckingham's chamber had a new door fitted. He was executed on charges of high treason on 17 May 1521 by Margaret's grandson, Henry VIII; Henry was created Earl of Wiltshire in 1510.

19. BL, Add MS 12060, f. 22v.

20. Fisher, 'Mornynge Remembraunce', 2.

21. His mother was Joan Hill. Somerset married Elizabeth, the daughter of William Herbert by Mary Wydeville; Jones and Underwood suggest that Somerset's change of name may have been for Henry VII to present himself as the true Beaufort heir. See Jones and Underwood, *King's Mother*, 72.

22. Kibre, 'Lewis of Caerleon', 102–103.

23. CPR 1485–1494, 15. This grant took place on 23 September 1485.

24. Ibid., 67.

25. Ibid., 55.

26. Ibid., 61, 45.

27. Given-Wilson et al., *Parliament Rolls of Medieval England*, Henry VII: November 1485, Part 1.

28. On 13 December, he was also given the office of chief justice of South Wales. See CPR 1485–1494, 47.

29. Ibid.

30. Given-Wilson et al., *Parliament Rolls of Medieval England*, Henry VII: November 1485, Part 1.

31. Ibid.

32. Ibid.

33. Ibid.

34. Lewis, 'Lathom House', 161.

35. From 1464, Cecily had also begun styling herself 'queen by rights' in her letters. This was undoubtedly as a result of her husband's earlier claims.

36. See also S. Fisher, '"Margaret R".

37. Fisher, 'Mornynge Remembraunce', 3.

38. Given-Wilson et al., *Parliament Rolls of Medieval England*, Henry VII: November 1485, Part 1.

39. André, *Life of Henry VII*, 35.

40. BL, Royal 2 A XVIII, f. 28.

41. Stow, *Annales or Generall Chronicle of England*, 472.

42. André, *Life of Henry VII*, 34.

43. TNA, E 36/210, f. 30, for an offering made at the tomb of Henry VI.

44. CPR 1485–1494, 128.

45. Rosenthal, *Purchase of Paradise*, 31.

46. CSPS, I, 178.

47. Ibid., 153–167.

48. SJLM/9/2/1.

49. Halliwell, *Letters of the Kings*, I:181.

50. Hay, *Anglica Historia*, 7.

51. CSPS, I, 163.

52. Bacon, *History of the Reign of King Henry VII*, 206.

53. M. Underwood, 'The Pope, the Queen and the King's Mother', in *The Reign of Henry VII*, Vol. V, ed. B. Thompson (Stamford: Paul Watkins, 1995), 73.

54. Bacon, *History of the Reign of King Henry VII*, 207.

55. Ibid., 42.

56. BL, Add MS 7099, f. 4; TNA, E 101/414/6, f. 73v; TNA, E 101/415/3, f. 72v.

57. Cavell, *Heralds' Memoir 1486–1490*, 98.

58. Cecily Neville lived in quiet retirement following Henry VII's accession. She died on 31 May 1495 at Berkhamsted Castle. In her will, Cecily bequeathed Margaret 'a portuos with claspes of gold covered with blacke cloth of golde'.

59. Fisher, 'Mornynge Remembraunce', 2.

60. BL, Add MS 4712, ff. 3–22.

61. Olson, 'Margaret Beaufort, Royal Tapestries', 237; Leland, *Antiquarii de Rebus Britannicis Collectanea*, IV:179–180.

62. Leland, *Antiquarii de Rebus Britannicis Collectanea*, IV:179–180.

63. BL, Royal 2 A XVIII, f. 32.

64. Bacon, *History of the Reign of King Henry VII*, 44.

65. André, *Life of Henry VII*, 36.

66. Leland, *Antiquarii de Rebus Britannicis Collectanea*, IV:2; André, *Life of Henry VII*, 37.

67. Leland, *Antiquarii de Rebus Britannicis Collectanea*, IV:205.

68. Ibid., 206.

69. Ibid., 207.

CHAPTER 17: PRESERVATION OF YOUR MOST NOBLE AND ROYAL ESTATE

1. Given-Wilson et al., *Parliament Rolls of Medieval England*, Henry VII: November 1485, Part 1.

2. Cavell, *Heralds' Memoir*, 117; Given-Wilson et al., *Parliament Rolls of Medieval England*, Henry VII: November 1487. The name has been much disputed, and it is improbable that 'Lambert Simnel' was his real name. Simnel was described as being ten years old.

3. Hay, *Anglica Historia*, 13.

4. A splendid double monument to the couple can be seen in Wingfield Church, Suffolk.

5. It has been suggested that Lincoln's appointment to this post may have signified Richard regarded Lincoln as his heir.

6. Hay, *Anglica Historia*, 19.

7. That same year there was talk of arranging a marriage for Elizabeth with James III of Scotland, who had been widowed following the death of his wife, Margaret of Denmark, in 1486. The plans came to nothing as a consequence of James's death in 1488; Williams, *Henry VII*, 60.

8. Cavell, *Heralds' Memoir*, 109.

9. Margaret had been born at Fotheringhay Castle on 3 May 1446. On 3 July 1468, she was married to Charles the Bold of Burgundy at Damme in modern-day Belgium. They would have no children, and Charles died in 1477. Margaret never remarried.

10. Hay, *Anglica Historia*, 17.

11. Ellis, *Original Letters Illustrative of English History*, I:19–20.

12. Halliwell, *Letters of the Kings of England*, I:171.

13. Ibid.

14. Fisher, 'Mornynge Remembraunce', 6.

15. Cavell, *Heralds' Memoir*, 110–111.

16. Ibid., 110.

17. Hay, *Anglica Historia*, 25; Cavell, *Heralds' Memoir*, 118. The heralds' account states that Lovell was 'put to flight' (118).

18. Vergil claims that Simnel was still alive in 1534. Richard Symonds was imprisoned for life and only evaded execution because he was a priest.

19. BL, Royal 2 A XVIII, f. 30.

20. Cavell, *Heralds' Memoir*, 128.

21. Their union was seemingly very happy, but though two daughters, Elizabeth and Anne, were born to the couple, neither survived.

22. Richard's father was Sir Geoffrey Pole. Margaret Pole's biographer, Hazel Pierce, states that Geoffrey was a councillor of Jasper Tudor, so he may also have had some hand in the marriage. See Pierce, *Margaret Pole*, 15.

23. Jones and Underwood, *King's Mother*, 82.

24. Anne's wedding took place on 4 February 1495 at Westminster Abbey. Sadly, the only child born of the marriage died in 1508, and Anne herself died on 22 November 1511. Her husband later became the third Duke of Norfolk and uncle to Anne Boleyn and Katherine Howard. See TNA, E 327/191, for their marriage contract. On one occasion, Margaret's accounts note a payment to Katherine, although the reason is not stipulated.

25. TNA, E 101/425/19, ff. 1–10.

26. Cavell, *Heralds' Memoir*, 129.

27. Leland, *Antiquarii de Rebus Britannicis Collectanea*, IV:218.

28. Ibid., 219.

29. Cavell, *Heralds' Memoir*, 131.

30. Ibid., 131–132.

31. Sir David Owen appears to have died in around 1535. He was buried in St Mary's Church in Easebourne, West Sussex, where his tomb effigy can be seen.

32. Cavell, *Heralds' Memoir*, 134–135.

33. Leland, *Antiquarii de Rebus Britannicis Collectanea*, IV:223.

34. Cavell, *Heralds' Memoir*, 136.

35. Leland, *Antiquarii de Rebus Britannicis Collectanea*, IV:224.

36. Cavell, *Heralds' Memoir*, 140.

37. Leland, *Antiquarii de Rebus Britannicis Collectanea*, IV:226.

38. Ibid., 227.

39. Cavell, *Heralds' Memoir*, 143.

40. Leland, *Antiquarii de Rebus Britannicis Collectanea*, IV:227.

41. Ibid., 228.

42. Anne was the only surviving child of John Mowbray, Duke of Norfolk, and his wife, Elizabeth Talbot. When her father died in 1476, she became a wealthy heiress, but she died at the age of eight in 1481. She was initially buried

in Westminster Abbey, but her coffin was later moved to the Minoresses convent in Aldgate. It was discovered in 1964 and reburied in Westminster Abbey the following year.

43. Cavell, *Heralds' Memoir*, 145.

44. Hayward, *Dress at the Court of King Henry VIII*, 84.

45. SJLM/2/3/3/4, ff. 1–3.

46. Ibid.

47. SJLM/1/1/3, f. 9.

48. SJLM/2/3/3/1, ff. 1, 3

49. SJLM/2/1/2, f. 3. SJLM/2/1/2, ff. 3–10.

50. Fisher, 'Mornynge Remembraunce', 2.

51. SJLM/1, 3 series.

52. Leland, *Antiquarii de Rebus Britannicis Collectanea*, IV:235.

53. TNA, E 101/414/16, f. 7r; TNA, E 36/214, 13r.

54. Ibid., 234.

55. Cavell, *Heralds' Memoir*, 153.

56. Leland, *Antiquarii de Rebus Britannicis Collectanea*, IV:235.

57. Ibid., 236.

CHAPTER 18: TOO MUCH FOR MY HAND

1. The next woman to be invested with this prestigious order was Queen Alexandra, consort of Edward VII.

2. Other ladies who had been appointed included Edward III's wife Queen Philippa, Constance of Castile, Katherine Swynford, Margaret of Anjou and Elizabeth Wydeville.

3. Leland, *Antiquarii de Rebus Britannicis Collectanea*, IV:242.

4. BL, Egerton MS 2341.

5. Leland, *Antiquarii de Rebus Britannicis Collectanea*, IV:243.

6. Hertford was a Norman castle that had been granted to Elizabeth of York in 1487. Elizabeth I was later fond of it, and it is now used as a venue for weddings and private events.

7. Cavell, *Heralds' Memoir*, 174.

8. Leland, *Antiquarii de Rebus Britannicis Collectanea*, IV:254.

9. Cavell, *Heralds' Memoir*, 180.

10. Ibid.

11. Ibid., 181. Alcock had once been the tutor of Edward V. He had been arrested by Richard III but was later restored to the council. He was appointed Bishop of Ely in 1486.

12. Ibid.

13. Ibid., 182.

14. This tradition is generally considered to have begun when Edward I invested his heir, Edward, with the title of Prince of Wales. Since the late fourteenth century, the title of Earl of Chester has only been granted alongside that of Prince of Wales.

15. Leland, *Antiquarii de Rebus Britannicis Collectanea*, IV:254.

16. Cavell, *Heralds' Memoir*, 183.

17. Jones and Underwood emphasize that Margaret was the only person to donate grain to the expedition. See Jones and Underwood, *King's Mother*, 81.

18. Katherine had three elder sisters, Isabella, Juana and Maria. She also had a brother, Juan, who died at the age of eighteen.

19. BL, Royal 2 A XVIII, f. 30.

20. L & P, IV:5791.

21. Lawson, *Eltham Palace*, 3. Eltham had been acquired by Edward II in 1305 and was given to his queen, Isabella of France.

22. An account of the visit is given in Nichols, *Epistles of Erasmus*, II:201.

23. See Flood, '"White Queen" Died of Plague'.

24. TNA, PROB 11/9/207, f. 74.

25. André, *Life of Henry VII*, 4.

26. Hutchinson, *Young Henry*, 37.

27. Cunningham, *Prince Arthur*, 71.

28. SJLM/1/1/2/1, f. 25.

29. Palgrave, *Antient Kalendars and Inventories*, 395.

30. Bacon, *History of the Reign of King Henry VII*, 207.

31. André, *Life of Henry VII*, 60.

32. Pollard, *Reign of Henry VII*, I:94.

33. Hay, *Anglica Historia*, 67.

34. Ibid.

35. On 8 May 1491, Arthur had been created a Knight of the Garter, and Henry's creation followed in May 1495.

36. Kingsford, *Chronicles of London*, 204.

37. André, *Life of Henry VII*, 64.

38. Hay, *Anglica Historia*, 75.

39. Ibid.

40. Ibid.

41. Ibid., 75.

42. Ibid., 75, 77.

43. BL, Add MS 7099, f. 23. A payment of £10 is also listed to William at the time of his execution, possibly for the purpose of tipping his executioner.

44. TNA, E 101/414/16, f. 58v.

45. André, *Life of Henry VII*, 65.

46. BL, Add MS 7099, f. 29. At the beginning of September, Henry returned to visit his mother at Collyweston.

47. André, *Life of Henry VII*, 62.

48. Katherine Gordon was the daughter of George Gordon, second Earl of Huntly. She had probably been born in around 1474.

49. An effigy once adorned the tomb but has since disappeared. The Latin inscription still survives, part of which reads 'Attrapos, the most severe messenger of Death, snatched her away but may she have eternal life in Heaven'.

50. Thornbury Castle is now a hotel.

51. Jasper left detailed instructions in his will for the construction of a tomb, though it no longer survives. See Nichols, *Testamenta Vetusta*, I:430. His entrails were buried in the church at Thornbury.

52. Upon Jasper's death, the mighty Pembroke Castle—the scene of Margaret's confinement almost forty years earlier—became Crown property, although neither Margaret nor her son would ever visit it again.

53. TNA, SC 1/51/189. The letter is dated from Sheen on 25 April.

54. TNA, E 101/414/6, f. 39r.

55. BL, Add MS 29976, ff. 65–80.

56. Ibid., f. 40r.

57. Ibid., f. 41r.

58. TNA, E 135/3/21.

59. Pollard, *Reign of Henry VII*, I:147.

60. BL, Royal 2 A XVIII, f. 30.

61. Pollard, *Reign of Henry VII*, I:161.

62. Ibid., I:162.

63. Ibid.

64. Hay, *Anglica Historia*, 111.

65. Ibid.

66. Ibid.

67. Ibid.

68. CSPV, I (760).

69. Hinds, *Calendar of State Papers, Milan*, I:550.

70. Kingsford, *Chronicles of London*, 222.

71. Ibid.

72. Ibid.

73. BL, Add MS 7099, f. 44.

74. Today, the gateway is the only part of Henry's magnificent palace that survives; it features his arms.

CHAPTER 19: THE RIGHT NOBLE PUISSANT AND EXCELLENT PRINCESS

1. CSPS, I:156.
2. Ibid.
3. Pollard, *Reign of Henry VII*, I:188.
4. SJLM/9/2/1.
5. See Wroe, *Perkin*, 455–457.
6. CSPS, I:156.
7. Ibid., I:190.
8. CPR 1485–1494, 236.
9. Nichols, *Testamenta Vetusta*, I:437.
10. CSPS, I:205.
11. Ibid.
12. TNA, E 101/414/16, f. 54r.
13. St John Hope, *Windsor Castle*, 241.
14. CPR 1494–1509, 79.
15. SGC, XV.58.C.13.
16. Wilkinson, *Henry VII's Lady Chapel*, 4.
17. CPR 1494–1509, 79. Margaret's cousin Charles Somerset and his wife later chose to be buried in St George's Chapel, and their tomb can be seen in what is now called the Beaufort Chantry.
18. CCR 1500–1509, 290–291.
19. Fisher, 'Mornynge Remembraunce', 2.
20. N. Beckett, 'Henry VII and Sheen Charterhouse', in *The Reign of Henry VII*, Vol. V, ed. B. Thompson (Stamford: Paul Watkins, 1995), 117.
21. See Powell, 'Margaret Pole and Syon Abbey', 563–567. Henry VII had lent Lady Pole money for the burial of her husband. See BL, Add MS 21480, f. 113v. Margaret Windsor was the daughter of Thomas Windsor, the constable of Windsor Castle.
22. Fisher, 'Mornynge Remembraunce', 4.
23. Ibid., 2.
24. SJLM/2/3/2/1, f. 20v. Most of these books were bequeathed to Christ's College, Cambridge.
25. Fisher, 'Mornynge Remembraunce', 3.
26. J. Backhouse, 'Founders of the Royal Library: Edward IV and Henry VII as Collectors of Illuminated Manuscripts', in *England in the Fifteenth Century*, ed. D. Williams (Woodbridge: Boydell Press, 1987), 32.
27. See SJLM/1/1/2/1, f. 57r, for example.
28. Although he was English, Caxton first established himself in Bruges before returning to London.

29. *Eneydos* was dedicated to Prince Arthur.

30. See Laynesmith, *Last Medieval Queens*, 212.

31. See Jones and Underwood, *King's Mother*, 182.

32. Kellner, *Blanchardin and Eglantine*.

33. Sitwell, *Scale of Perfection*.

34. Jones and Underwood, *King's Mother*, 183. Mary Roos's first husband, Hugh Denys, was Henry VII's Groom of the Stole. She later served Katherine of Aragon.

35. Schutte, 'Royal Tudor Women', 81.

36. In 1508, for example, twelve books were ordered from Pynson. TNA, E36/214, f. 138v.

37. SJLM/1/1/3/2, f. 27.

38. Ibid., f. 142. Jones and Underwood have pointed out that these were probably copies of the *Mirror of Gold for the Sinful Soul*. See Jones and Underwood, *King's Mother*, 183.

39. SJLM/1/1/3/3, f. 18.

40. Westminster Abbey MS 39.

41. St John's College, MS N.24, f. 12v.

42. See Backhouse, 'Founders of the Royal Library', 184–185.

43. Nichols, *Chronicle of the Grey Friars*, 26.

44. See TNA, E 101/415/3, f. 66v, for example.

45. Katherine's husbands were James Strangways, Sir Matthew Cradock and Christopher Ashton. It is Ashton whom Katherine is buried with in Fyfield, Berkshire. The effigies of the couple were destroyed by fire.

46. Hay, *Anglica Historia*, 119.

47. TNA, E 101/415/3, f. 6r.

48. CSPS, I:213.

49. Ibid.

50. Pollard, *Reign of Henry VII*, I:216.

51. In 1480 Thomas Bourchier, who had completed substantial building work at Knole, gave the property to the See of Canterbury. From then, archbishops of Canterbury, including Morton, whom Henry VII is known to have visited there, occupied it. Today Knole is cared for by the National Trust.

52. Fox hailed from Grantham and was of humble origin.

CHAPTER 20: MY GODLY MISTRESS, THE LADY MARGARET

1. Collyweston was largely pulled down in the eighteenth century. Both Henry VIII and Elizabeth I visited it. Excavations are currently under way in an attempt to discover more about the palace.

2. Toulmin Smith, *John Leland's Itinerary*, I:22.

3. Jones and Underwood point out that a local craftsman accidentally depicted the Beaufort yale as an antelope. Another craftsman had to be paid to rectify this mistake. See Jones and Underwood, *King's Mother*, 84.

4. SJLM/2/3/2/1, f. 10.

5. Ibid., f. 11.

6. Ibid., f. 16.

7. Ibid., ff. 10–38.

8. On one occasion the goldsmith of Stamford was also paid for making 'the pyx of the sacrament'.

9. SJLM/2/1/2–3, f. 18.

10. As a result of Margaret's influence, Oldham later became Bishop of Exeter.

11. In the Ante-Chapel of Christ's College, Cambridge, the monumental brass of Edith and her husband Thomas can still be seen. It is the only medieval brass to a husband and wife that can be found in any College Chapel in Oxford or Cambridge.

12. Fisher, 'Mornynge Remembraunce', 2.

13. Ibid., 3.

14. Likewise, Margaret's treasurer William Bedell later credited Margaret for 'all that I have'. See Norton, *Lives of Tudor Women*, 98.

15. BL, Add MS 12060, f. 9.

16. Ibid., f. 20v.

17. Ibid., f. 21r.

18. Fisher, 'Mornynge Remembraunce', 3.

19. Ibid.

20. Ibid., 5.

21. Kisby, 'Mirror of Monarchy', 204. On one occasion, Margaret's accounts note the payment of a pair of organs bought for her chapel from London.

22. Kisby, 'Officers and Office-Holding at the English Court', 24.

23. In 1506 grammar books were purchased for their use.

24. BL, Add MS 12060, f. 21v.

25. SJLM/1/1/3, f. 47.

26. Ibid.

27. Fisher, 'Mornynge Remembraunce', 4.

28. Jones and Underwood, *King's Mother*, 89.

29. Jones, Michael K., and Malcolm G. Underwood, 'Beaufort, Margaret', in *Oxford Dictionary of National Biography* (New York: Oxford University Press, 2004); Jones and Underwood, *King's Mother*, 87.

30. TNA, REQ 2/4/246.

31. Bentley, *Excerpta Historica*, 167–168.

32. Fisher, 'Mornynge Remembraunce', 4.

33. Ibid., 2.
34. TNA, E 101/415/3, f. 51r.
35. Beer, 'Practices and Performances of Queenship', 20.

CHAPTER 21: RIGHT ROYAL AND PLEASANTLY BESEEN

1. BL, Royal 2 A XVIII, f. 32; Hays, *Anglica Historia*, 123.
2. Kipling, *Receyt of the Ladie Kateryne*, 7.
3. Ibid.
4. Ibid., 8.
5. Ibid., 9.
6. Ibid., 26.
7. Ibid., 31.
8. Ibid., 32.
9. Ibid.
10. Ibid., 37.
11. Ibid., 38.
12. Ibid., 39.
13. Kingsford, *Chronicles of London*, 249.
14. Ibid.
15. Ibid., 248.
16. Kipling, *Receyt of the Ladie Kateryne*, 43–44.
17. Fisher, 'Mornynge Remembraunce', 6.
18. SJLM/1/1/4/1.
19. Kipling, *Receyt of the Ladie Kateryne*, 47–48.
20. Ibid., 48.
21. Ibid.
22. Ibid., 53.
23. Ibid., 55.
24. Ibid.
25. Ibid., 58.
26. Ibid.
27. CSPS, I:176.
28. Ibid.
29. Ibid., 169.
30. BL, Add MS 59899, f. 27r.
31. Fisher, 'Mornynge Remembraunce', 2.
32. This visit has often been dated to 1501, but as Jones has shown, there is good evidence to suggest that it took place in 1502. See Jones, 'Henry VII, Lady Margaret Beaufort'.

33. Following the death of Thomas, Duke of Clarence, in 1421, Margaret's grandmother Margaret Holland had inherited the custody of a valuable French prisoner, John, Count of Angoulême, who was primarily housed at Maxey Castle. He and six others had been given to the English as hostages to guarantee payment from his brother, Louis, Duke of Orléans, which he had promised in 1412 to ensure that the English left Gascony. Though a relatively small amount had been paid off, the balance was by no means settled at Margaret Holland's death. Thus, Margaret's father had inherited the debt, which he gave Angoulême the opportunity to pay off. A new agreement was drawn up with Orléans, and though much of the debt remained outstanding, Angoulême was returned to Cherbourg in March 1444. When Somerset died, Margaret's mother tried her best to pursue the debt, enlisting the help of her husband Lord Welles. Yet the payments began to fall further into arrears and were inherited by Margaret upon her mother's death.

34. As the son of the Duke of Orléans, Louis inherited the debt.

35. Ellis, *Original Letters*, 46–47.

36. Ibid., 47–8.

37. Ibid., 44–45. Henry chose not to press the debt, but his son, Henry VIII, felt differently. It would not be settled until after both Margaret and her son were dead.

38. See Weir, *Elizabeth of York*, 371–374.

39. BL, Royal 2 A XVIII, f. 29.

40. Kipling, *Receyt of the Ladie Kateryne*, 80.

41. Ibid., 81.

42. Ibid.

43. Ibid., 82.

44. TNA, E 101/415/3, f. 98v.

CHAPTER 22: IN EVERYTHING LIKE TO THE QUEEN

1. Somerset inherited the castle in right of his wife, Elizabeth Herbert. Elizabeth was the daughter of William Herbert, Earl of Huntingdon, the heir of Henry VII's former guardian.

2. TNA, E 36/210, f. 85.

3. Alison Weir has pointed out that at the end of the month the queen's accounts show that she visited Coldharbour, but Margaret was not present. That she visited, however, is further evidence of their close relationship. See Weir, *Elizabeth of York*, 402.

4. Ibid., 403–404.

5. Margaret noted the queen's death in her Book of Hours. BL, Royal 2 A XVIII, f. 28.

6. BL, Add MS 45133, f. 141v.

7. Ibid.

8. Part of the effigy still survives in the abbey today.

9. Elizabeth of York had probably supervised their earliest lessons, and the resemblance that Henry VIII's handwriting bore to that of his mother has been noted. See Starkey, *Henry: Virtuous Prince*, 119.

10. Leland, *Antiquarii de Rebus Britannicis Collectanea*, IV:265; BL, Royal 2 A XVIII, f. 31.

11. Thomas and Thornley, *Great Chronicle of London*, 323.

12. SJLM/1/1/3/1, f. 117.

13. M. Jones, 'Collyweston—an Early Tudor Palace', in *England in the Fifteenth Century*, ed. D. Williams (Woodbridge: Boydell Press, 1987), 129.

14. Ibid.

15. Leland, *Antiquarii de Rebus Britannicis Collectanea*, IV:267.

16. Ibid., 324.

17. James died on 27 February 1508. Margaret's second child, Arthur, was born on 20 October 1509, but died on 14 July 1510.

18. Harris, 'Women and Politics', 264.

19. It was probably at her instigation that, in around 1500, a match had been arranged between Margaret's niece, Eleanor St John, and Henry Grey, the son and heir of the Marquess of Dorset. Eleanor was the daughter of Margaret's half-brother Oliver St John and his wife, Elizabeth Scrope. Eleanor died childless, and Henry Grey became second Marquess of Dorset and grandfather to the ill-fated Lady Jane Grey. Margaret may also have had a hand in arranging the marriage of the queen's first cousin, Anne St Leger, to George Manners.

20. CCR 1500–1509, 89; in December, Margaret's accounts noted a reward to a servant of Kildare's who brought her a gift. SJLM/1/1/3/1, f. 122. The newly-weds would eventually move to Ireland.

21. SJLM/1/1/3/1, f. 122, notes a payment to a servant of Princess Mary.

22. Nichols, *Testamenta Vetusta*, I:446.

23. SJLM/1/1/3/1, f. 128. Stanley is referenced at various points throughout Margaret's accounts. On one occasion, for example, she rewarded his minstrels, while on another she paid the goldsmith of Stamford for repairing candlesticks from Stanley's chapel.

24. Nichols, *Testamenta Vetusta*, II:460.

25. Ibid., 459.

26. Ibid., 458; Stanley's son and heir, George, Lord Strange, had died just months earlier in December 1503—having reportedly been poisoned following a banquet at Derby House. In consequence, Stanley's eldest grandson succeeded him.

27. Cooper, *Lady Margaret*, 97–98.

28. CSPS, I:295.

CHAPTER 23: *NOS MARGARETA*

1. Fisher's father died in his youth, and though his mother remarried and sired further children, she remained devoted to John and his brother.

2. Bayne, *Life of Fisher MS.*, 9–10.

3. The architecture has long since changed and includes buildings designed by Nicholas Hawksmoor and Sir Christopher Wren.

4. Marie was the wife of Aymer de Valence, the half-brother of Henry III, whose tomb can still be seen in Westminster Abbey. Marie's licence to found Pembroke was granted on Christmas Eve 1347. It was originally known as the Hall of Valence Mary.

5. Twigg, *History of Queens' College*, 1.

6. Cooper, *Lady Margaret*, 46–47.

7. CPR 1494–1509, 371.

8. Ibid., 79. These are the modern Lady Margaret Professorships. See Jones and Underwood, *King's Mother*, 205. Lady Margaret Hall, Oxford, still commemorates her.

9. CPR 1494–1509, 79.

10. Anstey, *Epistolae Academicae Oxon*, II:614.

11. Underwood, 'Lady Margaret and Her Cambridge Connections', 69.

12. CPR 1494–1509, 415.

13. TNA, E 36/281.

14. Schroder, 'Royal Tudor Rock-Crystal and Silver-Gilt Vase', 363.

15. SJLM/1/1/3/3, f. 8.

16. CPR 1494–1509, 543.

17. See Rackham, *Early Statutes of Christ's College*, iv.

18. Ibid., 87.

19. Ibid., 89.

20. Fisher, 'Mornynge Remembraunce', 7.

21. Hatfield later served as a royal palace before Robert Cecil acquired it in 1607. He tore down much of the old palace and transformed it into what is now Hatfield House. Croydon Palace now forms part of an independent girls' school.

22. SJLM/2/3/1/3, ff. 24, 9.

23. SJLM/2/3/1/4, ff. 1–4.

24. Philip was the son of Maximilian and Mary of Burgundy. He married Juana on 20 October 1496, and following the death of her mother, Isabella of Castile, she became queen. However, her father, Ferdinand, contested this, necessitating the couple's journey to Spain.

25. TNA, E 36/214, f. 16r.

26. SJLM/9/2/2.

27. Edmund succeeded his father to the dukedom of Suffolk in 1492. Because he did not have the financial means to support his title, he instead became known as the Earl of Suffolk.

28. TNA, E 36/214, f. 19r.

29. Ibid., f. 23r.

30. Eleanor instead married first Manuel I of Portugal, and in 1530, Francis I, King of France. Charles married Isabella of Portugal.

31. Suffolk had been exempted from Henry VIII's general pardon in 1509 and was executed on 30 April 1513 on Tower Hill.

32. In 1525 Richard had joined the King of France's army at Pavia. He was buried in the church there following his death in the battle.

33. Jones and Underwood, *King's Mother*, 79.

34. SJLM/1/1/3, f. 93.

35. Philip died suddenly on 25 September of natural causes, although whispers of poison abounded. He was laid to rest in the Royal Chapel of Granada, where his wife and her parents are also entombed.

36. Margaret had continued to make payments for the upkeep of Coldharbour in recent years, including for a broken chimney, a bar of iron 'for my lady's closet' and 'a great new key made for the great door' standing next to the front gate. SJLM/1/2/3.

CHAPTER 24: A WOMAN MOST OUTSTANDING

1. Astle, *Will of Henry VII*, 42.

2. L & P, I:17.

3. Hay, *Anglica Historia*, 151.

4. L & P, I:17.

5. Gristwood, *Blood Sisters*, 330.

6. L & P, I:4.

7. Cooper, *Lady Margaret*, 135. Jones and Underwood suggest that Perrot may first have been employed to help with Margaret's command of the French language, or else Katherine of Aragon's (Jones and Underwood, *King's Mother*, 164). In her will, Margaret left Perrot an annuity 'if she tarry within this realm'.

8. Mayor, *English Works of John Fisher*, 268.

9. L & P, I:4.

10. Henry VII had left money in his will for the completion of the Lady Chapel and his tomb. The eventual cost of the tomb totalled over £9 million in modern money; the vault would be opened in 1625 for the burial of James I.

11. L & P, I:34.

12. TNA, LC 9/50; L & P, I:82.

13. SJLM/1/1/5, f. 14r. See also Hayward, *Dress at the Court of King Henry VIII*, 44.

14. SJLM/1/1/5, f. 17r.

15. Fisher, 'Mornynge Remembraunce', 6.

16. Hay, *Anglica Historia*, 151.

17. Fisher, 'Mornynge Remembraunce', 6.

18. Hay, *Anglica Historia*, 151.

19. BL, Add MS 12060, f. 24r.

20. Two rooms of the abbot's house (Cheyneygates) still survive and are often used for corporate events.

21. Fisher, 'Mornynge Remembraunce', 7.

22. BL, Add MS 12060, f. 24r.

23. Ibid.

24. Fisher, 'Mornynge Remembraunce', 5.

25. Ibid.

26. Hay, *Anglica Historia*, 151.

27. St John's College, *Collegium Divi Johannis Evangelistae*, 118–120.

28. Ibid., 121.

29. SJLM/2/3/5, ff. 1–10.

30. Cooper, *Lady Margaret*, 117.

31. SJLM/2/3/2/1, f. 30.

32. Hayward, *Dress at the Court of King Henry VIII*, 65.

33. Fisher, 'Mornynge Remembraunce', 1.

34. Torrigiano was born in 1472. Though he had completed other commissions, Margaret's is likely to have been the first tomb of his creation.

35. Scott, 'On the Contracts for the Tomb', 370.

36. Ibid.

37. Fisher, 'Mornynge Remembraunce', 7.

EPILOGUE

1. James V had been born on 10 April 1512 at Linlithgow Palace. He was the only one of James IV and Margaret Tudor's six children to survive infancy.

2. L & P, I:3151.

3. John Stewart, second Duke of Albany, was a blood relative to James V, his grandfather having been James II of Scotland. Though Albany had been born and raised in France, he became regent of Scotland in July 1515. He was ousted from his position in 1524, and died in France in 1536.

4. Mary's two sons, both named Henry, predeceased her.

5. The eldest of James's sons, also named James, was born on 22 May 1540. The younger, Robert, was born on 12 April 1541. Tragically, he died eight days

after his birth on 20 April at Falkland Palace. The following day, his elder brother died at St Andrews.

6. Following her death, Margaret was buried in the Charterhouse at Perth. Unfortunately, this was destroyed in 1559 during the course of the Reformation.

7. James VI was the only son of Mary, Queen of Scots, as a result of her second marriage to Henry Stuart, Lord Darnley. Darnley was the son of Margaret Douglas, Queen Margaret's daughter by Archibald Douglas.

8. Margaret is also distantly related to the dukes of Beaufort, who are descended from her cousin, Charles Somerset. The title of Duke of Beaufort was bestowed upon Henry Somerset, third Marquess of Worcester, by Charles II in 1682.

9. Cited in Ballard, *Memoirs of Several Ladies of Great Britain*, 26–27. Originally composed in Latin, the elegy was intended to hang next to Margaret's tomb.

NOTES ON SOURCES

1. Alice was the granddaughter of Margaret's half-brother John St John. She was also a beneficiary of Margaret's will. One of Alice and Parker's daughters, Jane, married Anne Boleyn's brother, George, Viscount Rochford. Jane was executed in February 1542 alongside Katherine Howard for aiding and abetting the queen's adulterous behaviour.

2. Fisher, 'Mornynge Remembraunce', 3.

3. Pronay and Cox, *Crowland Chronicle Continuations*; see also Riley, *Ingulph's Chronicle*.

4. Mancini, *Usurpation of Richard III*.

5. Hay, *Anglica Historia*; Ellis, *Three Books*.

6. André, *Life of Henry VII*.

ACKNOWLEDGEMENTS

UNCROWNED QUEEN HAS TAKEN ME on an incredible journey: it has challenged me, frustrated me, shocked me, inspired me, but most of all it has given me the opportunity to work with and meet some amazing people—many have had a greater impact than they will realise. This is my chance to thank them. The book is dedicated to my grandparents, but I would like to share that dedication with someone else. My superb—now former—UK editor (and forever friend!), Fiona Slater, has been as enthralled by Margaret as I have, and has stuck by me and inspired me throughout my writing career to date. I cannot thank her enough for all her commitment both to me and to my books: *Uncrowned Queen* is for you too, Fiona, with heartfelt thanks.

I would like to express my sincerest gratitude to everyone at Basic Books for their dedication and commitment both to myself and the book. Especial thanks to my editor Claire Potter, who has been instrumental in the construction of the book, and has been incredibly supportive. Thanks also to Rachel Field for pulling the text into such good shape and for all of her thought provoking insights. Huge thanks are also due to Christina Palaia for all her hard work on my behalf.

Thanks to the team at Watson Little, but most particularly my agent, Donald Winchester. Thank you so much for all of your support, and for patiently listening when panic set in! Your calm words of reassurance made the world of difference.

I'm very grateful to Jean Follett from the Friends of Woking Palace for taking the time to show me around the remains of Margaret's former home, and to Chris Close of Collyweston Historical Society for updating me on the archaeological evidence uncovered at the site of Margaret's splendid palace. Thanks to Christine

Reynolds of the Westminster Abbey Muniments, and to the patient staff at the British Library and the National Archives. Also to Tracy Deakin and her assistants at the St John's College archives, who were incredibly helpful during my visits.

Alison Weir was kind enough to draw my attention to the jumbled glass portraying Margaret in the church at Landbeach, and sent me several photographs. I'd also like to thank her for her unwavering support, and for the many conversations we've shared about Margaret. Likewise to Tracy Borman and Sarah Gristwood, who have both been incredibly generous with their time, enthusiasm and encouragement. Julian Humphrys was a star for reading an early draft of the book and sending me useful pointers, and thanks to John Cooper for his thorough feedback. I have also been fortunate enough to draw on the expertise of Michael Jones, whose knowledge of Margaret is second to none. Thank you for inspiring me. Thanks are also due to Elizabeth Norton, Kate Williams and Joanne Paul.

Particular thanks go to my wonderful mother, Sylvia, for taking the time to share her extensive medical knowledge with me—you are the most amazing woman I know, and I'm privileged to call you my mother. I am also indebted to Suzanne Schuld for listening to my medical theories and for going to great lengths to help me obtain answers—thank you to you and your colleagues.

My friends are all superstars, but especial thanks go to Chris Warwick for his endless championing of me. Also to Keita Weston, Kerrie Britten, Amelia Douchet and Donna Kelly for all of your warmth, loyalty and love. I'd also like to thank your beautiful girls: Ava, Manon and Amelia respectively, who are wonderful friends to my stepdaughter Olivia, and who I have been proud to watch growing into such lovely young ladies.

As always, my family are the ones who have been forced to put up with me (and Margaret) for the last two years, and no words can express my gratitude. Our newest addition, Nell, has brought some much-needed sunshine into our lives, and my two lovely stepchildren, Charlie and Olivia, have been the best. Particular thanks to my Dad, who has driven me across the country in pursuit of Margaret, read drafts of the book and given me endless support. Finally, my amazing fiancé, Matt, I can say nothing other than you rock my world! To everyone that has been a part of my journey, my sincerest thanks.

INDEX

Joey Menghini

Nicola Tallis received her doctorate in history from the University of Winchester. The author of several books, she has previously lectured at the University of Winchester and has worked with Historic Royal Palaces and the National Trust. She lives just outside Bath, UK.